Sugar Snub™ Food Guide

The ultimate advice and supermarket
food shopping guide for those who
wish to reduce sugar in their diets

By
Claire White

Published by
Claire White

ISBN: 978-0-9933849-0-5

Published by
Claire White

Traffic light food guide

The SugarSnub™ advice and Traffic Light Guide, will help you enjoy a reduced sugar lifestyle. Foods from five large supermarkets have been categorised, and using the Food Standards Agency's recognised system, arranged in order of sugar quantities. Included are the other essential markers for food advice: Fat, Saturated Fat, Salt and Calories.

Low
%per
100g/100ml

Medium
%per
100g/100ml

High
%per
100g/100ml

Contents

Disclaimer

This guide does not replace professional health and nutrition advice. It is not intended to diagnose or treat any medical condition. It should be used as information to support your own good judgement and the professional advice of qualified healthcare professionals. If you are concerned about any aspect of your health you should see your GP or other appropriate qualified healthcare provider. All information is given in good faith and is correct to the best of our knowledge as of June 2015, and is purely informational.

About Sugar Snub™

I have created this book out of frustration while becoming sugar free. I wanted to produce a guide that would be helpful to me, my family and friends, and ultimately, anyone who wishes to find out where the sugar is hiding in our foods.

Diagnosed with breast cancer in my late 30s, when my son was 18 months old, was a devastating experience. Following fantastic, but intensive treatment, I wanted to find a way to get back on my feet.

Research and consultations led me to eliminate sugar from my diet, but I had no idea how hard that would be!

Being sugar free has been an eye opener. Despite the challenges, I now feel fantastic. At the time of writing I've lost 10kg (1st 8lb). I no longer feel bloated; it's the first time I've had a waist since before I was pregnant! I sleep better and have more energy all day.

Prior to marriage and having a family I was a personal trainer and nutrition advisor. I thought I ate very healthily; I had more than my 5 a day, I was cautious what my son ate, and I was very aware of saturated fat and salt.

However, I put on weight during pregnancy and chemotherapy. Tiredness during the early months of motherhood and then cancer treatment led me to be more habitual about eating sugary snacks to keep me going.

I was shocked when I started researching how sugar has a negative effect on our health & wellbeing. And I was horrified to learn how much sugar had crept into my food cupboard.

What to do for the best?

We are in a state of confusion when it comes to diets.
Should we go fat free, carb free, high protein?
There are so many contradictory messages.

- We are bombarded more than ever with headlines containing health warnings; different foods linked to dementia, cancer, heart disease and childhood behavioral problems

- We can buy super foods and supplements promising miraculous results and cures

- We are advised to cook from scratch, but we are busier and in demand more than ever

So what should we do for the best, and where is the real problem?

Sugar is a very big issue, and it's everywhere. I want to help you live a sugar free or limited sugar lifestyle and this book will help you do it.

Cutting out or even just reducing your sugar intake will make a huge difference to you.

If you want to make the change, have more energy than ever, lose weight, look and feel fantastic, then SugarSnub™ can help you every step of the way.

Claire White
Founder of SugarSnub™

Sugar - the reality

Sugar has been taking over our diet without us realising how much we are consuming. Food experts agree that the amount of sugar in the British diet is too high, but sugar seems to be added to so many foods that are readily available on supermarket shelves.

The reality is that you and your family are the only ones who can control the amount of sugar you eat.

We have an emotional attachment to sugary foods. As children we were offered sweets and chocolate as a treat if we hurt ourselves, did well, or were brave at the dentist (how ironic). With pocket money we would raid the pick'n'mix at Woolworths or the cinema. I, personally would stock up on Toffee Cushions and Wham bars from the corner shop (I'm showing my age!) As we get older sugary foods become a comfort; if we're feeling down, bored, or celebrating. We give chocolates for presents, Easter, Christmas, or to show someone we care.

We know about these obvious sugary foods and we eat them with a slight guilt. To break away from this relationship is emotional as well as physical.

But what about other sugars?

Many of us know about the sugar in condiments, tomato sauce, BBQ sauce, baked beans etc., but did you know the second ingredient listed in some soy sauces is sugar?

Often from an early age, our taste buds are trained to like and expect a sweet taste from many foods and snacks we eat. We need to re-train our taste buds to embrace and enjoy savoury flavours.

I'm not saying you should live your lives completely without sugar, without chocolate or treats, but to learn to live without a dependence on sugar.

To buy and cook knowing exactly what's on the menu. To make informed choices.

Sugar comes in many different forms,
not all are bad for us.

Naturally occurring sugars are found in fruit and in some vegetables, such as peas and sweetcorn. There's also a type of sugar found in milk and dairy products – lactose - it makes up around 2-8% of milk.

We need energy for living, and glucose is the main source. It can either be burned immediately, or the body will store excess for later. If we take in more than we need however, it can cause problems long-term.

This storage is in two forms – glycogen and fat.

Glycogen is stored in the liver and in muscles. When we need it the body can easily break it down to provide more glucose. This will provide enough energy for around half an hour of exercise.

Fat is the main long-term energy reserve. The more excess sugar we have, the more fat we will store. Breaking down fat to make glucose for energy can happen when we reduce our intake and exercise regularly. Managing this balance is key to staying a healthy weight.

Concentrated sources of sugar include table sugar, honey, golden syrup, maple syrups, agave syrup and molasses. These are naturally very sweet foods and they provide a very quick source of glucose to the body. If we eat too much of these, the extra energy they supply will turn to fat and body weight will increase.

Sugar is also released when we eat starchy foods – carbohydrates or 'carbs'.

Choosing these wisely can also make a difference.

Good and bad carbs

Many foods in the modern diet contain carbohydrates. Some are better than others. The typical British diet contains carbs made from grains such as wheat, rye, oats and rice, and from root vegetables like potatoes.

Refined carbohydrates

These have had the fibre removed. Their simple composition means your body will break them down quickly. This fast digestion causes sugar to be released into the blood stream quickly, causing a 'high' in the body's energy level followed by a crash.

Think about the common post-lunch slump mid-afternoon when you are likely to grab a sugary pick me up.

Examples of simple carbs are: white bread, white pasta, white rice, crisps, chips, cakes and biscuits, fruit juices.

Good carbs

Also known as complex carbs or 'slow carbs'. These still contain the fibre and usually other nutrients as well. Their complexity causes the body to take longer to digest them. This means glucose is released into the blood stream more slowly than from refined carbs. We also benefit from the fibre and other nutrients in complex carbs.

> **Examples of complex carbs are: wholemeal bread, oats, beans, root vegetables with the skin on, and whole fruits.**

These carbs are also part of what are considered 'whole foods'. This means they don't just provide sugar but also vitamins, minerals and fibre.

The human body evolved to eat these kinds of foods, and when we choose these 'slow carbs' we have a better chance of maintaining a healthy weight.

How much sugar should I be eating?

Several health expert bodies are now telling us that we are eating too much sugar. For example The World Health Organization and the UK government's advisory body on nutrition, SACN, is strongly advising we cut our added sugar intake to no more than 5% of our daily calories.

> **For example, a daily intake of 2000 calories, no more than 100 calories should be from added sugar.**
>
> **That's about 6-7 tsp, or 25g (1tsp=4g)**

In the UK we currently eat much more than that, which is contributing to many health problems, including weight problems, diabetes, and tooth decay.

Fructose can also be a problem

Fructose is a very sweet sugar found naturally in fruit. It isn't a problem eaten in moderation in a piece of fruit, as it comes with fibre and several vitamins and minerals. However, a lot of manufactured food, and especially drinks, contain a processed sugar syrup called high fructose corn syrup. This contains both glucose and fructose. It's also used to add texture to foods and drinks.

It's in soft drinks, sports drinks, fruit drinks, processed foods, jars of pasta sauce and BBQ sauce to name a few. It's also used in some bakery goods like cakes, biscuits and even bread.

However, some studies are raising alarm bells about fructose in these processed foods. This is because a high intake of fructose seems to have an effect on controlling appetite.

Appetite is a complex function. It's affected by our mood, upbringing, habits and some very clever body chemistry.

Having an appetite was essential for humans to survive in harsh times; it made us go out and find food. When we've eaten enough, there's an orchestra of hormones involved that should send a signal to the brain saying 'we're full now, stop eating'.

Some types of food are good at triggering this signal, especially protein foods like chicken or nuts. However, fructose doesn't trigger this 'stop eating' signal very well. That means we can easily keep drinking those sugary drinks or eating those sweets.

It seems that humans have evolved without an appetite 'off switch' for fructose.

Sugary and starchy foods in general are not good at triggering the appetite 'off switch'. This was all very well when sugar was rare, but now it's abundant and in so many things. Having no 'off switch' is a problem.

That's why it's so easy to eat more than we need and why so many people struggle with weight and over eating. Modern processed foods are often high in calories, but low in good nutrients like vitamins and minerals. It's easy to take in too many calories very quickly from these calorie-dense foods.

Have you ever tried to make fresh orange juice?

It takes a lot of effort and oranges to squeeze out the juice for 1 glass. Can you imagine sitting down and eating a plate of 10 oranges? That seems an impossible task.

> **It's all too easy to drink a glass of juice, which doesn't contain the additional fibre to slow down the sugar release, but contains the same amount of sugar as a can of coke!**

330 ml can = 35g / 9 tsp sugar

The same caution should be applied to smoothies. These seemingly healthy drinks have also had the fibre removed and are therefore loaded with fructose.

Taking all of these food factors into account, when we eat a lot of sugar and refined starches, we have a high sugar load.

In fact there's a name for this type of diet – 'high glycaemic load diet', which means it pushes the level of sugar in the blood too high, for too long, and that isn't good for any of us. There has been much research to demonstrate the effects of excess sugar intake on our body.

It:

- Speeds up the ageing process
- Is linked to dementia
- Is linked to type 2 diabetes
- Causes fat to build up in the liver
- May increase the risks of several cancers, including cancers of breast, ovaries, prostate, digestive system, pancreas and liver
- Inhibits our immune system
- Causes a rapid rise in adrenalin, anxiety & loss of concentration

and

- It makes us FAT – especially around the middle – where the fat produces hormones that are linked to a lot of chronic diseases

When the excess sugar is flying around the blood stream, if left unused the molecules latch onto protein molecules that are everywhere in the body.

This causes inflammation and tissue damage, and that's how it causes so many health problems.

Healthy human bodies can handle sweet foods in small amounts. We evolved mechanisms to manage this, but overloading with sugar on a regular basis is paving the way to poor health.

The Sugar Snub™ way

The thought of cutting back sugar in your diet may seem like a daunting task.

You may question whether it is the right thing to do?
If this is the case, answer these questions:

- Do you have a mid afternoon slump when you would normally grab something sweet to 'pick you up'?

- Do you worry about cutting certain foods out of your diet?

- Do you eat foods even if you aren't hungry and mostly because you crave them?

- Do you often over eat?

- Do you feel tired and sluggish when you do?

- Do you have mood swings if you go too long without sugar?

If you go sugar free – what happens?

When no sugar is available for your body to burn energy, the liver cleverly takes the converted glycogen stored in your body's muscles and liver and changes it back to glucose. This is the system for blood sugar balance. When the glycogen is all used up, the body breaks down some fat to make some burnable sugar for energy.

When you cut out sugar, your cravings for it will increase. They will peak at around 3-4 days. It will take all your willpower not to dive into the goody cupboard.

This was certainly the case for me. I felt grumpy for a few days and had headaches. I was shocked as it made me realise how addicted my body was to sugar. But by day 5 these symptoms had passed and my energy levels were on the up.

In the long term you will experience:

- Increased consistent energy
- Better sleep
- Healthier skin
- Less bloating
- Fat loss
- Increase sense of wellbeing
- A feeling of pride

In the short term some people may experience:

- Headaches
- Dizziness
- Anxiety
- Cravings
- Grumpiness
- Lack of energy

It takes about 21 days to change a habit.
You will have tough days, but it will be worth the effort.

Family and friends

You may wonder what other people will think?

In my experience this can be a tricky one. I was initially embarrassed to tell people. I felt like I was being awkward at a play date when the plate of biscuits were being handed around, or a party pooper at a dinner party when the hostess didn't think I liked her dessert. This may have been true, or was it my interpretation?

Some people may make fun of your resolve, some may be quite cynical, but I found most people were actually very supportive, intrigued, and some envious. By reading this book you are a step ahead, and when they get to where you will be, you can help them along the way. We all make our own choices, but if you want to improve your health, and take good care of your family's health, then taking a close look at your sugar intake will be a move worth making.

Getting started

Step 1 - Cut out the obvious

It is completely up to you whether you wish to go cold turkey on sugar, or cut it down slowly.

I'm not dictating to you what to do, but to inform and advise. Everyone knows how they best respond to advice and diet change, so I will leave it to you to take it forward as you see fit.

Firstly, if you have a major health problem, are very overweight or diabetic, you have a lot to gain from making these changes. But you may need some help, from a qualified nutrition professional, to guide you.

First step is to target the obvious sugars:

- Chocolate
- Sweets
- Added sugar to cereal, tea & coffee
- Fizzy drinks

This will be enough to get going!

Step 2 – Time to swap

This is where the Traffic Light System will help you make simple substitutions.

Look through this guide and start making changes to your food shopping.

These are a good start and every swap helps to reduce your sugar load and get a better handle on your blood sugar balance.

From:	To:
White bread	Wholemeal bread
White pasta	Wholemeal pasta
White rice	Brown basmati rice
Jam & Marmalade	Peanut butter or mashed banana
Biscuits & cakes	Oat cakes
Salad Cream	Full fat Mayonnaise
Fruit juice	Fizzy water with slice of lemon
Chocolate nut spread	Nut butter
Soy Sauce	Tamari Sauce
Dried fruit	Fresh fruit
Bottled salad dressings	Oil & Vinegar dressing

Step 3 - Fruit and alcohol

Fruit is an essential part of a balanced diet; it contains vitamins and minerals needed for a healthy body.

However, some fruit is higher in fructose than others. The list on page 22 will help you understand the fruit you can eat more of, on a daily basis, and those that you should consume less often and in smaller portions.

Alcohol

I have a feeling some may have skipped a few paragraphs to get to this section!

There is sugar in alcohol. Some drinks contain a little, some have a substantial amount.

If you wish to carry on drinking alcohol, pick from the first list.

Alcohol with the least amounts of sugar:

- Red wine
- White wine (dry not sweet)
- White spirits, e.g. vodka, gin, rum
- Whisky
- Lager
- Champagne
- Mixers:
- Soda water

Red Wine:
175ml glass = 0.5 tsp (1.5g)

Avoid these:

- Whisky
- Dessert wines
- Cider
- Baileys & other creamy drinks
- Mixers:
- Fizzy drinks
- Fruit juice
- Tonic water

Cider:
1 pint = 5 tsp (20.5g)

A word of caution –
even low-sugar alcoholic drinks in excess have unhealthy consequences. Everything in moderation.

Step 4 – A balanced diet

Eliminating or reducing your sugar content is a fantastic way to become healthier. However, you must ensure you are consuming a balanced diet.

Protein:

Aim to eat a portion of protein with each meal; e.g. for breakfast these could be; milk, yoghurt, eggs, nuts and seeds. For lunch and dinner; lean meat, fish, tofu or quorn.

Carbohydrate:

For each meal choose a portion of 'Good Carbs' from the list on page 8.

Fruit & vegetables:

Aim for at least 5 portions a day, ideally making up a rainbow of colours, thus ensuring you will consume a wider variety of vitamins and minerals.

Fat:

We have been trained by diet clubs and the media to steer clear of fat and to opt for 'reduced' or 'low' fat food options. However, often when fat has been removed, sugar is added.

Fat is essential to our diet. Don't be afraid of higher fat options, e.g. nuts, avocados & eggs. These are fantastic snack & meal options. They fill you up and provide you with essential nutrients.

Portion sizes:

Visualise your plate. Aim for a quarter protein, a quarter good carbohydrates, and half vegetables or salads. Add some healthy fats, such as a drizzle of olive oil.

Understand food labelling

Ingredients are listed in order of quantities with the largest listed first.

Therefore, if sugar is included in the first few, you know it is likely to have larger amounts, except, of course if there are only 2 or 3 ingredients! You will find an exception occasionally to the general rule.

Sugar can be listed in many different guises. Added sugar isn't always called 'sugar'.

Keep an eye out for the following as these are all sugar:

Agave	Invert Sugar
Acesulfame	Isoglucose
Agave Nectar	Levulose
Aspartame	Maltodextrin
Barley Malt	Maltose
Beet Sugar	Mannutol
Caramel	Maltose
Coconut Nectar	Malt Syrup
Corn Sugar	Maple Syrup
Date Syrup	Molasses
Dextran	Palm Sugar
Dextrose	Saccharine
Fructose	Sorbitol
Glucose	Stevia
Golden Syrup	Sucralose
High-Fructose Corn Syrup	Sucrose
Honey	Xylitol

The ones listed in red are artificial sweeteners.

I think this list perfectly demonstrates why there is such a big problem. Sugar is everywhere and is listed under many different pseudonyms!

How to use this guide

I've found supermarket shopping very frustrating.
It is great to cook from scratch every time, but
we all have busy lifestyles so opening a jar to speed
up a meal is beneficial.

Listed in the next section are the categories of food I believe
contain many of the hidden and obvious sugars. I decided
to use the Food Standards Agency rating system to make
it visually easier to make informed choices.

Sugar per 100g / 100ml

Fat per 100g / 100ml

Saturated Fat per 100g / 100ml

Salt per 100g / 100ml

I have listed the sugar and other values as grams per 100g / 100ml of product, rather than portion size.

It's important to take a look at the packet and understand the amount of the food you will be consuming. It may appear low sugar per 100g but are you about to eat 250g of it?

Also the portion size used by the manufacturer is often much smaller than the amount a typical person will eat. Think of those large bags of snacks 'made for sharing', which often disappear alarmingly rapidly without anyone to help!

Some of the foods with a low sugar value may still contain added sugar. If you wish your diet to be completely free of added sugar you will need to read the ingredients list carefully.

The Food Standards Agency recommends sugar to be 5g or below per 100g. However if you wish to be sugar free this ideally would be lower in most situations.

But this is where it becomes a bit tricky. A product may have a higher amount of sugar per 100g but it is from natural sources, e.g. nuts or tomatoes. This is of course an exception to the rule and where a little common sense and food label reading needs to be employed.

Remember, we are on the look out to compare added sugar, which we don't need!

Ideally, you want to be choosing a food that is green or amber for each element, rather than red, which shows a high level.

Remember, it's all about balance

If you are eating a high sugar cereal at breakfast, you'll be wise to choose lower sugar foods for other meals. If you know you'll be eating cake at a party, then cut back on the sugar at other meals. And portion size is important. A sprinkle of granola and some fresh berries on a bowl of plain yoghurt will have less sugar than a 'fruit corner yoghurt'.

Fruit

Fruit is an important part of your diet.

This list is a guide of the fruits you can eat more of on a daily basis, and those you should consume less often and in smaller portions.

To help you make the best choices, fruits are listed with the least sugar first.

Product	Sugar per 100g	Product	Sugar per 100g
Limes	0.4	Watermelon	9
Avocado	0.7	Orange	9.2
Lemon	2.5	Apricots	9.3
Starfruit	4	Raspberries	9.5
Strawberries	5.8	Pears	10
Grapefruit	6.2	Pomegranate	10.1
Figs	6.9	Kiwi	10.5
Blueberries	7.3	Tangerine	11
Plum	7.5	Apple	11.8
Honeydew Melon	8	Pineapple	11.9
Papaya	8	Cherries	13
Blackberries	8.1	Mango	14.8
Peaches	8.4	Banana	15.6
Nectarine	8.5	Grapes	18.1
Cantaloupe Melon	8.7		

Sugar Snub™ food plan

Often when you start to look at food in a new light or embark on a new diet regime, it's useful to have some ideas of what to actually cook and snack on.

I hope these ideas and tips are helpful.

Tips for time-saving:

- Cook rice in large batches and freeze immediately. Reheat thoroughly. Can be used for stuffed peppers and to make a quick rice pudding

- If you have a few potatoes and other vegetables left over from dinner, use in a Spanish omelette for lunch the following day

- Canned fish is great in a salad or stirred through pasta for a quick healthy meal

- Quinoa is a slow carb grain and cooks in 15 minutes

- Children usually love brightly coloured foods and also often enjoy helping to make meals

- Boost your vegetable intake by having a plate of celery and carrot sticks on the table at dinner time

Breakfast:

- Muesli base with added nuts and seeds with natural yoghurt and berries
- Porridge with semi skimmed milk and berries
- Shredded Wheat with added nuts and seeds with semi skimmed milk
- Scrambled eggs on toast
- Grilled bacon with tomatoes
- Sardines on toast
- Pancakes made with spelt flour, natural yogurt and berries
- Yoghurt with fresh fruit, nuts and seeds
- Smoothie made from plain yoghurt or coconut milk, ground almonds, berries and a dash of natural vanilla essence or ground cinnamon

Food Plan

Snacks:

- Oat cakes with nut butter, or mashed avocado, or cheese
- Cheese and celery sticks
- Grilled halloumi
- Piece of fruit and a few nuts & seeds
- Natural yogurt with berries
- Natural yogurt with nuts
- Pistachios

Lunch:

- Chicken and avocado salad
- Chicken or ham salad in wholemeal pitta
- Ham & tomato toastie on wholemeal bread
- Cheese & tomato toastie on wholemeal bread
- Chicken and quinoa salad with peppers and spring onion
- Tinned fish (tuna, salmon, sardines or mackerel), salad and wholemeal flatbread
- Home made chicken and wholemeal noodle soup
- Mushroom omelette or frittata with salad
- Omelette of leftover vegetables

Dinner:

- Pan fried salmon with tamari, chilli flakes, lime and sesame seeds. Stir fried veg with brown basmati rice
- Lamb curry with spinach and chapati
- Jacket potato with chilli con carne and side salad
- Cottage pie topped with slices of potatoes with skin on, and vegetables
- Chicken stuffed with mozzarella, wrapped in bacon or parma ham with green beans or asparagus and new potatoes
- Spaghetti bolognese with wholemeal spaghetti or tagliatelli and a side salad
- Lasagna with wholemeal pasta sheets and a side salad
- Beef and veg stir fry with wholemeal noodles (sauce - chilli, garlic, tamari)
- Chicken and vegetable kebabs with salad and new potatoes
- Beef & vegetable hot pot with skin on potato slices and vegetables
- Steak with homemade peppercorn sauce with paprika potato wedges and French beans
- Left over roast and veg stir fry with basmati rice
- Peppers stuffed with brown rice and cubes of left over roast

Desserts:

- Fruit kebabs
- Live plain yoghurt with berries and a sprinkle of cinnamon
- Baked custard made with coconut milk, eggs and vanilla

Bakery

There are quite a few surprises on this list.

You may know some of these items contain high amounts of fat, but did you realise how much sugar is in them! Many contain dried fruit, which you are trying to avoid.

To help you make the best choices, products are listed starting with the least sugar first.

Product	Sugar	Fat	Sat per 100g	Salt	Cals
Sainsbury's Crumpets, Taste the Difference	1.8	0.9	0.2	1.02	178
Tesco Free From Crumpets	1.9	4.3	0.5	1.3	194
Warburtons Crumpets	2	0.7	0.2	1.48	178
Morrisons Cheddar Cheese Muffins	2.3	3.6	2	0.8	253
Morrisons Butter Muffins	2.5	5.1	2.8	0.7	263
Genius Gluten Free Crumpets	2.6	7.4	0.6	1.17	209
Sainsbury's Farmhouse Cheese Scone, Taste the Difference	2.6	16	9.6	1.75	336
Tesco Finest All Butter Toasting Muffins	2.8	9.4	5.8	1	296
Warburtons Toasting Muffins	2.9	2.1	0.4	0.78	228
Tesco Pikelets	2.9	0.6	0.2	1.4	193
Sainsbury's Cheese & Black Pepper Muffins, Taste the Difference	3.1	6.7	4.1	1.13	258
Tesco Finest Cheese Scones	3.1	14.9	9.4	1.7	333
Morrisons Crumpets	3.2	1.1	0.2	1.2	234
Tesco Everyday Value Crumpets	3.3	0.5	0.1	1	183
Tesco Crumpets	3.3	0.5	0.1	1	183
Tesco Teddy Bear Crumpets	3.4	1	0.2	1	186
Sainsbury's Crumpets, Basics	3.5	1.2	0.2	1.04	218
Morrisons Savers Crumpets	3.5	1.3	0.2	1.2	242
Haywood & Padgett Sultana Scones	3.7	9.7	3.7	1.6	340
Waitrose Essential Crumpets	3.8	1.1	0.3	0.75	182
Sainsbury's Crumpets	3.9	1.1	0.2	1.12	212
Asda Chosen by You Oven Bottom Muffins	4.2	2.7	0.4	1	267
Asda Chosen by You Muffins	4.3	1.8	0.3	0.8	230
Warburtons Round Potato Cakes	4.4	10.1	3.2	1.98	260

Bakery

Product	Sugar	Fat	Sat	Salt	Cals
			per 100g		
Tesco White Muffins	4.4	1.5	0.5	1	219
Asda Chosen by You Crumpets	4.4	1.2	0.2	1.1	213
Sainsbury's Muffins, Basics	4.6	1.9	0.3	0.8	247
Waitrose French Butter Croissants	4.6	23.8	15	0.8	430
Waitrose LoveLife Calorie Ctrl French Butter Croissants	5.1	16.7	10.8	0.79	381
Waitrose Charentes Butter Croissants	5.3	25.3	17.2	0.88	426
Duchy Originals from Waitrose Organic Wholemeal Muffins	5.3	5.4	2.4	0.9	276
Waitrose Charentes Butter Croissants	5.3	25.3	17.2	0.88	426
Sainsbury's Wholemeal Muffins	5.4	2.9	0.9	0.95	240
Sainsbury's Croissants, Taste the Difference	5.6	26.1	17.5	0.97	438
Sainsbury's Lighter All Butter Croissants	5.7	11.8	7.9	0.73	347
Waitrose Essential Butter Croissants	5.8	22.7	13.9	0.75	412
Sainsbury's Croissants	5.9	23.4	15.9	0.75	420
Sainsbury's Mini Croissants	5.9	23.4	15.9	0.75	420
Tesco Finest All Butter Croissants	6.1	28.2	17	0.8	453
Morrisons Signature All Butter Croissants	6.5	24.2	14.9	0.8	425
Asda Chosen by You Reduced Fat Croissants	6.6	13.8	7.7	0.9	357
Morrisons All Butter Croissants	6.8	20.3	11.6	0.7	410
Asda Chosen by You All Butter Croissants	6.8	20.3	11.6	0.9	410
Asda Chosen by You Croissants	6.8	20	12	0.9	406
Tesco Canadian Maple Pancakes	6.9	9.3	1.6	0.9	266
Tesco All Butter Croissants	6.9	19.1	12	0.8	388
Tesco Mini Croissants	6.9	19.1	12	0.8	388
Genius Gluten Free English Muffins	7	5.6	0.4	0.95	288
Waitrose All Butter Scones	7.5	9.9	6.6	0.9	314
Tesco Lemon And Poppy Seed Pancakes	8.2	8.2	1	0.8	259
Sainsbury's White Muffins	8.3	1.4	0.2	1	245
Tesco Potato Cakes	8.5	3.3	0.3	1	207
Morrisons Pancakes	8.5	10.7	4.8	1.5	212
Genius Gluten Free Croissants	9	28.8	12.4	0.8	457

Bakery

Product	Sugar	Fat	Sat	Salt	Cals
			per 100g		
Waitrose Maple Syrup Panckes	10.1	4.2	0.4	0.93	238
Waitrose Pains au Chocolat	10.3	26.2	17.1	0.61	442
Sainsbury's Cornish Clotted Cream Scones, Taste the Difference	10.4	15.2	9.9	1.25	368
Genesis Big Pancakes	11	4.1	0.7	1.3	213
Waitrose Essential Sliced Brioche Loaf	11.2	11.3	5.5	0.88	343
Asda Chosen by You Sweet Pancakes	11.2	10	4.6	0.5	263
Waitrose Essential Brioche Rolls	11.4	12.9	5.7	0.88	377
Waitrose Pains Aux Raisins	11.6	13.6	8.9	0.45	316
Asda Chosen by You English Classic Pancakes	11.9	10	4.2	0.8	263
Sainsbury's Butter Brioche Loaf	12	16.3	6.3	1	386
Tesco Finest Brioche Loaf	12.2	14.1	8.5	0.8	371
Sainsbury's Butter Brioche Roll	12.5	11.3	4.7	0.95	352
Tesco Finest All Butter Scones	12.6	15	9.6	1.5	369
La Boulangere Pains Au Choc	12.7	22.9	11.9	0.8	419
Tesco Finest Butter Briochettes	12.7	12.5	8.5	1	354
Morrisons Butter Brioche Rolls	13	11.6	4.8	0.88	357
Morrisons Sliced Fruited Teacakes	13.2	3.5	0.5	0.8	275
Sainsbury's Pain au Chocolat, Taste the Difference	13.3	23.3	14.1	0.78	435
Asda Chosen by You Brioche Rolls	13.3	12.2	1.7	1.2	360
Waitrose LoveLife Fruit, Nut & Seed Muffins	13.4	9.1	3.6	0.6	325
Waitrose All Butter Sultana Scones	13.4	9	5.8	0.95	302
Morrisons Brioche Pain au Chocolat	13.5	26.4	14	0.97	448
Waitrose Mini Pains au Chocolat	13.5	28.1	18.3	0.57	469
Morrisons Cinnamon & Sultana Muffins	13.7	1.4	0.4	0.5	244
Sainsbury's Mini Pain Au Chocolat	13.9	24.1	14.4	0.73	439
Waitrose Charentes Butter Pains Au Chocolat	13.9	24.4	16.2	0.67	437
Tesco Butter Brioche Rolls	14	11.4	5.5	1	355
Asda Chosen by You All Butter Chocolatines	14.2	21.8	14.4	0.9	418
Warburtons Teacakes	14.3	3	0.5	0.75	262
Warburtons Fruit Loaf With Orange	14.5	3	0.6	0.85	266

Bakery

Product	Sugar	Fat	Sat per 100g	Salt	Cals
Brioche Pasquier Milk Brioche Rolls	15	12.9	6.4	1.275	360
Brioche Pasquier Sliced Brioche Loaf	15	12	4.5	0.95	363
Asda Chosen by You Butter Brioche Loaf	15	13.5	5.5	1	364
Waitrose Essential Fruited Teacakes	15	6.6	2.6	0.4	301
Tesco Sliced Brioche Loaf	15.3	10.5	4	1.2	344
Tesco Finest All Butter Pains Au Chocolate	15.5	23.7	14.1	0.7	432
Asda Chosen by You Mini All Butter Pain au Chocolat	15.9	20.3	11.7	0.8	415
Tesco Finest Belgian Chocolate Briochettes	16	13.9	9.2	0.8	360
Waitrose Essential Chocolate Chip Brioche Rolls	16.1	12.9	3.9	0.98	362
Waitrose Essential Chocolate Chip Wrapped Brioche Rolls	16.1	12.9	3.9	0.98	362
Brioche Pasquier Croissants	16.4	21.7	14.8	1.08	420
Morrisons Hot Cross Buns	16.4	3.2	0.6	0.7	271
Genius Gluten Free Spicy Fruit Loaf	16.5	8	1	0.5	294
Tesco Large Pancakes	16.8	12.1	1.3	0.5	288
Sainsbury's Freefrom Hot Cross Buns	16.8	8.3	0.9	0.59	300
Asda Chosen by You Sliced Plain Brioche Loaf	16.9	11.3	4.2	1.2	344
Warburtons Pancakes	17.2	6.4	0.9	1.18	254
Tesco Pains Au Chocolate	17.2	25.5	15.4	0.6	446
Sainsbury's All Butter Scones	17.2	12.7	7.3	0.95	366
Asda Chosen by You Butter Scones	17.3	14.5	9.6	1.1	380
Sainsbury's Milk Chocolate Chip Brioche Roll	17.4	12.2	4.6	0.95	353
Morrisons All Butter Pain Au Chocolat	17.8	20.5	11.9	0.7	416
Tesco Scotch Pancakes	17.9	5.9	0.5	1	262
Asda Chosen by You Cinnamon & Raisin Fruit Loaf	18	3.1	1.2	0.4	275
Tesco All Butter Scones	18.3	13.7	8.4	0.9	372
Asda Smart Price Sultana Scones	18.3	7.8	2.4	0.8	332
Waitrose Essential Raspberry Jam Doughnuts	18.4	11.1	5.7	0.36	328
Morrisons Choc Chip Brioche Rolls	18.5	12.9	4.1	0.89	356
La Boulangere Raisin Swirls	18.6	6.6	1	0.69	286
Tesco Choc Chip Brioche Swirls	18.8	8.1	2.5	0.7	301

Product	Sugar	Fat	Sat per 100g	Salt	Cals
Sainsbury's Iced Buns	18.8	9.3	3.6	0.48	336
Tesco Raisin Brioche Swirls	19	6.3	1	0.7	283
Asda Chosen by You Chocolate Chip Brioche Rolls	19	12.4	3.8	1	357
Sainsbury's Scotch Pancakes	19.2	4.4	0.4	1	260
La Boulangere Choc Chip Spiralos	19.2	8	2.5	0.6	294
Sainsbury's Spiced Fruit Muffins, Taste the Difference	19.3	6	3.4	0.58	285
Sainsbury's Freefrom Syrup Pancakes	19.4	3.4	0.4	1.26	261
Sainsbury's Fruit Loaf	19.5	5.1	0.9	0.36	287
Tesco Everyday Value Sultana Scone	19.5	9	3.9	1.1	335
Asda Chosen by You Derby Scones	19.6	10.6	6.5	0.9	353
Tesco Finest Large Teacakes	19.9	5.7	3.1	0.6	281
Sainsbury's Hot Cross Buns	20.1	5.1	1.2	0.44	289
Sainsbury's Hot Cross Buns, Be Good To Yourself	20.1	2.7	0.7	0.39	267
Soreen Banana Loaf	20.2	4.9	0.9	0.7	316
Tesco Brioche Chocolate Chip Rolls	20.3	13.5	4.6	0.8	376
Soreen Fruity Malt Loaf, Sliced	20.6	2	0.3	0.6	313
Waitrose Lemon & Raisin Panckes	20.7	4	0.8	0.95	226
Tesco Finest Sultana Scones	20.9	12.7	8	1.3	359
Tesco Teacakes	20.9	4	1.7	0.5	275
Sainsbury's Pancakes, Basics	21	5.1	0.4	0.73	258
Soreen Orange Loaf	21	4.7	0.9	0.6	324
Sainsbury's Scones, Sultana	21.1	11.8	6.7	0.94	363
Sainsbury's Freefrom Fruit Loaf	21.2	5.2	0.6	0.68	274
Sainsbury's Sultana Scones, Taste the Difference	21.3	11.1	7.1	1.5	340
Tesco White Hot Cross Buns	21.3	4.7	1	0.5	284
Sainsbury's Teacakes	21.4	4.9	0.6	0.47	291
Morrisons Scotch Pancakes	21.5	6	0.8	0.7	279
Warburtons Raisin Loaf With Cinnamon	21.6	3.7	0.6	0.83	273
Soreen Large Fruit Loaf	21.7	2.6	0.5	0.7	306
Tesco Sliced Fruit Loaf	21.7	4.2	0.7	0.4	279

Bakery

Product	Sugar	Fat	Sat per 100g	Salt	Cals
Asda Chosen by You Fruit Loaf	21.7	4.2	0.7	0.4	279
Waitrose Essential Sweet Yum Yums	21.8	28.2	13.3	0.4	453
Waitrose Richly Fruited Loaf	22.1	4.4	1.7	0.6	292
Waitrose Essential Scotch Pancakes	22.3	5.4	0.5	0.88	257
Waitrose Essential Hot Cross Buns	22.4	4.4	1.3	0.35	273
Kingsmill Perfect Pancakes	22.5	4.7	0.7	1.25	269
Sainsbury's Large Teacakes, Taste the Difference	22.6	6.2	3.8	0.75	321
Tesco Finest All Butter And Cherry Scones	22.9	10.3	6.5	1.2	349
Tesco Blueberry Muffins	23.2	19.2	1.5	0.6	396
Waitrose Richly Fruited Hot Cross Buns	23.4	4.3	1.8	0.57	275
Waitrose Cinnamon & Raisin Hot Cross Buns	24.4	3.7	0.6	0.6	267
Tesco Sultana Scones	24.5	10.7	6.6	0.9	351
Asda Chosen by You Scotch Pancakes	24.6	5.2	0.8	0.8	281
Morrisons Fruited Loaf	24.9	5	0.9	0.75	305
Tesco Finest White Hot Cross Buns	25.1	5.4	2.8	0.6	283
Haywood & Padgett Cherry & Sultana Scones	25.3	9.3	3.6	1.1	338
Sainsbury's Hot Cross Buns Fruity, Taste the Difference	25.7	5	1.3	0.65	298
Waitrose Essential Blueberry Muffins	25.9	19.7	3.1	0.5	380
Tesco Lemon And Raisin Pancakes	26.1	6.6	1	0.9	284
Asda Chosen by You Butter & Sultana Scones	26.3	12.6	7.7	1	375
Morrisons Lemon & Raisin Pancakes	27.1	5	0.7	0.7	279
Asda Chosen by You Individually Wrapped Plain Crepes	28	20	3.5	1.5	428
Asda Chosen by You Chocolate Waffles	28	25.2	15.2	0.5	467
Tesco Finest Welsh Cakes	28.1	15.2	9.6	1	393
Tesco Belgian Liege Sugar Waffles	28.4	22.3	9.1	0.6	445
Sainsbury's Lemon & Raisin Pancakes	28.7	23.1	4.1	0.93	269
Asda Chosen by You Sugared Waffles	28.7	23.3	12.3	0.5	453
Tesco Sweet Butter Crepes	29	17	11	1.2	414
McVitie's Toasting Waffles	29.5	25.5	10.2	0.73	461
Pitch Chocolate Brioche	29.8	11 g	2.6	1.05	350

Product	Sugar	Fat	Sat	Salt	Cals
			per 100g		
Asda Chosen by You Individually Wrapped Crunchy Crepes	32	23	11	0.73	466
Kingsmill Waffles	32.4	25.8	7.1	0.75	467
Asda Chosen by You Sugared Waffle	32.5	21.6	4.1	0.5	446
Asda Chosen by You Waffles	33.2	21.3	3.8	0.8	442
Sainsbury's Freefrom Sultana Scones	33.2	6.9	2.6	0.9	342
Sainsbury's Belgian Waffles, Taste the Difference	33.5	29.2	18.6	0.65	499
Asda Chosen by You Caramel Waffles	34	21	12	0.6	457
Tesco Chocolate Zig Zag Crepes	35	22	8	0.6	462
Tesco Chocolate Filled Crepes	35.1	17.4	4	1	429
Morrisons Strawberry Crepes	37.3	8.3	1.9	0.8	362
Sainsbury's Chocolate Filled Crepes	37.6	18.4	5.5	0.93	449
Asda Chosen by You Toffee Crepes	38	17	5.3	1.1	420
Tesco Strawberry Zig Zag Crepes	39	8.5	4.9	0.7	362
Asda Chosen by You Double Chocolate Crepes	39	21	6.1	0.6	459
Asda Chosen by You Chocolate Crepes	40	23	7.4	0.65	492
Morrisons Chocolate & Hazelnut Filled Crêpes	40.1	22.3	5.8	0.6	467

Biscuits

We know biscuits contain very high amounts of sugar, but I've included them so you can choose the best of a bad bunch.

To help you make the best choices, products are listed starting with the least sugar first.

Product	Sugar	Fat	Sat per 100g	Salt	Cals
Tesco Finest Lemon Shortbread Thins	8.7	27.5	18.7	0.7	526
Asda Chosen by You Shortbread Fingers	10.4	27.2	17.3	0.5	515
Sainsbury's Freefrom Shortcake	12.8	23.6	11	0.25	486
Tesco Finest Shortbread Fingers	13.7	25.8	16.6	0.7	515
Nature Valley Protein Seeds Bars	14	23.3	3.2	0.77	465
Asda Extra Special Scottish Shortbread Fingers	14	27.4	16.6	0.6	520
Harvest Chewee Milk Chocolate Chip	14.5	14.5	6.1	0.5	436
Tesco Thick All Butter Shortbread Fingers	14.6	26.4	16.2	0.7	507
Waitrose Scottish Shortbread Fingers	14.9	29.2	18.4	0.57	525
Sainsbury's Highland Shortbread Fingers, SO Organic	15	30	19.3	0.75	530
Quaker Oat So Simple Morning Bars, Raspberry & Pomegranate	15	9.6	2.8	0.43	403
Weetabix Oaty Milk Chocolate Cereal Bars	15	6.5	2.1	0.13	343
Quaker Oat So Simple Morning Bars, Golden Syrup	15.4	10	3	0.51	407
Morrisons Shortbread Fingers	15.5	30.8	15.5	0.7	530
Nairn's Gluten Free Biscuit Break, Oats & Stem Ginger	15.7	18.6	7.7	1.28	459
Asda Chosen by You Shortcake Biscuits	15.8	25.4	11.1	0.5	502
Jordans Absolute Nut Cereal Bars	15.9	43.6	3.9	<.01	578
Quaker Oat So Simple Morning Bars, Strawberry & Yoghurt	16.1	9.3	3	0.62	426
McVitie's Digestives	16.6	21.3	10.1	1.3	481
Nairn's Gluten Free Biscuit Break, Oat & Syrup	16.6	20.4	8.3	1.17	469
Asda Chosen by You Mini Malted Milks	16.6	18.7	8.8	0.8	461
Asda Chosen by You Gluten Free Shortbread	16.7	28	11	0.8	501
Nairn's Wheat Free Ginger Biscuits	17.2	14.4	5.9	0.91	438
Eat Natural Bar, Almond, Apricot & Yogurt Gluten Free	17.6	25.6	16.8	0.08	462

Biscuits

Product	Sugar	Fat	Sat	Salt	Cals
			per 100g		
9 Bar Peanut	17.7	43	7.7	1	576
Asda Gluten Free Digestives Biscuits	17.7	24.3	8.8	0.5	490
Tesco Shortcake Biscuits	17.9	24.8	11.3	0.6	509
Waitrose Mini Shortbread	17.9	28.1	16.6	0.60	522
Morrisons Digestives	18	20.3	9.9	0.9	483
Morrisons Pink Wafers	18	34.1	22.4	0.1	558
Deans All Butter Petticoat	18.2	25.8	15.6	0.6	514
Deans All Butter Shortbread Fingers	18.2	25.8	15.6	0.6	514
Tesco Everyday Value Rich Tea	18.3	13.6	5.4	0.6	449
Alpen Light Cherry Bakewell Bars	18.4	5.6	1.7	0.16	342
Tesco Breakfast Biscuits Milk and Cereal	18.5	16	6.7	1.3	451
Tesco Digestives	18.5	22.4	10.1	0.9	491
Waitrose Essential Shortcake Biscuits	18.5	23.7	10.1	0.78	496
Waitrose Essential Malted Milk Biscuits	18.6	21.2	10.2	0.83	479
Quaker Oat So Simple Bar, Fruit Muesli	18.7	9.1	2.7	0.46	398
Sainsbury's Giant Shortbread Fingers	18.7	28.8	18.8	0.78	521
Sainsbury's Freefrom Digestive Biscuits	18.8	21.1	8.7	0.55	485
Tesco Everyday Value Digestive Biscuits	18.8	22.3	10	1	493
Morrisons Malted Milk Biscuits	18.8	20.8	9.8	0.8	490
Hovis Digestive Biscuits	18.9	20.1	9.4	1.1	479
Tesco Everyday Value Shortbread Fingers	18.9	24.1	10.2	0.5	500
Belvita Breakfast Biscuits, Crunchy Hazelnut	19	12	1.2	0.57	420
Tesco Scottish All Butter Chocolate Chip Shortbread	19	29.1	18.1	0.5	522
Waitrose Essential Digestive Biscuits	19	18.4	8.7	1.02	470
Fox's Moos Malted Milk Biscuit	19.1	21.8	10	0.97	489
Tesco Malted Milk Biscuits	19.1	21.8	10	0.9	494
Tesco Mini Malted Milk	19.2	20.5	9.5	0.9	478
Waitrose Butter Almond Viennese Swirls	19.2	30.1	19.3	0.65	531
Quaker Oat So Simple Crunchy Bar, Golden Syrup	19.5	16.2	1.5	0.36	469
Weetabix Oaty Bars, Toffee	19.6	6.7	2.9	0.21	348

Biscuits

Product	Sugar	Fat	Sat	Salt	Cals
			per 100g		
Quaker Oat So Simple Crunchy Bar, Ginger	19.6	16.1	1.5	0.39	470
Quaker Oat So Simple Crunchy Bar, Maple & Pecan	19.8	17.5	1.6	0.22	478
Waitrose Essential Belgian Chocolate Eclairs	19.8	28.8	12.3	0.25	426
Nature Valley Protein Peanut Chocolate Bars	19.9	22.9	4.5	0.55	466
McVitie's Thin Arrowroot	20	15.2	7.2	1.1	448
Belvita Breakfast Biscuits, Milk & Cereal	20	14	1.4	0.98	440
Morrisons Rich Tea	20	15	6.9	0.9	467
Tesco Reduced Fat Rich Tea Biscuits	20.1	8.7	3.3	0.7	425
McVitie's Light Digestive Biscuits	20.2	14.4	1.5	1.2	447
McVitie's Rich Tea Biscuits	20.2	15.5	1.5	0.8	459
Sainsbury's Eric The Elephant Malted Milk Biscuits	20.2	19.4	9	0.64	476
Sainsbury's Lemon Shortbread Thins, Taste the Difference	20.2	26.3	17.5	0.63	508
Tesco Everyday Value Hazelnut & Raisin Cereal Bars	20.2	16.3	3.2	0.2	422
McVitie's Light Rich Tea	20.3	10.8	1.2	0.9	436
Sainsbury's Digestive Biscuits, SO Organic	20.3	25.3	11.7	0.7	507
Morrisons Signature Shortbread Fingers	20.3	28.1	18	0.6	513
McVitie's Marie	20.4	15.6	7.3	1.1	458
Morrisons Nice Biscuits	20.4	21.1	11	0.7	485
Waitrose Duchy Originals Organic Butter Shortbread Fingers	20.4	32.8	20.6	0.80	546
Rakusen's Sweetmeal Digestive Biscuits	20.5	24.8	12.3	0.42	500
Morrisons Rich Tea Fingers	20.5	13.4	6.2	1	449
Waitrose Seriously Delicate All Butter Rose Shortbread	20.5	29	18.3	0.60	527
Sainsbury's Scottie Shortbread Chocolate Chip	20.7	27.5	15.9	0.75	515
Tesco Rich Tea Fingers	20.7	14.4	6.7	1	455
Asda Chosen by You Rich Tea Fingers	20.7	14.3	6.7	0.9	454
Morrisons Shorties	20.7	22.6	10.5	0.9	490
Waitrose Essential Rich Tea Finger Biscuits	20.8	14.4	6.7	0.98	455
Sainsbury's Highland Shortbread Fingers, Taste the Difference	20.9	27.4	17.1	0.88	515
Asda Chosen by You Rich Tea Biscuits	20.9	13.4	6.2	1	447
Alpen Light Chocolate & Fudge Bars	21	6.5	2.7	0.17	342

Biscuits

Product	Sugar	Fat	Sat	Salt	Cals
			per 100g		
Alpen Light Double Chocolate Bars	21	6.2	2.6	0.21	344
Kellogg's Special K Dark Chocolate Chewy	21	14	6	0.35	404
Tesco Reduced Fat Digestive Biscuits	21	15.6	6.9	1	460
Waitrose Essential Rich Tea Biscuits	21.1	13.4	6.2	1.00	448
Waitrose Seriously Earl Grey and lemon shortbread	21.2	28	18.2	0.48	519
Udi's Gluten Free Chocolate Sandwich Cookies	21.3	18.1	9.1	0.4	473
Waitrose Seriously Coffee Shortbread	21.4	28.1	17.6	0.57	525
Waitrose Seriously Lavender Shortbread	21.6	29.5	18.5	0.59	532
Eat Natural Protein Bar Peanuts & Chocolate	21.7	29.5	10.4	0.5	477
Weight Watchers Oat & Digestive Biscuits	22	14.2	22	0.7	443
Belvita Breakfast Biscuits, Crunchy Oats	22	14.5	1.3	1.38	440
Belvita Breakfast Biscuits, Forest Fruits	22	15	1.7	0.33	450
Alpen Light Lemon Drizzle Bar	22	4	1.5	0.13	328
Kellogg's All-Bran Biscuits, Original	22	20	5	0.65	440
Kellogg's Crunchy Nut Peanut & Chocolate	22	25	10	0.88	485
Kellogg's Nutri-Grain Crunchy Oat Granola Cinnamon Bars	22	19	2.5	0.93	465
Tesco Nice	22	22.2	10.2	0.6	497
Jordans Crunchy Cereal Bars, Honey & Almond	22.2	16.6	1.6	0.12	445
Asda Chosen by You Milk & Oat Breakfast Biscuits 8 Snack Packs	22.3	15.8	7.6	0.8	461
Waitrose All Butter Vanilla Viennese Swirls	22.5	33.7	21.6	0.65	548
Nairn's Chocolate Biscuit Breaks	22.7	20.1	9.2	1.03	470
Nairn's Gluten Free Biscuit Break, Chocolate	22.7	20.1	9.2	1.03	470
Asda Chosen by You Rich Highland Shortie	22.7	21.8	10.4	0.9	486
Waitrose Essential Rich Highland Shortie Biscuits	22.7	21.8	10.4	0.88	487
Sainsbury's Scottie Dogs Chocolate Dipped	22.8	30.5	19.6	0.53	532
Belvita Breakfast Biscuits Crunchy Chocolate Chip	23	12	2.9	0.57	420
Belvita Breakfast Biscuits, Fruit & Fibre	23	14	1.5	0.38	435
Alpen Light Summer Fruit Bars	23	4.1	1.5	0.2	335
Kellogg's All-Bran Biscuits, Chocolate Chip	23	16	5	0.5	418
Weight Watchers Double Chocolate Chip Cookies	23.1	18.4	4.5	0.5	456

Biscuits

Product	Sugar	Fat	Sat per 100g	Salt	Cals
Tesco Everyday Value Nice Biscuits	23.2	20.4	9.3	0.7	488
Tesco Rice Cakes Milk Chocolate	23.2	21.4	13	0.1	480
McVitie's Breakfast Oats Biscuits, Oat & Honey	23.3	14	3.9	1	452
Arden & Amici Cantuccini	23.3	17.6	3.1	0.2	458
Jammie Dodgers Bakes Apricot	23.4	15	7.5	1	421
Kallo Organic Dark Chocolate Ricecakes	23.4	24.1	14.6	trace	488
9 Bar Pumpkin Bars	23.5	34.6	6.6	0.3	510
Waitrose Duchy Originals Organic Sicilian Lemon All Butter Shortbread	23.5	25.5	15.1	0.98	505
Sainsbury's Coconut Cookies	23.6	31.1	19.9	0.23	525
Tesco Rich Shorties Biscuits	23.6	23.2	10.6	0.8	499
Asda Chosen by You Fruit & Fibre Breakfast Biscuits Snack Packs	23.6	16.2	5	0.7	473
Asda Chosen by You Mini Strawberry Flavour Swirls	23.7	23.7	14.4	0.7	500
Belvita Breakfast Biscuits, Crunchy Apricot	24	9.1	1.1	0.63	400
Kellogg's Special K Milk Chocolate Chewy	24	13	5.1	0.43	398
Maryland Gooeys Hazelnut	24	24	10.9	0.59	495
Tesco Chocolate Chip Digestives	24.2	21.6	8.8	1	488
Tesco Finest Earal Grey Shortbread	24.2	30.4	18.9	0.5	537
Weight Watchers Custard Cream Biscuits	24.3	20.2	7	0.6	472
Asda Gluten Free Chocolate Digestives Biscuits	24.3	25	10.2	0.5	493
Sainsbury's Eric The Elephant Party Biscuits	24.5	11.9	7.4	0.86	445
Tesco Peanut Cookies	24.5	29	10	0.5	539
Asda Chosen by You Mini Chocolate Animals	24.5	22.2	10.8	0.6	491
Sainsbury's Chocolate Chip Cereal Bars, Basics	24.6	9	4.3	0.25	397
Waitrose Duchy Originals Organic Stem Ginger All Butter Shortbread	24.7	25	17.3	0.78	502
Tesco Finest Rose Shortbread	24.8	28.5	19.2	0.4	528
Waitrose Duchy Originals Organic Highland All Butter Shortbread	24.8	26.9	16.2	0.85	518
Alpen Light Sultana & Apple Bars	25	3.6	1.5	0.17	329
Kellogg's Special K Cereal Bars, Double Chocolate	25	9	5	0.63	396
Sainsbury's Salted Caramel Cookies, Taste the Difference	25	26	17.2	0.93	502
Tesco Everyday Value Chocolate & Coconut Cereal Bar	25	15.5	9.2	0.3	433

Biscuits

Product	Sugar	Fat	Sat per 100g	Salt	Cals
Asda Chosen by You Peanut Cookies	25	29.5	11	0.4	541
Waitrose Essential Nice Biscuits	25	23.9	13.3	0.30	498
McVitie's Breakfast Oats Biscuits, Apple, Sultana & Cinnamon	25.1	13.3	3.7	1	447
Waitrose Cherry & Almond Cookies	25.2	21	11.1	0.77	460
Sainsbury's Oat & Raisin Bars, Basics	25.4	8.8	3.2	0.03	398
McVitie's HobNobs	25.5	20.3	2.1	0.8	470
Tesco Fruit Shortcake Biscuits	25.6	19.4	8.1	1	465
Asda Chosen by You Fruit Shortcake Biscuits	25.6	19.4	8.1	1	464
Asda Chosen by You Nice Biscuits	25.6	23.9	13.5	0.3	505
Waitrose Essential Fruit Shortcake Biscuits	25.6	19.4	8.1	0.95	465
Cadbury Dairy Milk Biscuit	25.7	25.7	13.6	0.48	470
McVitie's Breakfast Biscuits Raspberry & Yoghurt	25.7	21.1	9.3	0.7	487
Jammie Dodgers Jam & Custard	25.7	13.1	6.2	0.19	420
Kallo Yoghurt & Muesli Thin Rice Cake	25.8	23	12.8	0.1	491
Tesco Finest Treacle Oat Biscuits	25.8	23.4	15.2	1.2	505
Tesco Oaties	25.8	20.6	8.6	0.8	483
Asda Chosen by You Oatie Crumbles	25.8	20.6	8.6	0.8	483
Bonne Maman Traditional French Butter Galette	26	26	15	0.8	513
Kellogg's Special K Hazelnut & Almond Cereal Bars	26	12	2.3	0.8	404
Morrisons Custard Creams	26	21.6	12.5	0.5	491
Waitrose Scottish Chocolate Chip Shortbread	26	25.9	15.4	0.68	505
Asda Smart Price Milk Chocolate Digestives	26.1	22.7	11.7	0.8	491
9 Bar Original Bars	26.2	40.6	10.1	0.3	555
Sainsbury's Oat & Treacle Cookies, Taste the Difference	26.2	23.6	14.1	0.65	490
Asda Chosen by You Coconut Rings	26.2	21.4	11	0.9	485
Waitrose Essential Coconut Ring Biscuits	26.2	21.4	11	0.85	485
McVitie's Fruit Shortcake	26.3	18.9	6.3	0.9	462
Weight Watchers Bourbon Cream Biscuits	26.3	19.5	6.8	0.6	460
Sainsbury's Pink Wafer	26.3	32.9	21.9	0.38	552
Morrisons Oat Nobblies	26.3	19.7	8.7	0.8	490

Biscuits

Product	Sugar	Fat	Sat	Salt	Cals
			per 100g		
Waitrose Viennese Vanilla Swirls	26.3	34.4	18.2	0.05	546
McVitie's Breakfast Biscuits Oat & Yoghurt	26.5	21.3	9.3	0.8	489
Arden & Amici Biscotti	26.5	13.1	3.8	0.18	426
Nature Valley Crunchy Bars, Oats & Hazelnut	26.6	20.3	3.8	0.9	469
Morrisons Fruit Shortcake	26.6	17.3	8.1	0.9	455
Waitrose Essential Plain Chocolate Digestive Biscuits	26.7	23.8	12.2	0.75	499
Sainsbury's Chewy & Crisp Roasted Nut Bar	26.8	19.4	7	0.43	458
Waitrose Duchy Originals Organic Choc & Vanilla All Butter Shortbread	26.9	26.9	16.4	0.65	515
Belvita Breakfast Biscuits, Honey & Nut	27	15.5	1.7	0.9	450
Belvita Breakfast Biscuits, Honey Yogurt	27	16	4.8	0.55	450
Kellogg's Special K Biscuit Moments Chocolate	27	9	3.8	0.73	394
Sainsbury's Chocolate Chip Balance Cereal Bars	27	5.6	3.2	0.46	381
Kallo Organic Milk Chocolate Thin Rice Cakes	27	23	14.3	trace	495
Morrisons Milk Chocolate Digestives	27	23.2	11.8	0.9	497
Fox's Favourites, Cream	27.1	22.1	12.9	0.6	496
Waitrose Essential Chocolate Chip Digestives	27.1	24.4	8.8	0.98	512
Sainsbury's Peanut Cookies	27.2	28.2	8.7	0.4	528
Trek Cocoa Coconut Flapjack	27.2	25.3	27.2	0.8	468
Tesco Vanilla Kube	27.3	6.5	3.3	0.4	381
Weight Watchers Dark Chocolate Digestive Biscuits	27.4	17.8	10.3	0.4	459
Cadbury Animals Chocolate Biscuits	27.4	19.6	9.3	0.6	474
Sainsbury's Belgian Chocolate Chunk Shortbread, Taste the Difference	27.4	31.1	21.7	0.48	536
Cadbury Animals Dinosaurs Minipack	27.5	19.8	9.3	0.64	475
Belvita Breakfast Biscuits, Yogurt Crunch Cocoa	27.5	15	5	0.6	450
9 Bar Cocoa Hazelnut Bars	27.5	40.4	10.9	0.25	573
Morrisons Savers Chocolate Chip Cookies	27.5	23.4	11.6	0.6	499
McVitie's Dark Chocolate Digestive Biscuits	27.6	24.2	12.8	0.9	495
Weight Watchers Ginger & Lemon Cookies	27.7	16.5	3.3	0.6	446
McVitie's Hobnobs Chocolate Chip	27.7	21	9.8	0.7	471
Morrisons Caramel Rice Cakes	27.8	2.1	0.7	trace	394

Biscuits

Product	Sugar	Fat	Sat	Salt	Cals
			per 100g		
Nature Valley Crunchy Bars, Oats & Chocolate	27.9	19.4	5.3	0.6	466
Jordans Breakfast Maple & Pecans Multigrain Bars	27.9	8.3	1.5	0.01	388
Trek Cocoa Oat Flapjack	27.9	22	10.3	0.9	454
9 Bar Cocoa Raspberry Bars	27.9	38.1	10.9	0.25	561
Nature Valley Oats & Choco Bites	27.9	19.4	5.3	0.6	466
Waitrose Mini Oat Biscuits	27.9	21.9	13.7	0.55	482
Fox's Rich Tea Finger Cream Biscuits	28	20	11	0.57	489
Bonne Maman Chocolate Butter Galette	28	27	18	0.8	522
Sainsbury's Plain Chocolate Digestive Biscuits	28	24.1	12.4	0.99	498
Belvita Cocoa & Chocolate Chip	28	14.5	3.3	0.63	440
Kellogg's Special K Biscuit Moments Caramel	28	9	3.8	0.75	382
Nature Valley Crunchy Bars, Canadian Maple Syrup	28	17.1	2.7	0.7	457
Snack a Jacks Caramel	28	2.1	0.4	0.5	392
Alpen Coconut & Chocolate Bars	28	15.6	7.9	0.17	432
Loacker Chocolate Wafer	28	26	22	0.31	511
Tesco Plain Chocolate Digestives	28	24.1	12.4	1	498
Asda Chosen by You Dark Chocolate Digestives	28	24	12	1	508
Cadbury Milk Choc Digestives	28.1	24.3	13	1.44	490
Tracker Roast Nut	28.1	25.1	9.4	28.1	489
Jammie Dodgers Mini Lunchpack	28.2	15.1	7	0.18	445
Cadbury Salted Caramel Biscuit Fingers	28.2	25.6	14.3	0.8	473
Sainsbury's Milk Chocolate Digestives, Basics	28.2	23.7	12.1	0.93	496
Cadbury Salted Peanut Biscuit Fingers	28.3	26.5	14.7	0.6	478
Nature Valley Crunchy Bars, Oat & Honey	28.3	17.2	2.4	0.8	456
Nature Valley Oats & Honey Bites	28.3	17.2	2.4	0.8	456
Tesco Everyday Value Ginger Nuts	28.3	16.2	7.6	1	456
Waitrose Essential Milk Chocolate Digestive Biscuits	28.3	23.7	12.1	1.00	498
Sainsbury's Basics Chocolate & Raisin Bars	28.5	7.7	3.5	0.28	400
Sainsbury's Chewy Chocolate Chip & Nut Bar	28.5	17.3	6.9	0.45	448
Tesco Custard Cream Biscuits	28.5	20.9	10.8	0.5	493

Product	Sugar	Fat	Sat per 100g	Salt	Cals
Tesco Everyday Value Custard Cream Biscuits	28.5	20.9	10.7	0.5	493
Waitrose Essential Custard Creams	28.5	20.9	10.8	0.47	491
Sainsbury's 30% Less Fat Plain Chocolate Digestives	28.6	16	8.3	0.93	455
Asda Chosen by You Mini Chocolate Chip Cookies	28.6	25.5	12.8	0.5	512
Morrisons Bourbon Creams	28.6	20.6	12.1	0.2	486
Sainsbury's Peach & Apricot Balance Cereal Bars	28.7	3.8	2.2	0.4	370
Waitrose Essential Milk Chocolate Malted Milk Biscuits	28.7	23.2	12.1	0.63	500
Nature Valley Sweet & Nutty Bars, Peanut	28.9	27	8.4	0.7	499
Barny Bear Biscuits Milk	29	15	2.2	0.83	390
Fox's Favourites Malted Creams	29	23.2	12	0.5	503
Nature's Path Gluten Free Granola Bars Dark Chocolate Chip	29	10	2.9	0.5	400
Sainsbury's Chocolate Chunk & Hazelnut Cookies, Taste the Difference	29	30.8	13.8	0.8	527
Bahlsen Hit Chocolate Crème Sandwich Biscuit	29	25	17	0.51	508
Dietary Special Gluten Free Bourbon Biscuits	29	24	14	0.48	507
Tesco Mini Chocolate Breakfast Biscuit	29	20	9.5	0.8	473
Asda Chosen by You Malted Milk	29	23.5	12.3	0.6	500
Morrisons Milk Chocolate Biscuit Malted Milk	29	23.5	12.3	0.6	496
McVitie's Orange Chocolate Digestives	29.1	24.7	13	1.1	499
Sainsbury's Ginger Nut Biscuits, SO Organic	29.1	22.6	13.8	0.35	493
Sainbury's Eric the Elephant Chocolate Animal Biscuits	29.2	23.2	12.5	0.5	502
Sainsbury's Muesli Breakfast Biscuit	29.3	13	3.7	0.96	421
Sainsbury's Strawberry & Yogurt Cereal Bars	29.3	11.6	7.6	0.3	416
Sainsbury's Cookies, Basics	29.3	23.9	11.7	0.27	496
Waitrose Seriously White Chocolate & Lemon Biscuits	29.3	29.8	19	0.43	512
Berry Dodgers Mini Snack Biscuits	29.4	14.8	7.2	0.1	447
McVitie's Milk Chocolate Digestive Biscuits	29.5	23.6	12.4	1	495
Lyons Viscount Mint Chocolate Biscuit	29.5	29.5	16	0.51	529
Tesco Dark Chocolate & Hazelnut Cookies	29.5	30.9	12.6	0.8	530
Waitrose Vanilla Viennese Fingers	29.5	28.6	17.4	0.35	531
Sainsbury's Milk Chocolate Malted Milk Biscuits	29.6	24.2	12.4	0.7	505

Biscuits

Product	Sugar	Fat	Sat per 100g	Salt	Cals
Tesco Chocolate Coated Malted Milk	29.6	24.2	12.4	0.7	506
Tesco Everyday Value Bourbon Creams	29.6	21.4	12.8	0.3	490
Asda Chosen by You Chocolate Malted Milks	29.6	24.2	12.4	0.7	501
Asda Chosen by You Mini Milk Chocolate Digestives	29.6	23.7	12.1	0.9	494
Waitrose Pecan & Maple Syrup Cookies	29.6	23.9	10.6	1.26	490
Waitrose Seriously Triple Chocolate Biscuits	29.6	29.3	18.2	0.37	522
Sainsbury's Milk Chocolate Digestive Biscuits	29.7	23.9	12.3	1.09	499
Tesco Milk Chocolate Digestives	29.7	23.9	12.3	1.1	498
Morrisons Milk Chocolate Wafer	29.7	33.4	20.7	0.1	551
Waitrose Seriously Chocolate and Ginger Biscuits	29.8	26.7	16.7	0.52	504
Kallo Kids Mini Milk Chocolate Rice Cakes	29.9	23.8	14.2	0.1	496
Tesco Strawberry & Yoghurt Flavoured Bars	29.9	12.3	9.6	0.2	425
Weight Watchers Milk Chocolate Digestive Biscuits	30	19.5	11.7	0.5	474
Kellogg's Special K Biscuit Moments Raspberry	30	8.7	3.4	0.88	383
Snack a Jacks Choc Chip	30	7	3.5	0.05	414
Barny Bear Biscuits Strawberry	30	11	1.5	0.78	355
9 Bar Flax Seed Bars	30	35.5	10	0.3	523
Tesco Finest Cantuccini Biscuits	30	19	3.2	0.2	457
Asda Chosen by You Milk Chocolate Digestives	30	24	12	1.1	511
Sainsbury's Chocolate Chip Cookies	30.1	25.2	12.9	0.45	504
Sainsbury's Freefrom Rich Tea Biscuits	30.1	18	6.6	0.8	474
Tesco Chocolate Chip Cookies	30.1	25.2	12.8	0.5	505
Nature Valley Crunchy Bars, Oats & Berries	30.2	16.9	2.7	0.7	453
Morrisons Choc Chip Cookies	30.2	25.6	13	0.5	508
Sainsbury's Raspberry & Yogurt Cereal Bars	30.3	11	7.3	0.31	412
Tesco Bourbon Cream	30.3	21.6	13.1	0.3	490
Asda Chosen by You Bourbon Creams	30.3	21.6	13.1	0.3	487
Waitrose Essential Bourbon Creams	30.3	21.6	13.1	0.25	487
McVitie's Mini Gingerbread Men	30.4	16.9	7.9	0.9	462
Cadbury Fingers	30.5	27.1	14.8	0.4	516

Biscuits

Product	Sugar	Fat	Sat	Salt	Cals
			per 100g		
Cadbury Milk Chocolate Fingers	30.5	27.1	14.8	0.4	516
Sainsbury's Red Fruit Balance Cereal Bars	30.5	5.5	3.1	0.43	379
Sainsbury's Giant Chocolate & Hazelnut Cookies	30.5	29.3	11.3	0.45	521
Asda Chosen by You Custard Creams	30.6	21.5	13.5	0.5	493
Asda Chosen by You Chocolate Chip Cookies	30.6	24.3	13	0.7	508
Waitrose Essential Custard Cream Biscuits	30.6	21.1	11.3	0.47	487
McVitie's Ginger Nut	30.8	16.6	7.9	0.9	461
Tracker Chocolate Chip	30.8	23.7	10.2	0.43	483
McVitie's Double Chocolate Digestives	30.9	24.3	12.9	1	497
Jammie Dodgers Bakes Raspberry	30.9	15	7.5	1	421
Tesco Apple Crumble Cereal Bars	30.9	12.8	6.7	0.1	418
Asda Smart Price Chocolate Chip Cookies	30.9	22.6	11	0.8	492
Waitrose Chocolate Viennese Fingers	30.9	32.4	19.1	0.35	549
Fox's Jam Ring Creams	31	23	13	0.45	500
Cadbury Dream Fingers	31	27.9	15.4	0.6	518
Kellogg's Special K Biscuit Moments Blueberry	31	9	3.3	0.78	395
Kellogg's Special K Biscuit Moments Strawberry	31	8	2.8	0.75	390
Jordans Breakfast In a Bar Fruit & Nut	31	12.8	2.7	0.01	411
Kellogg's Nutri-Grain Oat Bakes Bars Totally Oaty	31	15	1.5	0.25	413
Waitrose Essential Jam Sandwich Creams	31.1	22.4	12.9	0.55	488
Cadbury Dairy Mily Biscuit	31.2	25.7	13.6	0.48	470
Tesco Jam Sandwich Creams	31.2	22.5	12.1	0.5	496
Tesco Everyday Value Chocolate Chip Cookie	31.3	22.7	11.3	0.6	495
McVitie's Hobnobs Dark Chocolate	31.4	23.8	11.9	0.7	492
Tesco Buttery Viennese Fingers	31.4	29.4	16.4	0.6	533
Waitrose Belgian Chocolate & Hazelnut Cookies	31.4	30	13.9	0.67	524
Maryland Big & Chunky Hazelnut Crunch	31.5	29.8	13.1	0.8	520
Sainsbury's Milk Chocolate Rich Tea Biscuits	31.6	19.8	10.1	0.55	482
Waitrose Scottish Stem Ginger Shortbread	31.6	22	14	0.50	478
Asda Extra Special Belgian Double Chocolate & Hazelnut Cookies	31.7	30.6	12.4	0.9	537

Biscuits

Product	Sugar	Fat	Sat	Salt	Cals
			per 100g		
Alpen Fruit & Nut Bars	31.8	7.7	1.5	0.28	389
Tesco Finest Fruit & Oat Cookies	31.8	20.2	13.9	0.9	454
Fox's Chocolate Viennese Melts	31.9	28.3	16.1	0.65	526
Chips Ahoy! Crispy Choco Caramel Cookies	32	24	12.5	1.38	495
Jammie Dodger Biscuits	32	11.7	5.5	0.3	420
Barny Bear Biscuits Chocolate	32	15.5	4.5	0.83	390
Cadbury Snack Shortcake	32	27	14.5	0.6	515
Kellogg's Frosties Cereal & Milk Bars	32	11	7.5	0.75	411
Kellogg's Pop Tarts Strawberry	32	11	5	0.88	400
Kellogg's Rice Krispies Squares Marshmallow	32	12	7	0.75	424
Kellogg's Rice Krispies Totally Chcolatey Scares	32	12	7	0.75	424
Bahlsen First Class Plainchoco Late	32	37	22	0.12	560
Dietary Special Gluten Free Chocolate Fingers	32	28	15	0.75	521
Waitrose Duchy Originals Organic Orange Biscuits Coated in Dark Chocolate	32	29.3	17.4	0.45	526
Jordans Frusli Raisin & Hazelnut Cereal Bars	32.1	12.2	1.8	0.03	399
McVitie's BN Chocolate	32.2	16.8	9.4	0.5	465
Maryland Double Chocolate	32.3	23	11.4	0.39	488
Tesco Finest Stem Ginger Cookies	32.4	19.9	11.3	1.1	489
McVitie's Medley Digestive Bars, Caramel & Milk	32.5	14.5	8.3	0.7	428
McVitie's Medley Hobnob Double Chocolate Bars	32.6	14.1	7.7	0.7	427
Maryland Chocolate Chip & Hazelnut Biscuits	32.7	25.2	11.8	0.64	497
Cadbury Milk Chocolate Fingers Honeycomb	32.8	22.9	12.3	0.6	455
Sainsbury's Chocolate Digestive Bars, Basics	32.8	24.1	12.8	0.93	503
Fudges Dipped Ginger Biscuits	32.8	28.3	17.1	0.61	525
Tesco Everyday Value Milk Chocolate Digestive Biscuit Bars	32.8	24.1	12.8	0.8	504
Asda Smart Price Milk Chocolate Digestive Bars	32.8	24.1	12.8	0.8	503
Fox's Crinkles Butter Biscuits	33	18	9.1	0.96	468
Cadbury Milk Chocolate Rich Tea	33	19.7	10.2	0.22	480
Fox's Chocolatey Viennese Sandwich	33	28	15	0.55	526
McVitie's Hobnobs Milk Chocolate	33	23.3	11.5	0.7	491

Biscuits

Product	Sugar	Fat	Sat per 100g	Salt	Cals
Fruitus Apricot Oat Bars	33	14	2.8	trace	382
Kellogg's Fruity Breakfast Bars, Apple	33	7.7	2.9	0.78	353
Kellogg's Fruity Breakfast Bars, Blackberry & Apple	33	7.7	2.9	0.88	354
Kellogg's Nutri-Grain Morning Bar Strawberry	33	7.7	2.9	0.78	354
Kellogg's Nutri-Grain Soft & Fruity Bars, Blueberry	33	7.7	2.9	0.78	353
Kellogg's Nutri-Grain Soft & Fruity Bars, Strawberry	33	7.7	2.9	0.78	354
Kellogg's Nutri-Grain Strawberry	33	7.7	2.9	0.78	354
Kellogg's Pop Tarts Choctastic	33	11	5	1.13	396
Nakd Bar Ginger Bread	33	20.8	2.5	<1	450
Fox's Chunkie Cookie, Fruit & Nut	33	24	11	0.37	493
Bahlsen Choco Leibniz Biscuits, Dark Chocolate	33	25	16	0.53	498
Dietary Special Gluten Free Custard Creams	33	22	13	0.55	500
De Beukelaer Chocolate Milk	33	20	12	0.63	486
Fox's Chocolatey Fruit & Nut Chunkies	33	24	11	0.37	493
Nakd Ginger Bread	33	30.8	2.5	<1	450
Asda Chosen by You Cocoa Creams	33	19	12	0.4	477
Jordans Frusli Blueberries Cereal Bars	33.1	7.1	1.4	0.03	375
Waitrose Essential Milk Chocolate Digestive Bars	33.1	24.8	13.4	0.79	507
Waitrose Essential Chocolate Chip Muffins	33.1	18.8	5.1	0.38	399
Nature's Store White Chocolate Rice Cake	33.3	22.5	13.3	0.13	493
Nature's Store White Chocolate Rice Cake	33.3	22.5	13.3	0.13	493
Sainsbury's Giant White Chocolate & Raspberry Cookies	33.3	26.1	13	0.65	499
Tesco Berry & Almond Bakewell Cereal Bars	33.3	14.5	6.8	0.1	427
Tesco Milk Chocolate Oaties	33.3	22.9	10.9	0.7	495
Fox's Coconut Crinkles Biscuits	33.5	22.6	13.5	0.59	487
Maryland Chocolate Chip Cookies	33.5	22.6	10.2	0.5	487
Tesco Ginger Nuts	33.5	14.7	6.9	1	450
Tesco Cranberry Crispy Slices	33.5	3.9	1.1	0.7	380
Tesco Raisin Crispy Slices	33.5	3.9	1.1	0.7	380
Sainsbury's 35% Reduced Fat Ginger Snaps	33.6	9	4.2	0.83	421

Biscuits

Product	Sugar	Fat	Sat	Salt	Cals
			per 100g		
Sainsbury's Almond Cantucci, Taste the Difference	33.6	18.9	4.4	0.18	459
Pink Panther Gluten Free Wafers	33.6	36.7	24.7	0.1	576
Asda Chosen by You Fig Rolls	33.6	11.1	5.1	0.4	382
Asda Chosen by You Ginger Nuts	33.6	14.7	6.9	1	452
Waitrose Essential Ginger Nuts	33.6	14.7	7	0.98	452
Waitrose Stem Ginger All Butter Cookies	33.7	18.8	11.8	0.99	460
Jordans Frusli Red Berries Cereal Bars	33.8	7.2	1.5	0.25	374
Prewett's Gluten & Wheat Free Jammy Wheels	33.9	23.2	9.1	0.4	470
Asda Free From Jammy Wheels	33.9	23.2	9.1	0.4	479
Fox's Caramel Waffles	34	21	12	0.63	457
Fox's Chunkie Cookie Bites Chocolate Chip	34	22	12	0.63	491
Fox's Chunkie Cookie Bites White Chocolate	34	22	12	0.65	493
Kellogg's Special K Peach & Apricot Bars	34	6.1	3.4	0.63	389
Fox's Raspberry & Cream Viennese Melts	34	28	17	0.67	517
Kambly Butterfly Almond Biscuits	34	18	7.6	0.47	476
Waitrose Mini Choc Chip Cookies	34	26.4	17	0.65	508
Sainsbury's All Butter Sultana Cookies, Taste the Difference	34.1	20	13.3	0.75	459
Tesco Sticky Toffee Cereal Bites	34.1	13.6	7.5	0.1	429
Tesco Finest Quadruple Chocolate Cookie	34.1	23.9	14.6	0.7	485
Asda Chosen by You Mini Beanies	34.1	24.2	12.7	0.6	510
Waitrose Belgian White Chocolate Cookies	34.1	27.2	17	1.07	512
Prewett's Gluten & Wheat Free Chocolate Cookies	34.2	30	15.7	0.3	530
Asda Chosen by You Milk Chocolate Oatie Crumbles	34.2	22.7	11.3	0.7	497
Asda Chosen by You Apple and Raisin Slices	34.2	10.7	7.5	0.5	423
Morrisons Ginger Nuts	34.2	16.2	7.7	0.8	464
Waitrose Flapjack All Butter Cookies	34.2	19.1	12.6	0.70	441
Sainsbury's White Chocolate Cookies, Taste the Difference	34.3	25.8	16.8	0.93	507
Asda Chosen by You Apple & Raisin Crispy Slices	34.3	7.7	1.4	0.6	400
Nakd Bar Pecan Pie	34.4	31.4	2.6	<1	477
Maryland Milk & Dark Chocolate Chunk Cookie Snack Packs	34.4	28	14.8	0.8	513

Biscuits

Product	Sugar	Fat	Sat	Salt	Cals
			per 100g		
Maryland Big & Chunky Milk & Dark Chocolate	34.4	28	14.8	34.4	513
Sainsbury's Freefrom Stem Ginger Cookies	34.5	21.8	10.6	0.1	482
Jordans Breakfast In a Bar Cranberry & Raspberry	34.6	5.6	1.2	0.01	370
Tunnock's Caramel Wafers	34.7	17.4	12.7	0.67	448
Jordans Frusli Cranberries & Apples Cereal Bars	34.7	7.1	1.4	0.03	397
Cadbury Chocolate Mini Fingers	34.9	27.1	10.8	0.5	515
Alpen Blueberry, Cranberry, Yoghurt Bar	34.9	11	6.3	0.15	422
Chips Ahoy! Popcorn Candy Chip Cookies	35	25	13	1.27	505
Mikado Milk Chocolate Biscuits	35	19.5	11.5	0.7	480
Alpen Strawberry & Yoghurt Bars	35	10	5.4	0.18	415
Fruitus Mixed Berry Oat Bars	35	17	3.2	trace	407
Kellogg's Rice Krispies Squares, Totally Chocolate	35	13	10	0.63	432
Kellogg's Special K Red Berry Bars	35	5.1	3	0.63	386
Bahlsen Pick Up!	35	26	15	0.49	511
Lazy Day Foods Millionnaire's Shortbread	35	29	12	1	497
Waitrose Essential jam tarts	35	12.7	5.3	0.04	399
McVitie's Choc Gems	35.1	23	12.7	0.8	495
Maryland Big & Chunky White Chocolate Brownie	35.1	26.9	14.2	0.8	509
Asda Gluten Free Chocolate Chip Cookies Biscuits	35.1	22.5	9.7	0.5	487
McVitie's Victoria Biscuits	35.1	25.9	14	0.7	510
Lyons Toffypops	35.2	19.9	10.4	0.46	451
Tesco Finest Free From Chocolate & Cranberry Cookies	35.2	24	14.5	0.6	497
Little Treats Co Chocolate Mini Men Biscuits	35.3	14.2	7	0.3	429
Tunnock's Dark Chocolate Wafers	35.4	17.9	12	0.63	455
Go Ahead Apple Bakes	35.4	8.3	3.8	0.6	380
Sainsbury's Freefrom Gingerbread Man	35.4	16.7	4.4	0.53	451
Cadbury Peanut Brunch Bar	35.5	20	9	0.57	460
Prewett's Gluten & Wheat Free Chocolate Digestives	35.5	24.7	11.7	0.3	490
Fudges Decadent Dark Chocolate Florentines	35.6	37.3	15.3	0.22	565
Waitrose Milk Chocolate Chip Cookies	35.7	28.8	18.1	0.53	524

Biscuits

Product	Sugar	Fat	Sat	Salt	Cals
			per 100g		
Jammie Dodgers	35.8	13.5	6.5	0.36	420
Sainsbury's Milk Chocolate Shortbread Rings, Taste the Difference	35.8	31.8	19.5	0.5	541
Tesco Garibaldi Biscuits	35.8	8.9	4.1	0.3	388
Asda Extra Special Belgian Chocolate Florentine Selection	35.9	36.9	16.3	0.3	567
Fox's Milk Chocolate Chunk Cookie	36	25	13	0.57	502
Tunnock's Milk Chocolate Biscuits	36	19.2	10.5	0.7	440
Alpen Fruit & Nut with Milk Chocolate Bars	36	13	5.1	0.2	431
Kellogg's Rice Krispies Cereal & Milk Bars	36	11	8	0.63	411
Kellogg's Special K Chocolate & Mint Bars	36	10	5	0.5	410
Kellogg's Special K Chocolate & Raspberry Bars	36	10	5	0.63	411
Sainsbury's Giant Extremely Chocolatey Cookies	36	29	15	0.57	524
Bahlsen First Class Milk	36	36	21	0.21	561
McVitie's BN Raspberry	36.1	8.6	4.1	0.5	396
Jordans Frusli Bars, Juicey Apples & Sultanas	36.1	7.8	1.7	0.03	379
Asda Chosen by You Forest Fruit & Raisin Slices	36.4	7.3	1.2	0.6	394
Morrisons Signature All Butter Stem Ginger Cookies	36.4	20.8	12.7	0.8	473
Morrisons Chocolate Cereal Bar	36.4	14.4	8.1	0.7	433
Waitrose Belgian Double Chocolate Cookies	36.5	23.6	14.9	0.73	493
Morrisons Signature All Butter Sultana Cookies	36.7	19.4	12	0.7	449
Go Ahead Apple & Sultana Crispy Slices	36.8	7.2	0.9	0.5	392
Morrisons Garibaldi	36.8	9.6	4.5	0.3	399
Waitrose Belgian Triple Chocolate Cookies	36.8	25.8	15.2	0.86	501
Asda Chosen by You Garibaldi	36.9	9.1	4.2	0.3	375
Waitrose Essential Garibaldi Biscuits	36.9	9.2	4.2	0.31	378
Oreo Chocolate Cream Cookies	37	19	9.2	0.9	465
Bahlsen Pick Up! Black N White	37	27	16	0.64	522
Mikado Daim Chocolate Biscuits	37	17.5	10.5	0.7	470
Alpen Raspberry & Yoghurt Bars	37	11	6.1	0.19	425
Kellogg's Nutri-Grain Breakfast Bars, Chocolate Chip	37	13	3	0.53	404
Kellogg's Nutri-Grain Breakfast Bakes, Ginger	37	10	0.9	0.43	377

Product	Sugar	Fat	Sat per 100g	Salt	Cals
Kellogg's Rice Krispies Cereal Bars, Squares Rocky Road	37	11	7	0.55	420
Lazy Day Foods Belgian Dark Chocolate Tiffin	37	30	15	1	488
De Beukelaer Cookies Bakery Creamy	37	23	13	0.68	481
Kellogg's Elevenses Chocolate Chip	37	13	3	0.53	404
Kellogg's Elevenses Ginger	37	10	0.9	0.43	377
Tesco Dark Chocolate Coated Biscuits	37	25	16	0.3	495
Waitrose Continental Dark Chocolate Butter Biscuits	37	25	15.8	0.25	502
Waitrose Chocolate Chip & Hazelnut Cookies	37	31.4	15.5	0.68	529
Go Ahead Blueberry Crispy Slices	37.1	7.1	0.8	0.6	392
Go Ahead Orange & Sultana Crispy Slices	37.1	7	0.8	0.6	392
Go Ahead Forest Fruit Crispy Slices	37.2	7	0.8	0.6	392
Jacob's Fig Roll	37.3	8	3.5	0.5	372
Cadbury Bournville Biscuits	37.3	30.7	18	0.45	520
Go Ahead Raspberry Crispy Slices	37.3	7	0.8	0.6	392
Go Ahead Red Cherry Crispy Slices	37.3	7	0.8	0.5	392
Morrisons Signature All Butter Triple Chocolate Cookies	37.3	27.4	16.9	0.8	513
Sainsbury's Freefrom Chocolate Chip Cookies	37.4	24.6	12.9	0.16	503
Asda Chosen by You Smileys	37.4	21	7.6	0.5	487
Cadbury Brunch Bar, Chocolate Chip	37.5	17	8.9	0.63	445
Kallo Milk Chocolate & Caramel Thin Rice Cake	37.6	21.8	13.5	0.1	485
Asda Extra Special Belgian Dark Chocolate Cookies	37.6	24.2	14.7	0.9	505
Tesco Orange Chocolate Biscuits	37.8	27.3	15.6	0.4	519
Go Ahead Strawberry Crispy Slices	37.9	7.2	0.8	0.6	392
Oreo Cookies	38	20	9.8	0.9	480
Fox's Chunkie Cookies White Chocolate Chunks	38	25	14	0.57	509
Fox's Double Chocolate Crunch Cream	38	25	14	0.95	511
Kellogg's Rice Krispies Squares Totally Chocolatey Mint	38	14	9	0.75	437
Kellogg's Special K Bar	38	5	3.5	0.65	383
Bahlsen Choco Leibniz Biscuits, Orange Chocolate	38	25	16	0.62	500
Sainsbury's Belgian Almond Florentines, Taste the Difference	38	30.7	14.8	0.25	538

Biscuits

Product	Sugar	Fat	Sat	Salt	Cals
			per 100g		
Fox's White Chocolate Chunkie	38	25	14	0.57	509
Kambly Coeur Truffle Dark Chocolate	38	30	18	0.13	532
Lotus Biscuit Pocket Pack	38.1	19	8.8	0.92	484
Lotus Caramelised Biscuits	38.1	19	8.8	0.92	484
Sainsbury's Quadruple Chocolate Cookies, Taste the Difference	38.1	27.9	17.9	0.75	522
Lotus Biscoff	38.1	19	8.8	0.92	484
Sainsbury's Almond Thins, Taste the Difference	38.2	15.9	7	0.98	458
Tesco Jammy Rings	38.2	14.3	6.4	0.4	438
Waitrose Duchy Originals Organic Stem Ginger Biscuits Coated in Dark Chocolate	38.2	30.1	18.4	0.40	534
Cadury Wispa Biscuits	38.3	26	13.8	0.4	505
Sainsbury's Dark Chocolate & Ginger Cookers, Taste the Difference	38.3	26.9	17	0.63	516
Asda Chosen by You Gluten & Dairy Free Chocolate Rocky Road	38.3	27	12.5	0.6	475
Waitrose Chocolate Chip & Orange Cookies	38.3	28.9	13.3	0.63	524
Waitrose Vanilla & Chocolate Mini Cupcakes	38.3	23.7	5.6	0.45	450
Trek Peanut Power Wholefood Energy Bar	38.4	10.9	1.8	0.8	369
Tesco Finest White Chocolate Cookie	38.4	27.7	17.7	0.9	515
Wagon Wheels Original	38.6	14.5	8.2	0.26	441
Merba Chocolate Cookies	38.7	27.4	14.6	0.6	510
Cadbury Fabulous Fingers	38.8	28.6	17.1	0.38	495
Eat Natural Bar, Brazil Nut Almond & Hazelnut Gluten Free	38.8	22.6	3.6	0.03	454
Nakd Bar Cocoa Orange	38.9	20	4.2	<1	415
Nakd Cocoa Orange Bars	38.9	20	4.2	<1	415
Tesco Fig Rolls	38.9	10	4.7	0.3	377
Asda Chosen by You Puffin Chocolate Orange Bars	38.9	29.3	16.9	0.3	532
Morrisons Fig Rolls	38.9	10	4.7	0.3	377
Kellogg's Rice Krispies Squares, Honeycomb Crunch Bars	39	10	7	0.75	418
Lazy Day Foods Belgian Rocky Road Chocolate	39	28	13	1	474
De Beukelaer Cookies Bakery Brownie	39	23	39	0.45	474
Fox's Crinkles Ginger	39	13	6	1	441
Tesco Milk Chocolate Butter Biscuits	39	26	16	0.4	510

Biscuits

Product	Sugar	Fat	Sat	Salt	Cals
			per 100g		
Waitrose Continental Milk Chocolate Butter Biscuits	39	26	16	0.38	511
Maryland Gooeys Hazelnut Cookies	39.1	24	10.9	0.59	495
Go Ahead Fruit Bakes Strawberry	39.1	8.4	3.6	0.6	381
Weight Watchers Caramel Mallows	39.2	2.1	1.1	0.3	332
Nakd Bar Cashew Cookie	39.2	23.4	4.6	<.1	410
Nakd Cashew Gluten Free Cookie Bar	39.2	23.4	4.6	<.1	410
Tesco Everyday Value Milk Chocolate Digestives	39.2	22.3	11.1	1	494
Weight Watchers Caramel Wafer Biscuits	39.3	20.2	12.5	0.3	427
Morrisons Milk Chocolate Eskimo Biscuits	39.3	28.2	16	0.4	527
McVitie's Club Orange	39.4	26.6	16.6	0.75	512
Lotus Chocolate Original Caramel Biscuits	39.5	22	13.5	0.8	496
McVitie's Club Honeycomb	39.5	26.3	16.3	0.7	510
McVitie's Club Mint	39.5	26.4	16.4	0.7	510
Lotus Biscoff Belgian Chocolate	39.5	22	13.5	0.8	496
Asda Caramel & Biscuit Bars	39.6	20.4	11.6	0.5	461
Asda Chunky Chocolate Biscuit Bars	39.6	24.7	13.7	0.9	502
Fox's Chunkie Half Coated Chocolate Cookies	39.7	25.8	14.4	0.54	509
Maryland Soft Double Chocolate Cookies	39.8	19	9.6	0.6	449
Tesco Finest Dark Chocolate Ginger Cookies	39.9	24.2	14.9	0.9	493
Fox's Golden Crunch Creams	40	24	14	0.58	506
McVitie's Penguin	40	27.1	15.5	0.23	521
Mikado King Chocolate Biscuits	40	26	16	0.4	505
Kellogg's Nutri-Grain Breakfast Bakes, Raisin	40	9	0.8	0.45	372
Kellogg's Rice Krispies Squares, Caramel & Chocolate	40	12	9	0.75	424
Kambly Coeur Noissette Milk Chocolate	40	26	13	0.23	501
Kambly Eclats Noisettes Chocolate	40	40	19	0.23	548
Kellogg's Elevenses Raisin	40	9	0.8	0.45	372
Sainsbury's Polar Bar Milk	40.1	27.9	16.3	0.34	524
Morrisons Milk Chocolate Continental	40.3	26.4	16.9	0.4	514
Go Ahead Raspberry Yoghurt Breaks	40.4	10.2	4.6	0.4	411

Biscuits

Product	Sugar	Fat	Sat	Salt	Cals
			per 100g		
Go Ahead Forest Fruit Yoghurt Break	40.5	10.1	4.6	0.4	410
Sainsbury's Polar Bar Orange	40.6	28.2	16.5	0.33	527
Go Ahead Cherry Yoghurt Breaks	40.6	10.2	4.6	0.4	411
Fudges Belgian Milk Chocolate Florentines	40.6	33.8	13	0.28	540
Eat Natural Bar, Cranberry Macadamia & Chocolate Gluten Free	40.7	24.6	14.2	0.07	478
Eat Natural Bar, Dark Chocolate with Cranberries & Macadamias	40.7	24.6	14.2	0.07	478
Asda Extra Special Belgian White Chocolate Cookies	40.7	26.1	16	0.9	514
Cadbury Fab Fingers Honeycomb	40.8	28.6	17.2	0.57	490
Maryland Soft Caramel & Chocolate Cookies	40.8	18.7	9.5	0.6	453
Fox's Ginger Crunch Cream Biscuits	41	23	13	0.85	501
Sainsbury's Raisin & Apple Fruit Slices	41	6.2	1.3	0.65	390
Bahlsen Choco Leibniz Biscuits, Milk Chocolate	41	25	16	0.64	505
Go Ahead Strawberry Yogurt Breaks	41.1	10.1	4.6	0.5	410
Tesco Popcorn Bar Cranberry & Cashew Nut	41.4	10.4	1.4	0.1	392
Asda Chosen by You Raspberry Baked Bars	41.4	7.6	3.6	0.3	385
Waitrose Dark Chocolate Ginger Biscuits	41.4	29.8	17.5	0.24	530
McVitie's Club Fruit	41.5	24.7	15.5	0.3	496
Sainsbury's Polar Mint Bar	41.5	27.9	16.1	0.35	524
Asda Extra Special Belgian Double Chocolate Cookies	41.5	23.9	13.1	0.7	503
Asda Chosen by You Puffin Milk Chocolate Bars	41.5	27.8	16.1	0.3	523
Maryland Gooeys Chocolate Cookies	41.6	25.4	10.4	0.7	504
Asda Chosen by You Mint Puffin Bar With Choc Chips	41.6	28.2	16.3	0.4	525
Bahlsen Chocolate Leibniz White	42	25	15	0.53	508
Fox's Rocky Big Eat	42	26	15	0.83	507
Kellogg's Cereal & Milk Bars, Coco Pops	42	12	9	0.53	419
Kellogg's Rice Krispies Squares, Choc-Marshmallow Mash-up	42	14	8.4	0.58	438
Fox's Rocky Chocolate	42.1	25.5	14.8	0.83	507
Tesco Milk Chocolate Crunch Biscuits	42.1	25.5	14.8	0.8	507
Sainsbury's Hazelnut Meringue Biscuits, Taste the Difference	42.2	34	3.3	0.1	549
Asda Chosen by You Apple Baked Bars	42.2	7.8	3.7	0.3	382

Biscuits

Product	Sugar	Fat	Sat per 100g	Salt	Cals
Borders Biscuits Dark Chocolate & Ginger	42.5	22.3	6.1	0.8	470
Tesco Apple Fruity Bakes	42.5	7.4	3.7	0.6	386
Breakaway Milk	42.7	25.2	13.6	0.28	511
Nakd Cocoa Crunch Bars	42.9	8.8	2	0.6	351
Nakd Choco Crunch	42.9	8.8	2	0.6	351
Oreo Double Stuff Cookies	43	23	12	0.7	500
Sainsbury's Forest Fruit Yogurt Slices	43	12	7.6	0.6	421
Bahlsen Choco Leibniz Caramel	43	25	15	0.64	499
Kambly Intense Orange Dark Chocolate	43	33	18	0.25	548
The Biscuit Collection Rainbow Cookies	43.1	24.6	12.9	0.63	498
Nakd Banana Bread Bars	43.2	7.2	1	<1	314
Waitrose Belgian Dark Chocolate Ginger Thins	43.4	22.5	14.4	0.43	481
Tesco Strawberry Fruity Bakes	43.5	7.4	3.7	0.6	386
Fox's Hazelnut Slices	43.8	29.8	15	0.59	535
Fox's Rocky Caramel	43.9	23.5	13.8	0.67	489
Fox's Classic	44	27	16	0.78	517
Fox's Mini Party Rings	44	12	5.7	0.54	446
Sainsbury's Eric The Elephant Iced Biscuits	44.3	8.1	4	0.74	426
Yum Chocolate Wafers	44.3	30	21.5	0.24	542
Sainsbury's Chocolate Wafers	44.4	25.9	17	0.4	514
Nakd Banana Crunch Bars	44.4	8.1	1.6	0.6	343
Yorkie Biscuits	44.5	24.8	13.4	0.13	505
Waitrose Belgian Milk Chocolate Hazelnut Thins	44.5	26.6	14.7	0.43	514
Sainsbury's Caramel Wafers, Basics	44.7	21.6	13.2	0.3	489
Tesco Everyday Value Caramel Wafer Biscuit	44.7	21.6	13.2	0.3	489
Asda Extra Special Fruit & Oat Cookies	44.7	17.1	10.9	0.8	447
Nakd Bar Strawberry Crunch	44.8	9.1	1.8	0.6	357
Asda Chosen by You Milk Chocolate Butter Biscuits	44.8	26.1	16	0.5	524
Kit Kat Dark Chocolate Finger	45	25	14.4	0.07	502
Fox's Rocky Chocolate Orange	45.2	28.7	17.6	0.74	527

Biscuits

Product	Sugar	Fat	Sat	Salt	Cals
			per 100g		
Wagon Wheels Wheelies Jammie	45.2	15.2	8.3	0.19	434
Asda Chunky Caramel Biscuit Bars	45.2	22.2	12.3	0.6	485
Nakd Bar Cocoa Delight	45.3	15.1	3.1	<.1	386
Nakd Cocoa Delight Wholefood Cereal Bars	45.3	15.1	3.1	<.1	386
Tesco Caramel Crunch	45.3	23.4	13.8	0.7	495
Cadbury Time Out Biscuit Bars	45.5	30	19.5	0.2	535
Sainsbury's Dark Chocolate Double Take	45.6	28	17.7	0.05	530
Nakd Bakewell Tart	45.6	17	3.3	<.1	391
Arden & Amici Soft	45.7	24.8	1.7	0.1	470
Cadbury Double Chocolate Fingers	45.8	27.4	14.9	0.3	514
Fox's Party Ring Biscuits	46	11	5.4	0.52	443
Blue Riband Coffee & Cream Biscuits	46	24.6	14.6	0.13	514
Blue Riband Original	46	24.6	14.6	0.13	514
Fox's Party Fairytales	46	12	5.5	0.52	443
Fox's Party Rings Footballs	46.1	11.5	5.5	0.52	444
Tesco Snappy Milk Chocolate Finger Biscuit	46.2	28.3	17.8	0.2	528
Asda Chosen by You Dark Chocolate Butter Biscuits	46.2	24.1	14.9	0.5	521
Waitrose Milk Chocolate Shortcake Biscuits	46.2	27.1	16.2	0.36	522
Fox's Caramel Slices	46.3	24.6	14.4	0.73	494
Asda Smart Price Caramel Wafers	46.3	20.4	12.5	0.3	479
Kelkin Gluten Free Belgian Milk Chocolate Snacks	46.5	35	21.4	0.04	554
Fox's Chocolate Shortcake Rings	46.7	26.7	16	0.58	517
Fox's Rocky Big Eat Caramel	47	23	14	0.64	483
Nakd Café Mocha Bar	47	13.4	2.9	<.1	371
Asda Chosen by You Take A Break Milk Chocolate Wafer Bars	47	26.9	17	0.2	521
Jules Destrooper Chocolate Delight	47.1	24.3	12.9	0.5	507
Nakd Apple Crunch Bars	47.1	8	1.6	0.6	355
Lees Snowballs	47.3	16.6	14.2	0.2	432
Tesco Chunky Chocolate Shortcakes	47.3	28.4	16.9	0.4	527
Nakd Bar Berry Delight Cereal Bars	47.4	14.8	2.9	<.1	385

Biscuits

Product	Sugar	Fat	Sat	Salt	Cals
			per 100g		
Nakd Berry Delight	47.4	14.8	2.9	<.1	385
Nakd Nibbles Toffee Treat	47.6	12	2.6	<.1	348
Asda Chosen by You Take A Break Mint Chocolate Wafer Bars	47.6	29.1	18.3	0.1	532
Asda Free From Belgian Choc Twin Wafer Bars	47.7	29.9	18.9	0.3	531
Asda Chosen by You Take A Break Orange Chocolate Wafer Bars	47.8	28.1	17.4	0.2	527
Cadbury Dairy Milk Sandwich Lu	48	26.5	16	0.48	515
Cadbury Dairy Milk with Lu Biscuit Chocolate Bar	48	26.5	16	0.48	515
Cadbury Dairy Milk Sandwich Ritz	48.5	29	17	0.63	525
Cadbury Dairy Milk with Ritz Biscuit Chocolate Bar	48.5	29	17	0.63	525
Perkier Tiffin Crunchy Chocolate Biscuit Bars	48.5	60	48.5	1	487
Little Treats Co Gingerbread Mini Biscuits	48.5	11.1	4.8	0.5	440
Toffee Crisp Biscuits	48.8	27.8	17.5	0.26	519
Twix	48.8	23.9	13.9	0.44	495
Fox's Milk Chocolate Rounds	49	26	15	0.47	512
Lees Teacakes	49	15.8	12.4	0.23	449
Waitrose Milk Chocolate Orange Biscuits	49.3	27.2	16	0.44	521
McVitie's Gold Chocolate Bar	49.8	25.8	20.7	0.49	516
Tesco Chewy Caramel Wafer Biscuit	49.8	20	12.5	0.3	472
Cadbury Crunchie Biscuits	50.3	23.6	14.1	0.47	495
Nakd Nibbles Salted Caramel	50.5	11.8	2.4	0.4	345
Sainsbury's Jaffa Cakes, Basics	51	9.7	5.6	0.22	385
Kit Kat Cookies & Cream Chocolate Finger	51.3	25	14.3	0.25	510
Kit Kat Finger Toffee Biscuits	51.3	25.4	14.5	0.27	514
Caxton's Pink & Whites	51.4	0.8	0.3	0.18	350
Kit Kat Milk Chocolate Finger	51.6	24.5	14	0.2	508
Kit Kat Orange Chocolate Finger	51.6	24.5	14	0.2	508
McVitie's Iced Gems	51.6	3.1	1.3	0.7	399
Nakd Rhubarb & Custard	51.7	12.1	2.4	<.1	365
Sainsbury's Milk Chocolate Double Take	51.8	29.3	18.8	0.15	534
Asda Smart Price Jaffa Cakes	51.9	9	5.2	0.1	384

Biscuits

Product	Sugar	Fat	Sat	Salt	Cals
			per 100g		
Morrisons Savers Jaffa Cakes	51.9	9	5.2	0.1	385
Tesco Everyday Value Jaffa Cakes	52	12	7.1	0.2	394
Asda Chosen by You Jaffa Cakes	52	10	6	0.2	381
Waitrose Mini Jaffa Cakes	52	12	6.7	0.13	397
Sainsbury's Jaffa Cakes	52.2	8.9	4.9	0.25	380
McVitie's Jaffa Cakes	52.5	8	4	0.3	374
Nakd Nibbles Fruit Salad	52.7	11.8	2.4	<.1	344
Nakd Nibbles Strawberries & Cream	52.8	11.8	2.4	<.1	344
Tesco Jaffa Cakes	53	10.3	6.1	0.2	378
Aero Biscuits	53.4	29.6	16.8	0.23	534
Kelkin Gluten Free Jaffa Cakes	54.2	7.6	2.3	0.68	354
McVitie's Café Noir	54.5	4.3	2.1	0.37	377
Aero Biscuit Peppermint	54.9	29.3	18.9	0.3	534
Morrisons Jaffa Cakes	55.1	8.2	4.7	0.1	378
Geobar Trail Cocoa Crunch	57	2	1	1.6	336
Doria Amaretti	74	7.5	0.7	0.32	414
Doria Italian Ratafias	74	7.5	0.7	0.32	414

Breakfast Cereals

For many of us we believe eating muesli and granola is healthy. However they are often produced with sugar or honey and are loaded with dried fruit. There are some good cereal options, add some fresh berries for a sweet kick and added vitamins.

To help you make the best choices, products are listed starting with the least sugar first.

Product	Sugar	Fat	Sat	Salt	Cals
			per 100g		
Nature's Path Gluten Free Porridge Sachets	0	6.3	1.3	0	425
Sainsbury's Wholegrain Mini Wheats	0.6	1.8	0.4	0.04	359
Nestle Shredded Wheat	0.7	2.2	0.5	0.05	363
Nestle Shredded Wheat Bitesize	0.7	3	1.4	0.18	208
Flahavan's Organic Jumbo Oats	0.9	5.8	1	trace	371
Tesco Micro Oats Original	0.9	8.3	1.3	0.1	377
Scott's Porridge Oats	1	8	1.5	trace	372
Jordan's Organic Porridge Oats	1	9.3	1.8	trace	364
Quaker Oat So Simple Original Porridge	1	7.7	1.3	trace	370
Ready Brek Original Porridge	1	8.7	1.2	0.03	374
Jordans Organic Porridge Oats	1	9.3	1.8	trace	364
Mornflake Medium Oatmeal	1	8.4	1.3	<.01	367
Ready Brek Original	1	8.7	1.2	0.03	374
Sainsbury's Express Porridge Original	1	8	1.2	<.01	370
Mornflake Superfast Oats	1	8.4	1.3	<.01	367
Tesco Finest Scottish Porridge Oats	1.1	7	1	<.01	368
Tesco Scottish Porridge Oats	1.1	7	1	<.01	363
Quaker Porridge Oats	1.1	8	1.5	trace	374
Waitrose Essential Original Instant Oats	1.1	7.4	1.2	trace	374
Mornflake Oatbran	1.2	9.4	1.8	<.00	364
Flahavan's Irish Organic Porridge Oats	1.3	5.5	1.1	0.25	374
Tesco Whole Oat Bran Cereal	1.3	10	1.6	<.01	369
Morrisons Puffed Wheat	1.3	1.3	0.3	trace	360
Mornflake Toasted Oatbran	1.5	10.3	1.6	<.01	366
Sainsbury's Express Porridge Jumbo Oats & Barley	1.8	4.4	0.7	0.03	352

Breakfast Cereals

Product	Sugar	Fat	Sat	Salt	Cals
			per 100g		
Sainsbury's Cornflakes, SO Organic	2.1	0.7	<.1	0.8	381
Sainsbury's Wholewheat Biscuits, Basics	2.5	2.1	0.6	0.68	359
Tesco Everyday Wheat Biscuits	2.5	2.5	0.4	0.8	370
Morrisons Saver Wheat Biscuits	2.5	2.2	0.4	0.7	357
Weetabix Oatibix	3.2	8	1.3	0.28	395
Tesco Bircher Muesli Base	3.5	9.1	1.4	0.1	380
Sainsbury's Cornflakes, Basics	3.6	0.7	<.1	1	377
Morrisons Savers Cornflakes	3.7	1.1	0.3	0.5	386
Asda Smart Price Corn Flakes	3.9	0.3	0.1	0.7	379
Tesco Everyday Cornflakes Cereal	4	1	0.2	0.8	373
Sharpham Park Bran Flakes	4.3	2.7	0.1	0	369
Weetabix Cereal	4.4	2	0.6	0.65	358
Sainsbury's Wholewheat Biscuits Cereal	4.4	2	0.6	0.65	358
Tesco Wheat Biscuits	4.4	2	0.6	0.7	358
Morrisons Wheat Biscuits	4.4	2	0.6	0.7	358
Asda Wheat Bisks	4.4	2	0.6	0.7	362
Waitrose Essential Wholewheat Biscuits	4.4	2	0.6	0.65	358
Asda Smart Price Wheat Bisks	5.2	1.7	0.3	0.7	357
Ruse Health Honey & Nuts	5.6	6.8	1.2	trace	182.8
Morrisons Original Porridge Pot	6	1.2	0.2	trace	91
Asda Smart Price Crispy Rice	6.2	0.9	0.3	0.7	378
Morrisons Apple & Blueberry Porridge Pot	6.4	1.2	0.2	trace	89
Nature's Path Gluten Free Crispy Rice	6.7	5	0	1	367
Sainsbury's Cornflakes	7.2	0.9	0.3	1.05	381
Sainsbury's Muesli, Basics	7.8	5.1	0.8	<.01	355
Tesco Everyday Muesli	7.8	4.4	0.7	<.01	353
Kellogg's Cornflakes	8	0.9	0.2	1.25	378
Tesco Cornflakes	8.1	1.1	0.3	1	384
Asda Cornflakes	8.1	1.1	0.3	1	384
Morrisons Golden Syrup Flavour Porridge Pot	8.5	1.2	0.2	trace	91

Breakfast Cereals

Product	Sugar	Fat	Sat	Salt	Cals
			per 100g		
Morrisons Cornflakes	8.6	0.4	0.1	0.7	367
Rude Multigrain Flakes	8.7	1.3	0.3	<.01	363
Waitrose Essential Corn Flakes	8.9	1.1	0.3	0.74	385
Lizi's Original Granola	9.1	29.3	7.5	0	496
Tesco Rice Snaps	9.7	1.2	0.4	0.7	385
Asda Rice Snaps	9.7	1.2	0.4	0.7	385
Waitrose Essential Rice Pops	9.7	1.2	0.4	0.74	385
Oatibix Flakes with Fruit	10	2	0.4	0.1	152
Quaker Oat Crisp	10	6.5	1	0.84	375
Kellogg's Rice Crispies	10	1	0.2	1.13	383
Tesco Everyday Rice Snaps Cereal	10	1	0.2	0.1	391
Bear Alphabites	10.1	2.8	1.5	trace	171
Bear Alphabites Multigrain	10.1	2.7	1.5	trace	170
Morrisons Rice Crackles	10.1	0.9	0.2	0.7	382
Sainsbury's Rice Pops	11	1.4	0.5	0.72	391
Tesco Wheat Flakes Cluster	11.8	17	5.2	0.5	440
Morrisons Special Flakes	12	1.3	0.3	0.6	367
Eat Natural Crunchy Toasted Muesli, Nuts & Seeds	12.9	22.2	5.6	0.29	438
Kellogg's Special K Multigrain Porridge Red Berries	13	4.5	0.8	0.08	385
Kellogg's Raisin Wheats	13	2	0.4	0.08	345
Dorset Cereals Honey Granola	13	25	2.8	0.04	484
Dorset Cereals Simply Nut Granola	13	27	5.6	0.1	500
Sainsbury's High Fibre Bran	13.3	3.6	0.7	0.5	341
Asda High Bran	13.3	3.6	0.7	0.5	341
Nature's Path Gluten Free Mesa Sunrise	13.3	3.3	0	1	400
Nature's Path Gluten Free O's	13.3	5	0	1	400
Tesco Swiss Style Fruit Muesli	13.4	8.8	1.1	0.1	369
Tesco Finest Scottish Porridge Oats with Flame Raisin & Hazelnut	13.5	7.6	2.3	<.01	369
Mornflake Oatbran Granola Nuts & Seeds	13.6	22.8	4.7	0.03	473
Sainsbury's Banana, Date & Coconut Muesli	13.8	15.2	9	trace	405

Breakfast Cereals

Product	Sugar	Fat	Sat	Salt	Cals
			per 100g		
Kellogg's Special K Multigrain Porridge Original	14	5	0.9	0.08	385
Weetabix Crunchy Bran	14	3.6	0.6	0.9	352
Dorset Cereals Simply Nutty	14	9.2	1.5	0.02	378
Morrisons Red Fruit Special Flakes	14	1.5	0.3	0.6	364
Oatibix Flakes	14.3	5.6	0.9	0.3	381
Weetabix Baked with Golden Syrup	14.5	1.9	0.4	0.23	363
Morrisons No Added Sugar Swiss Style Muesli	14.5	6	0.7	0.1	362
Sainsbury's Rice Pops, Basics	14.6	2.5	0.8	<.01	382
Sainsbury's Swiss Style Muesli, No Added Salt & Sugar	14.7	4.9	0.6	trace	356
Tesco Instant Oats Porridge Multigrain	14.7	3.7	0.7	0.2	357
Nestle Shreddies	14.9	2.1	0.3	0.75	208
Weetabix Cereal, Banana	15	2	0.4	0.23	357
Dorset Cereals Oat Granola	15	17	2.1	0.2	443
Dorset Cereals Toasted Hazelnut & Brazil Muesli	15	14	5.5	0.4	409
Pertwood Farm Organic Muesli Fruit & Seeds	15	9.5	1.2	0.03	388
Tesco Everyday Malt Wheats Cereal	15	2	0.3	0.6	371
Tesco No Added Sugar Muesli	15	6.4	0.8	0.1	361
Mornflake Oatbran Flakes	15.4	5.2	0.8	0.53	372
Jordans Muesli, Natural	15.6	5	0.7	0.03	357
Morrisons Fantastic Fibre	15.6	3.3	0.6	0.5	341
Tesco Malt Wheats Cereal	15.7	1.9	0.3	0.6	366
Morrisons Mighty Malties	15.7	1.9	0.3	0.6	366
Waitrose Essential Malted Wheats	15.7	1.9	0.3	0.6	366
Waitrose Essential Bran Flakes	15.7	2.4	0.5	0.75	356
Nestle Honey Nut Shredded Wheat	15.9	5	1.7	0.05	385
Tesco Finest Dark Chocolate & Amerena Cherry Granola	15.9	23.8	5	0.1	483
Alpen No Added Sugar Swiss Recipe	16	6.2	0.9	0.29	375
Sainsbury's Wholegrain Malties Cereal	16	1.9	0.3	0.6	366
Asda Malted Wheaties	16	1.9	0.3	0.6	366
Tesco Raspberry Wheat Cereal	16.1	1.4	0.3	0.2	335

Breakfast Cereals

Product	Sugar	Fat	Sat per 100g	Salt	Cals
Asda Wholegrain Raspberry Wheats	16.1	1.4	0.3	0.2	335
Sainsbury's Balance	16.3	1.3	0.3	0.85	371
Sainsbury's Wholegrain Bran Flakes	16.3	2	0.4	0.78	365
Tesco Special Flake Cereal	16.3	1.3	0.3	0.9	371
Jordans Super Nutty Granola	16.6	21	3.6	<.03	470
Lizi's On The Go Granola Original	16.6	27.5	8.6	0.24	500
Tesco Everyday Bran Flakes Cereal	16.6	2	0.4	0.6	359
Tesco Finest Multigrain Raspberry & Blueberry Granola	16.7	15.7	1.5	0.1	444
Waitrose Essential Wholegrain Cranberry Wheats	16.7	1.5	0.3	0.22	336
Kellogg's Special K	17	1.5	0.3	1	375
Ready Brek Chocolate Porridge	17	7.9	1.8	0.03	374
Ready Brek Gingerbread Porridge	17	7.1	1.2	0.03	372
Kellogg's Frosted Wheats	17	2	0.6	0.03	364
Kellogg's Special K Granola Cranberries, Pumpkin Seeds & Almonds	17	7.5	1.2	0.75	387
Morrisons Bran Flakes	17	2	0.5	0.7	356
Asda Bran Flakes	17	2	0.5	0.7	356
Tesco Oat Crispies Cereal	17.1	14.7	4.1	0.3	448
Mornflake Cranberry & Nut Muesli	17.2	9.6	1.2	0.03	371
Sainsbury's Maple & Pecan Crisp Cereal	17.2	16.8	5.3	0.03	461
Tesco Swiss Style Muesli	17.4	6.1	0.8	0.3	366
Morrisons Savers Bran Flakes	17.5	2.4	0.5	0.7	364
Morrisons Strawberry & Raspberry Clusters	17.7	12.4	5	trace	432
Tesco Apricot Wheats Cereal	17.8	1.4	0.3	0.2	337
Tesco Superberry Granola	17.8	13.5	5	0.1	444
Asda Wholegrain Apricot Wheats	17.8	1.4	0.3	0.2	337
Waitrose Essential Wholegrain Apricot Wheats	17.8	1.4	0.3	0.16	337
Kellogg's Special K Hazelnut & Almond	18	5	0.8	1	394
Kellogg's Special K Oats & Honey	18	3	0.5	0.63	381
Weetabix Chocolate	18	4	1.7	0.2	368
Kellogg's All Bran	18	3.5	0.7	0.95	334

Breakfast Cereals

Product	Sugar	Fat	Sat	Salt	Cals
			per 100g		
Kellogg's Mini Max Cereal	18	2	0.3	0.03	370
Tesco Raisin Wheats Cereal	18	1.5	0.3	0.3	340
Nestle Shredded Wheat Raspberry, Strawberry & Cranberry	18.1	1.5	0.3	0.23	346
Sainsbury's Wholegrain Red Cherry Wheats	18.1	1.2	0.3	0.23	332
Tesco Bran Flakes	18.2	2.6	0.4	0.7	364
Morrisons Mini Cranberry Wheats	18.2	1.3	0.3	0.2	333
Perkier Apple, Cinnamon & Raisin Porridge Pot	18.3	4.5	0.8	0.1	359
Sainsbury's Granola, Strawberry	18.3	11.4	4.5	0.03	433
Tesco Maple & Peacan Crisp	18.3	18.7	1.6	0.1	469
Tesco Special Flake Fruit	18.3	1.5	0.4	0.8	377
Jordans Simply Granola	18.4	12.5	2.5	0.03	428
Tesco Blueberry Wheats Cereal	18.4	1.5	0.3	0.2	336
Morrisons Mini Blueberry Wheats	18.4	1.3	0.3	0.2	326
Asda Wholegrain Blueberry Wheats	18.4	1.5	0.3	0.2	336
Sainsbury's Balance with Red Fruit	18.5	1.3	0.4	0.83	374
Tesco Fruit & Nut Granola	18.5	16.4	6.9	0.1	449
Tesco Micro Oats Golden Syrup	18.6	5.5	1	0.1	375
Quaker Oat So Simple Honey & Vanilla Flavour Porridge	18.8	6.4	1.2	0.03	381
Sainsbury's Wholegrain Apricot Wheats	18.9	1.3	0.3	0.23	334
Sainsbury's Wholegrain Raisin Wheats	18.9	1.4	0.3	0.05	331
Kellogg's Special K Chocolate & Strawberry	19	3.1	0.7	0.95	384
Kellogg's Special K Red Berries	19	1.5	0.2	0.95	379
Quaker Oat So Simple Porridge, Raspberry & Pomegranate	19	6.6	1.2	trace	381
Quaker Oat So Simple Porridge, Sweet Cinnamon	19	6.6	1.2	trace	379
Dorset Cereals Toasted Raspberry & Apple Muesli	19	5.2	0.9	0.5	365
Kellogg's All-Bran Choc Wheats	19	9	5	0.05	397
Sainsbury's Golden Syrup Wheats	19	1	0.2	0.34	336
Sainsbury's Multigrain Hooplas	19	4.5	0.7	0.68	386
Tesco Red Cherry Wheat Cereal	19	1.5	0.3	0.2	337
Asda Multigrain High 5s	19	4.5	0.7	0.68	386

Breakfast Cereals

Product	Sugar	Fat	Sat	Salt	Cals
			per 100g		
Waitrose Essential Multigrain Hoops	19	4.5	0.7	0.68	386
Sainsbury's Balance Peach & Apricot	19.2	1.3	0.3	0.8	374
Perkier Porridge Pot Golden Syrup Gluten Free	19.3	4.6	0.9	0.23	384
Tesco Everyday Multigrain Hoop Cereal	19.3	4.5	0.7	0.7	384
Tesco Instant Oats Porridge Multigrain with Red Berries	19.3	3.9	0.7	0.1	360
Tesco Multigrain Hoops	19.3	3.5	0.7	0.7	384
Morrisons Super Hoops	19.3	4	0.6	0.7	386
Sainsbury's Multigrain Flakes & Fruit	19.4	2.2	0.3	0.73	367
Tesco Multigrain Flake Fruit	19.4	2.2	0.3	0.7	367
Mornflake Oatbran Flakes Very Berry	19.5	4.2	0.8	0.42	378
Sainsbury's Wholegrain Blueberry Wheats	19.7	1.3	0.3	0.23	331
Morrisons Maple & Pecan Clusters	19.7	17.5	5.5	trace	457
Asda Starting Right	19.7	2.1	0.3	0.8	367
Morrisons Wholewheat Muesli	19.8	10.3	4.2	trace	378
Sainsbury's Granola, Raisin, Nut & Honey	19.9	16.8	6.4	trace	449
Tesco Finest Nut Granola	19.9	26	4.9	0.1	500
Kellogg's Coco Pops Porridge	20	6.9	1.2	0.08	397
Kellogg's Special K Creamy Berry Crunch	20	3.1	1.5	0.93	382
Weetabix Minis Banana	20	4.9	3	0.18	389
Kellogg's All Bran Flakes	20	2	0.5	1	356
Asda Chosen by You Swiss Style Muesli	20	5.8	0.9	0.2	363
Mornflake Oatbran Crisp, Nut & Honey	20.1	18	4.8	0.03	428
Tesco Oat Crispies Strawberry Cereal	20.2	15.4	4.8	0.3	453
Morrisons Swiss Style Muesli	20.2	6.1	0.7	0.3	370
Quaker Oat So Simple Cuppa Porridge Original	20.3	6.1	1.6	0.22	378
Morrisons Right Balance	20.3	1.9	0.3	0.8	363
Sainsbury's Wholegrain Fruit & Fibre	20.4	5.6	3.3	0.7	376
Sainsbury's Weekend Granola, Taste The Difference	20.5	18.6	5.9	trace	454
Tesco Finest Summer Fruit Granola	20.6	21	2.7	0.1	473
Jordans Nut & Seed Muesli	20.7	7.9	1.1	0.01	363

Breakfast Cereals

Product	Sugar	Fat	Sat	Salt	Cals
			per 100g		
Nestle Cheerios	20.8	3.6	0.8	1	378
Quaker Oat So Simple Porridge Pot Apple & Blueberry	20.9	6.4	1.1	0.2	376
Jordans Crunchy Oat Granola Tropical	20.9	15.4	6.7	0.03	447
Kellogg's Special K Peach & Apricot	21	1.5	0.2	0.95	375
Kellogg's Special K Yoghurty	21	3.1	1.5	1.03	384
Weetabix Minis Chocolate	21	5.4	2.6	0.18	391
Kellogg's All Bran Golden Crunch	21	11	1.5	0.9	405
Kellogg's All Bran Red Berry Crunch	21	11	1.5	0.8	405
Kellogg's Honey Loops	21	3	0.05	0.35	379
Kellogg's Honey Pops	21	3	0.05	0.35	379
Kellogg's Rice Krispies Multigrain	21	2.5	0.5	0.38	379
Tesco Golden Syrup Wheat Cereal	21	1.4	0.3	0.3	336
Jordans Super Berry Granola	21.1	14.4	2.6	0.03	438
Quaker Oat So Simple Porridge, Golden Syrup	21.5	6.5	1.1	0.5	376
Asda Crisp Maple & Pecan	21.5	20.5	3.9	trace	469
Quaker Oat So Simple Porridge, Banana & Strawberry	21.7	6.2	1.2	0.18	376
Sainsbury's Apple & Cinnamon Crisp	21.8	12.6	5.6	0.05	434
Tesco Crunchy Oat Cereal Fruit & Nut	21.8	18.6	8.6	0.1	462
Asda Crisp Strawberry	21.8	15.5	3.5	trace	443
Jordans Country Crisp with Chunky Nuts	21.9	22.9	5.4	0.03	492
Mornflake Oatbran Muesli Very Berry	21.9	4.3	0.7	0.03	342
Tesco Everyday Maple & Pecan Cereal	21.9	16.3	1.5	0.1	458
Kellogg's Crunchy Nut, Granola Caramel & Hazelnut	22	24	10	0.78	511
Kellogg's Special K Granola Apple & Raisin	22	7.4	1.1	0.65	389
Tesco Honey Nut Clusters	22	14.4	1.8	0.5	441
Quaker Oat So Simple Porridge, Blackberry & Apple	22.2	6.1	1.1	0.05	372
Jordans Lighter Granola Raspberry & Apple	22.2	7.5	1.4	0.03	398
Quaker Oat So Simple Porridge Pot Original	22.3	7.2	1.2	0.22	379
Quaker Oat So Simple Porridge, Apple & Cherry	22.3	6.1	1.2	0.08	375
Jordans Country Crisp with Honey Nut	22.3	16.8	3.2	<.03	449

Breakfast Cereals

Product	Sugar	Fat	Sat	Salt	Cals
			per 100g		
Sainsbury's Granola, SO Organic	22.4	12.2	4.3	trace	419
Tesco Strawberry Yoghurt Crisp	22.6	13.5	2.8	0.1	440
Waitrose Essential Fruit & Fibre	22.7	7.6	4.8	0.33	383
Sainsbury's Granola, Tropical	22.8	14.5	7.8	0.05	435
Weetabix Minis Fruit & Nut	23	4.1	0.8	0.18	373
Kellogg's Just Right Cereal	23	2	0.3	0.98	371
Alpen Original	23	5.8	0.8	0.28	378
Dorset Cereals Roasted Nuts & Seeds	23	8.9	1.1	0.02	383
Jordans Lighter Granola Strawberry & Blueberry	23	7.5	1.4	0.03	399
Quaker Oat Granola	23	9.5	1.2	trace	420
Sainsbury's Express Porridge Blueberry & Raspberry	23	6.2	1	trace	381
Waitrose Essential Fruit & Nut Muesli	23	13.5	3.9	0	384
Quaker Oat So Simple Porridge Pot Caramel	23.3	5.7	1.1	0.15	377
Nature's Path Gluten Free Maple Sunrise	23.3	3.3	0	1.2	367
Sainsbury's Fruit & Fibre, Basics	23.4	6.2	4.2	0.75	382
Jordans Country Crisp with Strawberries	23.5	15.6	4.8	<.03	453
Tesco Apple & Cinnamon Crisp	23.5	13.1	3.1	0.1	433
Nestle Clusters Cereal	23.6	3.8	1.6	1.05	378
Tesco Crunchy Cookie Cereal	23.6	4	0.7	0.5	379
Kellogg's Special K Breakfast Cereal, Chocolate	24	6	3	0.85	398
Kellogg's Start Cereal	24	3.5	2	1	390
Nestle Honey Cheerios	24	3.2	0.6	1.06	377
Kellogg's Special K Multigrain Porridge Pot Original	24	4.5	0.8	0.2	387
Kellogg's Fruit 'n' Fibre Cereal	24	6	3.5	1	380
Dorset Cereals Chocolate, Macadamia & Almond Granola	24	22	4.1	0.15	456
Dorset Cereals Gloriously Nutty	24	13	1.7	0.02	388
Nestle Toffee Crisp Cereal	24	10	4.6	0.29	421
Weetabix Weetox Chocolatey	24	4.9	1	0.09	390
Tesco Choco Hoops	24	4	2.4	0.3	385
Tesco Everyday Fruit & Fibre Cereal	24	5.8	3.5	0.7	383

Product	Sugar	Fat	Sat	Salt	Cals
			per 100g		
Nestle Cookie Crisp	24.2	3.2	1.2	0.84	383
Sainsbury's Raspberry & Yogurt Crisp Cereal	24.2	13.5	6.6	trace	439
Sainsbury's Express Porridge Apple & Cinnamon	24.3	5.9	0.9	trace	383
Asda Choco Balls Cereal	24.3	3.3	1.2	0.4	379
Asda Honey Nut Crunch	24.4	14.7	2.7	0.6	446
Asda Hawaiian Crunch	24.4	14.5	5.1	trace	433
Sainsbury's Nut & Flame Raisin Crisp	24.5	13	4.1	trace	431
Mornflake Luxury Fruit & Nut Muesli	24.5	8.8	2.4	0.02	365
Nestle Curiously Cinnemon	24.8	10.1	3.8	1.11	419
Jordans Fruit & Nut Muesli	24.9	6.6	2.4	0.03	357
Sainsbury's Express Porridge Golden Syrup	24.9	5.9	0.9	<.01	384
Kellogg's Special K Multigrain Porridge Pot Honey & Almond	25	5	0.9	0.2	389
Alpen Raspberry & Apple	25	4.1	0.8	0.23	372
Kellogg's Fruit Loops	25	3.5	0.09	1.13	391
Nestle Golden Nuggets	25	1.5	0.3	0.73	379
Sainsbury's Multigrain Boulders	25	1.3	0.3	0.76	382
Asda Choco Hoops	25	4.3	1.1	0.4	389
Nestle Golden Grahams	25.1	3.1	1.1	1.07	384
Nestle Nesquick Chocolate Cereal	25.1	4	1.7	0.58	381
Sainsbury's Granola, Red Apple & Raisin	25.1	10.9	4.4	0.05	422
Morrisons Spooky Hoops	25.1	4.3	1.1	0.4	390
Nestle Chocolatey Cheerios	25.2	4.9	1.1	1.01	385
Tesco Malt Wheats Raspberry	25.3	1.4	0.3	0.6	367
Tesco Finest Fruit & Fibre	25.5	6.6	2.9	0.6	382
Quaker Oat So Simple Cuppa Porridge Apple & Blueberry	25.7	6.4	1.6	0.29	381
Morrisons Fruit & Fibre	25.8	6.7	4	0.6	388
Asda Gluten Free Golden Syrup Flavour Porridge	25.8	4.5	0.8	0.1	377
Sainsbury's Orchard Fruit Muesli	25.9	4.1	0.6	trace	339
Tesco Fruit & Fibre	25.9	6.6	3.9	0.7	387
Kellogg's Special K Multigrain Porridge Pot Red Berries	26	4.5	0.8	0.2	387

Breakfast Cereals

Product	Sugar	Fat	Sat	Salt	Cals
			per 100g		
Dorset Cereals Simple Fruity Muesli	26	2.4	0.4	0.06	337
Kellogg's Crunchy Nut Clusters Honey & Nut	26	15	3	0.95	447
Kellogg's Coco Pops Mini Crocs	26	2.5	1	0.45	377
Sainsbury's Express Porridge Honey	26	6.5	1	trace	390
Tesco Cinnamon Squares	26	8	4	0.5	406
Tesco Golden Syrup Porridge Pots	26	4.9	0.8	0.2	380
Asda Raisin Honey & Almond Crunch Cereal	26	13	2.9	<.1	421
Tesco Apple & Cinnamon Muesli	26.1	4.8	0.7	0.1	343
Tesco Fruit Nut Muesli	26.1	12.5	5.6	0.1	387
Tesco Honey Nut Chocolate Clusters	26.1	16.7	4.3	0.5	454
Quaker Oat So Simple Porridge, Sultana, Raisin, Cranberry & Apple	26.2	5.7	0.9	0.23	371
Sainsbury's Lighter Granola Raisin & Almond	26.2	8.4	2.7	trace	402
Tesco Crunchy Tropical Cereal	26.3	16.3	8.3	0.1	450
Quaker Oat So Simple Porridge Pot Summer Berries	26.4	4.7	0.8	0.24	375
Tesco Pillows Original	26.5	11.7	5.3	0.6	440
Nature's Path Gluten Free Granola Mixed Berry	26.7	13.3	1.7	0	467
Sainsbury's Wholewheat Muesli	26.7	7.6	2.4	0.03	350
Tesco Multigrain Boulders	26.7	1.7	0.4	0.8	386
Alpen Creamy Porridge Pot Fruit & Nut	26.8	10	3.5	0.25	399
Tesco Finest Oat Sachet Cranberry & Raspberry	26.8	5.7	0.9	<.01	376
Nestle Honey Shreddies	26.9	1.8	0.2	0.64	372
Tesco Finest Oat Sachet Aplple & Raisin	26.9	4.7	0.7	<.01	370
Quaker Oat So Simple Porridge Pot Strawberry Raspberry & Cranberry	27	5.1	1	0.3	374
Dorset Cereals Toasted Spelt, Fruit & Nut Muesli	27	9.2	1.1	0.72	380
Kellogg's Crunchy Nut Bites, Nut & Caramel	27	15	7	1.13	450
Kellogg's Coco Pops Rocks	27	8	3	0.75	410
Asda Sultana Bran	27	2	0.4	0.5	352
Quaker Oat So Simple Porridge Pot Honey & Vanilla	27.1	5.1	1	0.33	374
Quaker Oat So Simple Porridge Pot Apple & Cherry	27.2	4.8	0.8	0.3	377
Quaker Oat So Simple Porridge Pot Banana & Strawberry	27.3	5	0.8	0.22	376

Breakfast Cereals

Product	Sugar	Fat	Sat per 100g	Salt	Cals
Morrisons Chunky Triple Chocolate Clusters	27.3	15.6	7.4	trace	449
Morrisons Syrup Oat Sachets	27.3	6.3	1	0	382
Tesco Micro Oats Apple & Blueberry	27.4	4.9	0.8	0.1	376
Nestle Oats & More Almond	27.5	8.8	1.3	0.64	407
Morrisons Fruit & Nut Muesli	27.5	9.9	3.6	trace	372
Asda Choco Curls	27.5	2.8	1.2	0.3	382
Jordans Crunchy Oat Granola Raisin & Almond	27.6	11.9	2.1	0.03	415
Morrisons Loopy Bees	27.9	3.6	0.6	0.6	389
Asda Honey Nut Crunch with Milk Chocolate Curls	27.9	16.1	4.1	0.6	454
Kellogg's Special K Fruit & Nut	28	2.5	0.4	0.75	375
Sainsbury's Fruit & Nut Muesli	28	9	1.8	0.03	359
Sainsbury's Muesli Fruit & Nut	28	9	1.8	0.03	361
Asda Honey Hoops	28	3.6	0.6	0.6	388
Waitrose Essential Golden Syrup Instant Oats	28	6	0.9	0.3	384
Sainsbury's Balance Crinnamon, Apple & Raisins	28.1	1	0.2	0.6	358
Sainsbury's Chocolate Hazelnut Squares	28.1	12.7	3.8	0.58	415
Morrisons Sultana Bran	28.2	2	0.4	0.5	354
Quaker Oat So Simple Cuppa Porridge Golden Syrup	28.3	5.2	1	0.52	375
Tesco Finest Chunky Fruit Nut Muesli	28.3	11.3	3.6	0.1	394
Asda Milk Choc Coco Locos	28.3	11	2.7	0.6	416
Nestle Shreddies Coco Caramel	28.4	2.2	0.6	0.62	374
Nestle Shreddies Frosted	28.4	1.7	0.2	0.63	373
Quaker Oat So Simple Porridge Pot Sweet Cinnamon	28.4	5.2	1.1	0.31	376
Nestle Coco Shreddies	28.5	2.2	0.6	0.62	374
Tesco Everyday Coco Snaps Cereal	28.5	1.2	0.8	0.4	388
Weight Watchers Rice & Wheat Flakes with Mixed Fruit	28.5	1.6	0.3	0.4	362
Asda Smart Price Coco Rice	28.5	3	1.6	0.5	384
Waitrose Essential Sultana Bran	28.6	1.9	0.4	0.53	339
Alpen Creamy Porridge Pot Cranberry & Blueberry	28.8	9.6	3.5	0.24	399
Nestle Chocolate Lion Cereal	28.8	7.6	3	0.5	412

Breakfast Cereals

Product	Sugar	Fat	Sat	Salt	Cals
			per 100g		
Kellogg's Crunchy Nut Granola, Fruit & Nut	29	21	8.7	6	477
Honey Monster Puffs	29	1.2	0.4	0.01	379
Kellogg's Krave Chocolate Hazelnut	29	16	4	1.13	452
Tesco Mini Chocolate Breakfast Buscuit	29	20	9.5	0.8	473
Tesco Pillows Chocolate Nut Cereal	29	12.5	3.1	0.6	444
Asda Chosen by You Luxury Fruit & Nut Muesli	29	8.9	3.1	0.05	371
Quaker Oat So Simple Porridge Pot Golden Syrup	29.5	4.9	0.8	0.58	372
Alpen Creamy Porridge Pot Raspberry & Apple	29.6	8.7	3.3	0.25	394
Kellogg's Krave Choco Roulette	30	15	3.8	1.2	443
Kellogg's Krave Milk Chocolate	30	15	5.1	1	445
Kellogg's Sultana Bran	30	2	0.5	0.83	344
Waitrose Essential Apple & Raspberry Instant Oats	30	5.8	0.9	trace	382
Sainsbury's Lighter Granola Raisin, Apple & Apricot	30.2	7.3	2.5	trace	387
Tesco 50% Fruit Muesli	30.3	2.5	0.5	0.1	330
Waitrose Essential Fruit Muesli	30.7	4.5	2.1	0.1	342
Jordans Crunchy Nut Granola, Fruit & Nut	30.8	13.2	4	0.03	422
Kellogg's Crunchy Nut Clusters Chocolate	31	17	5	0.83	460
Tesco Finest Tropical Muesli	31.1	9	4.4	0.1	369
Mornflake Luxury Fruit Muesli	31.1	3.9	1.1	0.02	333
Sainsbury's Luxury Fruit & Nut Muesli, Taste The Difference	31.2	9	2.6	trace	376
Nestle Oats & More Raisin	31.3	4.7	0.9	0.64	381
Sainsbury's Wholegrain Sultana Bran	31.4	1.6	0.4	0.55	350
Asda Honey Numbers	31.4	4.7	0.5	0.9	397
Asda Choco Milk Hoops	31.9	2	1.8	0.6	380
Jordans Country Criso with Flame Raspberry	32	13.4	4.1	0.01	433
Tesco Sultana Bran	32	2	0.3	0.6	356
Tesco Crispy Seedy Nutty Bites	32.2	31.2	7	0.1	527
Mornflake Chocolatey Squares	32.6	20.5	4	0.03	476
Tesco Choco Snaps Cereal	32.7	2.8	1.5	0.7	389
Sainsbury's Choco Caramel Duo	33	2.6	1.3	0.5	389

Breakfast Cereals

Product	Sugar	Fat	Sat	Salt	Cals
			per 100g		
Morrisons Golden Honey Balls	33	1.3	0.3	0.8	383
Asda Golden Balls	33	1.3	0.3	0.8	383
Asda Jungle Bites	33	2.6	1.3	0.5	389
Tesco Honey Nut Cereal	33.3	4.5	1	0.7	403
Asda Honey Nut Cornflakes	33.3	4.5	1	0.8	403
Asda Choco Squares	33.3	19.5	3.8	trace	467
Waitrose Essential Honey Nut Corn Flakes	33.3	4.5	1	0.74	403
Morrisons Honey Nut Cornflakes	33.5	4.3	0.8	0.7	398
Tesco Finest Berry Muesli	33.8	3.9	0.7	0.1	345
Kellogg's Riccicles	34	0.8	0.1	0.88	383
Tesco Everyday Honey Nut Cornflakes	34.1	4	0.9	0.5	401
Sainsbury's 50% Fruit Muesli	34.6	2.2	0.4	0.05	327
Tesco Frosted Flakes Cereal	34.9	0.8	0.2	0.5	386
Kellogg's Crunchy Nut Cornflakes	35	5	0.9	0.88	402
Kellogg's Coco Pops	35	2.5	1	0.75	389
Sainsbury's Choco Rice Pops	35	3	1.6	0.73	390
Morrisons Choco Crackles	35	2	1.1	0.7	386
Asda Choco Snaps	35	2.9	1.6	0.8	389
Waitrose Essential Choco Pops	35	2.9	1.6	0.74	389
Sainsbury's Freefrom Oaty Muesli	35.1	8.3	1.1	0.04	358
Morrisons Extra Fruity Muesli	35.5	3.3	1.6	trace	330
Dorset Cereals Berries & Cherries	36	2.1	0.3	0.02	332
Morrisons Choco Pillows	36.1	18.6	3.6	0.5	466
Sainsbury's Honey Nut Cornflakes	36.3	4.5	0.7	0.76	403
Asda Choco Flakes	36.8	1	0.4	0.6	384
Kellogg's Frosties	37	0.06	0.01	0.88	375
Sainsbury's Frosted Flakes Cereal	37	0.6	0.2	0.55	381
Asda Frosted Flakes	37	0.8	0.2	0.5	386
Morrisons Ice Flakes	37.5	0.4	0.1	0.5	385
Kellogg's Crunchy Nut Chocolate Curls	40	12	6	0.7	432

Cakes

As you will see, this list is pretty 'red'. There won't be any surprises that these items contain sugar, but the amount may be shocking to some.

Hopefully this list will help you choose a better occasional treat.

To help you make the best choices, products are listed starting with the least sugar first.

Product	Sugar	Fat	Sat per 100g	Salt	Cals
Waitrose Essential Custard Yum Yums	11.2	30.7	14.5	0.44	452
Waitrose Essential Bramley Apple & Cream Turnovers	13.2	17.1	9.2	0.37	307
Waitrose Doughnuts with Cream & Strawberry Jam	13.5	16.7	7.3	0.57	328
Waitrose Essential Egg Custard Tarts	14.4	11.7	5.2	0.16	276
Tesco Jam Doughnuts	15.1	16	5.7	0.8	349
Asda Extra Special Egg Custards	15.2	21	11.8	0.2	367
Waitrose Essential Belgian Chocolate Choux Buns	15.3	30.1	12.5	0.25	427
Morrisons Large Chocolate Eclairs	16.4	27.4	13.7	0.2	390
Waitrose Essential Coffee & Caramel Eclairs	16.5	25.2	11.7	0.18	368
Morrisons Egg Custard Tarts	17.2	13.3	5.3	0.1	288
Waitrose Essential Raspberry Jam Doughnuts	18.4	11.1	5.7	0.36	328
Waitrose Essential Belgian Chocolate Eclairs	18.5	29.2	12.6	0.25	422
Morrisons Signature New York Vanilla Cheesecake	19.3	27.3	14.5	0.16	393
Morrisons Signature Berry Indulgence Cheesecake	19.9	23.2	11.8	0.15	364
Waitrose Fresh Fruit Tarts	20	13.5	8	0.13	272
Waitrose Richly Fruited Buns	20.1	4.3	1.5	0.63	279
Morrisons Banoffee Pie	21.3	13.7	6.1	0.08	264
Waitrose Essential Sultana Scones	21.5	9.2	3.3	0.5	335
Asda Chosen by You Free From Madeira Cake	21.7	19.5	1.8	0.8	404
Tesco Lemon Loaf Cake	21.8	18.7	2.1	0.4	392
Waitrose Essential Sweet Yum Yums	21.8	28.2	13.3	0.4	453
Tesco Madeleines	22	28	3.4	0.9	477
Tesco Iced Finger Buns	22	9	3.6	0.6	338
Sainsbury's Apple Pies, Basics	22.4	16.8	5.5	0.3	401

Cakes

Product	Sugar	Fat	Sat	Salt	Cals
			per 100g		
Morrisons Key Lime Pie	22.5	13	5.7	0.08	284
Sainsbury's Freefrom Blueberry Muffins	22.5	17	2.1	0.42	382
Waitrose Lemon Fruited Buns	22.7	3.9	1.7	0.6	276
Asda Chosen by You Coconut Tarts	23	24.7	9.6	0.3	453
Sainsbury's Lemon Meringue Doughnut	23.2	22.7	11.5	0.22	422
Sainsbury's Victoria Sponge Cake, Taste the Difference	23.4	18.3	5.2	0.54	399
Tesco Everyday Value Chocolate Chip Cake	23.4	21.4	2.5	0.3	432
Waitrose Richly Fruited Mini Hot Cross Buns	23.4	4.3	1.8	0.57	275
Sainsbury's Freefrom Chocolate Muffins	23.9	20.5	4.1	0.88	404
Waitrose Cream Scones with Strawberry Jam	24	13.1	8.2	0.5	333
Morrisons Chocolate Mississippi Mud Pie	24.2	17.7	8.4	0.13	324
Waitrose Saffron Buns	24.2	17.3	8	0.5	385
Asda Smart Price Madeira Cake	24.4	21	1.9	0.5	406
Asda Smart Price Apple Pies	24.6	17.8	5.7	0.3	404
Asda Chosen by You Plain Fairy Cakes	24.6	20.7	1.8	0.5	396
Asda Smart Price Apple Pies	24.6	17.8	5.7	0.3	404
Mr Kipling Apple Pies	24.7	13.1	4.5	0.3	349
Sainsbury's Apple & Blackcurrant Pies	24.7	15	4.6	0.22	378
Tesco Everyday Value Fairy Cakes	24.7	22.8	2	0.4	415
Sainsbury's Bramley Apple Pies	24.8	14.1	4.1	0.22	365
Tesco Chocolate Chip Madeleines	25	25	4.3	0.9	457
Morrisons Signature Triple Chocolate Cheesecake	25	27.8	14.9	0.13	428
Waitrose Richly Fruited Teacakes	25	5.8	1.4	0.65	303
We Love Cake Gluten Free Raspberry Macaroon Slices	25.2	23.6	12.5	0.19	450
Morrisons Chocolate Cheesecake	25.2	23.2	11.4	0.2	386
Tesco Coffee And Chocolate Chip Loaf Cake	25.3	20.5	2.4	0.3	399
Asda Chosen by You Chocolate Fairy Cakes	25.3	20.7	2	0.4	397
Waitrose Apple & Cinnamon Muffins	25.3	17.5	2.6	0.43	370
Waitrose Essential Salted Caramel & Chocolate Eclairs	25.5	23	11.2	0.23	387
Morrisons Apple & Blackcurrant Pies	25.6	13.1	3.8	0.2	351

Cakes

Product	Sugar	Fat	Sat per 100g	Salt	Cals
Pink Rose Cupcake	25.7	15	4.8	0.37	304
Dina Hand Made Baklawa Snack Pack	25.8	30.6	11.3	0.32	509
Tesco Mini Shortbread Bites	25.8	29.3	13.1	0.5	528
Tesco Double Chocolate Mini Muffins	25.8	19	2.9	0.4	395
Bonne Maman Madeleines	25.9	26.8	15.2	0.63	453
Morrisons Chocolate Éclairs	26	26.9	13.2	0.2	391
McVitie's Snickers Duo Flapjack	26.1	28.2	11.1	0.5	488
Asda Chosen by You Bramley Apple & Blackcurrant Pies	26.1	14.2	4.6	0.3	367
Waitrose Essential Iced Finger Buns	26.1	8.7	4.2	0.6	347
Sainsbury's Vanilla Sponge Fairy Cakes	26.2	21.7	1.9	0.45	421
Asda Chosen by You Bramley Apple Pies	26.2	14.2	4.8	0.3	371
Waitrose Essential Apple Yum Yums	26.2	21.3	9.8	0.33	382
Morrisons Bramley Apple Pies	26.3	13.7	4	0.2	372
Waitrose Madeira loaf cake	26.3	21	13.5	0.38	409
Asda Gluten Free Assorted Jam Tart Cakes	26.4	15	7	0.3	409
Asda Extra Special Kirsch Cherry Frangipane Tart	26.4	18.7	8.8	0.1	404
Asda Gluten Free Assorted Jam Tart Cakes	26.4	15	7	0.3	409
Tesco Free From Jam Tarts	26.4	15	7	0.2	401
Dina Luxury Baklawa	26.5	28.7	11.5	0.46	486
Morrisons Chocolate Cake	26.6	23.4	5.5	0.3	407
Sainsbury's Chocolate Fairy Cakes	26.9	22.9	2.3	0.46	430
Waitrose Date & Walnut Loaf Cake	27	20.6	1.9	0.5	416
Morrisons Plain Fairy Cakes	27.2	21.9	1.8	0.5	431
Mr Kipling Apple & Blackcurrant Pies	27.3	13.2	4.5	0.33	361
Tesco Bramley Apple Pies	27.3	12.5	3.8	0.2	362
Heston from Waitrose Earl Grey Mandarin Teacake	27.3	8.3	2.7	0.45	319
Asda Chosen by You Viennese Whirls	27.4	30	17	0.1	524
Waitrose Essential iced Belgian Buns	27.4	6.1	2.8	0.54	323
Waitrose Seriously Chocolate Fudge Cake	27.4	24.4	8.6	0.4	433
Waitrose Lardy Cake	27.7	15.6	6.6	0.35	380

Cakes

Product	Sugar	Fat	Sat per 100g	Salt	Cals
Sainsbury's Freefrom Lemon Cake Slices	27.7	27.1	4.8	0.3	457
Tesco Everyday Value Apple Pies	27.8	14.4	3.3	0.1	393
Mr Kipling Viennese Whirls	27.9	30.2	12.3	0.59	514
Sainsbury's Freefrom Coffee & Walnut Cake Slices	27.9	28.7	5	0.32	463
Tesco Free From Bramley Apple Pies	27.9	12.5	5.9	0.2	376
Mr Kipling Fruit Pie Selection	28	13.2	4.5	0.31	361
Respect Organic Banana Loaf Cake	28	21	2.7	1	384
Chorley Cakes	28	19	6.6	0.22	420
Tesco Apple And Blackcurrant Pies	28	12.6	3.9	0.3	366
Morrisons Date & Walnut Loaf Cake	28	20.7	1.8	0.5	413
Thorntons Toffee Cake Slice	28	28.4	7.7	0.2	467
Waitrose Essential Custard Slices	28	12.5	7.1	0.42	288
Tesco Free From Bakewell Slices	28.2	17.8	1.6	0.5	409
Tesco Finest Free From Carrot Cake	28.2	20.9	5.7	0.8	407
Waitrose Marlborough Bun	28.4	3.5	0.9	0.6	304
Sainsbury's Muffins, Lemon	28.5	18.4	1.6	0.39	384
Tesco Giant Chocolate Cupcake	28.6	19.8	4.6	0.5	401
Tesco Chocolate And Vanilla Jumbo Swiss Roll	28.6	13.8	5.9	0.6	381
Morrisons Chorley Cakes	28.6	19.3	7.1	0.3	429
Asda Smart Price Chocolate Mini Rolls	28.7	15.9	4.5	0.4	385
Asda Chosen by You Triple Chocolate Giant Doughnut Cake	28.8	14.2	5.5	0.5	376
Asda Chosen by You Triple Chocolate Giant Doughnut Cake	28.8	14.2	5.5	0.5	376
Sainsbury's Freefrom Cherry & Almond Slices	28.9	24.3	4.3	0.11	442
We Love Cake Gluten Free Raspberry Macaroon Slices	28.9	23.6	12.5	0.19	450
Sainsbury's Chocolate Sponge Sandwich	29	22.3	9.3	0.58	426
Tesco Viennese Whirls	29	33.4	22.4	0.2	538
Sainsbury's Freefrom Jam Tarts	29	13.8	3.8	0.38	420
Sainsbury's Caramel & Pecan Nut Slices, Taste The Difference	29.1	29.9	12	0.3	508
Tesco Toffee Loaf Cake	29.1	16.1	1.5	0.4	384
Tesco Fairy Cakes	29.1	24.1	2.2	0.5	442

Cakes

Product	Sugar	Fat	Sat	Salt	Cals
			per 100g		
Sainsbury's Belgian Chocolate Fudge Cake, Taste the Difference	29.2	21.7	6.9	0.58	428
Sainsbury's Carrot Cake, Taste the Difference	29.2	19	5.3	0.51	398
Tesco Mini Chocolate Muffins	29.5	20.5	4	0.4	417
Tesco Chocolate Chip Muffins	29.5	20.5	4	0.4	417
Waitrose Lemon & Poppy Seed Muffins	29.5	19.1	1.6	0.6	380
Tesco Butterscotch And Pecan Cake Slices	29.6	21.5	2.3	0.4	417
Waitrose Double Chocolate Loaf Cake	29.6	20.3	2.8	0.5	413
Asda Chosen by You Large Chocolate Birthday Cake	29.9	22.7	7.1	0.5	438
Sainsbury's Madeira Cake	30	15	9.2	0.48	379
Tesco Finest Free From Victoria Sponge Cake	30	16.1	8	0.6	389
Tesco Red Velvet Slab Cake	30.2	24.2	6.8	0.4	432
Asda Chosen by You Iced Madeira Cake	30.2	14.9	9.1	0.3	396
Tesco Free From Lemon Drizzle Loaf Cake	30.3	19.6	3.4	0.5	398
Tesco Triple Layer Chocolate Cake	30.5	23.4	6.1	0.5	427
Morrisons Lemon Curd Tarts	30.5	14	5	0.1	395
Waitrose Essential Plain Cup Cakes	30.5	20.2	1.8	0.49	414
Sainsbury's Freefrom Ginger Cake Slices	30.5	19	3.5	0.15	419
Tesco Everyday Value Flapjack Traybake	30.6	14.3	5.1	0.1	401
Asda Chosen by You Chocolate Party Cake	30.6	22.5	6.8	0.5	436
Waitrose Lemon Loaf Cake	30.6	17.9	3.9	0.33	396
Waitrose Carrot Cake	30.7	22.8	4.1	0.45	414
Sainsbury's Madeira Cake, Basics	30.8	13.6	5.9	0.6	367
Bonne Maman Chocolate Madeleines	30.9	27.6	15.8	0.57	469
Tesco Everyday Value Lightly Fruited Slab Cake	30.9	9	4	0.3	332
Waitrose Windmill Round Fruited Bun	30.9	3.7	1.8	0.53	294
Tesco Free From Coffee And Walnut Slices]	30.9	19.2	2.6	0.5	418
Asda Chosen by You All Butter Madeira Cake	31	14.7	9.6	0.7	384
Morrisons Chocolate Cake Slices	31	18	3.7	0.3	388
Asda Chosen by You All Butter Madeira Cake	31	14.7	9.6	0.7	384
Tesco Big Chocolate Cake	31.1	20.4	4.3	0.5	405

Cakes

Product	Sugar	Fat	Sat per 100g	Salt	Cals
Asda Chosen by You Giant Chocolate Cupcake	31.3	18.9	4.9	0.4	404
Tesco Everyday Value Chocolate And Vanilla Swiss Roll	31.4	13.4	6.4	0.6	383
Sainsbury's Triple Layer Chocolate Cake	31.4	24	8.2	0.49	432
Morrisons Madeira Slab Cake	31.5	15	9.5	0.7	388
Morrisons Signature Belgian Chocolate Millionaires Tart	31.8	23.7	15.3	0.3	423
Waitrose Pecan & Walnut Squares	31.8	29.6	10.8	0.14	485
Asda Chosen by You Mega Chocolate Cake	31.9	17.3	4.1	0.5	399
Mr Kipling Jam Tarts	32	13	4.5	0.1	394
Sainsbury's Mince Puffs, Basics	32	19	9.5	0.5	430
Mr Kipling Almond Slices	32.1	18.6	5.7	0.25	412
Sainsbury's Large Victoria Sponge, Taste the Difference	32.3	17.1	4.1	0.57	392
Sainsbury's Giant Chocolate Cupcake	32.3	21.2	5.3	0.49	423
Tesco Double Chocolate Swiss Roll	32.4	13.3	6.4	0.6	396
Tesco Pack Lunchbox Flapjacks	32.4	16.8	6.1	0.1	420
Tesco Finest Victoria Sponge Cake	32.6	17.6	10.5	0.4	403
Asda Chosen by You Triple Layer Milk Chocolate Cake	32.6	18.4	8.2	0.4	396
Asda Chosen by You Chocolate Chip Cake Bars	32.6	25.5	6.1	0.4	461
Waitrose Blackcurrant Sundaes	32.6	17.4	10.6	0.31	415
Sainsbury's Muffins, Double Chocolate Chip	32.7	21.7	3.9	0.6	422
Asda Gluten Free Chocolate Muffins Cakes	32.8	19.5	4.6	0.7	403
Sainsbury's Coffee Cake, Taste the Difference	32.9	21.9	7.6	0.4	422
Sainsbury's Chocolate Swiss Roll, Basics	32.9	15.1	5.1	0.5	383
Sainsbury's Coffee Cake, Taste the Difference	32.9	21.9	7.6	0.4	422
Respect Organic Carrot Cake	33	23	4.8	1	401
Sainsbury's Walnut Cake	33	18.1	7.3	0.5	398
Tesco Pack Sponge Tops	33	20	3.2	0.3	432
Morrisons Toffee Bakewells	33	19.2	7.9	0.13	437
Asda Gluten Free Toffee Slices	33	19.8	2.9	0.7	443
Waitrose Essential Chocolate Chip Muffins	33.1	18.8	5.1	0.38	399
Thorntons Triple Chocolate Cake Slices	33.2	21.2	5.4	0.23	402

Product	Sugar	Fat	Sat	Salt	Cals
			per 100g		
Morrisons Coconut Slices	33.2	19.9	3.1	0.4	428
Asda Chosen by You Chocolate Slices	33.2	15	4.1	0.5	393
Asda Chosen by You Chocolate Cake Slice	33.3	17.5	6.1	0.5	395
Asda Extra Special Hand Finished Salted Caramel Cake	33.3	19.8	5.3	0.5	438
Asda Chosen by You Chocolate Cake Slice	33.3	17.5	6.1	0.5	395
Waitrose Seriously Carrot Cake	33.3	22.5	6.6	0.57	416
Sainsbury's Frangipanes	33.4	21.1	9.9	0.33	444
Tesco Frangipanes	33.4	21.1	9.9	0.5	444
Asda Chosen by You Teatime Treat Frangipanes	33.4	21.1	9.9	0.5	444
Morrisons Lemon Bakewells	33.4	18.1	7.1	0.18	427
Asda Chosen by You Teatime Treat Frangipanes	33.4	21.1	9.9	0.5	444
Waitrose Salted Caramel Cake	33.4	21.4	5.7	0.35	426
Tesco Free From Chocolate Muffins	33.4	20.8	5.1	0.7	434
Sainsbury's Lemon Loaf Cake	33.5	17.7	1.5	0.42	403
Morrisons Chocolate Swiss Roll	33.5	12.9	6.5	0.4	381
Waitrose Essential Double Chocolate Muffins	33.5	22.1	6.1	0.33	424
Sainsbury's Freefrom Fruit Cake Slices	33.5	13.3	1.3	0.14	377
Sainsbury's Rich Chocolate Slices	33.6	22.5	3.6	0.3	436
Sainsbury's Angel Cake	33.6	14.5	4.7	0.48	383
Tesco Cornflake Clusters	33.6	19.3	11.6	0.4	476
Asda Gluten Free Cherry Bakewells Cakes	33.6	14.5	5.8	0.3	402
Asda Chosen by You Walnut Cake	33.6	15.7	5.3	0.5	393
Asda Gluten Free Cherry Bakewells Cakes	33.6	14.5	5.8	0.3	402
Asda Chosen by You Walnut Cake	33.6	15.7	5.3	0.5	393
McVitie's Galaxy Mini Muffins	33.7	25.5	7.9	0.62	449
Thorntons Chocolate Celebration Cake	33.7	24.1	8.9	0.4	426
Sainsbury's Belgian Chocolate Mini Loaf Cakes	33.8	26.9	8.1	0.22	454
Tesco Large Chocolate Celebration Cake	33.8	21.9	6.5	0.5	430
Tesco Chocolate Stuffed Crust Cake	33.8	21.6	10.4	0.5	439
Waitrose Stem Ginger Loaf Cake	33.8	13.7	1.1	0.35	384

Cakes

Product	Sugar	Fat	Sat per 100g	Salt	Cals
Sainsbury's Victoria Fairy Cakes	33.9	21.5	4	0.53	436
Sainsbury's Chocolate Brownie, Taste the Difference	34	25	15	0.1	449
Sainsbury's Mini Caramel Wafers	34	21	12	0.78	477
Asda Chosen by You Strawberry Jam Tarts	34	13.4	6.7	0.1	401
Asda Chosen by You Iced Fairy Cakes	34	18.3	2.1	0.4	399
Asda Chosen by You Strawberry Jam Tarts	34	13.4	6.7	0.1	401
Tesco Mr Or Mrs Gingerbread People	34.1	14.3	6.2	0.6	447
Asda Chosen by You Decorate-It Cake Kit	34.1	21.4	4.1	0.5	425
Asda Chosen by You Mega Madeira Cake	34.1	15.2	3.6	0.6	381
Mr Kipling Manor House Cake	34.2	20.2	7.2	0.3	403
McVitie's Chocolate Hobnobs Flapjacks	34.2	17.4	8.7	0.5	440
Tesco Madeira Cake	34.2	15.2	9.2	0.7	386
Tesco Free From Lemon Slices	34.2	17.5	2.5	0.5	410
Tesco Finest Free From Chocolate Cake	34.2	16.6	8.5	0.5	386
Tesco Small Chocolate Celebration Cake	34.3	21.7	7.1	0.5	421
Morrisons Walnut Cake	34.3	15.9	5.1	0.6	395
Asda Extra Special Hand Finished Victoria Sponge	34.3	20.7	9.6	0.5	423
Waitrose Belgian Chocolate Cake	34.3	23.3	8.1	0.5	447
Waitrose Lemon Drizzle Cake	34.4	15.8	3.1	0.5	387
Waitrose Chocolate Orange Sponge Bakes	34.4	20.3	8.3	0.57	435
Sainsbury's Large Carrot Cake, Taste the Difference	34.5	19.8	5.6	0.51	407
Sainsbury's Jumbo Chocolate Swiss Roll	34.5	19.4	6.6	0.48	411
M&M's Chocolate Brownie	34.5	17.7	8.5	0.3	409
Asda Assorted Jam Tarts	34.5	13.1	6.5	0.1	403
Morrisons Cherry Bakewells	34.5	16.1	6.5	0.2	410
Asda Extra Special Hand-Finished Strawberry & White Chocolate Cake	34.5	18.6	4.8	0.4	413
Asda Assorted Jam Tarts	34.5	13.1	6.5	0.1	403
Waitrose Chocolate & Vanilla Butterfly Cakes	34.5	21.8	6.1	0.49	456
McVitie's Chocolate Hobnob Flapjack	34.6	17.5	8.8	0.5	441
Fabulous Bakin' Boys Choccy Cupcakes	34.6	25.8	11.8	0.8	456

Product	Sugar	Fat	Sat	Salt	Cals
			per 100g		
Tesco Finest Carrot Cake	34.6	17.9	2.6	0.4	385
Tesco Angel Layer Cak	34.6	14.8	4.8	0.6	387
Tesco Iced Fairy Cakes	34.6	21.3	2.8	0.5	436
Asda Chosen by You Angel Cake	34.6	14.8	4.8	0.5	387
Morrisons Angel Layer Cake	34.6	14.8	4.8	0.6	387
Asda Chosen by You Angel Cake	34.6	14.8	4.8	0.5	387
Asda Chocolate Cornflake Mini Bites	34.7	16.8	10.1	0.5	460
Tesco Free From Chocolate Brownie Cake Bars	34.8	20.3	4.1	0.8	430
Sainsbury's Raspberry Sponge Sandwich	34.9	15.1	5.2	0.6	383
Sainsbury's Jam Tarts	35	12.7	5.3	0.02	399
Sainsbury's Pecan Tarts	35	23.6	5.8	0.22	461
Sainsbury's Caramel Wafers	35	21	13	0.65	483
Tesco Cherry Madeira Slab Cake	35	11	5.4	0.5	357
Sainsbury's Chocolate Party Cake	35	17	2.9	0.48	393
Morrisons Strawberry Tarts	35	12.1	4.6	0.2	392
Waitrose Essential Jam Tarts	35	12.7	5.3	0.04	399
Sainsbury's Freefrom Pecan Tarts	35	23.6	5.8	0.22	461
Mr Kipling Bakewell Slices	35.2	17.4	7.8	0.45	408
Sainsbury's Strawberry & Vanilla Swiss Roll	35.2	13.7	4.6	0.3	381
Asda Extra Special Hand Finished Apple & Blackcurrant Cake	35.2	16.7	3.9	0.5	385
Asda Chosen by You Teatime Fairy Cakes	35.2	21.5	4.7	0.4	434
Tesco Free From Cherry Bakewell Tarts	35.2	17.4	4.9	0.2	445
Tesco Finest Free From Chocolate And Cranberry	35.2	24	14.5	0.6	497
Mr Kipling Treacle Tart	35.3	12.4	4.2	0.52	383
Thorntons Toffee Cake	35.3	20.6	7.5	0.52	425
Sainsbury's Marble Loaf Cake	35.4	19	1.8	0.44	409
Mr Kipling Caramel Slice	35.6	23	8.1	0.55	447
Asda Extra Special Hand Finished Lemon Cake	35.6	20	4.8	0.4	413
Waitrose Happy Birthday Cake	35.6	23.7	9	0.38	439
Waitrose Victoria Sponge Cake	35.7	18.8	10.6	0.45	406

Cakes

Product	Sugar	Fat	Sat	Salt	Cals
			per 100g		
Mrs. Crimble's Gluten Free Bakewell Slices	35.7	23.8	13.5	0.4	465
Morrisons Ginger Buns	35.8	11.5	0.9	0.4	373
Waitrose Seriously Apple & Blackcurrant Crumble Cake	35.8	19.3	6.1	0.45	402
Waitrose Vanilla Butterfly Cakes	35.8	18.4	5.1	0.51	447
Asda Chosen by You Mega Malty Chocolate Factory Ultimate Cupcake	35.9	18.7	5.8	0.3	407
Asda Smart Price Raspberry Mini Rolls	35.9	13.7	4.4	0.3	393
Bonne Maman Chocolate Caramel	36	23	13	0.6	490
Sainsbury's Buttery Flapjacks	36	20	10	0.48	445
Tesco Mini Chocolate Cornflake Bites	36	18.2	11	0.4	467
Tesco Crispy Caramel Bites	36	12.2	7.2	0.3	434
Asda Chosen by You Jumbo Strawberry Swiss Roll	36	12.1	4	0.6	373
Sainsbury's Freefrom Bramley Apple Pies	36	12.6	5.8	1	367
Tesco Finest Millionaire Shortbread	36.1	28.1	15.8	0.4	509
Asda Chosen by You Jumbo Chocolate Swiss Roll	36.1	18.9	6.8	0.6	409
Sainsbury's Cherry Bakewells	36.2	17	6.5	0.35	424
Tesco Chocolate Slices	36.2	22.5	3.8	0.3	439
Asda Chosen by You Jazzie Raspberry Giant Doughnut Cake	36.2	12.1	3.5	0.4	376
Morrisons Assorted Jam Tarts	36.2	13.4	6.7	0.1	403
Morrisons Cherry Cake	36.2	8.9	4.6	0.6	347
Asda Chosen by You Jazzie Raspberry Giant Doughnut Cake	36.2	12.1	3.5	0.4	376
Tesco Belgian Bun	36.3	10.6	4.2	0.5	373
Waitrose White Chocolate & Strawberry Cake	36.4	20.3	5.4	0.48	432
Tesco Caramel Shortcake Traybake	36.5	27.9	17	0.4	527
Morrisons Butterfly Buns	36.5	24.7	5.5	0.5	450
Sainsbury's Carrot Cake Slices	36.6	20.7	4.6	0.33	428
Tesco Millionaire Bites	36.6	28	15.2	0.5	500
Tesco Marble Madeira Cake	36.6	18.7	1.6	0.5	409
Tesco Granola Traybake	36.6	15	4.9	0.1	404
Morrisons Iced Fairy Cakes	36.6	19.2	2.5	0.5	422
Tesco Free From Angel Slices	36.6	18.1	2.5	0.5	421

Cakes

Product	Sugar	Fat	Sat	Salt	Cals
			per 100g		
Sainsbury's Almond Slices	36.7	17.8	17.8	0.4	406
Tesco Finest Lemon Meringue Cake	36.7	14.8	3.9	0.5	368
Morrisons Iced Madeira Cake	36.7	14.4	8.1	0.7	397
Waitrose Chocolate Cake	36.7	20.4	6.4	0.48	424
Waitrose Triple Chocolate Muffins	36.7	22.2	5.4	0.48	425
Morrisons Mini Chocolate Cakes	36.8	26.4	7.2	0.4	478
Morrisons Free From Flapjack Tray Bake	36.8	17	5.1	0.1	432
Asda Extra Special Hand Finished Chocolate Fudge Cake	36.8	23.9	7.4	0.5	451
Mr Kipling Trifle Bakewells	36.9	17.3	6.9	0.31	422
Tesco Everyday Value Raspberry Flavoured Sponge Cake	36.9	10.4	3	0.5	353
Waitrose Almond Frangipane Tarts	36.9	26.3	13.1	0.3	474
Sainsbury's Cherry Madeira Cake	37	10	5.1	0.53	362
Sainsbury's Lemon Iced Madeira Cake	37	14	9.1	0.5	389
Tesco Mini Flapjack Bites	37	21.9	9.6	0.4	458
Morrisons Signature Decadent Belgian Chocolate Fudge Cake	37	20.2	5.7	0.4	413
Waitrose Seriously Victoria Sponge Sandwich	37	19.4	12.5	0.4	402
Waitrose Seriously Cherry & Marzipan Cake	37	21	9.7	0.07	427
McVitie's Chocolate Digestive Slice	37.1	26.8	13.1	0.8	500
Asda Chosen by You Sultana & Cherry Cake	37.1	9.5	4.6	0.2	348
Tesco Strawberry And Vanilla Jumbo Swiss Roll	37.2	9.3	4.5	0.5	364
Tesco Assorted Jam Tarts	37.2	13.6	6.4	0.2	408
Waitrose Rocky Road Bites	37.2	24.9	14.8	0.43	498
Waitrose Walnut, Chocolate, Raisin & Oat Cookies	37.2	17.5	8.2	0.5	430
Morrisons Chocolate Celebration Cake	37.3	23.4	6.9	0.5	440
Twix Caramel Slice	37.4	26.4	13.8	0.55	492
Asda Chosen by You Genoa Cake	37.4	9	4.4	0.2	346
Morrisons Iced Teatime Buns	37.4	22.7	6.1	0.5	446
Asda Chosen by You Genoa Cake	37.4	9	4.4	0.2	346
Tesco Almond Slices	37.5	17.6	3.4	0.5	404
Waitrose Ginger Mini Loaf Cakes	37.5	18.9	1.5	0.48	415

Cakes

Product	Sugar	Fat	Sat	Salt	Cals
			per 100g		
Mr Kipling Bakewell Tart	37.6	16.7	6.6	0.33	414
McVitie's Jamaica Ginger Cake	37.6	10.4	3.2	0.61	362
Sainsbury's Swiss Roll Raspberry	37.6	11.3	6.5	0.64	356
Tesco Iced Madeira Cake	37.7	14.6	8.8	0.6	393
Tesco Finest Purple Velvet Cake	37.7	21.3	4.4	0.5	437
Tesco Almond Fingers	37.7	14.9	5.9	0.5	405
Asda Chosen by You Cherry Madeira Cake	37.7	10.7	5.4	0.5	356
Tesco Assorted Party Selection	37.9	20.8	4.3	0.4	435
Asda Extra Special Hand Finished Carrot Cake	37.9	19.7	4.6	0.5	406
Tesco Free From Chocolate Celebration Cake	37.9	17.4	9.4	0.6	394
Sainsbury's Lightly Fruited Cake	38	15	7.1	0.43	386
Sainsbury's Raisin Fruit Slab Cake, Basics	38	13	4.5	0.13	372
Sainsbury's Fruit Flapjacks	38	19	9.2	0.45	435
Sainsbury's Rose Cup Cake	38	19	7.5	0.46	413
Sainsbury's Seriously Chocolatey Cake	38	24	9.5	0.35	442
Sainsbury's Sweetie Traybake	38	20	6.2	0.5	434
Morrisons Belgian Chocolate Button Party Cake	38	18.9	5.6	0.5	413
Asda Mini Fairycakes	38	24.7	6.3	0.4	468
Peppa Pig Cupcakes	38.1	28.8	8.8	0.5	495
Mr Kipling Banoffee Slice	38.2	18.1	6	0.57	413
Sainsbury's Lemon Slices	38.2	22.3	4.8	0.33	438
Mr Kipling Banoffee Slice	38.2	18.1	6	0.57	413
Morrisons Lemon Cake Slices	38.2	19.1	2.5	0.4	418
Mr Kipling Cherry Bakewells	38.3	17.1	7.1	0.35	423
McVitie's Lyle's Golden Syrup Cake	38.3	11	3.4	0.92	361
Waitrose Vanilla & Chocolate Mini Cupcakes	38.3	23.7	5.6	0.45	450
McVitie's Digestive Caramel Slices	38.4	25.8	14	0.7	484
Sainsbury's Bramley Apple Turnovers	38.4	16.9	8.9	0.4	410
Tesco Madeira Party Cake	38.4	17.7	4.3	0.5	415
Tesco Finest Chocolate Cake	38.4	22.3	6.4	0.4	422

Product	Sugar	Fat	Sat per 100g	Salt	Cals
Tesco Pack Cranberry And Seed Flapjacks	38.4	18.5	6.6	0.1	429
Asda Lemon Curd Tarts	38.4	16	8.2	trace	427
Asda Smart Price Chocolate Swiss Roll	38.4	16.3	5.6	0.3	402
Asda Lemon Curd Tarts	38.4	16	8.2	trace	427
Asda Smart Price Chocolate Swiss Roll	38.4	16.3	5.6	0.3	402
Mr Kipling Chocolate Slice	38.5	18.5	6.2	0.57	412
Tesco Everyday Value Jam And Vanilla Mini Rolls	38.5	7.9	2.8	0.3	354
Asda Chosen by You Iced Lemon Madeira Cake	38.5	15.7	6.8	0.5	389
Morrisons Iced Lemon Madeira Cake	38.5	15.7	6.3	0.5	395
Asda Chosen by You Iced Lemon Madeira Cake	38.5	15.7	6.8	0.5	389
Sainsbury's Mini Bite Millionaire Flapjack	38.7	20.4	9.7	0.35	455
Asda Extra Special Hand Finished Chocolate Cake	38.7	22.8	6.7	0.4	441
Tesco Free From Lightly Fruited Loaf Cake	38.7	10.8	6.3	0.5	351
Tesco Finest Cherry Bakewell Cake	38.8	15.3	7.7	0.6	389
Asda Extra Special Hand Finished Coffee Cake	38.8	20.9	6.4	0.5	431
Genius Gluten Free Lemon Cupcakes	38.8	31.7	8.7	0.8	500
Sainsbury's Angel Cake Slices	38.9	18.2	3.8	0.3	410
Mr Kipling Chocolate Chip Cake Bars	38.9	20.5	8.1	0.4	440
Tesco Swiss Gateau Cake	38.9	19.3	9.2	0.5	440
Sainsbury's Freefrom Mini Cherry Bakewell	38.9	19.8	6.2	0.19	456
Mr Kipling Chocolate & Vanilla Milkshake Slice	39	16	4.8	0.5	401
Sainsbury's Swiss Roll Cappucino	39	15.6	7.5	0.35	389
Mr Kipling Chocolate & Vanilla Milkshake Slice	39	16	4.8	0.5	401
Tesco Lemon Slices	39	17.1	3.8	0.3	394
Tesco Carrot Slices	39	21.7	4.2	0.2	431
Sainsbury's Hugo The Hedgehog Cake	39	22	9	0.26	437
Asda Chosen by You Cherry Bakewells	39	16.2	6.3	0.4	415
Asda Chosen by You Toffee Popcorn Surprise Cake	39	15	3	0.59	384
Asda Chosen by You Cherry Bakewells	39	16.2	6.3	0.4	415
Mr Kipling Banana Milkshake Slice	39.1	16	4.8	0.5	402

Cakes

Product	Sugar	Fat	Sat	Salt	Cals
			per 100g		
Mr Kipling Strawberry Milkshake Slice	39.1	16	4.8	0.5	402
Tesco Finest Lemon Drizzle Cake	39.1	16.5	4.6	0.4	391
Sainsbury's Millionaire Square Flapjacks	39.2	20.2	9.4	0.34	445
Tesco Country Slices	39.2	17.2	1.5	0.4	397
Just Love Food Company Nut Safe Chocolate Partybake	39.2	22.9	4.1	0.5	442
Asda Giant Ice Cream Cupcake	39.2	18.6	4.6	0.4	421
Sainsbury's Freefrom Oaty Flapjack Slices	39.2	14.6	4.2	0.03	429
Tesco Red Velvet Slices	39.3	18.2	3.6	0.3	427
Tesco Cherry Bakewell Tarts	39.3	15.9	5.2	0.1	417
Sainsbury's Madeira Party Cake	39.3	20.2	4.1	0.54	427
Waitrose Orange & Lemon Mini Loaf Cakes	39.3	18.9	4.8	0.45	413
Sainsbury's Triple Layer Blackcurrant Cake, Taste the Difference	39.4	21.6	9.7	0.4	439
Tesco Finest Praline Belgian Chocolate Brownies	39.4	25	7.8	0.1	473
Sainsbury's Freefrom Chocolate Brownies	39.4	26.1	6	0.15	467
Sainsbury's Country Slices	39.5	17	1.4	0.45	396
Tesco Lemon Iced Madeira Cake	39.5	18.2	8	0.5	418
Tesco Finest White Chocolate And Strawberry Cake	39.5	20.8	6.9	0.3	422
Tesco Angel Slices	39.6	19.6	4.4	0.3	419
Waitrose Jelly Bean Cake	39.6	15.1	7.5	0.5	397
McVitie's Jaffa Cakes 'The Big One'	39.7	11.1	6.8	0.5	373
Sainsbury's Mini Bite Rocky Road	39.8	27.9	13.5	0.24	495
Tesco Finest Coffee And Walnut Cake	39.8	24.9	7.7	0.4	460
Mr Kipling Country Slices	39.9	15.1	5.1	0.39	384
Sainsbury's Lemon Curd Tarts	39.9	15.9	6.9	0.2	424
Asda Chosen by You Victoria Sponge	39.9	8.5	3.2	0.5	348
Bonne Maman Lemon Tartlets	40	17	9.5	0.3	439
Sainsbury's Coffee Iced Madeira Cake	40	14	5.7	0.55	394
Sainsbury's Freefrom Mini Chocolate Logs	40	24	6.5	0.2	450
Sainsbury's Seriously Chocolate Cake, Large	40	25	10	0.33	454
Morrisons Iced Coffee Cake	40	14.1	5.7	0.6	391

Product	Sugar	Fat	Sat	Salt	Cals
			per 100g		
Asda Chosen by You Chocolate Star Tray Bake	40	16	3.9	0.5	405
Asda Chosen by You Vanilla Traybake	40	13	4.3	0.4	381
Waitrose Coffee & Walnut Cake	40	19.8	5.1	0.43	420
Sainsbury's Freefrom Mini Chocolate Logs	40	24	6.5	0.2	450
Sainsbury's Caramel Brownies	40.2	24.3	13.7	0.63	463
Galaxy Cookie Crumble Slice	40.2	24.7	12.3	0.6	492
Sainsbury's Caramel Brownies	40.2	24.3	13.7	0.63	463
Sainsbury's Bakewell Cake Slices	40.3	17.5	5.3	0.35	411
Cadbury Chocolate Cake Bars	40.3	24.1	12	0.63	450
Cadbury Milk Chocolate Cake Bars	40.3	24.1	12	0.63	450
Sainsbury's Jam & Coconut Square Slices	40.3	23.6	16.8	0.2	435
Waitrose Red Velvet Mini Cupcakes	40.3	21.3	3.2	0.45	436
Asda Chosen by You Iced Coffee Cake	40.4	14	5.4	0.5	392
Tesco Finest Free From Triple Chocolate Cookies	40.4	26.2	15.8	0.8	508
Tesco Lemon Sponge	40.5	9.8	4.4	0.5	352
Waitrose Chcolate Tiffin	40.5	26.3	15.4	0.33	498
Morrisons Carrot Slices	40.6	16.7	2.6	0.4	403
Mr Kipling Victoria Slices	40.7	16	5.6	0.6	442
Asda Extra Special Hand Finished Red Velvet Cake	40.7	22.6	6.2	0.4	448
Mrs. Crimble's Gluten Free Cranberry Macaroons	40.7	26.4	22.2	0.1	470
Sainsbury's Freefrom Cherry Bakewells Tarts	40.7	22.3	6.6	0.23	476
Cadbury Caramel Cake Bars	40.9	19.5	11.7	0.78	435
Sainsbury's Belgian Choc Billionaire Slice, Taste the Difference	41	29	17	0.4	518
Bonne Maman Lemon & Poppy Seed Cakes	41	22	9.9	0.48	439
Tesco Chocolate Party Tray Bake	41	24.4	9.4	0.4	454
Sainsbury's Chocolate Party Traybake	41	24	10	0.44	458
Sainsbury's Mega Chocolate Traybake	41	22	8.6	0.5	426
Waitrose Seriously Ginger Cake	41	20.2	12.7	0.56	436
Tesco Mini Milk Chocolate Cookie Bites	41.1	21.6	7.2	0.7	482
Sainsbury's Lemon & Pistachio Mini Loaf Cakes	41.2	16.9	2.6	0.53	403

Cakes

Product	Sugar	Fat	Sat	Salt	Cals
			per 100g		
Sainsbury's Iced Madeira Cake	41.2	14.9	9.1	0.58	396
Sainsbury's Milk Choc Chip Cookie	41.2	20.7	10.2	0.6	457
Sainsbury's Lemon & Pistachio Mini Loaf Cakes	41.2	16.9	2.6	0.53	403
Sainsbury's Milk Choc Chip Cookie	41.2	20.7	10.2	0.6	457
Morrisons Free From Choc Chip Brownies	41.2	25.9	6.1	0.1	475
Asda Caramel Shortcake Bites	41.2	25.5	14.3	0.5	494
Sainsbury's Iced Fairy Cakes	41.4	18.2	2.8	0.36	422
Tesco Rose Bouquet Cake	41.4	19.7	7.6	0.5	431
Tesco Vanilla Party Tray Bake	41.5	21	7.1	0.4	446
Tesco Finest Red Velvet Cake	41.5	20.4	3.7	0.4	431
Morrisons Vanilla Traybake	41.5	13.3	6.3	0.5	387
Thorntons Caramel Shortcake	41.6	30.8	17.5	0.72	508
Real Lancashire Eccles Cakes	41.6	17.6	9.3	0.4	401
Tesco Coffee Iced Madeira Cake	41.6	14.2	5.8	0.6	391
Sainsbury's Ultimate Pink Madeira Cupcake	41.7	16.7	4.9	0.41	417
Tesco Lemon Curd Tarts	41.7	15.8	5.9	0.2	428
Sainsbury's Raspberry Swiss Roll	41.9	1.7	0.9	0.43	301
Sainsbury's Rocky Road, Taste the Difference	42	26	15	0.37	491
Mr Kipling Angel Slice	42	18.2	6.1	0.57	431
Sainsbury's Coconut & Jam Loaf Cake	42	22.5	4.9	0.4	424
Mr Kipling Angel Slice	42	18.2	6.1	0.57	431
Sainsbury's Rocky Road, Taste the Difference	42	26	15	0.37	491
Mrs. Crimble's Stem Ginger Cake	42	2.1	0.4	0.5	319
Tesco Rocky Road Traybake	42.1	25.4	16.5	0.4	508
Nestle Smarties Little Gift Cake	42.1	24.5	10.1	0.5	461
Asda Chosen by You Carrot Cake Slices	42.1	14.8	1.9	0.3	396
Waitrose Cornflake Cluster Bites	42.1	19.4	11.8	0.3	481
Waitrose Caramel Crispy Bites	42.1	12.7	7.9	0.39	412
Waitrose Millionaire's Shortbreads	42.1	26.6	14.6	0.48	498
Tesco Milk Chocolate Mini Rolls	42.2	21.5	13.6	0.5	451

Cakes

Product	Sugar	Fat	Sat per 100g	Salt	Cals
Morrisons Chocolate Sponge Cake	42.2	10.1	5	0.5	358
Cadbury Swiss Gateau	42.3	17.5	10.2	0.6	425
Waitrose Cherry Medeira Cake	42.3	11.7	5.4	0.23	362
Waitrose Caramel Fudge Mini Cupcakes	42.3	24.6	6.2	0.5	462
Cadbury Chocolate Mini Rolls	42.4	23	11.3	0.68	435
Cadbury Mini Roll Selection	42.4	23	11.3	0.68	435
Cadbury's Orange Mini Rolls	42.4	23	11.3	0.68	435
Tesco Large White Chocolate Celebration Cake	42.4	25.9	10.1	0.3	485
Tesco Coconut Sponge Cake	42.4	17.2	7.3	0.4	400
Asda Chosen by You Lemon Sponge	42.4	14.8	6.1	0.4	387
Morrisons Coconut Sponge Cake	42.4	17.2	7.3	0.4	400
Asda Chosen by You Lemon Sponge	42.4	14.8	6.1	0.4	387
Tesco Genoa Cake	42.5	9	4.2	0.3	349
Asda Chosen by You All American Ice Cream Sundae Cake	42.7	18.5	6.1	0.4	416
Sainsbury's Red Velvet Triple Layer Cake, Taste the Difference	42.8	22.7	7.3	0.37	428
McVitie's Ginger Nuts Slices	42.8	21.8	10.8	0.8	478
Sainsbury's Swiss Roll Lemon Curd	42.8	8.9	4.5	0.41	367
Waitrose Chocolate Brownies	42.8	25.1	11.1	0.1	469
Tesco Strawberry Cheesecake Cake Slices	42.9	21.1	3.1	0.4	432
Waitrose White & Plain Chocolate Cookies	42.9	19.4	11.9	0.65	454
Genius Gluten Free Chocolate Cupcakes	43	24.9	7.1	0.8	471
Tesco Free From Madeira Mini Gift Cake	43.2	17	7.3	0.5	421
Weight Watchers Carrot Cake Slices	43.3	5.6	3.5	0.3	323
Cadbury Boost Cake Bars	43.3	26.8	16.6	0.5	480
Cadbury Flake Cake	43.3	15.4	9.3	0.38	385
Waitrose Essential Iced Fairy Cakes	43.3	20.5	4.5	0.38	429
Asda Chosen by You Strawberry Mini Rolls	43.4	20.5	10.3	0.3	441
Wiggles The Caterpillar Cake	43.5	19	11.9	0.45	425
Waitrose Nutty Caramel Flapjack	43.5	19.1	10.7	0.35	443
Tesco Curly The Caterpillar Cake	43.7	17.1	10.5	0.5	410

Cakes

Product	Sugar	Fat	Sat	Salt	Cals
			per 100g		
Waitrose Caterpillar Cake	43.7	21.4	13	0.25	448
Sainsbury's Chocolate Flavoured Cupcakes	43.8	16.4	3	0.44	408
Morrisons Signature Divine Red Velvet Cake	43.8	17	3.7	0.4	411
Cadbury Triple Chocolate Roll	43.9	15.7	9.6	0.5	405
Tesco Chocolate Chunk Brownie Bites	43.9	18.8	11.3	0.2	428
Sainsbury's All Butter Fruit & Seed Flapjack, Taste the Difference	44	17	8.3	0.15	432
Sainsbury's Football Crazy Cake	44	12	2.8	0.25	406
Mrs. Crimble's Dutch Apple Cake	44	1.8	0.4	0.63	319
Kelkin Gluten Free Tea Cakes	44	16	13	0.38	407
McVitie's Galaxy Caramel Cake Bars	44.1	20.5	10.1	0.7	440
Sainsbury's Belgian Chocolate Cupcakes, Taste the Difference	44.2	27.6	14.4	0.27	486
Waitrose Cranberry & White Chocolate Cookies	44.2	11.6	7	0.57	410
Mr Kipling Lemon Layer Slices	44.3	15	3.3	0.56	403
Cadbury's Raspberry Mini Roll	44.5	19.6	9.9	0.54	410
Tesco Raspberry Sponge Cake	44.5	9.2	4	0.5	348
Tesco Iced Bakewell Slices	44.5	18.2	5.4	0.4	419
Tesco Mini Gingerbread Men	44.5	10.5	4.2	0.5	429
Just Love Food Company Nut Safe Vanilla Party Bake	44.5	21	6.8	0.7	437
Morrisons Raspberry Sponge Cake	44.5	9.2	4	0.5	346
Thorntons Triple Layer Chocolate Cakes	44.6	25.7	10.9	0.19	463
Heart Strawberry Cupcake	44.7	24.7	10.9	0.52	458
Tesco Banana Loaf Cake	44.8	17.2	1.7	0.3	377
Waitrose Chocolate Cupcakes	44.8	21.5	8.4	0.33	449
Tesco Mini Gingerbread Men	44.9	10.8	4.3	0.5	436
McVitie's Galaxy Cake Bars	45	26.8	13.5	0.5	485
McVitie's Mars Cake Bars	45	22.9	11.4	0.6	457
Tesco Mini Chocolate Brownie Bites	45	19.8	11.9	0.3	430
Disney Princess Traybake	45	11.2	4.3	0.45	373
Morrisons Coconut Cakes	45	22	20	0.1	470
Waitrose Chocolate Mini Rolls	45	23.6	14.6	0.48	464

Cakes

Product	Sugar	Fat	Sat	Salt	Cals
			per 100g		
Morrisons Sultana & Cherry Cake Slice	45.3	7.6	3.9	0.2	353
Sainsbury's Lemon Drizzle Cake, Taste the Difference	45.4	13.9	3.8	0.55	379
Sainsbury's Seriously White Chocolate Pearl Cake	45.5	22.2	10.4	0.43	447
Asda Chosen by You Candyland Ultimate Cupcake	45.6	23.6	6.9	0.4	455
Tesco Rocky Road	45.7	21.7	12.9	0.4	480
Tesco Hidden Sweetie Cake	45.7	19.3	7.3	0.3	451
Tesco Bagged Jaffa Cake Bars	45.7	15	9.4	0.4	405
Tesco Pack Cupcakes	45.7	27.9	6.5	0.5	490
Keep Calm Celebration Cake	45.7	9.3	2.7	0.5	377
Morrisons Raspberry Swiss Roll	45.7	2.5	1.4	0.4	320
Tesco Battenberg Cake	46	11.3	2.7	0.4	375
Sainsbury's Lion Cake	46	32	14	0.23	498
Asda Chosen by You Clyde the Caterpillar	46	17	10	0.45	418
Waitrose Essential Brownie Bars	46	18.1	7.9	0.23	415
Waitrose Millionaire Bites	46	29.1	17.4	0.22	511
Tesco Bagged Chocolate Cake Bars	46.1	19.2	12	0.2	433
Morrisons Chocolate Cake Bars	46.1	19.2	12	0.2	433
Asda Chosen by You Football Party Cake	46.1	12.8	2.8	0.4	415
Asda Chosen by You Chocolate Cake Bars	46.1	19.2	12	0.2	433
Tesco Chocolate Brownie Traybake	46.4	18.4	9.1	0.3	428
Asda Chosen by You Irish Cream Flavour Cake	47	27	9.8	0.31	484
Asda Chosen by You Chocolate Mini Rolls	47	20	12.4	0.4	450
Candy Crush Celebration Cake	47.2	17	3.5	0.5	437
Thorntons Mini Chocolate Fudge Brownies	47.3	20	11.5	0.52	435
Tesco Raspberry Swiss Roll	47.4	2.4	0.9	0.6	303
Morrisons Large Shining Star Celebration Cake	47.4	14.6	2.8	0.4	409
Waitrose Seriously Dainty Cupcakes	47.4	16	5.4	0.52	448
Waitrose Raspberry Macaroon Tarts	47.5	15.2	7.4	0.3	423
Morrisons Vintage Cupcake	47.6	21.4	7.3	0.4	461
McVitie's Jaffa Cake Bars	47.9	14.5	7.6	0.5	395

Cakes

Product	Sugar	Fat	Sat per 100g	Salt	Cals
Waitrose Genoa Cake	47.9	13.8	5.6	0.45	380
Sainsbury's Chocolate Cupcakes	48	29	11	0.36	492
Tesco Princess Tiara Cake	48	11.2	4.1	0.4	384
Sainsbury's Happy Birthday Madeira Cake	48	12	2.6	0.44	399
Asda Chosen by You Pina Colada Mocktail Cake	48	24	7.6	0.3	478
Asda Chosen by You Strawberry Woo Woo Mocktail Cake	48	25	8.6	0.27	478
Asda Chosen by You American Waffles & Syrup Gravity Cake	48	15	3.2	0.32	416
Thorntons Triple Layer Toffee Cakes	48.1	25.5	12.5	0.36	468
Waitrose Fruit Cake	48.4	9.9	5.9	0.5	342
Tesco Football Cake	48.5	13.6	2.6	0.4	420
Tesco Chocolate Cubes Celebration Cake	48.6	18.8	12.2	0.5	427
Sainsbury's Lemon Cupcakes	48.7	25.5	8.8	0.4	483
Asda Chosen by You White Chocolate Birthday cake	48.7	22.8	8.2	0.4	467
Sainsbury's Caramel Brownie Triple Layer Cake, Taste the Difference	48.9	20.5	9.4	0.44	436
Morrisons Cheeky Caterpillar Cake	48.9	14.9	9	0.5	404
Sainsbury's Wedding Cake Tier, Extra Large	49	9.9	3.3	0.15	369
Waitrose Pineapple Tarts	49.1	11.3	6.9	0.19	400
Tesco Pack Chocolate Brownie	49.5	17.4	7.7	0.2	408
Tesco Rocky Road Cluster	49.7	20.3	12.1	0.3	470
Asda Chosen by You Happy Birthday Cake Cubes	49.7	19.1	12.1	0.6	434
Forever Friends Celebration Cake	49.8	16.1	4.4	0.5	437
Frozen Celebration Cake	49.8	12.7	2.9	0.42	400
One Direction Celebration Cake	49.8	11.8	2.5	0.44	393
Asda Chosen by You Pinata Surprise Cake	49.9	21.4	8.2	0.3	459
Sainsbury's Genoa Cake	50	9.3	5.4	0.3	350
Weight Watchers Chocolate Mini Rolls	50	13.9	8	0.44	411
Batman Cake	50	9.7	2.7	0.45	359
Sainsbury's Simply Butterflies Cake	50	9.8	3	0.39	388
Asda Chosen by You Decorate Your Own Cupcake Kit	50	15	2.5	0.3	400
Tesco Giant Cupcake	50.1	15.3	5.2	0.4	434

Cakes

Product	Sugar	Fat	Sat	Salt	Cals
			per 100g		
Asda Chosen by You Fruit Cake	50.1	5.7	3.8	0.1	340
Waitrose Parcel Cake	50.1	14.4	3.8	0.28	412
Tesco Shooting Stars Party Cake	50.3	13.9	2.4	0.4	425
Big Hero 6 Cake	50.3	12.5	2.9	0.41	400
Asda Chosen by You Party Cake	50.5	16.2	5	0.5	422
Tesco Loom Party Cake	50.6	13.1	3.4	0.3	388
Disney Minnie Mouse Cake	50.9	12	2.9	0.39	396
Mrs. Crimble's Gluten Free Jam Coconut Rings	51	21	20	0.09	433
Forever Friends Mini Gift Cake	51.3	16.7	4.9	0.43	441
Tesco White Chocolate And Vanilla Cupcakes	51.4	27.8	11.6	0.2	501
Tesco Raspberry Pavlova Cupcake	51.5	24.8	9.7	0.2	478
Asda Chosen by You Large Party Cake	51.5	15	4.1	0.4	421
Sainsbury's Ginger Loaf Cake	51.7	12.4	1.1	0.4	392
Mrs Crimble's Gluten Free Coconut Macaroons	51.8	22.7	20.9	0.08	471
Tesco Red Velvet Cupcake	51.9	27.7	9.1	0.4	489
Tesco Party Cupcakes	51.9	27.7	9.1	0.4	489
Sainsbury's Red Velvet Cupcakes	52	29	10	0.39	500
Tesco Small Celebration Cake	52	17.1	3.1	0.3	445
Asda Chosen by You Design a Cake with Edible Ink Pens	52	13	2	0.37	403
Me To You Celebration Cake	52.5	14	4.2	0.28	407
Star Wars Celebration Cake	52.6	11.3	2.5	0.4	396
Sainsbury's Decorate Your Own Cake	53	16	7.6	0.32	418
Sainsbury's Handbag & Shoe Madeira Cake	53	20.2	4.1	0.35	454
Asda Chosen by You Coconut Macaroons	53	19	18	0.1	453
Asda Chosen by You Iced Fruit Bar	53.1	6.3	2.9	0.1	361
Morrisons Fashionista Celebration Cake	53.3	19.2	4	0.3	445
Sainsbury's Owl Madeira Birthday Cake	53.6	11.1	2.6	0.32	411
Asda Be A Princess Cake	53.8	19.2	3.3	0.3	453
Waitrose Lucky Lamb Cake	53.8	16.2	3.7	0.48	416
Sainsbury's Coconut Macaroons	54	18	15.5	0.13	424

Cakes

Product	Sugar	Fat	Sat per 100g	Salt	Cals
Tesco Coconut Macaroons	54	18	15.5	0.1	424
Sainsbury's Princess Castle Cake	54	13	6	0.3	410
Sainsbury's Wedding Cake Tier	54	10	3	0.14	385
Asda Chosen by You Jolly Roger Pirate Ship Cake	54	15	3	0.28	422
Mrs Crimble's Gluten Free Giant Chocolate Macaroon	54.3	22	20.3	0.08	458
Avengers Celebration Cake	54.3	13.4	2.9	0.39	405
Tesco Everyday Value Party Cake	54.5	15	2.9	0.5	431
Morrisons Rose Celebration Cake	54.5	16.9	3.4	0.3	434
Waitrose Decorate Your Own Cake	54.9	12.7	2.9	0.45	407
Asda Chosen by You Pablo the Pug Cake	55	15	3	0.25	422
Spiderman Celebration Cake	55.3	12.8	2.6	0.36	399
Asda Chosen by You Two-Tier Blossom Cake	55.6	19.3	3.2	0.3	438
Waitrose Party Cake	55.6	13.3	2.9	0.45	411
Peppa Pig Celebration Cake	55.9	14.2	4.5	0.41	405
Morrisons Decorate at Home Maderia Cake	56	18	3.2	0.3	445
Fireman Sam Celebration Cake	56.1	14.2	3.4	0.3	413
Waitrose Hidden Treasure Cake	56.5	13.7	3.2	0.33	409
Mr Kipling Battenberg	56.6	11.9	3.1	0.56	416
Sainsbury's Fondant Fancies	56.7	9.1	4.2	0.48	373
Thomas & Friends Cake	56.9	10.8	2.7	0.37	397
Sainsbury's Small Party Cake	57	13	3.2	0.25	407
Sainsbury's Wedding Cake Tier, Medium	57	9.8	3.1	0.14	376
Asda Extra Special 3-Tier Occasion Fruit Cake	57	11	4.8	0.2	378
Waitrose Butterfly Cake	57	14.3	2.8	0.48	416
Mr Kipling French Fancies	57.5	9.8	4.4	0.5	379
Morrisons Shining Star Celebration Cake	57.7	16.5	3.2	0.3	440
Tesco Strawberries & Cream Cupcakes	57.8	24.3	9.6	0.4	468
Jammie Dodger Cake	57.9	10.8	2.1	0.33	390
Sainsbury's Vanilla Choc Cupcakes	58	27	11	0.39	496
Morrisons Football Crazy Celebration Cake	58	15.3	2.8	0.3	424

Cakes

Product	Sugar	Fat	Sat	Salt	Cals
			per 100g		
Asda Chosen by You Chocolate Stout Cake	58	15	9.2	0.4	412
Waitrose Fairy Cake	58	13.9	3.1	0.48	423
Mr Kipling Strawberry Fancies	58.1	9.6	4.7	0.54	378
Me To You Cake	58.8	14	4.3	0.39	418
Spongebob Celebration Cake	58.9	13.8	3.9	0.31	405
Asda Chosen by You New York Cheeseburger and Fries cake	59.7	11	2.3	0.3	407
Tesco Medium Rich Fruit Celebration Cake	59.8	8.4	3.6	0.1	370
Tesco Celebrate Bar Celebration Cake	60	15	2.7	0.4	427
Despicable Me Celebration Cake	61.4	12.4	2.9	0.24	415
Hello Kitty Celebration Cake	61.4	12.6	3.1	0.32	409
Waitrose Sports Cake	61.9	15.3	4.4	0.43	425
Mr Kipling Mini Battenburgs	62.1	10.4	4.2	0.41	410
Waitrose Time for Tea Cake	62.6	11.1	2.2	0.45	398
Tesco Bunting Cake	62.9	13.1	3.1	0.3	405
Sainsbury's Princess Fairy Cupcakes	63	19	3.8	0.43	447
Tesco Fish And Chips Cake	63.3	13.6	3.5	0.3	412
Sainsbury's Pirate Fairy Cupcakes	64	19	3.6	0.39	444
Asda Chosen by You Pub Grub Pie & Gravy Gravity Cake	66	20	5.1	0.24	457

Kids Meals & Snacks

There are some really good ready meals for children. In most cases they use fresh ingredients without added sugar or salt. Often the sugar listed will be naturally occurring from the vegetables and other ingredients. However although some of the snacks are ok, many contain high amounts of sugar in the form of added sugar and dried fruit.

To help you make the best choices, products are listed starting with the least sugar first.

Product	Sugar	Fat	Sat per 100g	Salt	Cals
Cow&Gate Pure Baby Rice, 4+ Mths	trace	1.2	0.4	0.03	388
Ella's Kitchen Wonderfully Warming Beef Stew With Spuds, 10+Mths	0.1	0.5	0.1	0.3	69
Cow&Gate Little Steamed Meal, Sweet Potato Mash & Chicken 10+Mths	0.5	1.9	0.3	0.1	67
Tilda Kids Rice, Sunshine Vegetable	0.6	2.8	0.7	0.4	137
Marmite Toddler Rice Cake Bag	0.8	2.2	0.4	0.7	384
Sainsbury's Kids Cheesy Pasta Sweetcorn & Broccoli	1	2.4	1.3	0.33	120
Heinz Mum's Own Recipe, Cheesy Tomato Pasta Stars	1	2.2	1.5	0.15	65
Sainsbury's Kids Cheesy Pasta Sweetcorn & Broccoli	1	2.4	1.3	0.33	120
Sainsbury's Kids Mild Beef Chilli With Rice	1.1	1.7	0.6	0.15	124
Cow&Gate Fisherman's Bake, 4+ Mths	1.1	2	0.3	0.1	75
HiPP Meals, Paella With Mixed Vegetables & Chicken	1.1	2.8	0.6	0.25	84
Sainsbury's Kids Mild Beef Chilli With Rice	1.1	1.7	0.6	0.15	124
Heinz Mum's Own, Spaghetti Bolognese	1.2	2.2	0.5	0.04	58
Heinz Pasta Bake, Tuna	1.2	1.3	0.8	0.11	66
HiPP Jars, Parsnip Potato & Turkey Casserole	1.3	2.4	0.4	0.05	67
HiPP Meals, Hearty Vegetable & Beef Casserole	1.3	2.4	1	0.23	72
HiPP Meals, Wholesome Vegetable & Chicken Risotto	1.3	2.6	0.6	0.23	77
Annabel Karmel Chicken & Potato Pie	1.4	4.8	2.2	0.1	114
Cow&Gate Little Steamed Meal, Creamy Vegetables & Cod 10+ Mths	1.4	1.9	0.8	0.07	63
Heinz Mashed Mum's Own, Cheesy Vegetable Bake 7+ Mths	1.4	3.1	2	0.2	79
HiPP Jars, Scrumptious Sunday Lunch	1.4	2	0.4	0.05	68
HiPP Meals, Mild Chilli Con Carne With Kidney Beans 18+ Mths	1.4	2.5	0.7	0.23	75
Annabel Karmel Beef Cottage Pie	1.5	3.8	1.9	0.1	98
Cow&Gate Creamed Cauliflower Cheese, 7+ Mths	1.5	2.7	1.6	0.18	63

Kids Meals & Snacks

Product	Sugar	Fat	Sat	Salt	Cals
			per 100g		
Ella's Kitchen Cheeky Greek-y Veg Moussaka & Red Lentils, 7+ Mths	1.5	2	1.1	0.1	57
Heinz Mediterranean Veggie & Chicken	1.5	2.5	0.3	0.05	56
Heinz Mum's Own, Sunday Chicken Dinner	1.5	2.5	0.3	0.05	63
HiPP Jars, Vegetables & Chicken Risotto	1.5	2.1	0.4	0.05	66
HiPP Jars, Vegetables with Rice & Chicken 4+ Mths	1.5	2.4	0.4	0.05	63
HiPP Meals, Potato Pumpkin & Chicken	1.5	2.4	0.6	0.23	73
HiPP Meals, Spaghetti Bolognese 12+ Mths	1.5	2.1	0.5	0.23	73
Ella's Cheese & Tomato Puffits	1.5	3.3	1.5	0.5	394
Cow&Gate Baby Cauliflower Cheese, 4+ Mths	1.6	2.8	1.8	0.2	78
Heinz Little Kidz, Tomato & Mozzarella Pasta	1.6	2.6	1.5	0.1	75
HiPP Jars, Star Pasta with Sweet Squash & Chicken, 7+ Mths	1.6	2.1	0.4	0.05	65
HiPP Pouches, Hearty Vegetable Pork & Apple Casserole	1.6	3	0.9	0.04	68
Cow&Gate Scrummy Spaghetti Bolognese, 7+ Mths	1.7	1.9	1	0.08	70
HiPP Meals, Risotto Garden Vegetables & White Fish	1.7	2.4	0.8	0.1	72
HiPP Meals, Squiggly Spaghetti With Tasty Tomato & Mozzarella Sauce	1.7	2.8	1.3	0.23	84
Annabel Karmel Disney Snack, Cheese & Onion	1.7	8.5	1	0.7	402
Morrisons Just for Kids Cottage Pie	1.8	1.7	0.9	0.3	77
Ella's Kitchen Lamb Roast Dinner With All Trimmings, 7+ Mths	1.8	1.9	0.9	0.06	53
Heinz Mum's Own Recipe, Cottage Pie, 7+ Mths	1.8	2	0.7	0.06	57
HiPP Jars, Cheesy Spinach & Potato Bake	1.8	3.1	1	0.08	80
HiPP Jars, Vegetables With Noodles & Chicken 7+ Mths	1.8	2.5	0.5	0.05	68
HiPP Meals, Ratatouille With Potato & Beef	1.8	2.2	1	0.23	66
HiPP Meals, Ravioli Bolognese Sauce	1.8	2.9	0.6	0.23	85
HiPP Pouches Vegetable & Chicken Risotto	1.8	2.9	0.6	0.08	74
HiPP Pouches, Hearty Cottage Pie	1.8	2.4	0.6	trace	67
Annabel Karmel Disney Cheesy Mini Bread Sticks, 12+ Mths	1.8	15	2.5	1.5	437
Sainsbury's Kids Cottage Pie	1.9	2.1	0.7	0.42	87
Cow&Gate Creamed Cottage Pie, 4+ Mths	1.9	2.4	1.1	0.05	76
Cow&Gate Little Steamed Meal, Sunday Lunch, Chicken 10+ Mths	1.9	2.2	0.3	0.06	75
Cow&Gate Succulent Pork Casserole, 7+ Mths	1.9	1.8	0.3	0.05	62

Kids Meals & Snacks

Product	Sugar	Fat	Sat	Salt	Cals
			per 100g		
Ella's Kitchen Beef Stew & Root Vegetables, 12+ Mths	1.9	1.2	0.4	0.1	59
Ella's Kitchen Creamy Chicken & Sweetcorn Mash with Herbs, 7+ Mths	1.9	1.5	0.7	0.06	71
Heinz Little Kidz, Chicken & Sweetcorn Risotto	1.9	0.8	0.2	0.2	67
HiPP Jars, Pasta Italienne With Ham	1.9	3	0.9	0.2	74
HiPP Jars, Spaghetti Bolognese	1.9	2.1	0.4	0.06	68
HiPP Meals, Three Cheese Macaroni With Carrot & Courgette	1.9	2.5	1.2	0.23	74
Sainsbury's Kids Cottage Pie	1.9	2.1	0.7	0.42	87
Sainsbury's Kids Chicken Dinner	2	3.2	0.6	0.41	109
Annabel Karmel Orient Pork Meatballs & Noodles	2	4.4	0.9	0.7	122
Cow&Gate Shepherd's Pie, 7+ Mths	2	2.5	0.9	0.08	63
Ella's Kitchen Beef Stew With Spuds, 7+ Mths	2	1.4	0.6	0.06	48
Ella's Kitchen Chicken Paella, 12+ Mths	2	1.4	0.3	0.05	64
HiPP Jars, Cottage Pie	2	2.4	0.6	0.06	67
HiPP Meals, Creamy Vegetable Lasagne	2	3.5	1	0.08	90
Sainsbury's Kids Chicken Dinner	2	3.2	0.6	0.41	109
Tilda Kids Rice, Cheese & Tomato	2	4	2	0.5	151
Morrisons Just for Kids Chicken Casserole	2.1	2.2	1	0.3	90
Ella's Kitchen Chicken Curry with Coconut & Mango, 12+ Mths	2.1	3.4	2.1	0.08	77
Ella's Kitchen Oodles Of Fun Chicken Noodles	2.1	0.8	0.2	0.06	55
Ella's Kitchen Pork & Apple Stew	2.1	1.4	0.4	0.08	59
Heinz Baby Rice Dinners, Garden Vegetables 4+ Mths	2.1	0.7	0.1	0.28	379
Ella's Kitchen Raspberry & Vanilla Puffits 7+ Mths	2.1	1.5	0.1	0.18	339
Cow&Gate Lancashire Hotpot, 4+ Mths	2.2	2.2	0.8	0.05	60
Cow&Gate My First Bolognese, 4+ Mths	2.2	3.4	1.1	0.8	82
Ella's Kitchen Lovely Lamb Roast Dinner, 10+ Mths	2.2	1.7	0.7	0.03	53
Ella's Kitchen Squished Squishy Fishy Cakes, 7+ Mths	2.2	2.5	1.2	0.07	71
HiPP Jars, Mixed Vegetables 4+ Mths	2.2	1.4	0.1	0.05	41
HiPP Jars, Pasta In A Ham & Tomato Sauce 4+ Mths	2.2	2	0.7	0.18	61
HiPP Jars, Vegetables With Cheese Pasta	2.2	2.2	0.8	0.13	69
HiPP Meals, Scrumptious Lasagne	2.2	3.1	0.8	0.23	92

Kids Meals & Snacks

Product	Sugar	Fat	Sat per 100g	Salt	Cals
Sainsbury's Kids Fish Pie	2.3	2.2	1.2	0.44	86
Sainsbury's Kids Sausage & Mash	2.3	3.4	1.3	0.41	90
Cow&Gate Little Steamed Meal, Spaghetti Bolognese 10+ Mths	2.3	2.7	0.9	0.05	81
HiPP Meals, Shell Pasta With Juicy Tomatoes & Courgettes 12+ Mths	2.3	2.7	0.3	0.23	81
HiPP Pouches, Mild Tomato & Chicken Curry	2.3	2.8	0.6	0.9	73
HiPP Pouches, Sweet Potato Cauliflower & Sweet Potato Bake	2.3	2.8	0.8	0.9	71
Sainsbury's Kids Fish Pie	2.3	2.2	1.2	0.44	86
Sainsbury's Kids Sausage & Mash	2.3	3.4	1.3	0.41	90
Annabel Karmel Disney Snack, Tasty Tomato Corn	2.3	6.8	0.4	0.8	400
Annabel Karmel Fish Pie	2.4	4.1	2.4	0.24	93
Heinz Cottage Pie	2.4	2.9	0.7	0.2	73
Heinz Mum's Own Recipe, Spaghetti Bolognese, 12-36 Mths	2.4	1.8	0.6	0.1	64
HiPP Jars, Rigatoni Napoli	2.4	2	0.3	1.5	68
HiPP Jars, Spaghetti Bolognese 6+ Mths	2.4	2.1	0.4	0.05	61
HiPP Jars, Vegetable Lasagne	2.4	2.8	0.6	0.05	72
Sainsbury's Kids Tomato & Mascarpone Pasta	2.5	2.3	0.8	0.19	127
Morrisons Just for Kids Spaghetti Bolognese	2.5	2.1	1.1	0.3	99
Morrisons Just For Kids Fish Pie	2.5	2.4	1.2	0.25	93
Cow&Gate Grandpa's Sunday Lunch, 4+ Mths	2.5	2.2	0.4	0.05	74
Ella's Kitchen Jammin' Jamaican Curried Pork, Rice & Peas, 7+ Mths	2.5	1.5	0.9	0.01	59
Ella's Kitchen Lip Smacking Spaghetti Bolognese with Cheese, 10+ Mths	2.5	2.5	1.1	0.3	66
Heinz Mum's Own Recipe Apple & Pork Casserole, 7+ Mths	2.5	2	0.5	0.04	60
HiPP Jars, Penne Tomato & Courgette 6+ Mths	2.5	1.7	0.1	0.05	61
Sainsbury's Kids Tomato & Mascarpone Pasta	2.5	2.3	0.8	0.19	127
Tilda Kids Wholegrain Rice, Sweet Vegetable	2.5	3.4	0.9	0.5	131
Sainsbury's Kids Spaghetti Bolognese	2.6	1.6	0.6	0.32	99
Cow&Gate Sweet Potato Bake, 4+ Mths	2.6	1.4	0.2	0.04	70
Ella's Kitchen Bangers & Mash, 7+ Mths	2.6	3.4	1.5	0.2	74
Ella's Kitchen Cheesy Pie With Veggies, 7+ Mths	2.6	3.1	1.9	0.21	69
Ella's Kitchen Roast Dinner, Cheery Chicken 7+ Mths	2.6	0.9	0.3	0.07	47

Kids Meals & Snacks

Product	Sugar	Fat	Sat	Salt	Cals
			per 100g		
Heinz Meals, Sweet Potato Chicken & Veggies	2.6	1.8	0.2	0.13	61
Sainsbury's Kids Spaghetti Bolognese	2.6	1.6	0.6	0.32	99
Annabel Karmel Beef Lasagne	2.7	5.2	3.2	0.3	116
Annabel Karmel Chicken Tikka	2.7	2.5	0.08	0.3	103
Annabel Karmel Eat Fussy Bolognese Pasta Bake	2.7	5.6	2.6	0.2	130
Ella's Kitchen Bolognese Bake	2.7	2.8	0.7	0.08	82
HiPP Carrot, Salmon & Dill Risotto 7+ Mths	2.7	2.5	0.3	0.08	65
HiPP Pouches, Mediterranean Vegetable Spaghetti	2.7	2.4	0.7	0.08	69
HiPP Vegetable Bake Jar	2.7	3.3	0.8	0.08	86
Ella's Kitchen Thai Curry With Lots of Veg, 10+ Mths	2.8	2.2	1.8	trace	53
Ella's Kitchen Veggie Moussaka, 12+ Mths	2.8	2.3	1.4	0.1	68
HiPP Jars, Spaghetti With Tomatoes & Mozzarella	2.8	2.4	0.6	0.1	70
HiPP Jars, Sweet Squash & Chicken 4+ Mths	2.8	2.3	0.5	0.08	68
HiPP Meals, Wholemeal Spaghetti & Mediterranean Vegetable Jar	2.8	2.6	0.7	0.05	67
Kiddylicious Fruity Puffs, Strawberry	2.8	8	1.1	0.01	415
Cow&Gate Little Steamed Meal, Pasta Tomato, Spinach & Cheese 10+ Mths	2.9	2.3	0.9	0.14	73
Ella's Kitchen Veggie Lasagne, 7+ Mths	3	1.7	0.8	0.13	46
Heinz Mum's Own Recipe, Sweet & Sour Chicken With Rice	3	2.3	0.4	0.1	79
HiPP Jars, Tender Carrots & Potatoes 4+ Mths	3	0.1	0	trace	32
HiPP Meals, Vegetable Ravioli In Tomato Sauce	3	3	0.4	0.25	90
HiPP Squash Jar	3	0.2	0	0.06	44
Annabel Karmel Pouches, Moroccan Chicken 6+ Mths	3.1	0.3	0.1	0.06	37
Ella's Kitchen Hearty Four Bean Feast With Big Flavour, 7+ Mths	3.1	0.2	0.1	0.03	43
Ella's Kitchen Lip Smacking Spaghetti Bolognese with Cheese, 7+ Mths	3.1	1.7	0.9	0.1	60
Ella's Kitchen Punchy Pork Roast Dinner With Apples	3.1	1.5	0.5	0.06	51
Annabel Karmel Meals, Shell Pasta Shapes	3.2	1.5	0.3	0.02	356
Sainsbury's Kids Beef Lasagne	3.3	3.5	1.5	0.5	116
Cow&Gate Orchard Chicken, 4+ Mths	3.3	2.3	1.4	0.05	80
Heinz Little Kidz, Tender Lamb 5 Veg & Rice	3.3	2	0.7	0.1	69
Heinz Mum's Own Recipe Casserole with Apple & Pork, 1-3 Years	3.3	1.7	0.3	0.1	67

Kids Meals & Snacks

Product	Sugar	Fat	Sat	Salt	Cals
			per 100g		
Sainsbury's Kids Beef Lasagne	3.3	3.5	1.5	0.5	116
Ella's Kitchen Perfectly Pleasing Tomato-y Pasta, 10-12 Mths	3.4	1.5	0.6	1.2	58
Heinz Mum's Own Recipe, Sweet Potato & Beef Hotpot	3.4	1.4	0.7	0.1	71
Tilda Kids Rice, Mild & Sweet Curry	3.4	5.6	3	0.3	155
Heinz Mums Own Baby Food, Pumpkin & Lamb Stew	3.5	2.2	0.7	0.05	63
Organix Finger Food, Sweetcorn Ring 7+ Mths	3.5	14.4	1.6	trace	450
Organix Goodies, Sweetcorn Salsa Snappy Crocs 12+ Mths	3.5	15	2.1	0.01	453
Ella's Kitchen Moreish Moroccan Chicken, Chickpeas & Cumin, 7+ Mths	3.6	2.2	0.1	0.08	81
Heinz Creamy Fish Pie Pouch	3.6	2.2	1.3	0.2	85
Annabel Karmel Sauce, Carrot & Lentil 7+ Mths	3.7	1.6	0.9	0.12	54
Ella's Kitchen Cool Caribbean Chicken, 10+ Mths	3.7	0.4	0.1	0.03	55
Annabel Karmel Pouches, Cosy Cottage Pie 6+ Mths	3.8	1.8	0.9	0.1	59
Ella's Kitchen Carrots Carrots, 4+ Mths	3.8	0.3	0.1	0.1	26
Organix Goodies, Cheese & Herb Puffs 12+ Mths	3.8	17	3.6	0.2	468
Morrisons Just for Kids Cheese & Tomato Pasta	3.9	3.3	1.5	0.3	107
Annabel Karmel Chicken Tomato & Veggie Risotto	3.9	3.8	2	0.3	125
Heinz Mum's Own Recipe, Juicy Apricot Chicken with Rice, 1-3 Years	3.9	1.8	0.4	0.2	71
Organix Goodies, Cheese Crackers 12+ Mths	3.9	15.8	7.1	0.56	459
Ella's Kitchen Vegetable Bake With Lentils, 7+ Mths	4.1	1.3	0.2	0.04	66
Heinz Casserole Pouch, Apple & Pork	4.1	0.3	trace	trace	56
Ella's Kitchen Chick-Chick Chicken Casserole With Rice, 7+ Mths	4.2	1	0.3	0.07	62
Ella's Kitchen Sweet Potato Sweet Potato	4.2	0.1	0.1	0.05	55
HiPP Jars, Tasty Vegetable Risotto 4+ Mths	4.2	3.9	1.7	0.1	88
HiPP Carrot Jar	4.3	0.1	0.02	1.2	30
Annabel Karmel Tomato & Mascarpone Pasta with Hidden Veggies	4.4	4.8	2.2	0.1	114
Ella's Kitchen Parsnips Parsnips, 4+ Mths	4.4	0.9	0.1	0.03	61
Annabel Karmel Meals, Chicken & Butternut Squash 6+ Mths	4.5	1.1	0.5	0.06	48
Annabel Karmel Puree, Banana Pear & Peach	4.5	0.2	0	0.05	73
Annabel Karmel Sauce, Tomato Sweet Potato & Cheese	4.5	2.4	1.2	0.26	58
Annabel Karmel Spaghetti With Meatballs	4.5	3.5	1.6	0.1	120

Product	Sugar	Fat	Sat	Salt	Cals
			per 100g		
HiPP Pouches, Pears & Baby Rice 4+ Mths	4.6	0.2	0	<.02	49
Organix Goodies Tomato, Cheese & Herb Puffs, 12+ Mths	4.8	17	2.8	0.09	456
HiPP Pouches, Peaches & Baby Rice	4.9	0.1	0	0.06	47
Annabel Karmel Disney Snack, Wheaty Mini Bread Sticks	5.1	15	3.6	2	455
Organix Finger Foods, Tomato Slices 7+ Mths	5.1	14.9	1.6	0.07	448
Ella's Kitchen Zingy Lamb & Cous Cous, 7+ Mths	5.2	1.9	0.9	0.06	57
Organix Goodies, Big Poppy Seed Crackers, 12+ Mths	5.2	14.2	3.6	0.16	455
Annabel Karmel Puree, Apple Blueberry & Vanilla	5.5	0.25	0	0.05	74
Ella's Kitchen Yummy Rice Pudding with Mangoes & Apples, 7+ Mths	5.8	3.3	2	trace	91
Annabel Karmel Puree, Carrot Apple & Parsnip	6	0.5	0.1	0.05	38
Organix Goodies Spicy Stars, 12+ Mths	6	15	2	0.07	448
Organix Goodies Saucy Tomato Noughts & Crosses, 12+ Mths	6.1	15	2.1	0.02	446
Ella's Kitchen Sweet Potato, Broccoli & Carrots	6.3	0.5	0.1	0.1	46
Heinz Fruity Pudding, Apple With Oats 4-36 Mths	6.5	0.3	0.1	trace	50
Heinz Smooth Egg Custard with Rice, 4-36 Mths	6.6	2	1.3	0.09	68
Organix Goodies Ricecake Strawberry	6.7	2.5	0.6	0.03	384
Organix Goodies, Raspberry & Peach Ripple Rice Cakes 12+ Mths	6.7	2.7	0.5	trace	386
Annabel Karmel Puree, Apple Banana & Mango	6.9	0.2	0	0.05	65
Heinz Smooth Rice Pudding, 4-36 Mths	7	1.6	1	0.06	70
Organix Finger Foods Carrot Sticks, 7+ Mths	7.1	14.4	1.5	0.12	442
Ella's Kitchen Carrots Peas & Pear, 4+ Mths	7.3	0.5	0.1	0.03	46
Ella's Kitchen Plums, Pears, Parsnips & Swedes, 4+ Mths	7.5	0.5	0.1	0.03	50
Heinz Multigrain Dinners, Carrot Sweetcorn & Cheese 7+ Mths	7.5	7.9	3.5	1	410
Ella's Kitchen Red Peppers Sweet Potatoes & Apples, 4+ Mths	7.6	0.5	0.1	0.03	46
HiPP Pouches, Mangoes & Baby Rice	7.6	0.2	0	0.06	57
Organix Goodies, Carrot Stix 12+ Mths	7.6	14.8	1.9	0.15	439
Cow&Gate Rice Pudding, 4+ Mths	7.7	2	1	0.09	89
Cow&Gate Rice Pudding, 7+ Mths	7.7	2	1	0.09	89
Ella's Kitchen Organic Broccoli Pear & Peas, 4+ Mths	7.9	0.5	0.1	0.03	52
HiPP Rice Pudding, 4+ Mths	8.1	1.9	1.2	0.05	85

Kids Meals & Snacks

Product	Sugar	Fat	Sat per 100g	Salt	Cals
Ella's Kitchen Peaches Pears & Baby Rice, 4+ Mths	8.3	0.5	0.1	0.02	55
Heinz Smooth Chocolate Pudding, 4-36 Mths	8.3	2.6	1.7	0.09	83
Ella's Kitchen Peaches Peaches, 4+ Mths	8.4	0.3	0.1	0.03	47
HiPP Banana & Baby Rice	8.5	0.1	0	trace	61
Ella's Kitchen Mangoes Pears & Papaya, 4+ Mths	8.6	0.5	0.1	0.03	44
HiPP William Christ Pears	8.7	0.2	0	trace	60
Cow&Gate Puree, A Taste of Apple, 4+ Mths	8.8	0.1	trace	0.003	42
Ella's Kitchen Organic Butternut Squash Carrot Apple & Prune, 4+ Mths	9	0.5	0.1	0.06	50
HiPP Rice Pudding, Apple & Pear	9	1.8	1.2	0.06	86
Cow&Gate Fruit Pouch, Apple Strawberry & Banana 4+ Mths	9.1	trace	trace	0.03	46
Ella's Kitchen Organic Carrot Apple & Parsnip, 6+ Mths	9.2	0.5	0.2	0.04	48
Ella's Kitchen Organic Sweet Potato Pumpkin Apple Blueberry, 4+ Mths	9.2	0.5	0.1	0.04	52
Yeo Valley Organic Little Yeos, Strawberry & Peach, Apple & Pear	9.2	2.6	1.4	0.12	91
Ella's Kitchen Pears Pears Pears, 4+ Mths	9.3	0.5	0.1	0.05	51
HiPP Fruit Pots, Apple & Pear 4+ Mths	9.3	0.1	0	0.06	50
Cow&Gate Banana & Cookie Crumble, 4+ Mths	9.4	0.7	0.3	0.03	75
Cow&Gate Banana & Cookie Crumble, 7+ Mths	9.4	0.7	0.3	0.03	75
HiPP Fruit Pots, Apple Peach & Mango	9.4	0.1	0	0.06	49
Ella's Kitchen Organic Peaches & Bananas, 4+ Mths	9.5	0.1	trace	0.03	46
Cow&Gate Apple Crumble, 7+ Mths	9.5	0.4	0.2	0.01	69
Ella's Kitchen Yummy Yoghurt, Strawberry, 6+ Mths	9.5	3.6	2.3	0.06	88
HiPP Banana Custard	9.5	2.5	1.6	0.1	91
Yeo Valley Organic Little Yeos, Mango & Vanilla, Strawberry & Vanilla	9.5	2.6	1.4	0.12	92
Ella's Kitchen Pears Apple & Baby Rice, 4+ Mths	9.7	0.5	0.2	0.02	60
Cow&Gate Fruit Pouch, Apple & Pear 4+ Mths	9.7	0.1	trace	0.03	45
Cow&Gate Fruit Pouches, Apple & Pear 4-36 Mths	9.7	0.1	trace	0.03	45
Cow&Gate Fruit Pots, Apple & Pear 4-36 Mths	9.7	0.1	trace	0.03	45
Organix Finger Foods, Carrot & Tomato Ricecake 7+ Mths	9.7	2.7	0.6	0.13	380
Organix Ricecakes, Banana	9.7	2.8	0.6	trace	397
Ella's Kitchen Strawberries & Apples, 4+ Mths	9.8	0.5	0.1	0.03	45

Product	Sugar	Fat	Sat per 100g	Salt	Cals
Rachel's My First Yogurt	9.8	3.5	2.1	0.3	88
Annabel Karmel Pouches, Salmon & Sweet Potato 6+ Mths	9.9	3.1	1.5	0.09	100
HiPP Puree, Apple & Strawberry	9.9	0.1	0	0.06	47
HiPP Baby Dessert, Apple & Pear Pudding	9.9	0.2	0	trace	62
HiPP Banana With Rice Pudding	9.9	0.2	0	0.05	70
HiPP Yogurt, Strawberry & Raspberry	9.9	1.4	0.8	0.05	75
Organix Goodies, Red Berry Burst Rice Cakes 12+ Mths	9.9	2.5	0.5	0.01	383
HiPP 100% Pear Jar	10	0.3	0	0.05	55
Cow&Gate Fruit Mix Pouch, 4+ Mths	10	trace	trace	0.03	48
Cow&Gate Fruit Pouches, Fruit Cocktail 4-36 Mths	10	trace	trace	0.01	48
Organix Finger Foods, Raspberry & Blueberry Ricecakes 7+ Mths	10	2.5	0.5	0.03	389
HiPP Jars, Mango & Banana Melba	10.2	0.2	trace	0.06	64
HiPP Fruit Pots, Peach Apple Blueberry & Raspberry 4+ Mths	10.2	0.1	0	0.06	49
Organix Fruit Pots, Pear & Raspberry 4+ Mths	10.2	0.5	0.1	0.02	57
Cow&Gate Fruit Pots, Apple Apricot & Strawberry 4-36 Mths	10.2	0.1	trace	0.03	50
Cow&Gate Fruit Pouch, Apple 4+ Mths	10.3	0.1	trace	0.03	46
Organix Fruit Pots, Apple & Blueberry Compote 4+ Mths	10.3	0.2	0.1	0.03	54
Ella's Kitchen Apples Apples Apples, 4+ Mths	10.5	0.5	0.1	0.02	50
Cow&Gate Fruit Pots, Fruit Cocktail 4-36 Mths	10.5	0.1	trace	0.03	50
Cow&Gate Yogurt, Apricot Apple & Banana 7+ Mths	10.5	1.9	1.2	0.08	89
Organix Fruit Pots, Apple & Raspberry Pieces 7+ Mths	10.5	0.5	0.1	0.06	51
Heinz Dinners, Mediterranean Vegetables & Rice 4+ Mths	10.6	6.5	3	0.88	401
Cow&Gate Fruit Pots, Plum & Apple 4-36 Mths	10.6	0.1	trace	0.03	57
Cow&Gate Summer Fruit Salad, 4+ Mths	10.6	0.1	trace	0.03	72
Organix Fruit Pots, Mashed Apple & Mango 7+ Mths	10.6	0.5	0.1	0.03	52
HiPP 100% Apple Jar	10.7	0.1	0	0.05	50
Cow&Gate Juicy Pear & Banana, 4+ Mths	10.7	0.1	trace	0.005	60
HiPP Fruit Pots, Apple Strawberry & Blueberry 4+ Mths	10.7	0.1	0	0.05	50
HiPP Compote, Red Fruit & Apple	10.8	0.2	0	0.02	66
HiPP Dessert, Apple & Blueberry 4+ Mths	10.8	0.2	0	0.05	71

Kids Meals & Snacks

Product	Sugar	Fat	Sat	Salt	Cals
			per 100g		
Yeo Valley Organic Little Yeos, Fruity Favourites	10.8	4.5	2.9	0.17	108
Cow&Gate Fruit Pots, Pear & Pineapple 4-36 Mths	10.8	0.05	trace	0.03	51
HiPP Apple & Banana Crumble	10.9	0.7	0.4	0.05	74
Heinz Fruit Pouch, Apple & Strawberry	11	0.3	0.1	trace	70
Cow&Gate Mango Surprise, 4+ Mths	11	0.1	trace	0.01	61
Ella's Kitchen Yummy Yoghurt, Berry, 6+ Mths	11.1	3.4	2.2	0.06	93
Ella's Kitchen Yummy Yoghurt, Mango, 6+ Mths	11.1	3.7	2.4	0.06	93
Cow&Gate Pear Pouch, 4+ Mths	11.3	0.1	trace	0.03	60
Cow&Gate Fruit Pots, Banana Peach & Strawberry 4-36 Mths	11.4	0.1	0.1	0.03	70
HiPP Jars, Mango Apple & Peach	11.5	0.2	0	0.06	55
Ella's Kitchen The Pink One	11.5	0.2	0.1	0.03	58
HiPP Apple & Banana With Fruit Pieces	11.5	0.1	0	0.06	56
Heinz Farley's Savoury Babies' Meal, Cauliflower Broccoli Cheese 4+ Mths	11.7	7.1	3.2	0.78	416
Heinz Fruity Custard, Pear & Apple 4-36 Mths	11.7	1.4	0.8	trace	76
HiPP Jars, Mango & Banana With Yogurt	11.7	1.4	0.8	0.05	87
Cow&Gate Fruit Cocktail, 7+ Mths	11.9	0.1	trace	0.01	63
Ella's Kitchen The White One 4+ Mths	11.9	3	2.4	0.03	96
Sainsbury's Kids Smoothie Strawberry & Banana	12.2	0.5	0.1	0.01	59
Kiddylicious Fruity Puffs, Banana	12.4	11.1	1.3	0.01	426
Cow&Gate Apple & Banana Pouch, 4+ Mths	12.5	trace	trace	0.03	57
Heinz Fruit Pouch, Apple & Blueberry	12.5	0.4	0.2	trace	64
Heinz Fruit Pouch, Apple & Mango	12.5	0.2	0.1	trace	63
Heinz Fruit Pouch, Peach Mango & Banana	12.5	0.4	0.2	trace	71
Cow&Gate Fruit Pouches, Apple & Banana 4-36 Mths	12.5	trace	trace	0.03	57
Cow&Gate Fruit Pots, Apple & Banana 4-36 Mths	12.5	0.1	trace	0.03	53
Heinz Fruit Pouch, Strawberry Raspberry & Banana	12.6	0.5	0.2	trace	68
Cow&Gate Fruit Pots, Apple Orange & Banana 4-36 Mths	12.7	0.1	trace	0.03	67
Sainsbury's Kids Smoothie Mango, Orange & Banana	12.8	0.5	0.1	0.01	62
Heinz Fruit Pouch, Mango Banana & Lime	13	0.3	0.1	trace	68
Heinz Fruit Pouch, Smooth Apple Pear & Banana	13	0.3	0.1	trace	69

Kids Meals & Snacks

Product	Sugar	Fat	Sat	Salt	Cals
			per 100g		
Organix Ricecakes, Cherry	13.1	2.7	0.5	0.03	385
Heinz Fruity Custard, Medley 4-36 Mths	13.4	1.3	0.7	trace	84
HiPP Banana, Pear & Mango	13.7	0.2	0	0.06	74
Sainsbury's Kids Smoothie Apple & Blackcurrant	13.7	0.5	0.1	0.01	65
Organix Finger Foods, Apple Rice Cakes 7+ Mths	14.1	2.6	0.5	0.03	393
HiPP Dessert, Cocoa & Vanilla	14.3	3.2	2	0.12	116
Heinz Fruity Custard, Banana, 4-36 Mths	15	1.4	0.9	trace	86
Ella's Kitchen Mangoes Mangoes Mangoes, 4+ Mths	16	0.6	0.3	0.02	77
Kiddylicious Wibble Wobble Jelly Pots, Pear & Raspberry	16	0.5	0.1	0.21	73
Kiddylicious Wibble Wobble Jelly Pots, Peach & Strawberry	16	0.5	0.1	0.21	74
Organix Goodies, Alphabet Biscuits 12+ Mths	16	14.6	3.8	0.43	446
Organix Goodies, Animal Biscuits 12+ Mths	16	13.5	4	0.4	426
Ella's Kitchen Baby Rice, Banana & Apricots 4+ Mths	16.3	0.5	0.1	0.02	86
Ella's Kitchen Organic Apples & Bananas, 4+ Mths	16.3	0.5	0.1	0.02	76
Ella's Kitchen Baby Rice, Bananas & Blueberry	17.1	0.5	0.1	0.04	97
Kiddylicious Wibble Wobble Jelly Pots, Apple & Blackcurrant	17.2	0.5	0.1	0.21	84
Annabel Karmel Disney Mini Biscotti Biscuits, Apple & Cinnamon	18	16	1.3	0.1	451
Organix Goodies, Gingerbread Men 12+ Mths	18.8	11.5	3.8	0.38	424
Organix Goodies, Mini Gingerbread Men 12+ Mths	18.8	11.5	3.8	0.38	424
Ella's Kitchen Bananas Bananas Bananas, 4+ Mths	19.5	0.5	0.1	0.09	90
Organix Baby Biscuits, Banana 7+ Mths	19.7	15.4	3.9	0.7	449
Heinz Apple Biscotti	20	9.7	4.5	0.5	423
Heinz Biscotti Finger Biscuits, Banana 7+ Mths	22	9.5	4.1	0.5	422
Organix Goodies, Apricot Cereal Bars	25.1	12.8	1.5	0.03	379
Ella's Kitchen Strawberries & Apples Nibbly Fingers, 12+ Mths	25.5	12.8	4.4	0.06	404
Organix Goodies, Cocoa & Raisin Soft Oaty Bars 15+ Mths	25.8	15.4	1.9	0.03	406
Organix Goodies Raspberry & Apple Soft Oaty Bars, 12+ Mths	25.9	14.9	1.8	0.03	403
Organix Goodies, Blackcurrant Soft Oaty Bars 12+ Mths	26	15	1.8	0.03	403
Organix Goodies, Strawberry Cereal Bars	26.1	15.1	1.8	0.03	405
Annabel Karmel Disney Fruity Bakes, Apple	26.3	10.7	3.7	0.43	415

Kids Meals & Snacks

Product	Sugar	Fat	Sat per 100g	Salt	Cals
Organix Goodies, Carrot Cake Soft Oaty Bars 12+ Mths	26.3	15.5	1.8	0.08	399
Organix Goodies, Apple & Orange Soft Oaty Bars 12+ Mths	26.9	14.9	1.7	0.03	410
Heinz Biscotti Finger Biscuits, Chocolate 7+ Mths	27	8.7	4.1	0.5	416
Organix Goodies, Soft Oaty Banana Bars	27.6	15.7	1.9	0.03	408
Heinz Biscotti Finger Biscuits, Organic 7+ Mths	28	8.5	3.9	0.43	423
Farley's Original Rusks, 4+ Mths	29	7.2	3.1	0.03	414
Heinz Farley's Rusks, Original, 4-6 Mths	29	7.2	3.1	0.03	414
Heinz Farleys Mini Rusks	29	7.2	3.1	trace	415
Heinz Breakfast, Creamy Oat Porridge 4+ Mths	30.2	10.2	4.5	0.35	423
Annabel Karmel Disney Fruity Bakes, Raspberry	30.5	10	3.5	0.43	408
Kiddylicious Fruit Snacks, Pineapple	35.1	25.1	12	0.19	503
Kiddylicious Fruit Crisps, Banana	35.2	26.8	12.6	0.04	495
Kiddylicious Fruit Crisps, Apple	47.3	25.6	11.5	0.22	497
Kiddylicious Fruit Wriggles, Tropical	48.4	0.8	0.2	0.09	326
Bear Arctic Paws Fruit Shapes, Raspberry & Blueberry	49	0.2	0	0	275
Bear Dino Paws Fruit Shapes	49	0.2	0	0	275
Bear Jungle Paws Fruit Shapes	49	0.2	0	0	275
Bear Safari Paws Fruit Shapes	49	0.2	0	0	275
Kiddylicious Strawberry Fruit Wriggles	54.8	0.7	0.1	0.08	299
Organix Goodies, Raspberry & Apple Fruit Moo's 12+ Mths	57.1	0.5	0.1	0.07	334
Organix Goodies, Banana & Date Fruit Bars 12+ Mths	58.5	0.5	0.1	trace	299
Kiddylicious Fruit Wriggles, Apple	60.6	0.5	0.1	0.08	301
Organix Goodies Raisin Mini boxes	62.3	0.6	0.2	0.13	315
Organix Goodies, Blackcurrant & Apple Fruit Stars 12+ Mths	62.8	0.5	0.1	0.06	331
Organix Goodies, Apple & Strawberry Fruit Gummies	67.2	0.5	0.1	0.06	266
Kiddylicious Fruit Melts, Strawberry & Banana	67.7	0.5	0.2	0.01	345
Kiddylicious Fruit Melts, Apple & Blackcurrant	68.5	0.9	0.2	0.02	349
Kiddylicious Fruit Melts, Mango & Passion	69.1	1.3	0.3	0.04	362

Crisps & Snacks

Many crisps contain a variable amount of sugar. You may think this is a good snack alternative but crisps don't contain any nutritional benefits and are also often high in salt.

Savoury popcorn is a more suitable snack option.

To help you make the best choices, products are listed starting with the least sugar first.

Product	Sugar	Fat	Sat	Salt	Cals
			per 100g		
Hula Hoops Original	<.5	26	2.5	1.8	507
Sainsbury's Ready Salted Crisps	<.5	2.8	1.18	1.18	537
Sainsbury's Ready Salted Potato Sticks	<.5	33	2.9	1.2	538
Sainsbury's Salted Tortilla Chips	<.5	23	1.9	0.8	491
Morrisons Ready Salted Flavour Crisps	0.1	33.9	3.1	1.4	545
Morrisons Sea Salt Ridge Crisps	0.1	26.3	1.9	1.3	504
Mr Porky Pork Crackles	0.2	45.7	16.8	2.9	616
Tesco Finest Lightly Salted Crisps	0.2	28.8	2.4	1.2	519
Tesco Twirls Salt And Vinegar Snacks	0.2	21.2	2.1	2.9	484
Asda Variety Fries	0.3	18.4	1.3	2.2	455
Walkers Ready Salted Crisps	0.4	31.9	2.6	1.4	526
Metcalfe's Popcorn Skinny Topcorn Sargent Salt	0.4	24.4	2	2.64	471
Sainsbury's Potato Rings	0.4	28.4	2.5	2.33	519
Walkers Deep Ridged Salted Crisps	0.4	32.1	2.6	1.24	528
Walkers Salt & Shake Crisps	0.4	32.3	2.6	2.5	533
Morrisons Signature Hand-Cooked Sea Salt Flavour Crisps	0.4	28.6	3.1	1.4	531
Morrisons Salt or Not Crisps	0.4	31.4	2.7	2	529
Asda Salt Your Own Crisps	0.4	33.1	4.8	1.2	538
Asda Potato Sticks Ready Salted	0.4	33.2	2.9	1	542
Waitrose Essential Salt Your Own Crisps	0.4	35.1	3	1.23	557
Tesco Potato Chips	0.4	33.2	2.9	1.1	542
Tesco Ready Salted Crisps	0.4	33.2	2.8	1.2	544
Kettle Chips Lightly Salted	0.5	30.1	3.5	0.9	513
Sainsbury's Taste the Difference Gourmet Sea Salt Crisps	0.5	30	3.5	1.2	498

Crisps & Snacks

Product	Sugar	Fat	Sat	Salt	Cals
			per 100g		
Twiglets Original	0.5	12.2	1.8	2	413
Walkers Deli Market Anglesy Sea Salt	0.5	21.8	1.8	1.22	473
Walkers Extra Crunchy Salted Crisps	0.5	21.8	1.8	1.22	473
Walkers Lights Ready Salted Crisps	0.5	22	2	1.52	480
Morrisons Salted Potato Sticks	0.5	29.8	2.6	1	518
Morrisons Mini Poppadoms	0.5	40.2	3.5	2.6	565
Morrisons Cheese Puffs	0.5	38.2	3.9	1.8	577
Asda Good & Counted Snacking Savoury Variety Popcorn	0.5	25.9	2.7	1.7	488
Waitrose Hand Cooked Sea Salt Crisps	0.5	30.1	3.5	0.9	513
Waitrose Giant Pretzels with Sea Salt	0.5	6.4	0.5	1.4	412
Waitrose LoveLife Lightly Salted Reduced Fat Crinkle Cut Crisps	0.5	23.8	1.9	1.02	483
Tesco Cheese Puff Snacks	0.5	34.6	3.9	1.7	550
Tesco Chipz Original	0.5	35.8	3	1	555
Tesco Everyday Value Potato Rings Snacks	0.5	21.5	1.9	1.2	484
Tesco Salted Popcorn	0.5	31.1	2.3	1.9	527
Tyrrells Popcorn Salted	0.6	25.5	2.8	1.3	487
Asda Chosen by You Ridge Cut Variety Flavour Crisps	0.6	28.4	2.8	1	508
Asda Sea Salt Crisps	0.6	29.8	3.5	1.3	523
Tesco Cheese Balls Snacks	0.6	32.8	3.8	1.6	545
Tesco Mini Poppadoms	0.6	40.2	3.5	2.6	565
Tesco Potato Rings Snacks	0.6	26.4	2.5	1.9	515
Sainsbury's Crunchy Fries	0.7	26.6	2.2	1.85	505
Sainsbury's Salt Your Own Potato Crisps	0.7	33.2	2.8	2.03	537
Morrisons Salt and Vinegar Flavour Crisps	0.7	32.2	3	2.1	533
Morrisons Bacon Crisps	0.7	32.4	3.1	1.5	537
Asda Meaty Crisps	0.7	32.7	3.9	1	533
Asda Ready Salted	0.7	32.7	3.9	1	533
Asda Chosen by You Salted Popcorn	0.7	29.2	4	0.8	508
Tesco Everyday Value Ready Salted Crisps	0.7	32.7	3.3	1	533
Tesco Finest Crinkle Cut Cream Cheese And Herb	0.7	28.8	2.4	1.3	519

Crisps & Snacks

Product	Sugar	Fat	Sat	Salt	Cals
			per 100g		
Tesco Salt And Vinegar Crisps	0.7	31	2.6	2.1	524
Tesco Shake To Salt Crisps	0.7	32.3	3.2	2.2	527
Kettle Chips Crushed Black Pepper	0.8	28.6	0.8	1.5	502
Kettle Chips Sea Salt & Cracked Black Pepper	0.8	28.6	3.3	1.5	502
Roysters T-Bone Steak Bubbled Chips	0.8	32	3.1	1.8	540
Sainsbury's Ready Salted Potato Fries	0.8	27.2	2.4	0.47	501
Walkers Mighty Lights Salted Crisps	0.8	18.9	1.8	1.1	455
Morrisons Savers Lightly Salted Tortillas	0.8	22.4	2.2	1.1	496
Morrisons Signature Sea Salt & Blacked Pepper Hand-Cooked Crisps	0.8	27.5	3	1.4	521
Morrisons Lightly Salted Tortillas	0.8	22.4	2.2	1.1	496
Asda Smart Price Snacks	0.8	26.6	2.4	1.8	500
Tesco Finest Lightly Sea Salt Tort Chips	0.8	26.8	2.8	0.8	503
Tesco Popcorn Salt And Vinegar	0.8	27.5	2.1	2.8	492
Doritos Lightly Salted Corn Chips	0.9	23.4	1.9	0.74	487
McCoy's Salt & Vinegar Crisps	0.9	31	2.8	2	524
Asda Potato Squares Variety	0.9	21.2	1.5	2.2	474
Asda Smart Price Ready Salted	0.9	34.3	2.6	1.2	541
Asda Chosen by You Wholefoods Popcorn	0.9	4.5	0.6	trace	374
Walkers Salt & Vinegar Crisps	1	30.8	2.5	1.65	520
Hula Hoops BBQ Beef Potato Rings	1	26	2.5	2.3	505
Sainsbury's Taste the Difference Sea Salt & Cider Vinegar Crisps	1	28.6	3.4	2	503
Waitrose Sea Salt with a Black Pepper Shock	1	24.3	1.9	2.05	486
Sainsbury's Taste the Difference Sea Salt & Peppercorn Crisps	1.1	29.2	3.2	1.3	509
Sainsbury's Taste the Difference Sea Salt & Peppercorn Tortillas	1.1	28.6	2.5	0.75	523
Asda Good & Counted Snacking Crinkle Cut Crisps Salt & Vinegar	1.1	19.6	1.9	2.1	452
Asda Salt & Pepper Crisps	1.1	28.4	3.5	1.4	517
Waitrose Essential Salt & Malt Vinegar Twirls	1.1	21.1	1.5	2.8	469
Waitrose Sea Salt & Vinegar Hand Cooked Crisps	1.1	28.5	3.3	2.1	502
Tesco Finest Beef Burrito	1.1	25.5	2.4	0.9	494
Tesco Finest Crinkle Crisps Smoky Habanero	1.1	28.8	2.4	1.3	519

Product	Sugar	Fat	Sat	Salt	Cals
			per 100g		
Pom-Bear Original Potato Snack	1.2	25	2.4	1.4	500
Walkers Cheese & Onion Crisps	1.2	30.5	2.5	1.45	518
French Fries Salt & Vinegar	1.2	16	1.4	2.3	438
Sainsbury's Cool Tortilla Chips	1.2	22.5	1.6	1.27	490
Sainsbury's Salt & Vinegar Crisps	1.2	32.9	2.9	2.38	5353
Asda Tortilla Chips Lightly Salted	1.2	23.3	2.6	0.9	496
Asda Smart Price Salted Tortillas	1.2	23.3	2.6	0.9	487
Tesco Chipz Salt And Vinegar	1.2	32.7	2.7	1.6	535
Tesco Lightly Salted Tortilla Chips	1.2	24.6	2.3	0.8	500
Kettle Chips Sea Salt & Balsamic Vinegar	1.3	28.4	3.3	1.9	502
French Fries Worester Sauce	1.3	16.8	1.9	1.98	441
Kettle Chips Salt & Vinegar	1.3	28.4	3.3	1.9	502
Sainsbury's Prawn Cocktail Crisps	1.3	34.1	3.1	1.33	542
Tyrrells Furrows Sea Salt & Vinegar Crisps	1.3	23	1.8	1	447
Waitrose Salted Tortilla Chips	1.3	24.7	2.4	0.8	499
Tesco Finest Hot Chilli Crisps	1.3	28.8	2.4	1.2	519
Pringles Original	1.4	33	3.4	1.4	516
Sainsbury's Salted Popped Potato Snacks	1.4	13.2	1.6	2	429
Walkers Chicken & Chorizo	1.4	32	2.6	1.45	526
Walkers Worcester Sauce Crisps	1.4	30.5	2.5	1.3	516
Waitrose Paprika Mix	1.4	28.3	2.3	1.99	509
Waitrose LoveLife Calorie Ctrl Unsalted Reduced Fat Crinkle Cut Crisps	1.4	23.9	1.9	trace	489
Pom Bear Cheese & Onion Potato Snack	1.5	25	2.3	1.4	499
Walkers Mighty Lights Cheese & Onion Crisps	1.5	19	1.9	1.1	454
Morrisons Prawn Cocktail Flavour Crisps	1.5	32.4	2.9	1	536
Asda Ready Salted Potato Loops	1.5	18.8	1.6	2	469
Asda Loops Ready Salted	1.5	18.8	1.6	2	469
Tesco Everyday Value Lightly Salted Tortillas	1.5	20	2	0.8	472
Tesco Finest Crinkle Cut Steak & Ale Crisps	1.5	28.8	2.4	1.1	519
Kettle Chips Thai Sweet Chilli	1.6	30.5	3.6	1.1	517

Crisps & Snacks

Product	Sugar	Fat	Sat	Salt	Cals
			per 100g		
Morrisons Lightly Salted Tortilla Chips	1.6	22.3	2.3	0.6	482
Sainsbury's Taste the Difference Harissa Chicken Crisps	1.7	28.3	3	0.93	506
Walkers Crinkles Simply Salt Crisps	1.7	34.8	2.8	1.2	545
Walkers Roast Chicken Crisps	1.7	30.5	2.5	1.27	518
Morrisons Cheese and Onion Flavour Crisps	1.7	32.3	3	1.3	536
Doritos Hint of Lime Corn Chips	1.8	25.9	2.2	1.25	498
Tesco Finest Smoky Ancho Chilli And Paprika	1.8	24.2	2.6	0.8	491
Sainsbury's Cheese & Onion Crisps	1.9	34.7	3	1.63	548
Walkers Prawn Cocktail Crisps	1.9	30.5	2.5	1.3	520
Tesco Finest Feature Flavour Ribs And Chilli Crisp	1.9	28.8	1.9	1.2	519
Popchips Original Chips	2	14	1.3	2.9	408
Sainsbury's Tangy Cheese Tortilla Chips	2	23.6	2.2	1.27	492
Tyrrells Furrows Mature Cheddar & Pickled Onion Crisps	2	26.4	3	0.8	492
Tyrrells Furrows Sea Salted Crisps	2	23.9	2.4	1	476
Tyrrells Lightly Sea Salted Crisps	2	24.4	2.5	0.5	501
Waitrose Ham Hock & English Mustard Hand Cooked Crisps	2	28.4	3.3	1.35	502
Waitrose Sour Cream & Chive Mix	2	26.5	2.1	1.69	501
Tesco Snack Mix Sour Cream And Chive	2	20.2	2	2.5	467
Walkers Deep Ridged Cheese & Onion Crisps	2.1	30.8	2.6	1.65	518
Walkers Deep Ridged Mature Cheddar & Onion Crisps	2.1	30.8	2.6	1.65	518
Walkers Deli Chilli & Tomato Tortilla Chips	2.1	27.2	2.4	1.05	529
Asda Prawn Cocktail	2.1	31	3.8	1	521
Waitrose Essential Bacon Rashers	2.1	20.3	1.5	1.9	468
Tesco Snakes And Ladders Salt And Vinegar	2.1	20.5	1.6	1.3	488
Walkers Mighty Lights Chicken Crisps	2.2	18.9	1.8	1.1	455
Walkers Mix Ups Cheese & Worcester Sauce Snacks	2.2	32.5	2.8	1.15	529
Asda Meaty Variety	2.2	30.9	3.7	1.5	521
McCoy's Flame Grilled Steak Crisps	2.3	31	2.8	1.5	526
Sainsbury's Bacon Crispies	2.3	21	2.3	2.1	480
Sainsbury's Salt Potato Twirls	2.3	24.6	2.2	2.68	491

Crisps & Snacks

Product	Sugar	Fat	Sat	Salt	Cals
			per 100g		
Tyrrells Cider Vinegar & Salt Crisps	2.3	22.6	2.5	0.6	447
Tesco Cheese And Onion Crisps	2.3	31.8	2.7	1.3	533
Tesco Chipz Sour Cream And Onion	2.3	34.2	2.9	1	550
Frazzles Crispy Bacon Corn Snacks	2.4	22.7	1.7	2.76	483
Sainsbury's Taste the Difference Sour Cream & Lime Tortillas	2.4	23.1	2	0.8	495
Sainsbury's Taste the Difference Spicy Chilli Salsa Tortillas	2.4	28.3	2.1	0.9	518
Walkers Deli Garlic & Herb Pita Chips	2.4	19.9	1.9	1.28	483
Waitrose Cheese with a Jalapeno Twist	2.4	26.7	2.2	1.66	502
Kettle Chips Mature Cheddar & Red Onion	2.5	28.9	3.3	1.1	505
Popchips Sea Salt & Vinegar Chips	2.5	14	1.3	2.2	411
Walkers Deli Red Pepper & Tomato Pita Chips	2.5	20	2	1.33	484
Morrisons Signature Sea Salt & Balsamic Vinegar Hand-Cooked Crisps	2.5	26.6	2.9	1.9	515
Asda Good & Counted Snacking Lentil Chips	2.5	19.2	1.8	2.2	461
Asda Salt & Vinegar Crisps	2.5	28.1	3.5	1.8	519
Tesco Finest Sea Salt And Cider Vinegar Crisps	2.5	28.8	2.4	2.1	519
Doritos Tangy Cheese Corn Chips	2.6	26.3	2.4	1.27	499
Sainsbury's Taste the Difference Sea Salt & Pepper Snacks	2.6	19.5	2	3.5	462
Morrisons Cool Tortillas	2.6	22.6	2.5	1.5	493
Morrisons Salt & Vinegar Flavour Sticks	2.6	26.1	2.1	2.5	509
Tesco Bacon Rashers Snacks	2.6	22.4	2.2	2.2	478
Tesco Finest Cheese And Onion Crisps	2.6	28.8	2.4	1.4	519
Tesco Finest Crinkle Cut Sea Salt & Vinegar Crisps	2.6	28.8	2.4	2.3	519
Tesco Finest Mature Cheddar And Onion Crisps	2.6	28.8	2.4	1.4	519
Sainsbury's Chilli Tortilla Chips	2.7	21.7	1.8	1.3	485
Sensations Chicken & Thyme Crisps	2.7	26.4	2.3	1.65	503
Walkers Deli Chorizo Chips	2.7	21	1.7	1.18	468
Morrisons Bacon Rasher Snacks	2.7	28.7	2.3	2.4	525
Waitrose Nacho Cheese Tortilla Chips	2.7	24.2	2.8	1.38	493
Pringles Sour Cream & Onion	2.8	32	3.6	1.4	511
Morrisons Signature Hand-Cooked Cheese & Caramelised Onion Crisps	2.8	27.7	3.1	1.4	528

Crisps & Snacks

Product	Sugar	Fat	Sat	Salt	Cals
			per 100g		
Asda Cheesy Curls	2.8	31.6	3.9	3	543
Waitrose Hand Cooked Cheddar & Onion Crisps	2.8	28.8	3.6	1.38	504
Sainsbury's Taste the Difference Cheddar & Spring Onion Crisps	2.9	29.2	3.8	1.4	507
Sensations BBQ Crisps	2.9	26.4	2.2	1.52	504
Tyrrells Summer Butter & Mint Crisps	2.9	25.7	2.7	0.8	492
Walkers Deli Ham & Cheddar Chutney Chips	2.9	21	1.8	1.18	468
Walkers Extra Crunchy Salt & Vinegar	2.9	20.8	1.7	1.3	463
Tesco Nacho Cheese Tortilla Chips	2.9	24.6	3	1.3	497
Monster Munch Pickled Onion	3	25	2.1	1.55	492
Monster Munch Roast Beef	3	25	2.2	1.73	492
Sensations Lime Chutney Poppadoms	3	22	17.6	3.05	471
Asda Good & Counted Crinkle Cut Crisps Cheese & Onion	3	19.8	1.9	1.4	456
Tesco Cheese Curls Snacks	3	32	3.3	2.5	530
Tesco Cool Tortilla Chips	3	23.6	2.4	1.3	493
Kettle Chips Mozzarella & Pesto	3.1	29.2	3.8	1.4	506
Pringles Paprika	3.1	3.2	52	2.1	503
Sensations Balsamic Vinegar & Onion Crisps	3.1	26.2	2.9	1.65	501
Tyrrells Cheddar Cheese & Chive Crisps	3.1	27.5	2.9	1	486
Phileas Fogg Sour Cream & Onion Taco Rolls	3.2	27	2.7	1.3	508
Sensations Cheddar & Chutney Crisps	3.2	25	2.2	1.65	496
Walkers Mix Ups Bacon & Cheese Snacks	3.2	32.5	2.8	1.16	530
Walkers Pops Prawn Cocktail	3.2	13.9	1.3	2.01	445
Asda Cheese & Onion	3.2	31.1	3.8	1.5	523
Asda Chosen by You Ridge Cut Meaty Flavour Crisps	3.2	28.9	3	1.3	534
Asda Tortilla Chips Nacho Cheese	3.2	22.3	2.6	1.5	486
Tesco Finest Sweet Chilli Crisps	3.2	28.8	2.4	1	519
Walkers Crinkles Salt & Vinegar Crisps	3.3	33.2	2.7	1.53	532
Asda Tortilla Chips Cool	3.3	22.1	2.3	1.5	481
Doritos BBQ Rib Corn Chips	3.4	25.6	2.1	1.78	493
Marmite Crisps	3.4	30.7	3.1	1.52	519

Product	Sugar	Fat	Sat per 100g	Salt	Cals
Pom Bear Cheesy Potato Snack	3.4	29	2.6	1.5	515
Morrisons Sour Cream & Chive Dip	3.4	36.5	11.7	0.8	364
Waitrose Spicy Chilli Tortilla Chips	3.4	23.6	2.3	1.08	490
Kettle Chips Sour Cream & Sweet Onion	3.5	29.2	3.9	1.2	507
Pringles Cheese & Onion	3.5	31	3.2	1.9	505
Pringles Tortilla Chips Nacho Cheese	3.5	29	3.1	2.3	472
Squares Salt & Vinegar	3.5	18	1.5	2.2	443
Walkers Deep Ridged Salt & Malt Vinegar Crisps	3.5	30	2.5	1.75	511
Walkers Deep Ridged Salt & Vinegar Crisps	3.5	30	2.5	1.75	511
Walkers Mix Ups Spicy Snacks	3.5	24	2.1	1.74	492
Asda Cheese & Onion Crisps	3.5	28.2	3.8	1.4	517
Pringles Tortilla Chips Original	3.6	30	2.8	1.4	479
Wheat Crunchies Bacon	3.6	25	2.4	1.8	495
Morrisons Cheese Savouries	3.6	30	11.6	1.6	520
Asda Cheese Savouries	3.6	30	11.6	1.6	520
McCoy's Cheddar & Onion Crisps	3.7	30	2.8	1.5	524
Sainsbury's Taste the Difference Thai Sweet Chilli Crisps	3.7	28.5	3.4	0.48	503
Sensations Chipotle Crisps	3.7	26.1	2.1	1.57	501
Sensations Thai Sweet Chilli Crisps	3.7	26.3	2.2	1.57	504
Tyrrells Sweet Chilli & Red Pepper Crisps	3.7	27	2.6	2	490
Walkers Deli Balsamic Vinegar Chips	3.7	20.8	1.7	1.18	467
Walkers Deli Cheddar Chips	3.7	20.8	1.7	1.18	467
Morrisons Cheese Curls	3.7	29.4	3.2	2.3	519
Popchips Tortilla Chips Cool Ranch	3.8	15.9	1.3	1.8	445
Pringles Salt & Vinegar	3.8	31	3.2	2.3	507
Sainsbury's Salt & Pepper Popped Potato Snacks	3.8	13	1.6	2	428
Walkers Extra Crunchy BBQ Ribs Crisps	3.8	19.7	1.6	1.19	434
Tesco Chilli Tortilla Chips	3.8	23.3	2.2	1.3	491
Doritos Cool Original Corn Chips	3.9	26.3	2.5	1.91	497
Sainsbury's Salt Crunch Sticks	3.9	22	2.2	2.9	479

Crisps & Snacks

Product	Sugar	Fat	Sat per 100g	Salt	Cals
Walkers Crinkles Cheddar & Onion Crisps	3.9	33.3	2.8	1.23	536
Asda Beastie Bites	3.9	25.9	3.2	1.7	504
Asda Bacon Bites	3.9	24.2	1.8	1.8	498
Waitrose Sea Salt & Cracked Black Pepper Pretzels	4	3.8	0.4	1.85	396
Tesco Cheese Savouries Snacks	4	30.9	12.2	1.5	523
Quavers Cheese	4.1	30.1	2.7	2.21	534
Popchips Tortilla Chips Crazy Hot	4.1	16.9	1.4	1.8	445
Tesco Finest Hoisin Duck Crisps	4.1	28.8	4.1	1.2	519
Tesco Healthy Living Red Thai Curry Popcorn	4.1	16	1.5	1.3	427
Kettle Chips Sweet Chilli & Sour Cream	4.3	28.4	3.5	1.1	505
Pringles Prawn Cocktail	4.3	31	3.3	1.6	509
Walkers Mix Ups Cheese Snacks	4.3	25	2.5	1.67	497
Asda Good & Counted Snacking Flavours of the Med Lentil Chips	4.3	19.5	1.7	2.2	459
Asda Salt & Vinegar Sticks	4.3	27.3	2.4	2.1	510
Popchips Tortilla Chips Nacho Cheese	4.4	16.7	2.3	1.7	455
Sainsbury's Cheddar & Onion Snacks, Be Good to Yourself	4.4	19.3	1.9	3.5	482
Sainsbury's Cheesy Curls	4.4	32.1	2.8	3.5	544
Walkers Deep Ridged Steak Crisps	4.4	30.1	2.5	1.55	515
Walkers Smokey Bacon Crisps	4.4	30.5	2.5	1.3	520
Asda Tortilla Chips Chilli	4.4	21.6	2.2	1.5	482
Popchips Sour Cream & Onion Chips	4.5	15	1.6	1.9	413
Pringles BBQ	4.5	31	3.2	1.6	506
Tesco Finest Goats Cheese And Chilli Crisps	4.5	28.8	2.4	1.2	519
Walkers Pops Sour Cream & Onion	4.7	13.8	1.3	1.97	445
Asda Party Mix Sour Cream & Chive	4.7	22.3	1.5	2.3	471
Doritos Chilli Heatwave Corn Chips	4.8	25.3	2	1.37	494
Tesco Healthy Living Sour Cream And Black Pepper Popcorn	4.8	16	1.5	1.4	438
Kettle Chips Smoky BBQ	4.9	28	3.1	1.4	500
Morrisons Cheese Balls	4.9	29.9	3.4	1.5	531
Tesco Salted Pretzels	4.9	4.2	0.4	1.6	399

Crisps & Snacks

Product	Sugar	Fat	Sat	Salt	Cals
			per 100g		
Tesco Sea Salt And Black Pepper Pretzel Mix	4.9	11.5	0.9	1	442
Pringles Tortilla Chips Spicy Chilli	5	29	2.7	1.8	474
Sainsbury's BGTY Cheese & Red Onion Soya & Potato Snacks	5	6	0.8	1.5	387
Sainsbury's Thai Chilli Soya & Potato Snacks, Be Good to Yourself	5	6	0.8	1.5	389
Walkers Sunbites Pitta Bakes Roasted Onion & Rosemary	5	17	1.7	1.39	462
Waitrose Essential Salt & Malt Vinegar Sticks	5	27.1	2.1	2.63	503
Jacob's Mini Cheddars	5.1	29.2	11.6	2.5	512
Walkers Sunbites Pitta Bakes Vintage Cheddar & Caramelised Onion	5.1	16.8	1.6	1.49	461
Asda Onion Rings	5.1	26.4	2.4	1.5	508
Walkers Sunbites Pitta Bakes Roasted Red Pepper & Chilli	5.2	16.9	1.6	1.48	461
Jacob's Cheese & Onion Mini Cheddars	5.3	29.9	11.2	1.8	524
Pringles Tortilla Chips Sour Cream	5.3	29	2.8	1.8	477
Asda Meaty Flavour Potato Loops	5.3	18.6	1.6	2	462
Walkers Pops Original	5.4	14	1.4	2.01	445
Tyrrells Sunday Best Roast Chicken Crisps	5.6	23.1	2.8	1	451
Phileas Fogg New York Deli Relish Bubble Chips	5.7	32	3	1.5	543
Sainsbury's Salt & Pepper Wholegrain Bites	5.7	22.2	2.1	1.58	478
Walkers Pops Cheese & Bacon	5.7	14	1.4	2	444
Waitrose Essential Onion Rings	5.7	28.3	2.1	2.25	509
Walkers Baked Hoops & Crosses Roast Beef Snacks	5.8	21	1.9	1.49	474
Walkers Baked Ready Salted Crisps	5.8	8	0.8	1.16	409
Waitrose Spicy Plantain Crisps with Sweet Chilli & Lime	5.8	27.1	3.2	0.88	493
Phileas Fogg Sweet & Smokey BBQ Bubble Chips	5.9	32.3	2.9	1.5	540
Asda Cheese Balls	6.1	28.6	2.9	1.8	509
Tesco Finest Jalapeno And Cheese Tort Chips	6.1	26.3	2.7	0.9	502
Tesco Onion Rings	6.1	24.6	2	2.3	500
Penn State Sour Cream & Chives Pretzels	6.2	11	0.9	1.7	423
Walkers Baked Salt & Vinegar	6.3	8	0.8	0.91	406
Morrisons Savers Bombay Mix	6.3	17.5	10.6	0.3	458
Penn Stars Smoky BBQ Pretzels	6.5	11	0.9	0.83	433

Crisps & Snacks

Product	Sugar	Fat	Sat	Salt	Cals
			per 100g		
Wotsits Cheese	6.6	33	4	1.96	546
Asda Prawn Shells	6.7	22	2.1	2.1	493
Walkers Baked Sour Cream & Chive Crisps	6.8	8.5	1.2	1.13	411
Walkers Salt & Vinegar Baked Stars	6.8	8	0.8	1.1	409
Sainsbury's Cheese Balls	6.9	30.1	3.3	1.83	530
Walkers Baked Cheese & Onion Crisps	7	8.3	0.8	0.93	411
Tesco Broad Beans	7	16.6	4.7	2.1	436
Asda Cheese Wiggles	7.2	29.6	2.7	1.9	519
Asda Wiggles	7.2	29.6	2.7	1.9	519
Waitrose Essential Cheese Puffs	7.2	26.5	2.2	1.75	518
Sainsbury's Spicy BBQ Popped Potato Snacks	7.3	13.5	1.6	2	432
Walkesr Sunbites Lighty Salted Crisps	7.3	21.6	2.2	0.94	480
Morrisons Onion Rings	7.4	26	2.4	2.1	504
Waitrose Essential Prawn Cocktail Shells	7.4	22.4	1.6	2.22	492
Walkers Cheese & Onion Baked Stars	7.5	8.2	0.9	1.1	410
Morrisons Prawn Crackers	7.6	32.1	2.7	1.9	541
Tesco Prawn Crackers	7.6	32.4	2.8	1.9	543
Sainsbury's Sour Cream & Sweet Chilli Wholegrain Bites	7.7	22.2	2.2	1.63	482
Skips Prawn Cocktail	7.8	32	2.9	2.3	544
Tesco Bombay Mix	8	25.9	3.4	2	477
Sainsbury's Prawn Crackers	8.2	31	2.7	2.4	530
Sainsbury's Onion Rings	8.4	24.7	2.6	2.25	502
Walkers Sunbites Sour Cream & Black Pepper Crisps	8.4	21.7	2.3	1.3	480
Waitrose Indonesian Cracker Mix	8.8	31.2	2.4	2.05	531
Sainsbury's Prawn Cocktail Shells	8.9	29.3	2.7	2.25	531
Tesco Prawn Cocktail Snacks	8.9	29.3	2.7	2.3	531
Walkers Sunbites Onion & Rosemary Crisps	9.1	21.7	2.3	0.97	481
Popchips Barbeque Chips	9.2	15	1.4	2.3	420
Walkers Sunbites Cheese & Onion Crisps	9.2	21.5	2.2	0.97	480
Sainsbury's Cheese Puffs	9.3	27.9	3.3	2.17	524

Crisps & Snacks

Product	Sugar	Fat	Sat per 100g	Salt	Cals
Sainsbury's Honey BBQ Wholegrain Bites	9.4	25.4	2.4	2.38	497
Morrisons Multigrain Sourcream & Black Pepper Chilli	9.5	16	1.4	2.1	455
Walkers Sunbites Sun Ripened Sweet Chilli Crisps	9.6	21.5	2.2	0.66	480
Walkers Sunbites Sweet Chilli	9.6	21.5	2.2	0.66	480
Tesco Thai Spicy Mix	9.7	4.9	1.2	1.4	400
Asda BBQ Triangles	10	20.9	1.5	2.2	475
Waitrose Vegetable Crackers Indonesian Style	10.4	30.4	2.5	2.65	522
Velvet Crunch Gourmet Bites Salt & Rich Balsamic Vinegar	11	10	1	2	429
Walkers Sunbites Crispy Crackers Lightly Salted	12	17	1.3	1.36	459
Tyrrells Thai Chilli Crackers	13	27	16.2	3	520
Velvet Crunch Gourmet Bites Cheese & Onion	13	10	1.1	1.5	429
Walkers Sunbites Crispy Crackers Roasted Onion & Rosemary	13	17	1.5	1.45	459
Velvet Crunch Thai Sweet Chilli	14	11	1.3	1.5	433
Walkers Sunbites Crispy Crackers Cream Cheese & Chive	14	17	1.6	1.5	458
Walkers Sunbites Crispy Crackers Sweet Chilli	14	17	1.3	1.41	456
Tesco Wasabi Mix	14.8	19.7	7.9	1.5	472
Tesco Sweet And Salted Popcorn	15.1	25.4	3.2	1.5	494
Tesco Sweet Popcorn	16.8	23.9	1.9	0.1	490
Tesco Baked Cracker Mix	17.1	8	3.9	2.5	418
Walkers Mix Ups Popcorn Sweet & Salty	17.4	29.8	3.4	1.12	553
Tyrrells Popcorn Sweet & Salty	17.6	28.4	3.3	1.6	517
Sainsbury's Taste the Difference Sweet Chilli & Lime Crisps	18.5	31.7	3.8	1	512
Tesco Barbeque Crackers	19.1	31.4	15.9	2.2	535
Walkers Mix Ups Popcorn Sweet & Spicy	20.1	27.1	3.3	0.51	541
Waitrose Vegetable Crisps	20.9	34.7	3.9	1.27	517
Morrisons Signature Hand-Cooked Vegetable Flavour Crisps	21.2	34.7	3.9	1.3	517
Tesco Finest Root Vegetable Crisps	21.6	33.4	3.8	0.8	513
Tyrrells Crinkly Mixed Root Vegetable Crisps	22.1	31.2	3.7	0.6	498
Tyrrells Mixed Root Vegetable Crisps	22.6	35.2	4.1	2	492
Tesco Peanut Cracker Mix	23.4	15.1	3.3	0.6	448

Crisps & Snacks

Product	Sugar	Fat	Sat per 100g	Salt	Cals
Waitrose Crinkle Cut Vegetable Crisps	24	35.7	4	1	518
Kettle Chips Vegetable	24.8	38.7	3.4	1	532
Tyrrells Vegetable Purple Sweet Potato, Beetroot & Parsnip Crisps	27.7	33.1	3.6	1	543
Asda Chosen by You Sweet & Salty Popcorn	31.7	28.6	4.2	1	517
Asda Chosen by You Sweet Popcorn	32.8	22	3.3	trace	486
Asda Good & Counted Snacking Popcorn Sweet Variety	40.4	20.1	2	trace	488
Morrisons NuMe Carrot Crisps	46.8	1	0.7	0.1	395
Tesco Toffee Popcorn	51	7.2	1.6	1.3	411
Asda Chosen by You Toffee Popcorn	54.9	8.1	1.8	1.6	413
Heston from Waitrose Salted Caramel Popcorn	58.4	11.3	3.3	1.5	433

Ice Cream & Lollies

You may still buy the occasional ice cream or lolly for your family. Some are better than others but all contain sugar.

Please check the ingredients carefully; some contain 'sugar' and some 'fructose syrup', which you want to completely avoid.

To help you make the best choices, products are listed starting with the least sugar first.

Product	Sugar	Fat	Sat	Salt	Cals
		per 100g / 100ml			
Waitrose Essential Soft Scoop Ice Cream Neapolitan	6.4	2.4	2	0.09	57
Morrisons Chocolate Ice Cream	7.3	2.7	2.3	trace	68
Waitrose Essential Vanilla Soft Ice Cream	7.9	2.9	2.5	0.08	64
Asda Smart Price Vanilla Soft Scoop Ice Cream	7.9	2.2	1.3	trace	57
Morrisons Neapolitan Ice Cream	8.1	2.8	2.3	trace	69
Morrisons Vanilla Ice Cream	8.2	2.6	2.2	trace	67
Waitrose Vanilla Dairy Ice Cream	8.6	5.4	3.6	0.06	93
Waitrose Essential Vanilla & Raspberry Ripple Ice Cream	8.8	2.3	1.7	0.08	66
Morrisons Raspberry Ripple Ice Cream	8.8	2.8	2.4	trace	77
Asda Vanilla Soft Scoop Ice Cream	9.1	3.2	1.9	0.1	71
Tesco Healthy Living Caramel Iced Dessert	9.3	5.4	3.9	0.2	135
Asda Neapolitan Soft Scoop Ice Cream	9.6	3	1.9	0.1	72
Asda My Really Creamy Vanilla Ice Cream	9.7	4.7	4.2	0.1	99
Asda Chosen by You Really Creamy Vanilla Ice Cream	9.7	4.7	4.2	0.1	99
Asda Chosen by You Soft Scoop Mint Choc Chip Neapolitan Ice Cream	9.9	3.5	2.1	0.05	78
Morrisons Cornish Dairy Ice Cream	9.9	4.8	3.2	trace	102
Waitrose Chocolate Mint Dairy Ice Cream	10	6	3.9	0.08	107
Philadelphia Lemon Cheesecake	10	26	11	0.3	370
Asda Chocolate Soft Scoop Ice Cream	10	3.3	2	0.1	79
Asda Chosen by Kids Chosen by Kids Monster Lollies	10.2	3.6	2.2	0.1	99
Asda Vanilla Cornish Soft Scoop Ice Cream	10.4	5.2	3.6	trace	107
Asda Good & Counted Vanilla Iced Dessert	10.4	1.3	1	0.1	75
Asda Raspberry Ripple Soft Scoop Ice Cream	10.7	3.1	1.9	0.1	78
Waitrose Vanilla Cornish Dairy Ice Cream	11.1	5.5	3.6	0.07	107

Ice Cream & Lollies

Product	Sugar	Fat	Sat	Salt	Cals
	per 100g / 100ml				
Waitrose Cornish Dairy Vanilla Ice Cream	11.1	5.5	3.6	0.08	107
Waitrose Seriously Fruity Mango & Lime Coulis	11.2	0.6	0.2	0.03	63
Waitrose Butterscotch Dairy Ice Cream	11.4	6.4	4.2	0.08	120
Asda Chosen by You Mango & Pineapple Smoothie Mix	12	0.5	0.1	0	59
Asda Chosen by You Really Creamy Rocky Road	12.1	5.1	4.1	0.1	121
Waitrose Chocolate Dairy Ice Cream	12.3	6.3	4	0.08	126
Waitrose Duchy Organic Vanilla Ice Cream	12.5	9.8	6	1.2	149
Waitrose LoveLife Calorie Ctrl R'berry & B'currant Frozen Yogurt	12.6	1.1	0.8	0.1	75
Claudi & Fin Frozen Yogurt Lollies Strawberry	12.8	4.6	3.2	0.1	104
Waitrose Strawberry Dairy Ice Cream	13	4.8	3.2	0.05	108
Waitrose Essential Chocolate & Vanilla Cones	13	8.5	7	0.08	194
Asda Good & Counted Chocolate Greek Style Frozen Yoghurt	13	1.7	1	0.1	84
Asda Chosen by You Really Creamy Cookie Crumble Ice Cream	13	4.8	3.9	0.13	120
Asda Chosen by You Really Creamy Black Forest Gteau Ice Cream	13	4.7	3.9	0.08	119
Asda Really Creamy Chocolate Truffle Ice Cream	13.1	4.9	4	0.1	119
Waitrose Toffee Fudge Dairy Ice Cream	13.2	6.1	4	0.08	127
Waitrose LoveLife Calorie Ctrl Belgian Chocolate Frozen Yogurt	13.2	1.7	1.1	0.1	89
Morrisons Double Chocolate Ice Cream Sundae	13.2	4.1	2.4	trace	109
Morrisons Chocolate & Raspberry Ice Cream Sundae	13.2	4.1	2.4	trace	109
Asda Really Creamy Raspberry Pavlova Ice Cream	13.4	4.2	3.7	0.1	110
Asda Chosen by You Really Creamy Chocolate Orange Ice Cream	13.4	4.6	3.8	0.1	120
Morrison Savers Assorted Fruit Flavour Lollies	13.4	0.2	0.1	trace	59
Asda Chosen by You Raspberry Ripple Screwballs	13.6	3.9	2.4	0.1	98
Asda Chosen by You Fruity Blackcurrant Moments	13.6	2.5	1.7	0.1	99
Claudi & Fin Frozen Yogurt Lollies Mango	13.7	4.7	3	0.12	112
Asda Strawberry & Vanilla Cones	13.9	5.9	5.1	0.1	153
Asda Chosen by You Loaded Chewy Peanut Butter Ice Cream	13.9	11.4	6.3	0.3	193
Asda Really Creamy Coconut & Chocolate Ice Cream	14	5.9	4.9	0.1	130
Asda Chosen by You Strawberry & Banana Smoothie Mix	14	0.5	0.1	0.09	71
Asda Chosen by You Really Creamy Key Lime Pie Ice Cream	14	4.9	4.2	0.15	124

Ice Cream & Lollies

Product	Sugar	Fat	Sat	Salt	Cals
	per 100g / 100ml				
Waitrose Duchy Organic Strawberry Ice Cream	14.1	7.7	4.8	0.08	136
Asda Chosen by You Lovely Bubbly Chocolate Frozen Mousse	14.1	6.7	5.1	0.1	138
Haagen Dazs Ice Cream Strawberries & Cream	14.2	13.9	8.6	0.12	221
Asda Chosen by You Dark Choc Ices	14.2	12.6	10	0.1	185
Waitrose LoveLife Calorie Ctrl Frozen Natural Yogurt Dessert	14.3	1.6	1.1	0.13	90
Haagen-Dazs Ice Cream Vanilla	14.3	17	10.4	0.15	251
Asda Good & Counted Strawberry Greek Style Frozen Yoghurt	14.4	1.5	1	0.1	84
Asda Chocolate & Hazelnut Cones	14.4	8	6.3	0.1	176
Morrisons Strawberry & Cream Ice Cream Sundae	14.4	4.2	3.3	0.1	109
Haagen Dazs Yuzu Citrus & Cream	14.7	13.4	8.3	0.16	233
Asda Really Creamy Caramel Fudge Ice Cream	15	4.8	4.2	0.1	121
Asda Fruity Tropical Moments	15	2.6	1.7	0.1	106
Asda Chosen by You Really Creamy White Choc & R'berry Ice Cream	15	4.7	3.9	0.05	121
Waitrose Seriously Clotted Cream & Raspberry Ice Cream	15.1	11.8	8.2	0.08	179
Waitrose Essential Rocket Lollies	15.1	0.2	0.1	0.05	72
Asda My Really Creamy Chocolate Truffle Ice Cream	15.2	5.2	4.1	0.1	128
Haagen-Dazs Ice Cream Cookies & Cream	15.2	17.1	10.8	0.21	263
Morrisons Toffee & Vanilla Ice Cream Sundae	15.2	4.2	3.5	trace	112
Waitrose Seriously Madagascan Vanilla Ice Cream	15.3	12.8	8.3	0.1	190
Waitrose Essential Strawberry Splits	15.3	2.7	1.4	0.08	99
Asda My Really Creamy Caramel Fudge Ice Cream	15.3	4.9	3.8	0.1	123
Asda Chosen by You Mint Cones	15.4	6.4	5.4	0.1	163
Asda Chosen by Kids Assorted Mini Milk Lollies	15.5	2.9	1.8	0.2	115
Tesco Frozen Yoghurt Mango And Passion Fruit	15.6	1.1	0.7	0.2	115
Asda Chosen by You Rocket Lollies	15.6	0	0	0	74
Asda Chosen by You Crazy Pop Push Ups	15.6	trace	trace	trace	64
Waitrose Essential Strawberry & Vanilla Cones	15.7	5.9	4.9	0.05	162
Tesco Frozen Yoghurt Mixed Berry	15.7	1.2	0.7	0.2	115
Sainsbury's Vanilla Ice Cream Slicing Block	15.7	7.1	5.6	0.18	151
Waitrose Seriously Intense Pistachio Italian Gelato	15.8	9	4.3	0.15	173

Product	Sugar	Fat	Sat	Salt	Cals
	per 100g / 100ml				
Asda Chosen by You Milk Choc Ices	15.8	13.6	10.9	0.1	198
Haagen-Dazs Ice Cream Strawberry Cheesecake	15.9	15.5	9.6	0.14	246
Asda Apple & Blackcurrant Licky Ice Lollies	15.9	0	0	trace	74
Asda Chosen by You Toffee Cones	16	7.6	6.1	0.1	174
Asda Chosen by You Ripplicious Café Latte Ice Cream	16	6.7	4.7	0.07	147
Asda Good & Counted Black Cherry Greek Style Frozen Yoghurt	16.1	1.5	1	0.1	91
Asda Chosen by You Orange Juice Lollies	16.2	0.2	trace	trace	69
Asda Refreshingly Tropical Mango Sorbet	16.3	0.3	0.2	trace	71
Asda Chosen by You Assorted Real Fruit Splits	16.5	3.1	1.9	0.1	108
Morrisons Orange Lollies	16.5	0.2	0.1	trace	76
Asda Smart Price Fruit Flavoured Lollies	16.6	0	0	trace	71
Asda Chosen by You Zesty Lemon Sorbet	16.7	0.1	0.1	0.1	77
Asda Chosen by You Loaded Choc Fudge Brownie	16.7	7.7	5.8	0.1	163
Waitrose Alphonso Mango Sorbet	16.9	0.3	0.2	0	75
Wall's Soft Scoop Vanilla Light Ice Cream	17	5.9	3.2	0.21	139
Asda Chosen by You Ripplicious Chocolate Hazelnut Truffle Ice Cream	17	11	5.8	0.11	199
Asda Chosen by You Banoffee Choccy Splits	17	10	5.4	0.13	176
Sainsbury's Strawberry Gateau	17.1	8.2	4.8	0.15	190
Tesco Everyday Value Strawberry Flavoured Splits	17.2	3.2	1.7	0.1	117
Sainsbury's Belgian Chocolate Ice Cream, Taste the Difference	17.2	12.7	6.8	0.11	230
Morrisons Strawberry Splits	17.2	3.1	1.8	trace	109
Heston from Waitrose Salted Caramel Popcorn Ice Cream	17.3	11.5	7.2	0.2	192
Sainsbury's Profiteroles With Chocolate Sauce	17.4	22.4	14.9	0.18	341
Waitrose Essential Dark Choc Ices	17.5	11.2	9.8	0.15	183
Tesco Everyday Value Soft Scoop Vanilla Ice Cream	17.5	5.1	3.2	0.2	135
Heston from Waitrose Choc & Nut Ice Cream	17.5	9.2	5.3	0.15	181
Waitrose Seriously Coconut & Lime Ice Cream	17.6	10.1	6.6	0.13	175
Tesco White Chocolate And Raspberry Ice Cream	17.6	8.5	5.8	0.2	202
Waitrose Seriously Creamy Santa Domingo Chocolate Ice Cream	17.9	19.5	12.3	0.09	262
Waitrose Seriously Creamy Dark Chocolate Choc-Ices	17.9	12.8	7.9	0.08	212

Ice Cream & Lollies

Product	Sugar	Fat	Sat	Salt	Cals
		per 100g / 100ml			
Morrisons Twisty Lollies	17.9	0.2	trace	0.1	79
Waitrose Essential Fruit Juice Lollies	18	0.2	0.1	0.1	95
Tesco Finest Madagascan Vanilla Ice Cream	18	16.3	10.5	0.1	235
Sainsbury's Vanilla Ice Cream, Taste the Difference	18	16	11	0.13	243
Coconut Co Snowconut Fro Yo Vanilla	18	7.5	6.6	5	843
Asda Chosen by You Ripplicious White Chocolate & Passion Fruit	18	6.9	4.7	0.08	168
Asda Chosen by You Ripplicious Raspberry & Cream Ice Cream	18	7	4.7	0.06	159
Asda Chosen by You Ripplicious Coconut & Chocolate Ice Cream	18	8.8	6.4	0.07	185
Asda Chosen by You Puzzle Popz	18	0.5	0.1	0.01	84
Asda Chosen by You Mini Mocktail Ice Lollies	18	1.8	1.6	0.03	91
Asda Chosen by You Loaded Mallow Mayhem	18	5.2	4.4	0.08	144
Asda Chosen by You Cola Floats	18	2.3	1.4	0.04	110
Asda Chosen by You Loaded Mint Choc Chip Cookie Dough	18.2	7.3	5.8	0.1	165
Tesco Raspberry Sorbet	18.3	0.4	0.2	0.2	118
Tesco Lemon Sorbet	18.3	0.2	0.1	0.1	95
Sainsbury's Salted Peanut & Caramel Ice Cream	18.3	14.5	6.2	0.36	260
Waitrose Lemon Sorbet	18.4	0.1	0.1	0.03	77
Yoomoo Frozen Yogurt Vanilla	18.6	1.2	0.7	0.1	124
Tesco Vanilla Ice Cream	18.6	10.1	6.9	0.1	198
Waitrose Essential Milk Choc Ices	18.7	11	9.7	0.15	186
Sainsbury's Strawberry Cheesecake	18.7	13	6.6	0.24	260
Asda Chosen by You Loaded Gingerbread Fudge	18.7	8.6	6.2	0.2	188
Asda Chosen by You Cider Flavour Lollies	18.7	trace	0	trace	82
Asda Chosen by You Loaded Cookie Dough	18.8	7.4	5.9	0.1	171
Sainsbury's Cornish Dairy Ice Cream	18.9	7.6	4.8	0.18	170
Sainsbury's Neapolitan Soft Scoop Ice Cream	19	6.2	5.1	0.15	164
Waitrose Seriously Intense Hazelnut Italian Gelato	19.1	5.9	0.6	0.13	150
Asda Assorted Mini Moments	19.2	13.9	9.9	0.1	216
Waitrose Coconut Water Lollies	19.3	0.2	trace	0.05	88
Mackie's Ice Cream Traditional Dairy Vanilla	19.3	10.8	6.8	0.2	204

Product	Sugar	Fat	Sat	Salt	Cals
			per 100g / 100ml		
Waitrose Seriously Creamy Milk Chocolate Choc-Ices	19.4	13.6	8.4	0.1	226
Tesco Mango And Vanilla Frozen Yoghurt	19.4	8.1	5.7	0.2	185
Tesco Finest Cornish Salted Caramel Ice Cream	19.4	16	10.5	0.5	236
Sainsbury's Vanilla Soft Scoop Ice Cream	19.4	6.5	5.6	0.14	165
Waitrose Belgian Milk Chocolate Ice Creams	19.5	14.7	9.9	0.27	235
Tesco Free From Creamy Iced Vanilla Dessert	19.5	12.3	11.2	0.2	220
Sainsbury's Vanilla Ice Cream, Be Good To Yourself	19.5	3.4	2.3	0.14	145
Sainsbury's Blackforest Gateau	19.6	8.5	5	0.15	207
Tesco Soft Scoop Vanilla	19.7	7.7	4.5	0.1	176
Tesco Soft Scoop Cornish Ice Cream	19.7	8.7	5.4	0.1	187
Tesco Cornish Ice Cream	19.7	8.7	5.4	0.1	187
Tesco Mixed Berry Frozen Yoghurt Lollies	19.8	2.3	1.4	0.1	117
Morrisons Chocolate Dipped Splits	19.8	6.7	3.2	0.1	149
Sainsbury's Cookie Dough Ice Cream	19.9	8.4	5.4	0.17	214
Viennetta Ice Cream Dessert, Strawberry	20	14	13	0.13	240
Viennetta Ice Cream Dessert, Mint	20	16	14	0.14	250
Sainsbury's Toffee Honeycomb Ice Cream	20	10.5	6.6	0.22	236
Asda Smart Price Raspberry Ripple Mousse	20	7	4.3	0.2	160
Waitrose Seriously Intense Zabaglione Italian Gelato	20.1	7.2	4.4	0.15	165
Waitrose Pineapple & Coconut Colada Lollies	20.1	2.1	1.8	0.05	108
Kelly's Cornish Clotted Ice Cream	20.1	14.9	9.5	0.1	227
Weight Watchers Salted Caramel Sundaes	20.2	4.6	3.2	0.4	192
Green & Black's Organic Vanilla Ice Cream	20.2	13.3	8	0.15	220
Cadbury Marvellous Ice Cream Salted Caramel	20.2	11.8	7.2	0.27	223
Asda Good & Counted Mini Fruit Moments	20.3	1.6	1.3	0.1	127
Tesco Caramel Shortcake Ice Cream	20.4	11.6	8	0.3	236
Waitrose Seriously Intense Espresso Italian Gelato	20.5	4.3	2.4	0.13	135
Asda Vanilla Ice Cream	20.5	6.9	4.2	0.1	177
Asda Chosen by You Loaded Chewy Chewy Caramel	20.5	9	7.3	0.2	178
Sainsbury's Vanilla Soft Scoop Ice Cream, Basics	20.8	5.2	3.1	0.2	146

Ice Cream & Lollies

Product	Sugar	Fat	Sat	Salt	Cals
	per 100g / 100ml				
Waitrose Seriously White Chocolate Ice Cream	20.9	14.9	9.5	0.1	231
Wall's Soft Scoop Vanilla Ice Cream	21	9.1	6	0.21	187
Viennetta Ice Cream Dessert, Vanilla	21	14	13	0.12	250
Tesco Ice Cream Roll	21	4.7	2.5	0.2	180
Snog Frozen Yogurt Original	21	6.2	5.4	0.14	171
Carte D'or Ice Cream Vanilla Light	21	4.5	4	0.16	140
Ben & Jerry's Greek Frozen Yogurt Strawberry Shortcake	21	7	4.5	0.14	190
Tesco Soft Scoop Neapolitan Ice Cream	21.1	5.8	3.1	0.1	158
Tesco Neapolitan Ice Cream Block	21.1	5.8	3.1	0.1	158
Mackie's Ice Cream Honeycomb	21.1	10.6	7	0.2	196
Asda Milk Chocolate Almond Moments	21.1	18	11.1	0.1	269
Sainsbury's Triple Chocolate Gateau	21.2	12.3	7.4	0.15	242
Asda White Chocolate Moments	21.2	17.5	12.3	0.1	260
Tesco Everyday Value 8 Raspberry Ripple Mousse	21.3	6.7	3.8	0.1	161
Heston from Waitrose Malted Milk & Marmalade Ice Cream	21.4	9.9	6.3	0.18	191
Sainsbury's Raspberry Ripple Soft Scoop Ice Cream	21.5	6.1	4.7	0.15	167
Waitrose Valencia Orange Lollies	21.6	0.2	0.1	0.05	95
Tesco Finest Chocolate Ice Cream	21.6	27.5	16.8	0.1	354
Sainsbury's Chocolate & Vanilla Ice Cream	21.7	6.5	5.1	0.15	188
Morrisons Mini Twirlers	21.7	2.2	1.9	0.1	124
Waitrose LoveLife Calorie Ctrl Mango and R'berry Fruit Sorbet Lollies	21.8	0.2	0.1	0.1	115
Haagen-Dazs Ice Cream Belgian Chocolate	21.8	20.6	12.4	0.17	313
Waitrose Seriously Colombian Coffee Ice Cream	21.9	10.7	6.8	0.1	197
Tesco Milk Chocolate Ices	21.9	23.3	20.1	0.1	314
Tesco Belgian White Chocolate Ice Creams	22	44.2	28.9	0.2	494
Sainsbury's Tarte Au Citron, Taste the Difference	22	11.5	7.7	0.32	290
Haagen Dazs Ice Cream Chocolate Salted Caramel	22	18.4	12	0.41	293
Carte D'or Ice Cream Rum & Raisins	22	8	5	0.14	200
Ben & Jerry's Greek Frozen Yogurt Vanilla Honey Caramel	22	7	4.5	0.17	200
Ben & Jerry's Cookie Core Ice Cream Speculoos? SpecuLove	22	20	11	0.22	310

Ice Cream & Lollies

Product	Sugar	Fat	Sat	Salt	Cals
	per 100g / 100ml				
Asda Milk Chocolate Moments	22.2	16.1	11.5	0.1	252
Tesco Mango Passion Fruit Frozen Yoghurt Lollies	22.3	2.2	1.4	0.1	129
Sainsbury's Lemon Cheesecake, Taste the Difference	22.3	24	14.4	0.5	377
Kelly's Cornish Vanilla Dairy Ice Cream	22.3	11.9	7.6	0.2	212
Asda Chocolate Orange Moments	22.3	14.2	9.8	0.1	242
Waitrose Seriously Intense Limoncello Italian Gelato	22.4	5	3	0.2	155
Sainsbury's Toffee & Vanilla Ice Cream	22.4	6.5	5.3	0.16	184
Haagen-Dazs Ice Cream Pralines & Cream	22.4	16.2	9.0	0.3	275
Cadbury Marvellous Ice Cream Zingy Raspberry Brownie	22.4	10.6	6.9	0.16	219
Tesco Cookie Dough Ice Cream	22.5	11.4	8	0.2	241
Haagen-Dazs Ice Cream Salted Caramel	22.5	17.3	11.1	0.48	284
Sainsbury's Strawberry & Cream Ice Cream	22.6	5.6	4.6	0.12	163
Kelly's Salted Caramel Ice Cream	22.6	11.7	7.7	0.44	228
Tesco Mississippi Mud Pie Ice Cream	22.7	8.5	5.9	0.3	216
Sainsbury's Mandarin Cheesecake	22.7	13.2	6.7	0.28	278
Morrisons Chocolate & Vanilla Milkshake Lollies	22.7	13.1	5.9	0.2	236
Waitrose Seriously Creamy Chocolate Cherry & Kirsch	22.8	13.2	8.3	0.08	228
Waitrose Almond & Milk Chocolate Ice Creams	22.9	17.9	11.9	0.1	281
Sainsbury's Cherry & Amaretto Ice Cream, Taste the Difference	22.9	10.7	7.1	0.1	205
Cadbury Marvellous Ice Cream Jelly Popping Candy	22.9	10.3	6.9	0.09	217
Wall's Cream Of Cornish Vanilla Ice Cream	23	7	4.5	0.18	180
Tesco Soft Scoop Raspberry Ripple Ice Cream	23	5.1	3	0.1	162
Snog Frozen Yogurt Strawberry & Raspberry	23	5.6	4.9	0.13	171
Snog Frozen Yogurt Passionfruit	23	5.6	4.9	0.13	172
Sainsbury's Sorbet Raspberry	23	0.5	0.1	0.08	105
Sainsbury's Salted Caramel Ice Cream, Taste the Difference	23	19	12	0.26	279
Carte D'or Ice Cream Vanilla	23	7	7	0.15	200
Ben & Jerry's Greek Blueberry Cheesecake	23	8.6	4.1	0.2	220
Ben & Jerry's Cookie Core Ice Cream Utter Peanut Butter Clutter	23	20	7.6	0.48	317
Asda Chosen by You Indulgent Moments Triple Choc Cookie Crumble	23	16	11	0.18	269

Ice Cream & Lollies

Product	Sugar	Fat	Sat	Salt	Cals
			per 100g / 100ml		
Sainsbury's Vanilla Ice Cream	23.1	7.2	5.5	0.1	181
Sainsbury's New York Cheesecake, Taste the Difference	23.1	24.6	14.5	0.5	379
Yoomoo Frozen Yogurt Strawberry	23.3	1.3	0.7	0.1	143
Tesco Cookies And Cream Ice Cream Roll	23.3	6.2	3.4	0.4	222
Morrisons Luxury Double Chocolate Stick	23.4	16.7	10.6	trace	277
Asda Smart Price Vanilla Cones	23.5	12.6	9.3	0.2	269
Tesco Finest Caffe Latte Ice Cream	23.6	19.1	12.2	0.1	280
Sainsbury's Toffee Swirl Cheesecake, Basics	23.7	15.6	5.1	0.3	318
Sainsbury's Chocolate Brownie Ice Cream	23.7	8.6	5.3	0.15	223
Tesco Chocolate Brownie Ice Cream	23.8	10.8	7.5	0.2	241
Sainsbury's Eton Mess, Taste the Difference	23.8	17.5	11.6	0.1	274
Tesco Dark Chocolate Ices	23.9	19.9	17.1	0.2	305
Swedish Glace Dairy Free Vanilla Dessert	24	11	6	0.25	208
Carte D'or Ice Cream Dessert Praline	24	11	8.3	0.15	225
Ben & Jerry's Ice Cream Peanut Butter Cup	24	21	12	0.43	320
Ben & Jerry's Core Ice Cream All Or Nut-ting	24	17	10	0.16	280
Asda Smart Price Choc Ices	24	19.9	17.4	0.3	297
Asda Chosen by You Indulgent Moments Peanut Butter & Salt Caramel	24	19	11	0.28	295
Tesco Soft Scoop Chocolate	24.2	6.3	4.1	0.1	170
Morrisons Cookie Dough Demolition Ice Cream	24.4	12	8.8	0.3	263
Tesco Soft Scoop Mint Chocolate Chip	24.5	8.3	4.9	0.1	196
Tesco Mini Stick Ice Cream	24.5	31.1	19.9	0.2	401
Sainsbury's Mint Choc Chip Ice Cream	24.7	7.6	6.1	0.13	182
Waitrose Seriously Stem Ginger Ice Cream	24.8	15.3	9.3	0.08	252
Tesco Mango Sorbet	24.9	0.5	0.3	0.1	108
Green & Black's Organic Chocolate Ice Cream	24.9	14.1	8.7	0.13	250
Carte D'or Ice Cream Gelateria Caffe Latte	25	9	7	0.13	210
Ben & Jerry's Ice Cream Cookie Dough	25	15	9	0.17	270
Ben & Jerry's Ice Cream Caramel Chew Chew	25	15	10	0.19	270
Ben & Jerry's Cookie Core Ice Cream What-a-lotta Chocolate	25	18	9.3	0.23	300

Ice Cream & Lollies

Product	Sugar	Fat	Sat	Salt	Cals
			per 100g / 100ml		
Tesco Raspberry Ripple Screwball	25.1	8	4.3	0.1	185
Tesco Triple Chocolate Ice Cream	25.2	7.7	5	0.2	205
Weight Watchers Double Chocolate Brownies	25.5	3.8	2.6	0.3	194
Waitrose Seriously Intense Strawberry Italian Gelato	25.5	4.1	2.5	0.1	158
Waitrose 4 Scottish Raspberry Lollies	25.6	0.2	0.1	0.05	112
Tesco Mint Chocolate Ice Cream	25.6	9.4	6.3	0.1	239
Morrisons Luxury Caramel & Hazelnut Stick	25.6	18.6	10	0.2	292
Sainsbury's Farmhouse Toffee Ice Cream, Taste the Difference	25.8	18.6	12.3	0.4	295
Sainsbury's Double Chocolate Gateau	25.8	9.9	5.9	0.33	256
Tesco Finest Sicilian Mandarin Sorbetto	25.9	0.3	0	0.1	112
Tesco Cherry Vanilla Ice Cream	25.9	6.7	4.6	0.1	210
Weight Watchers Mini Pot Swirls Choc Honeycomb & Toffee Fudge	26	2.7	1.1	0.1	163
Carte D'or Ice Cream Strawberry	26	8	7	0.16	200
Carte D'or Ice Cream Gelateria Mascarpone	26	9	8	0.11	210
Carte D'or Ice Cream Gelateria Chocolate Inspiration	26	9	7	0.14	210
Ben & Jerry's Core Ice Cream Karamel Sutra	26	14	10	0.11	260
Ben & Jerry's Core Ice Cream Blondie Brownie	26	14	9	0.16	260
Asda Chosen by You Bourbon 6 Ice Creams	26	12	7.9	0.19	302
Sainsbury's Sorbet Lemon	26.1	0.5	0.1	0.08	122
Morrisons Nutty Chocolate Ice Cream Cones	26.3	13.7	11.9	0.1	291
Weight Watchers Caramel Crunch	26.4	2.9	1.8	0.3	199
Tesco Everyday Value Chocolate Ices	26.4	17.3	14.5	0.3	276
Morrisons Lemon Sorbet	26.4	trace	0	trace	125
Tesco Peanut Caramel Ice Cream	26.5	12.3	8.2	0.2	236
Sainsbury's Blackcurrant Cheesecake	26.5	12.8	6.5	0.14	286
Tesco Belgian Milk Chocolate Ice Creams	26.6	21.2	13.7	0.2	342
Morrisons Mint Choc Ice Cream Cones	26.7	13.9	12	0.1	293
Carte D'or Ice Cream Gelateria Eton Mess	27	6	5	0.11	180
Ben & Jerry's Ice Cream Chocolate Fudge Brownie	27	12	8	0.23	260
Asda Chosen by You Custard Cream Ice Cream	27	13	7.8	0.22	324

Ice Cream & Lollies

Product	Sugar	Fat	Sat	Salt	Cals
	per 100g / 100ml				
Asda Chosen by You Bubblegum Bursts	27	8.8	5.6	0.18	215
Tesco Vanilla Caramel Ice Cream	27.1	8.3	5.6	0.2	223
Sainsbury's Ice Cream Roll	27.2	4.9	2.8	0.25	212
Kelly's Clotted Cream & Honeycomb Ice Cream	27.6	9.9	6.3	0.2	217
Tesco Chocolatino Almond	27.9	27.6	17.1	0.2	391
Carte D'or Ice Cream Gelateria Salted Caramel	28	9	7	0.32	210
Ben & Jerry's Ice Cream Phish Food	28	12	8	0.17	270
Morrisons Toffee Ice Cream Cones	28	11.9	10.2	0.2	286
Tesco Limited Edition Pigs In Mud Ice Cream	28.3	9.3	7.5	0.1	232
Tesco Finest Sicilian Lemon Curd Ice Cream	28.3	15.7	10.3	0.2	270
Tesco Caramel Vanilla Ice Cream	28.5	7.7	4.8	0.1	228
Morrisons Strawberry Ice Cream Cones	28.6	9.8	8.5	0.1	254
Morrisons Milk Chocolate & Almond Chockas	28.7	22.5	14.5	0.2	342
Tesco Belgian Chocolate And Mint Ice Cream	29	22.8	14.9	0.2	348
Asda Chosen by You Mini Vanilla Cones	29.1	21.9	17.8	0.2	378
Morrisons Milk Chockas	29.3	19.4	14.5	0.2	316
Weight Watchers Toffee & Honeycomb Sundae	29.7	2	0.8	0.2	162
Morrisons White Chockas	29.7	19.2	14.5	0.2	313
Sainsbury's Sorbet Mango	30	0.5	0.1	0.03	133
Morrisons Mini Belgian Chocolate-Coated Vanilla Ice Creams	30.1	21	15.4	0.2	334
Morrisons Milk Choc Ices	30.3	22.1	19.2	0.2	340
Sainsbury's Lemon Tart	30.6	10.3	3.6	0.2	292
Sainsbury's Chocolate Cheesecake	30.9	19.5	10.6	0.33	370
Tesco Cookies And Cream Ice Cream	31	8.8	8	0.2	225
Tesco Raspberry And Strawberry Mini Ice Cream	31.3	24.4	15.6	0.1	375
Sainsbury's Millionaires Cheesecake	33.1	19.1	10.4	0.33	375
Tesco Caramella	33.5	22.2	14.7	0.3	354
Sainsbury's Lemon Meringue Pie	33.6	8.3	4.2	0.25	284
Tesco 6 Mini Caramel Dairy Ice Creams	34	24.5	16.1	0.2	381
Sainsbury's Raspberry Pavlova	34.6	14.6	9.3	0.1	289

Ice Cream & Lollies

Product	Sugar	Fat	Sat	Salt	Cals
		per 100g / 100ml			
Carte D'or Ice Cream Classic Caramel	35	7.4	6.6	0.13	230
Sainsbury's Berry Meringue Roulade, Taste the Difference	43.1	9.3	5.9	0.1	293
Sainsbury's Lemon & Mascarpone Roulade, Taste the Difference	44.2	9.9	6.6	0.15	322
Sainsbury's Toffee & Pecan Roulade, Taste the Difference	46.4	17.4	10.3	0.18	391
Coconut Co Snowconut Fro Yo Chocolate	71.2	10	8.3	0.5	734

Jams, Honey & Spreads

Jams, marmalades and chocolate spreads contain high amounts of sugar and some contain other artificial sweeteners. Make sure you check the label to be sure. The nut butters listed are a fantastic addition to your food cupboard. Some are over 5g but naturally good sugar, so don't be put off.

To help you make the best choices, products are listed starting with the least sugar first.

Product	Sugar	Fat	Sat per 100g	Salt	Cals
Tesco Yeast Extract	0.4	0.1	0.1	6.8	229
Marmite Yeast Extract	1.1	0.1	0	9.75	252
Sainsbury's Yeast Extract Reduced Salt	1.9	<.5	<.1	6.5	246
Tesco Smooth Peanut Butter	1.9	58.8	11.3	1	672
Morrisons Yeast Extract	2.2	0.9	0.3	10	235
Tesco Crunchy Peanut Butter	2.3	57.8	10.8	0.7	663
Stute No Added Sugar Diabetic Strawberry Jam	2.4	0.2	<.1	0.02	154
Stute No Added Sugar Diabetic Fine Cut Marmalade	2.5	<.2	<.1	0.02	153
Waitrose Essential Wholenut Peanut Butter	3.1	46.2	7.1	1.08	599
Tesco Wholenut Peanut Butter	3.2	51.7	8.3	0.6	626
Sainsbury's Basics, Crunchy Peanut Butter	3.3	58.8	10.5	0.75	672
Waitrose Smooth & Spreadable Peanut Butter	3.3	51.6	11.8	0.95	636
Sun Pat Peanut Butter Smooth No Added Sugar	3.4	49.4	9.7	1.2	614
Sun Pat Peanut Butter Crunchy No Added Sugar	3.5	49.1	9.2	0.9	613
Waitrose Essential Crunchy Peanut Butter	3.6	46	6.8	1.10	603
Tesco Everyday Value Crunchy Peanut Butter	3.6	59.9	10.8	0.7	678
Sainsbury's Peanut Butter Crunchy	3.8	55.5	9.4	0.43	650
Whole Earth Peanut Butter Crunchy	3.8	54.3	7.9	1.1	643
Asda Chosen by You Smooth Peanut Butter	4	55	10.2	0.7	655
Meridian Almond Butter	4	55.5	4.4	0.5	650
Sainsbury's SO Organic Peanut Butter Crunchy	4	51	11.5	0.81	619
Waitrose Thick & Crunchy Peanut Butter	4	51	11.5	0.81	619
Asda Chosen by You Crunchy Peanut Butter	4.1	55	10.2	0.7	642
Sainsbury's SO Organic Peanut Butter Smooth	4.1	51.6	10.7	0.78	631

Jams, Honey & Spreads

Product	Sugar	Fat	Sat	Salt	Cals
			per 100g		
Whole Earth Peanut Butter Smooth	4.2	54.5	7.2	1	645
Sun Pat Peanut Butter Rich Roasted Crunchy	4.5	50.8	9.4	0.9	621
Morrisons Reduced Fat Smooth Peanut Butter	4.6	33.7	4.7	0.4	546
Sun Pat Peanut Butter Crunchy	4.8	48.2	8.7	1	609
Sun Pat Peanut Spread Crunchy	4.8	48.2	8.7	1	609
Sun Pat Peanut Butter Smooth	5.1	48.2	9.1	1.2	608
Sun Pat Smooth Peanut Butter	5.1	48.2	9.1	1.2	608
Waitrose Essential Smooth Peanut Butter	5.1	47.1	7.5	1.13	609
Morrisons Crunchy Peanut Butter	5.2	49.5	8.9	0.9	617
Morrisons Smooth Peanut Butter	5.5	49.8	9.3	1.1	618
Meridian Cashew Nut Butter	5.6	51.2	10.2	0	628
Meridian Crunchy Peanut Butter	5.9	46	8.2	0	596
Meridian Smooth Peanut Butter	5.9	46	8.2	0	596
Asda Smart Price Crunchy Peanut Butter	6	55.1	9.5	0.6	648
Asda Chosen by You Reduced Fat Smooth Peanut Butter	7.5	44.3	7.7	0.5	600
Sainsbury's Peanut Butter Smooth	7.7	50.7	5.3	0.68	622
Tesco Honey Roast Crunchy Peanut Butter	8.4	53.7	9.5	0.8	643
Whole Earth 3 Nut Butter	8.6	53.1	8.6	1.7	598
Tesco Reduced Fat Peanut Butter	8.8	37.9	7.2	0.4	570
Skippy Peanut Butter Crunchy	9.4	52.2	10	0.38	631
Skippy Peanut Butter Smooth	10.9	51.6	10	0.45	631
Morrisons Honey Roast Crunchy Peanut Butter	11.1	47	8.5	0.4	607
Asda Chosen by You Peanut Butter with Chocolate Chunks	15	48.1	10.7	0.6	618
Asda Extra Special Berry & Elderflower Coulis	22	0.5	0.2	0.03	127
Asda Good for You Reduced Sugar Orange Marmalade	24.5	0.1	0.1	0.1	113
Tesco Finest 30% Dark Chocolate Spread	28.9	44.4	7.1	0.1	588
Asda Chosen by You Reduced Sugar Strawberry Jam	29.4	0.2	0.1	0.1	130
Asda Good For You Reduced Sugar Raspberry Jam	30	0.1	0.1	0.2	133
Morrisons Reduced Sugar Fine Cut Orange Marmalade	33.2	0.5	0.4	0.1	169
Tesco Custard Cream Spread	34	40	9.8	0.4	591

Product	Sugar	Fat	Sat	Salt	Cals
			per 100g		
Sainsbury's Reduced Sugar Apricot Jam	34.5	<5	0.4	0.15	178
Tesco Chocolate Chip Cookie Spread	35	38	11	0.2	571
Tesco Reduced Sugar Raspberry Jam	35.5	0.2	0.1	0.1	169
Tesco Bourbon Biscuit Spread	37	40	9.6	0.1	592
Tesco Reduced Sugar Blackcurrant Jam	37.1	0.1	0.1	0.1	178
Hartley's Reduced Sugar Strawberry Jam	37.7	0.2	0.1	0.15	184
Asda Chosen by You Chocolate Spread with Crunchy Bites	37.8	31.9	7	0.2	545
Hartley's Reduced Sugar Blackcurrant Jam	37.9	0.1	0	0.3	181
Hartley's Reduced Sugar Raspberry Jam	38.1	0.2	0.1	0.23	184
Tesco Finest Smooth Almond Chocolate Spread	38.3	43.1	7.2	0.5	593
Hartley's Reducd Sugar Apricot Jam	38.6	0.1	0	0.12	181
Tesco Reduced Sugar Apricot Jam	38.6	0.1	0.1	0.1	178
Tesco Reduced Sugar Orange Marmalade	38.9	0.1	0.1	0.1	181
Sainsbury's Reduced Sugar Fine Cut Orange Marmalade	39.5	<5	0.2	0.13	181
Streamline Reduced Sugar Raspberry Seedless Jam	39.5	0.7	0.1	0	180
Sainsbury's Reduced Sugar Strawberry Jam	40	<5	0.3	0.15	182
Streamline Reduced Sugar Thick Cut Orange Marmalade	40	0.2	0	8	170
Waitrose Reduced Sugar Cherries & Berries Jam	40.2	0.5	0.3	0.14	188
Fruit Shoot Strawberry & Summer Fruit Squeezy Jam	40.4	0.3	0.1	0	177
Sainsbury's Reduced Sugar Thick Cut Orange Marmalade	40.4	<5	0.1	0.13	180
Streamline Reduced Sugar Blackcurrant Jam	40.4	0.7	0.1	0	185
Fruit Shoot Apple & Blackcurrant Squeezy Jam	40.9	0.3	0.1	0	176
Streamline Reduced Sugar Strawberry Jam	40.9	0.3	0	0	176
Fruit Shoot Orange Squeezy Jam	41.1	0.3	0.1	0	174
Waitrose Reduced Sugar Blackcurrant Jam	41.3	0.6	0.4	0.42	190
Streamline Reduced Sugar Thin Cut Marmalade	41.4	0.2	0.1	0	174
Waitrose Reduced Sugar Orange Marmalade	41.5	0.4	0.3	0.14	185
Streamline Reduced Sugar Black Cherry Jam	41.6	0.2	0	0	172
Waitrose Reduced Sugar Raspberries Jam	41.7	0.5	0.2	0.16	191
Waitrose Reduced Sugar Strawberry Jam	41.8	0.4	0.3	0.12	186

Jams, Honey & Spreads

Product	Sugar	Fat	Sat per 100g	Salt	Cals
Tesco Reduced Sugar Strawberry Jam	41.8	0.2	0.1	0.1	184
Waitrose Seriously Chocolatey Chocolate Spread	42	15.6	9.7	0.04	373
Morrisons Seedless Raspberry Jam	42.1	0.5	0.2	0.2	245
Waitrose Stem Ginger Preserve	42.2	0.6	0.5	0.10	258
Asda Chosen by You Bourbon Biscuit Spread	43.4	33.1	10.2	0.1	545
Waitrose Greengage Conserve	43.9	0.4	0.2	0.15	243
Frank Cooper's Oxford Red Cherry Conserve	44	0.3	0.2	0.2	256
Sainsbury's Taste the Difference Morello Cherry Conserve	44.1	<.5	0.2	0.18	256
Sainsbury's Raspberry Jam Seedless	44.8	0.1	trace	0.13	248
Waitrose Essential Seedless Raspberry Jam	45.5	0.3	0.1	0.12	262
Sainsbury's Basics Lemon Curd	46	5.3	2.4	trace	234
Waitrose Essential Blackcurrant Jam	46.1	0.5	0.2	0.20	261
Asda Chosen by You Chocolate & Caramel Spread	46.2	32.1	7.3	0.1	556
Waitrose Blackcurrant Conserve	46.8	0.6	0.2	0.13	238
Waitrose Essential Strawberry Jam	46.8	0.3	0.1	0.21	263
Waitrose Essential Apricot Jam	46.9	0.3	0.1	0.06	259
Sainsbury's Raspberry Jam	47	0.1	0.1	0.1	248
Morrisons Raspberry Jam	47.1	0.6	0.3	0.2	248
Sainsbury's Orange Curd	47.3	4.4	1.7	0.15	282
Asda Chosen by You Duo Chocolate Spread	47.4	33.7	7.1	0.2	560
Tesco Cookies And Cream Spread	48	38	9.8	0.5	573
Morrisons Thick Cut Orange Marmalade	48.1	0.3	0.2	0.2	268
Sainsbury's Blackcurrant Jam	48.1	0.3	trace	0.07	249
Sainsbury's Strawberry Jam	48.5	0.1	trace	0.1	254
Sainsbury's Basics Strawberry Jam	48.6	trace	trace	trace	246
Morrisons Blackcurrant Jam	48.7	0.7	0.4	0.2	255
Tesco Thick Cut Orange Marmalade	48.7	0.5	0.3	0.1	252
Waitrose Apricot Conserve	48.7	0.5	0.2	0.13	234
Tesco Finest Crunchy Hazelnut Choco Spread	48.7	40.2	5.4	0.1	588
Tesco Thick Cut Orange Marmalade	48.7	0.5	0.3	0.1	252

Jams, Honey & Spreads

Product	Sugar	Fat	Sat per 100g	Salt	Cals
Marshmallow Fluff	49	0.3	0	0.1	330
Morrisons Apricot Jam	49.3	0.2	0.1	trace	256
Waitrose Strawberry Conserve	49.5	0.3	0.1	0.13	239
Morrisons Strawberry Jam	49.9	0.5	0.3	0.1	259
Waitrose Black Cherry Conserve	49.9	0.4	0.2	0.13	248
Asda Chosen by You Jaffa Cake Flavour Spread	50	37	9.5	0.25	576
Sainsbury's Plum Jam	50	<.5	0.2	0.08	252
Waitrose Duchy Sicilian Lemon Curd	50	18.5	11.2	0.12	385
Waitrose Essential Raspberry Jam	50.1	0.5	0.3	0.15	261
Morrisons Hazelnut Chocolate Spread	50.9	38.2	8.9	0.2	573
Asda Smart Price Orange Marmalade	51.1	0	0	0.2	257
Waitrose Raspberry Conserve	51.1	0.6	0.3	0.13	247
Sainsbury's Lemon Curd	51.3	4.8	1.8	0.15	254
Hartley's Family Raspberry Jam Seedless	51.4	0.1	0	0.2	259
Duerr's Seveille Orange Marmalade Fine Cut	51.5	<.1	0	<.1	256
Sainsbury's Basics, Marmalade Medium Cut	51.5	trace	trace	trace	254
Tesco Blackcurrant Jam	51.6	0.1	0.1	0.1	239
Tesco Everyday Value Lemon Curd	51.7	5.7	2.7	0.2	296
Sainsbury's Apricot Jam	51.8	trace	trace	trace	246
Waitrose Seriously Zesty Lemon Curd	51.8	6.2	4	0.41	322
Asda Chosen by You Milk Chocolate Spread	51.9	35.3	8.1	0.2	565
Waitrose Red Plum Conserve	51.9	0.3	0.1	0.13	251
Asda Chosen by You Lemon Curd	52	5	1.9	0.28	310
Asda Smart Price Chocolate Hazelnut Spread	52	36.3	8.5	0.1	571
Frank Cooper's Oxford Red Plum Conserve	52	0.3	0.1	0.13	243
Hartley's Family Apricot Jam	52	0	0	trace	257
St Dalfour Apricot Fruit Spread	52	<.8	<.01	0.05	220
St Dalfour Black Cherry Fruit Spread	52	<.1	<.1	trace	212
St Dalfour Orange Thick Cut Fruit Spread	52	<.8	<.01	0.03	221
St Dalfour Strawberry Fruit Spread	52	<.8	<.01	0.03	219

Jams, Honey & Spreads

Product	Sugar	Fat	Sat	Salt	Cals
			per 100g		
St Dalfour Wild Blueberry Fruit Spread	52	<.8	<.1	0.03	220
Tesco Plum Jam	52.3	0.1	0.1	0.1	239
Asda Chosen by You Blackcurrant Jam	52.4	0	0	0.2	248
Sainsbury's Taste the Difference Red Plum Conserve	52.4	<.5	0.1	0.13	243
Sainsbury's Hazelnut Chocolate Spread	52.5	34.5	7	0.13	555
Roses Lemon & Lime Marmalade	52.8	0	0	0.24	261
Sainsbury's Lime Curd	52.8	4.6	1.7	0.25	296
Tesco Lemon And Lime Marmalade	52.8	0.1	0.1	0.3	261
Morrisons Lemon Curd	52.9	5.2	1.9	0.2	313
Tesco Everyday Value Mixed Fruit Jam	52.9	0.5	0.5	trace	250
Asda Chosen by You Raspberry Seedless Jam	53	0.5	0.1	0.08	261
Cadbury Chocolate Spread	53	38	8.7	0.1	573
Robertsons Golden Shred Marmalade	53	0	0	0.2	253
Waitrose Rhubarb & Ginger Preserve	53	0.1	0.1	0.10	241
Tesco Hazlenut Chocolate Spread	53	34	6.9	0.1	551
Asda Chosen by You Raspberry Jam	53.1	0.1	0	0.1	258
Hartley's Best Strawberry Jam	53.1	0.2	0.1	0.06	247
Waitrose Essential Thick Cut Seville Orange Marmalade	53.1	0.3	0.2	0.15	268
Tesco Bramble Jelly	53.2	0.1	0.1	0.1	244
Tesco Raspberry Jam	53.2	0.1	0.1	0.1	245
Waitrose Morello Cherry Conserve	53.3	0.5	0.3	0.13	248
Frank Cooper's Vintage Oxford Marmalade	53.5	0.2	0.1	0.13	253
Robertsons Golden Marmalade Shreddless	53.5	0	0	0.2	254
Robertsons Golden Shredless Marmalade	53.5	0	0	0.2	254
Sainsbury's Duo Chocolate Swirl Spread	53.5	36.5	9	0.18	570
Tesco Lemon Curd	53.5	4.9	1.8	0.3	294
Robertsons Silver Shred Marmalade	53.6	0	0	0.1	253
Tesco Apricot Jam	53.6	0.1	0.1	0.1	245
Frank Cooper's Original Oxford Marmalade	53.7	trace	trace	0.2	254
Asda Chosen by You Hazelnut Chocolate Spread	53.8	36.1	6.9	0.1	567

Jams, Honey & Spreads

Product	Sugar	Fat	Sat	Salt	Cals
			per 100g		
Roses Lime Marmalade	53.8	0	0	0.31	265
Tesco Everyday Value Strawberry Jam	53.8	0.1	trace	trace	250
Hartley's Best Black Cherry Jam	54.1	0.2	0	0.16	245
Duerr's Seville Orange Marmalade Thick Cut	54.3	<.1	0	<1	256
Hartley's Best Blackberry Jam	54.3	0.1	0	0.16	250
Sainsbury's Milk Chocolate Spread	54.3	37	8.6	0.15	571
Hartley's Best Pineapple Jam	54.5	0.1	0	0.09	246
Asda Extra Special Lemon Curd	54.6	8.6	5.5	0.2	343
Waitrose Essential no Peel Seville Orange Marmalade	54.6	0.3	0.2	0.09	281
Sainsbury's Strawberry Conserve, SO Organic	55	<.5	0.1	0.05	243
Tesco Everyday Value Chocolate Spread	55	36	8.3	0.1	563
Tesco Seedless Raspberry Jam	55	0.1	0.1	0.1	252
Hartley's Best Blackcurrant Jam	55.1	0	0	0.34	246
Asda Chosen by You Strawberry Jam	55.2	0	0	0.1	254
Hartley's Best Apricot Jam	55.3	0	0	0.08	244
Sainsbury's Taste the Differece Blackcurrant Preserve	55.3	1	0.5	0.3	255
Morrisons Chocolate Orange Spread	55.6	37.9	9.1	0.1	578
Sainsbury's Orange Marmalade Thick Cut	55.6	0.6	<.1	0.13	261
Morrisons Chocolate Spread	55.7	38	9.1	0.1	580
Tesco Finest Salted Caramel And Chocolate Spread	55.7	38	6.6	0.2	580
Milky Way Chocolate Spread	55.9	35.1	8.3	0.18	559
Tesco Finest Lime Curd	55.9	9.9	6.6	0.3	345
Sainsbury's Taste the Difference Apricot Preserve	56	<.5	<.1	<.01	239
St Dalfour Raspberry & Pomegranate Spread	56	<.8	<.01	0.02	237
St Dalfour Raspberry Fruit Spread	56	0.8	<.01	0.02	237
Asda Extra Special Blackcurrant Conserve	56.3	0.1	0.1	0.1	239
Waitrose Fresh Fruit Orange Marmalade	56.3	trace	trace	0.23	244
Morrisons Lime Marmalade	56.5	0.5	0.3	0.2	273
Sainsbury's Chocolate & Caramel Spread	56.5	37.5	9.5	0.14	580
Sainsbury's Popping Candy Chocolate Spread	56.5	35.2	8.2	0.14	562

Jams, Honey & Spreads

Product	Sugar	Fat	Sat	Salt	Cals
			per 100g		
Waitrose Orange & Ginger Marmalade	56.7	0.3	0.1	0.06	272
Nutella Chocolate Spread	56.8	31.6	11	0.11	546
Waitrose Essential Fine Cut Seville Orange Marmalade	56.8	0.3	0.2	0.11	273
Tesco Everyday Value Orange Marmalade	56.8	0.1	trace	trace	260
Tesco Shredless Orange Marmalade	56.8	0.1	0.1	0.1	276
Frank Cooper's Fine Cut Marmalade	56.9	trace	trace	0.1	254
Asda Chosen by You Shredless Marmalade	57	0.5	0.1	0.15	254
Asda Extra Special Plum Conserve	57	0.5	0.1	trace	242
Asda Ginger Preserve	57	0.5	0.4	0.40	262
Galaxy Hazelnut Spread	57	34.1	7.5	0.13	553
Tesco Chocolate Caramel Swirl Spread	57	38	9.5	1	583
Tesco White Chocolate Spread	57	37	9.9	0.2	575
Frank Cooper's Raspberry Conserve	57.1	0.1	0.1	0.2	240
Asda Chosen by You Apricot Jam	57.3	0	0	0.1	254
Sainsbury's Taste the Differenec Raspberry Conserve	57.4	0.9	0.5	0.2	254
Roses Orange Fine Cut Marmalade	57.8	0	0	0.16	253
Sainsbury's Taste the Difference Lemon Curd	57.8	10	5.8	0.25	362
Sainsbury's Taste the Difference Strawberry Conserve	57.8	0.6	0.3	0.13	252
Tesco Finest Scandinavian Blackcurrant Conserve	57.8	0.1	0.1	0.1	251
Tesco Strawberry Jam	57.8	0.1	0.1	0.1	259
Asda Chosen by You Thick Cut Marmalade	57.9	0	0	0.1	254
Hartley's Strawberry Jam, No Bits	57.9	0.1	0	0.2	259
Frank Cooper's Strawberry Conserve	58	0.6	0.3	0.13	252
Nature's Store Hazelnut & Chocolate Spread	58	31	11	0.013	539
Asda Extra Special Strawberry Conserve	58.1	0.2	0.1	0.1	239
Asda Extra Special Raspberry Conserve	58.5	0.2	0.1	0.1	248
Asda Chosen by You Fine Cut Lime Marmalade	58.7	0	0	0.3	253
Sainsbury's Thick Cut Orange & Ginger Marmalade	58.7	<.5	<.1	0.13	262
Tesco Finest Raspberry Conserve	58.7	0.2	0.1	0.1	252
Tesco Finest Orange Curd	58.8	9	5.9	0.3	348

Jams, Honey & Spreads

Product	Sugar	Fat	Sat	Salt	Cals
			per 100g		
Asda Extra Special Cherry Conserve	58.9	0.3	0.1	0.1	245
Tesco Finest Hedgerow Conserve	58.9	0.1	0.1	0.1	244
Morrisons Duo Chocolate Spread	59	35.8	9.5	0.1	570
Robertsons Ginger Preserve	59	0	0	0.1	266
St Dalfour Orange & Ginger Spread	59	<.1	<.1	trace	239
Tesco Chocolate And Orange Spread	59	35	7.5	0.1	563
Tesco Chocolate Duo Spread	59	36	9.5	0.1	573
Tesco Chocolate Spread	59	35	7.5	0.1	563
Tesco Raspberry Squeezy Jam	59	0.4	0.4	0.2	252
Waitrose 3 Fruits Fresh Fruit Marmalade	59.1	0.4	trace	0.38	253
Morrisons Savers Chocolate Hazelnut Spread	59.3	37.1	8.9	trace	579
Tesco Finest Apricot Conserve	59.3	0.1	0.1	0.1	246
Tesco Finest Greengage Conserve	59.3	0.3	0.1	0.1	251
Sainsbury's Taste the Difference Breakfast Marmalade	59.4	<.5	<.1	0.13	285
Tesco Finest Morello Cherry Conserve	59.5	0.1	0.1	0.1	243
Tesco Ginger Preserve	59.8	0.1	0.1	0.1	259
Asda Chosen by You White Chocolate Flavour Spread	59.9	36	9	0.2	578
Asda Chosen by You Fine Cut Marmalade	60	0.5	0.1	0.10	262
Bonne Maman Fig Conserve	60	0	0	0	250
Morrisons Blackberry Jam	60	0.4	0.3	0.1	276
Waitrose Lemon Fresh Fruit Marmalade	60	0.3	trace	0.30	256
Tesco Finest Lemon Curd	60	9.2	5.9	0.3	335
Tesco Finest Strawberry Conserve	60.1	0.2	0.1	0.1	253
Tesco Shredless Lemon Marmalade	60.1	0.1	0.1	0.1	272
Sainsbury's Orange Marmalade Fine Cut	60.3	<.5	<.1	0.13	264
Sainsbury's SO Organic Medium Cut Marmalade	60.4	<.5	<.1	0.13	270
Morrisons Shredless Orange Marmalade	60.7	0.2	0.1	0.1	270
Sainsbury's Bramble Jelly	60.8	0.1	0.1	0.05	266
Waitrose Luxury Jaffa Orange Curd	60.8	10.1	6	0.26	357
Waitrose Luxury Lemon Curd	60.8	10.6	6.3	0.25	355

Jams, Honey & Spreads

Product	Sugar	Fat	Sat	Salt	Cals
			per 100g		
Waitrose Gooseberry Preserve	61	0.1	0.1	0.10	249
Morrisons Fine Cut Orange Marmalade	61.1	0.5	0.4	0.1	288
Waitrose Seville Orange Fresh Fruit Marmalade	61.4	0.2	trace	0.10	267
Hartley's Smooth Apricot Jam	61.6	0	0	0.03	249
Tesco Strawberry Squeezy Jam	61.6	0.3	0.2	0.1	260
Tesco Fine Cut Orange Marmalade	61.7	0.1	0.1	0.1	259
Sainsbury's Taste the Difference Fresh Fruit Three Fruits Marmalade	63	0.2	trace	0.23	269
Waitrose Ruby Grapefruit Fresh Fruit Marmalade	63	trace	trace	0.20	259
Asda Chosen by You Bramble Jelly	63.3	0.1	0	trace	269
Tesco Finest Three Fruit Marmalade	63.6	0.2	0.1	0.2	261
Tesco Finest Bitter Orange Marmalade	63.7	0.1	0.1	0.1	258
Tesco Finest Seville Dark Orange Marmalade	63.7	0.1	0.1	0.1	258
Sainsbury's Taste the Difference Fresh Fruit Bitter Orange Marmalade	64.5	0.2	trace	0.2	273
Sainsbury's Orange Marmalade Medium Cut	64.7	<.5	<.1	0.13	271
Bonne Maman Apricot & Raspberry Conserve	65	0	0	0	250
Bonne Maman Apricot Conserve	65	0	0	0	250
Bonne Maman Berries Cherries Jelly	65	0	0	0	250
Bonne Maman Mixed Berries Conserve	65	0	0	0	250
Bonne Maman Raspberry Conserve	65	0	0	0	250
Bonne Maman Wild Blueberry Conserve	65	0	0	0	250
Waitrose Duchy Originals Organic Strawberry Preserve	65.1	0.1	0	0.03	268
Waitrose Duchy Originals Organic Raspberry Preserve	65.2	0.4	0.1	trace	273
Waitrose Duchy Originals Organic Thick Cut Seville Orange Marmalade	65.3	0.3	0.1	0.03	277
Waitrose Duchy Originals Organic Thin Cut Seville Orange Marmalade	65.4	0.5	0.1	trace	274
Asda Chosen by You Pure Canadian Maple Syrup	65.6	0.4	0.1	0.1	280
Waitrose Duchy Originals Organic Blackcurrant Preserve	66.2	0.2	0	trace	275
Mackays Rhubarb & Ginger Preserve	66.3	0	0	0	269
Mackays Scottish Raspberry Preserve	66.7	0	0	0	271
Mackays The Dundee Orange Marmalade	66.7	0	0	0	269
Mackays Three Fruit Marmalade	66.7	0	0	0	270

Jams, Honey & Spreads

Product	Sugar	Fat	Sat	Salt	Cals
			per 100g		
Mackays Vintage Orange Marmalade	66.7	0	0	0	269
Mackayx Natural Fruit Seville Orange Marmalade	66.7	0	0	0	269
Mackays Seedless Bramble Preserve	66.8	0	0	0	269
Mackays Scottish Strawberry Preserve	66.9	0	0	0	270
Mackays Scottish Three Berry Preserve	67.3	0	0	0	272
Sainsbury's Ginger Preserve	69.7	<.5	<.1	0.13	290
Morrisons Pure Set Honey	76.4	0	0	trace	307
Morrisons Savers Honey	76.4	0	0	trace	307
Morrisons Signature English Set Honey	76.4	0	0	trace	307
Morrisons Squeezy Acacia Honey	76.4	0	0	trace	307
Morrisons Squeezy Pure Honey	76.4	0	0	trace	307
Waitrose Acacia Honey	76.4	0	0	0.03	307
Waitrose Australian Blossom Honey	76.4	0	0	0.03	307
Waitrose English Country Honey	76.4	0	0	0.03	307
Waitrose Essential Pure Clear Coney	76.4	0	0	0.03	307
Waitrose Essential Pure Set Honey	76.4	0	0	0.03	307
Waitrose Orange Blossom Honey	76.4	0	0	0.03	307
Waitrose Pure Clear Honey	76.4	0	0	0.03	307
Waitrose Scottish Heather Honey	76.4	0	0	0.03	307
Rowse Greek Hill Honey	78.1	0.2	0.2	0.024	342
Asda Chosen by You Lemon Honey	78.4	0.3	0.2	trace	337
Rowse Acacia Honey	80.8	<.5	0.2	0.03	329
Rowse Clear Honey	80.8	<.5	0.2	0.03	329
Sainsbury's Basics, Honey	80.8	<.5	0.2	0.03	329
Sainsbury's Clear Honey, SO Organic	80.8	<.5	0.2	0.03	329
Sainsbury's Honey, Clear	80.8	<.5	0.2	0.03	329
Sainsbury's Honey, Set	80.8	<.5	0.2	0.03	329
Sainsbury's Manuka 15+ Honey	80.8	<.5	0.2	0.03	329
Sainsbury's Taste the Difference Acacia Honey	80.8	<.5	0.2	0.03	329
Sainsbury's Taste the Difference Australia Macadamia Honey	80.8	<.5	0.2	0.03	329

Jams, Honey & Spreads

Product	Sugar	Fat	Sat per 100g	Salt	Cals
Sainsbury's Taste the Difference New Zealand CLover Honey	80.8	<.5	0.2	0.03	329
Sainsbury's Taste the Difference Mexican Orange Blossom Honey	81	<.5	0.2	0.03	329
Sainsbury's Taste the Difference Spanish Forest Honey	81	<.5	0.2	0.03	329
Tesco Clear Honey	81	0.1	0.1	0.1	326
Tesco Everyday Value Clear Honey	81	0.1	0.1	0.1	326
Tesco Finest Acacia Honey	81	0.1	0	0.01	326
Tesco Finest Eucalyptus Honey	81	0.1	0	0.01	326
Tesco Finest Limited Edition Honey	81	0.1	0	0.01	326
Tesco Finest New Zealand Clover Honey	81	0.1	0	0.01	326
Tesco Finest Orange Blossom Honey	81	0.1	0	0.01	326
Tesco Organic Pure Set Honey	81	0.1	0.1	0.1	326
Tesco Organic Squeezy Clear Honey	81	0.1	0.1	0.1	326
Tesco Pure Set Honey	81	0.1	0.1	0.1	326
Tesco Squeezy Clear Honey	81	0.1	0	0.1	326
Asda Chosen by You Pure Clear Honey	82.1	0.4	0.2	trace	341
Asda Chosen by You Set Pure Honey	82.1	0.4	0.2	trace	341
Asda Chosen by You Squeezy Pure Acacia Honey	82.1	0.4	0.2	trace	341
Asda Chosen by You Squeezy Pure Clear Hone	82.1	0.4	0.2	trace	341
Asda Chosen by You Squeezy Pure Forest Honey	82.1	0.4	0.2	trace	341
Asda Extra Special English Set Honey	82.1	0.4	0.2	trace	341
Asda Extra Special Mexican Orange Blossom Honey	82.1	0.4	0.2	trace	341
Asda Smart Price Clear Honey	82.1	0.4	0.2	trace	341
Rowse Manuka 10+ Honey	85.9	0.1	<.1	<.1	348

Nuts, Seeds & Mixed Fruit

The plain nuts will only contain natural sugars, which are great for you.
Beware of the packets with dried fruit and especially those with honey or yogurt coatings!

To help you make the best choices, products are listed starting with the least sugar first.

Product	Sugar	Fat	Sat	Salt	Cals
			per 100g		
Waitrose Love Life Sesame Seeds	0.4	58	8.3	0.05	627
Waitrose Love Life Pumpkin Seeds	1.4	49.1	8.7	0.02	618
Waitrose Love Life Mixed Seeds	1.9	49.7	5.7	0.03	592
Waitrose Love Life Walnuts	2	66.4	5.4	0.03	702
Tesco Salt And Vinegar Jumbo Peanuts	2	50.3	8.9	1.9	616
Asda Good & Balanced Brazil Nuts	2.3	68.2	16.4	0	701
Waitrose Love Life Brazil Nuts	2.3	66.4	15.1	trace	689
Morrisons Brazils	2.4	68.2	16.4	trace	691
Waitrose Love Life Organic Brazil Nuts	2.4	66.4	15.1	0.01	689
Asda Good & Balanced Walnut Halves	2.5	69	5.6	0.10	708
Morrisons Wholefoods Walnut Halves	2.6	65.2	6.1	0.1	689
Tesco Sweet Chilli Coated Peanuts	2.8	33.6	8.2	3	533
Waitrose Essential Large Roasted & Salted Peanuts	3	54.6	8	0.91	631
Asda Good & Balanced Mixed Nuts	3.1	61.5	8.5	trace	665
Sainsbury's Bombay Mix	3.2	33.3	7.8	1.34	526
Sainsbury's Salted Almonds	3.3	56.2	6.6	0.8	644
Morrisons Wholefoods Mixed Nuts	3.4	63	8.2	trace	665
Waitrose Love Life Mixed Nuts	3.4	62.9	8	trace	669
Tesco Roasted And Salted Nut Assortment	3.5	57.9	6.2	0.5	653
Waitrose Love Life Organic Pine Kernels	3.6	68.4	4.9	trace	715
Tesco Wasabi Flavour Jumbo Peanuts	3.6	53.1	10.4	0.7	630
Sainsbury's Mixed Nuts	3.7	57.6	8.4	0.02	644
Morrisons Signature Chunky Mixed Nuts with Marcona Almonds	3.7	60.8	7.3	0.1	669
Waitrose Essential Salted Mixed Nuts	3.7	55.6	7.1	0.83	637

Nuts, Seeds & Mixed Fruit

Product	Sugar	Fat	Sat	Salt	Cals
			per 100g		
Waitrose Roasted Salted Pecan Nuts	3.7	72.7	6.3	0.55	733
Sainsbury's Salted Nut Selection	3.8	55.6	8.1	0.88	643
Waitrose Love Life Mixed Roasted Nuts	3.8	62.8	9.3	trace	673
Sainsbury's Unsalted Nut Selection	3.9	61	9	0.03	667
Morrisons Large Salted Peanuts	3.9	48.3	7.4	1	609
Morrisons Pine Nuts	3.9	68.6	4.6	0	693
Morrisons Salted Peanuts	3.9	53	9.5	1	615
Asda Chosen by You Roasted & Salted Almonds	3.9	54.2	4.5	1	631
Waitrose Love Life Organic Almonds	3.9	49.4	3.7	trace	592
Sainsbury's Roasted & Salted Peanuts	4	50.9	9.9	1	620
Morrisons Hazelnuts	4	63.5	4.7	trace	665
Asda Good & Balanced Almonds	4	56	4.7	0.10	645
Waitrose Love Life Pecans	4	72	6.2	trace	721
Waitrose Roasted Salted Almonds	4	58.4	4.9	0.83	649
Waitrose Love Life Hazelnuts	4	63.5	4.7	0.02	671
Waitrose Roasted Salted Macadamia Nuts	4	75.2	11.8	1.50	744
Morrisons Wholefoods Pecans	4.1	74.3	6.3	0	742
Waitrose Love Life Macadamia Nuts	4.1	76.1	12	0.01	754
Morrisons Wholefoods Almond Mix	4.2	55.8	4.4	trace	629
Morrisons Almonds	4.2	55.8	4.4	trace	629
Waitrose Essential Roasted Monkey Nuts	4.2	49.7	6.9	0.02	612
Waitrose Love Life Almonds	4.2	49.9	3.8	trace	595
Morrisons Smoked Almonds	4.3	52.9	4.6	0.7	633
Waitrose Love Life Organic Hazelnuts	4.3	60.8	4.5	0.02	655
Waitrose Roasted and Salted Mixed Nuts	4.3	61	6.3	0.63	667
Waitrose Roasted Salted Mixed Nut Selection	4.3	61	6.3	0.63	667
Blue Diamond Roasted Sea Salt Almonds	4.4	56	4.2	0.8	634
Blue Diamond Smokehouse Almonds	4.4	55	4.2	1.3	627
Sainsbury's Dry Roasted Peanuts	4.4	49.8	19.1	1.37	612
Waitrose Essential Large Dry Roasted Peanuts	4.4	47.2	9.3	1.34	599

Nuts, Seeds & Mixed Fruit

Product	Sugar	Fat	Sat	Salt	Cals
			per 100g		
Waitrose Love Life Roasted Peanuts	4.4	51.7	9.5	0.06	621
Blue Diamond Almond Krunchies Salt & Vinegar	4.5	36.6	2.9	2.69	548
Sainsbury's Jumbo Salted Peanuts & Cashews	4.5	50.4	9.9	1.01	620
Sainsbury's Sea Salt & Cider Vinegar Peanuts	4.6	51.4	7.8	1.39	617
Morrisons Salt & Pepper Cashews	4.6	46.3	8.8	0.4	595
Tesco Unsalted Mixed Nuts	4.6	59.2	9.6	0.1	657
KP Original Salted Peanuts	4.8	50.8	10.3	1.3	619
Waitrose Roasted Salted Savoury Mixed Nuts	4.8	47	7.2	0.82	597
Tesco Dry Roasted Peanuts	4.8	46.5	8.7	1.9	591
Tesco Jumbo Dry Roasted Peanuts	4.8	46.5	8.7	1.9	591
Asda Good & Balanced Mixed Almonds	4.9	54.2	4	0	626
Sainsbury's Roasted Salted Cashews, Basics	5	50	11	0.89	620
Tesco Jumbo Roasted & Salted Peanuts	5	41.8	6.6	1.8	576
Tesco Jumbo Roasted And Salted Peanuts And Cashews	5.1	46.9	8.5	0.5	588
Waitrose Love Life Nut Selection	5.2	53.7	6.4	0.15	627
Waitrose Love Life Nut Medley	5.2	53.1	6.1	0.02	624
KP Dry Roasted Peanuts	5.3	46	7.8	2	573
KP Jumbo Salted Peanuts	5.3	49	8.8	1.3	590
Tesco Piri Piri Coated Peanuts	5.3	31.1	5.4	1.6	513
KP Jumbo Salt & Vinegar Peanuts	5.4	48.2	8.7	1.5	587
Sainsbury's Indian Spiced Peanuts	5.4	51.9	7.8	0.84	624
Sainsbury's Jumbo Salted Cashews	5.4	49.3	9.8	0.86	617
Blue Diamond Wasabi & Soy Almonds	5.5	54.5	4.3	1.1	627
KP Jumbo Spicy Chilli Peanuts	5.5	47.8	8.6	1.5	585
Blue Diamond Almond Krunchies Spicy BBQ Flavour	5.6	34.9	2.8	1.86	537
Waitrose Essential Sea Salt & Vinegar Coated Peanuts	5.6	32.4	5.3	2.36	519
Tesco Roasted And Salted Macadamia Nuts	5.6	73.6	12	0.9	741
Asda Chosen by You Dry Roasted Peanuts	5.7	45.8	5	0.9	590
Asda Good & Balanced Redskin Peanuts	5.7	43.5	8.4	trace	571
Asda Dry Roasted Peanuts	5.7	45.8	5	0.9	590

Nuts, Seeds & Mixed Fruit

Product	Sugar	Fat	Sat per 100g	Salt	Cals
Waitrose Love Life Pistachios	5.7	55.4	7.4	trace	624
Tesco Unsalted Roasted Monkey Nuts	5.7	48.1	8.6	0.1	604
Asda Chosen by You Roasted & Salted Mixed Nuts	5.8	46.5	8.4	0.2	616
Sainsbury's Roasted Pistachios in Shells	5.8	49.4	5.3	0.13	588
Morrisons Wholefoods Unsalted Cashews	5.9	43.9	7.8	trace	582
Waitrose Love Life Cashew Nuts	5.9	43.9	7.8	0.03	582
Waitrose Love Life Organic Cashew Nuts	5.9	43.9	7.8	0.03	582
Sainsbury's Roasted Monkey Nuts in Shells	6	50.6	6.3	0.02	620
Sainsbury's Salted Peanuts, Basics	6	50.6	6.3	0.72	620
Sainsbury's Thai Chilli Peanuts	6.1	52.4	7.9	0.68	632
Walkers Salt & Vinegar Tiger Nuts	6.1	34	5.1	2.3	540
Morrisons Mixed Salted Nuts	6.1	50.8	6	0.3	617
Waitrose Essential BBQ Crunchy Coated Peanuts	6.1	30.6	5	1.67	517
Waitrose Love Life Roasted Cashew Nuts	6.1	41.7	7.4	0.03	566
Tesco Bbq Flavoured Coated Peanuts	6.1	30.6	5	1.7	517
Morrisons Monkey Nuts	6.2	46	8.7	trace	589
Morrisons Redskin Peanuts	6.2	46	8.7	trace	580
Asda Chosen by You BBQ Crispy Coated Peanuts	6.2	30.4	5.6	1.7	516
Morrisons Salted Cashews	6.3	47.7	8.2	0.8	602
Morrisons Jumbo Salted Cashews	6.3	47.7	8.2	1.3	602
Morrisons Jumbo Cashews	6.3	47.7	8.2	1.3	602
Morrisons BBQ Cashews	6.4	48.5	10.5	0.7	613
Tesco Finest Mixed Nuts With Halen Mon Sea Salt	6.4	53	6.8	1.8	623
Tesco Roasted Salted Peanuts	6.4	46.4	5.5	1	599
Tesco Vindaloo Jumbo Peanuts And Cashews	6.4	51.5	9	0.8	628
Sainsbury's Jumbo Roasted Unsalted Cashews	6.5	51.7	9.2	0.04	630
Sainsbury's Roasted & Salted Pistachios	6.5	48.8	6.1	1.63	602
Sainsbury's Roasted Salted Pistachios	6.5	48.8	6.1	1.63	602
Walkers Smoky Bacon Tiger Nuts	6.5	34	5.1	2.6	539
Sainsbury's Salted Peanuts	6.6	49.3	6.3	1.3	607

Nuts, Seeds & Mixed Fruit

Product	Sugar	Fat	Sat	Salt	Cals
			per 100g		
Sensations Mexican Smoked Chilli Peanuts	6.6	34	5	3.8	538
Morrisons Pistachios	6.7	48.1	6	trace	595
Walkers Sweet Chilli Tiger Nuts	6.8	34	5.1	2.2	541
Asda Chosen by You Salted Jumbo Peanuts	6.8	48.8	7.7	1.1	607
Asda Chosen by You Roasted & Salted Peanuts	6.8	48.8	7.7	1.1	607
Asda Smart Price Salted Peanuts	6.8	49.2	6.4	1.2	608
Asda Chosen by You Roasted & Salted Pistachios	6.9	48.6	6.2	1	594
Waitrose Essential Cashew Nuts Roasted and Salted	6.9	49.2	8.9	0.79	605
Waitrose Roasted Salted Cashew Nuts	6.9	49.2	8.9	0.79	605
Marmite Cashews	7.2	45.4	7.9	1.02	588
Sensations Thai Sweet Chilli Peanuts	7.2	34	5	2.3	541
Morrisons Salted Pistachios	7.3	46.4	5.9	1.3	579
Waitrose Essential Thai Sweet Chilli Coated Peanuts	7.3	30.9	5.1	0.87	518
Tesco Everyday Value Roasted Salted Peanut	7.3	47.8	6	1	596
Asda Good & Balanced Cashew Nuts	7.5	43.3	8.2	0.1	582
Sainsbury's Pistachios in Shells, SO Organic	7.6	45.7	5.8	<.01	586
Waitrose Roasted Salted Pistachio Nuts	7.6	44.1	5.4	1.47	576
Tesco Pistachio Nuts	7.6	49.3	6.2	1.2	612
Asda Chosen by You Habanero Chilli Peanuts	7.7	46.9	7.5	1.8	597
Waitrose Love Life Roasted Pistachios	7.7	44.8	5.5	0.02	585
Wonderful Pistachios Roasted & Salted	7.8	46	5.6	1.3	590
Wonderful Pistachios Salt & Pepper	7.8	46	5.6	2.5	590
Tesco Sea Salt And Black Pepper Cashew Nuts	7.8	47.2	7.5	1.1	601
Asda Chosen by You Roasted & Salted Cashew Nuts	8	46.8	8.8	0.7	605
Asda Smart Price Salted Cashew Nuts	8	49.4	9.4	1	637
Morrisons Dry Roast Peanuts	8.4	45.6	6.2	0.9	592
Tesco Everyday Value Roasted And Salted Cashew Nuts	8.6	48.3	9.3	1	616
Tesco Finest Sea Salt Black Pepper Colossal Cashews	8.6	46	8.2	1.1	601
Sensations Chinese Szechuan Pepper Peanuts	9	22	4	2.1	479
Morrisons Cheese & Onion Flavour Crunchy Coated Peanuts	9.1	31.1	4.3	3.1	514

Nuts, Seeds & Mixed Fruit

Product	Sugar	Fat	Sat	Salt	Cals
			per 100g		
Sainsbury's Chilli Coated Peanuts	10.1	23.2	2.5	2.13	487
Morrisons Smokey Bacon Flavour Crunchy Coated Peanuts	10.2	29.3	4	3.1	503
Waitrose Honey Roasted Peanuts	10.2	49.3	7	0.96	606
Wonderful Pistachios Sweet Chilli	10.3	45.2	5.8	2.4	577
Gefen Whole Chestnuts Roasted & Peeled	11	0.5	0	1	52
Sainsbury's Chip Shop Curry Coated Peanuts	11	23	2.5	1.55	489
Sainsbury's BBQ Coated Peanuts	11.4	23.1	2.5	1.6	488
Waitrose Honey Roasted Cashew Nuts	11.7	45.9	8.2	0.99	599
Waitrose Honey Roasted Mixed Nuts	14.9	45	6.6	trace	583
KP Jumbo Honey Roast Cashews	16.7	44.6	9.3	0.8	593
KP Honey Roast Jumbo Nut Mix	17	45	7.1	0.75	594
KP Honey Roast Peanuts	17.3	42.8	8.1	0.8	568
Tesco Honey Roasted Cashew Nuts	17.9	43.4	8.9	0.2	594
Asda Good & Balanced Mixed Peanuts & Raisins	18	31	4.1	trace	469
Tesco Honey Roasted Jumbo Cashews And Peanuts	18.6	41.9	7.8	0.2	583
Sainsbury's Jumbo Honey Roast Cashew Nuts	19	43.6	7	0.95	588
Blue Diamond Honey Roasted Almonds	19.2	47.6	3.6	0.5	601
Sainsbury's Jumbo Honey Roast Cashew & Peanuts	20	42.5	5.9	1	581
Morrisons Honey Roast Peanuts & Cashew Nuts	20.1	42.3	5.7	1	580
Asda Chosen by You Honey Roasted Peanuts & Cashews	20.1	42.2	5.7	1	580
Sainsbury's Honey Roast Peanuts	20.9	41.3	4.8	1	574
Waitrose Love Life Trail Mix	21.1	38	3.6	0.03	540
KP Triple Nut Grazing Mix	22	36	5.3	0.1	528
Tesco Unsalted Fruit And Nut Mix	24.1	33.5	6.7	0.1	497
Tesco Unsalted Mixed Nuts And Raisins	24.2	36.6	6.6	0	509
Waitrose Love Life Fruit, Nut & Seed Mix	24.3	34.8	3.3	0.02	520
Sensations Californian Honey & Salted Peanuts	25	40	5.8	1.4	561
Waitrose Love Life Mixed Nuts & Raisins	25	31.9	4.4	0.03	500
KP Grazing Mix Red Berry & Nut Crunch	26	32	5	0.05	510
Tesco Fruit And Nut Boost Mix	26	36.5	5.4	0.1	519

Nuts, Seeds & Mixed Fruit

Product	Sugar	Fat	Sat per 100g	Salt	Cals
Morrisons Mixed Nuts & Raisins	26.5	36.8	6.6	trace	524
Waitrose Love Life Mixed Peanuts & Raisins	26.5	29.7	3.8	0.04	487
Sainsbury's Unsalted Mixed Nuts & Raisins	28	35	5.1	0.03	514
Waitrose Love Life Almonds & Raisins	31.5	24.9	1.9	0.02	459
Waitrose Love Life Nut & Fruit Mix	31.9	36.3	5.6	0.03	516
Tesco Unsalted Peanut Raisin And Chocolate Peanut	32.2	29.2	7.1	0.1	492
Waitrose Love Life Cashew Nuts & Raisins	32.6	22.2	3.9	0.03	454
Tesco Finest Fruit Nut Mix	33.5	32.5	5.1	0.1	495
Asda Chosen by You Yogurt Fruit & Nut Mix	34	26	9.3	trace	466
Waitrose Love Life Nut & Dried Fruit Selection	36	31.1	4.8	0.03	486
Asda Chosen by You Fruit, Peanuts & Choc Peanuts	36.6	24.9	6.2	0.1	456
Sainsbury's Unsalted Jumbo Peanuts & Raisins	37	20	3.4	0.03	429
Morrisons Signature Cranberry Fruit & Nut	37.3	28.9	4.6	trace	470
Asda Chosen by You Fruit, Nut & Chocolate Buttons	40	26.6	6.6	trace	488
Sainsbury's Peanuts, Raisins & Milk Chocolate Chips	41.8	26	8.8	0.13	471
Wholesome 65 Cherries Raisins & Nuts	43.1	23.8	1.9	0.03	439
Morrisons Wholefoods Blueberry Fruit & Nut Mix	44.2	27.9	5.5	trace	465
Sainsbury's Fruit & Nut Mix with Yoghurt Cranberries	44.3	24.7	7	<.01	465
Waitrose Love Life Berries & Nuts	45	19.8	2.5	0.08	419
Waitrose Yogurt Coated Nuts & Raisins	46.9	33.9	21	0.25	540
Morrisons Signature Granola Mix	48.3	11.6	2.9	0.2	403
Asda Smart Price Fruit & Nut Mix	48.6	11.9	2.1	trace	392
Morrisons Wholefoods Cranberry Fruit & Nut Mix	51.5	15.3	1.8	0.1	394
Morrisons Wholefoods Almond Fruit & Nut Mix	52.1	12.1	0.9	trace	356

Pasta: Fresh

These quick to cook pasta meals are a good option. Some contain a little sugar, but often it's very low down on the ingredients list.

To help you make the best choices, products are listed starting with the least sugar first.

Product	Sugar	Fat	Sat	Salt	Cals
			per 100g		
Waitrose Proscuitto Cappaelletii	0.7	4.1	1.5	0.5	178
Tesco Italian Sausage & Ham Tortelloni	0.8	7	3.2	0.7	197
Waitrose Prosciutto & Emmental Ravioli	1	5.7	3.1	0.43	163
Waitrose Essential Spinach & Ricotta Fresh Pasta Tortelloni	1.1	3.5	1.9	0.47	159
Tesco Ham & Cheese Tortelloni	1.2	6.4	3.1	0.8	192
Waitrose Essential Cheese & Smoked Ham Tortelloni	1.2	4.9	2.9	0.56	187
Tesco Chicken & Bacon Tortelloni Pasta	1.3	6.6	2.2	0.7	205
Waitrose Ham Hock & Pea Fiorelli	1.3	4.5	2.5	0.54	160
Sainsbury's Taste the Difference King Prawn & Chilli Ravioli	1.4	5.5	2	0.91	171
Morrisons Kitchen Savoury Pork Tortelloni	1.4	5.3	2	0.9	204
Asda Italian Garlic & Herb Tortelloni	1.4	6.2	2.5	0.5	171
Waitrose Spinach & Ricotta Ravioli	1.4	6.4	3.9	0.44	194
Morrisons Kitchen Ham & Cheese Tortelloni	1.5	4.2	1.9	0.5	170
Tesco Finest Portabello Mushroom & Truffle Girasoli	1.5	4.4	1.2	1.1	171
Tesco Beef & Red Wine Ravioli	1.6	6.8	2.3	0.8	223
Waitrose Portabello Mushroom Ravioli	1.6	4.1	1.6	0.4	161
Pizza Express Spinach & Rocotta Cappelletti	1.7	4.1	1.3	1	188
Tesco Cheese, Tomato & Basil Tortelloni	1.7	5.5	2.9	0.8	193
Waitrose Pumpkin & Pine Nut Stuffed Fiorelli	1.7	6	3.4	0.54	180
Waitrose Essential Tomato, Mozzarella & Basil Tortelloni	1.7	3.7	2.2	0.5	161
Waitrose Menu Hot Smoked Salmon & Asparagus Ravioli	1.7	7.6	4.4	0.33	191
Morrisons Kitchen Chicken & Bacon Tortelloni	1.8	6.3	1.3	0.5	201
Morrisons Kitchen Spicy Chicken Tortelloni	1.8	5.2	1.1	0.6	194
Tesco Finest Scottish Crab & Chilli Ravioli	1.8	7.4	2.6	0.7	213

Pasta: Fresh

Product	Sugar	Fat	Sat	Salt	Cals
			per 100g		
Pizza Express Prosciutto Ham Cappelletti	1.8	3.5	1.5	0.8	173
Waitrose Beef & Red Wine Ravioli	1.8	2.9	1.5	0.45	170
Waitrose Menu Ricotta & Spinach Ravioli	1.8	6.7	4.5	1.02	175
Bertarini Cappalletti with Ham	1.9	11.5	6.9	1.7	315
Bertarini Lunette with Mushrooms	1.9	9	4.5	1.5	292
Sainsbury's Taste the Difference Chicken & Chorizo Ravioli	1.9	7.9	2.3	0.75	192
Tesco 4 Cheese Tortelloni	1.9	7	3.3	0.6	208
Giovanni Rana Selected Italian Cheeses Raviolli	2	11	7	1.3	272
Tesco Everday Value Spinach & Ricotta Tortelloni	2	3.6	1.4	0.9	189
Morrisons Kitchen Mushroom Tortelloni	2.1	5	2.2	0.5	179
Waitrose Spinach & Ricotta Cannelloni	2.1	5.8	3.7	0.44	171
Morrisons Kitchen Four Cheese Tortelloni	2.2	5.8	2.8	0.5	198
Morrisons Kitchen Garlic & Herb Tortelloni	2.2	6.8	3.1	0.7	199
Giovanni Rana Cured Ham & Cheese Tortelloni	2.3	9	5.5	1	277
Sainsbury's Taste the Difference Basil & Pine Nut Margherite	2.3	7.4	2.3	1.26	188
Morrisons Kitchen Bolognese Tortelloni	2.3	6.2	2	0.7	205
Morrisons Kitchen Sausage Tortelloni	2.3	6	2.2	0.7	198
Asda Italian Mozzarella & Tomato Girasole	2.3	7.9	3.6	0.5	216
Giovanni Rana Chicken, Mushroom & Pancetta Ravioli	2.4	11.5	7	0.75	272
Sainsbury's Taste the Difference Mushroom & Pinot Grigio Margherite	2.4	5.5	2.4	1	154
Morrisons Kitchen Spinach & Ricotta Tortelloni	2.4	5.1	2.3	0.5	194
Asda Italian Cheese & Tomato Tortelloni	2.4	6.1	2.9	0.4	207
Morrisons Kitchen Tomato & Mozzarella Tortelloni	2.5	6.3	2.3	0.5	206
Tesco Finest Prawn & Siciliam Lemon Tortelloni	2.5	4.3	1	0.8	186
Bertarini Tortelloni Spinach & Ricotta	2.6	7.4	4.3	1.6	282
Tesco Finest Italian Pea & Smoked Pancetta Ravioli	2.6	6.7	2.3	1.1	205
Asda Italian Chicken & Bacon Tortelloni	2.8	4.8	1.7	0.6	203
Waitrose Essential Bolognese Tortelloni	2.8	3.7	1.9	0.47	210
Giovanni Rana Large Ravioli Sun Ripened Tomato Olive & Mozzarella	2.9	12.7	5.8	1.3	267
Morrisons Kitchen Spicy Arrabbiata Tortelloni	2.9	4.3	1.9	0.7	176

Pasta: Fresh

Product	Sugar	Fat	Sat per 100g	Salt	Cals
Giovanni Rana Large Ravioli Mushroom Creamy Ricotta	3	10	4.5	1.5	265
Waitrose Goats Cheese & Red Onion Fiorelli	3	6	3.9	0.28	177
Bertarini Lunette with Cheese	3.3	9.2	4.9	1.5	298
Giovanni Rana Rich Bolognaise Tortelloni	3.4	9.5	3.2	1.3	288
Tesco Finest Italian Tomato & Buffalo Mozzarella Ravioli	3.4	5.6	2.5	1.1	190
Giovanni Rana Large Raviolli Chicken & Rosemary	3.5	9	5.8	1.3	248
Giovanni Rana Large Ravioli Ricotta Spinach & Mascarpone	3.5	9.5	6	1.3	257
Giovanni Rana Large Ravioli Gorgonzola & Walnut	3.6	11	5.5	1.4	296
Bertarini Tortelloni Chicken & Bacon	3.7	7.3	2	1.24	271
Sainsbury's Taste the Difference Pumpkin & Sage Quadrotti	3.7	5	2	1.08	163
Tesco Finest Chorizo & Chicken Girasoli	4	3.3	1.6	0.9	160

Pasta: Fresh Sauces

The sauces containing higher fat e.g. cheese sauce, are much lower in sugar.

Some of the tomato based sauces contain sugar as it 'brings out the tomato taste', check to be sure. High fructose corn syrup, labelled corn syrup, or glucose-fructose syrup, is often used.

To help you make the best choices, products are listed starting with the least sugar first.

Product	Sugar	Fat	Sat per 100g	Salt	Cals
Sainsbury's Fresh Green Pesto	<.5	38.6	9	1.25	403
Tesco Finest Pesto & Fresh Basil	0.4	46	7.9	1.6	459
Waitrose Green Basil Pesto	0.4	42.9	74	0.75	424
Morrisons Kitchen Italian Creamy Mushroom Sauce	0.7	3.6	2.3	0.6	59
Waitrose Mushroom Sauce with Porcini	0.7	5.4	3.1	0.73	75
Waitrose Essential Cheese Sauce	1	8.7	5.6	0.75	119
Tesco Finest Wild Mushroom Sauce	1.1	11.3	6.6	0.6	127
Sainsbury's Carbonara Sauce	1.2	7.5	4.4	0.7	110
Tesco Carbonara Sauce	1.2	8	4.8	0.8	113
Tesco Finest Carbonara Sauce	1.3	8.4	5	0.5	116
Tesco Cheese Sauce	1.3	7.9	5.1	0.8	119
Asda Italian Cheese Sauce	1.3	8.2	4.6	0.6	113
Morrisons Kitchen Italian Carbonara Pasta Sauce	1.4	6	3.9	0.8	103
Sainsbury's Spinach & Ricotta Sauce	1.7	5.8	3.7	0.38	81
Asda Italian Chicken & Bacon Sauce	1.7	6.1	3.9	0.6	107
Waitrose Carbonara Sauce	1.7	13.3	8.2	0.78	164
Sainsbury's Mushroom Sauce	1.8	4.1	2.1	0.78	73
Sainsbury's Three Cheese Sauce	2	8.4	5.6	0.68	124
Sainsbury's Taste the Difference Carbonara Sauce	2.1	14.3	7.9	0.75	179
Morrisons Signature Creamy Four Cheese Sauce	2.2	10.3	7.2	0.6	133
Waitrose Four Cheese Sauce	2.2	11.7	7.7	0.7	156
Morrisons Kitchen Bolognese Paste Sauce	2.4	8.1	3.4	0.5	111
Morrisons Signature Creamy Tomato & Mascarpone Sauce	2.5	6.9	4.3	0.7	94
Tesco Finest 4 Cheese Sauce	2.5	9.9	6.5	0.8	135

Pasta: Fresh Sauces

Product	Sugar	Fat	Sat	Salt	Cals
			per 100g		
Asda Italian Carbonara Sauce	2.5	7.1	4.1	0.6	117
Morrisons Kitchen Italian Tomato & Mascarpone Pasta Sauce	2.7	5.9	3.8	0.4	90
Morrisons Kitchen Tomato & Mascarpone Pasta Sauce	2.7	5.9	3.8	0.5	90
Waitrose Beef Bolognese Sauce	2.7	5.5	2.3	0.63	100
Morrisons Kitchen Italian Cheese Sauce	2.8	8.3	5.4	0.8	124
Asda Italian Chosen by You Red Pepper & Goats Cheese Sauce	3	3.4	2	0.38	58
Morrisons Kitchen Italian Tomato & Chorizo Pasta Sauce	3.1	6	1	0.5	81
Asda Italian Bolognese Sauce	3.1	5.8	2.5	0.7	103
Morrisons Kitchen Italian Tomato & Basil Pasta Sauce	3.2	2.3	0.2	0.3	46
Morrisons Kitchen Italian Tomao & Garlic Pasta Sauce	3.2	2.1	0.1	0.5	50
Sainsbury's Tomato & Mascarpone Sauce	3.4	4.7	2.5	0.7	73
Morrisons Kitchen Italian Roasted Vegetable Pasta Sauce	3.7	2.2	1.2	0.6	50
Tesco Finest Tomato Mascarpone Sauce	3.8	7.5	4	0.8	97
Tesco Tomato & Mascarpone Sauce	3.9	8	3.9	0.8	110
Waitrose Essential Tomato & Mascarpone Sauce	3.9	7.2	3.7	0.75	101
Sainsbury's Beef Bolognaise Sauce	4	3.9	1.8	0.6	81
Morrisons Kitchen Italian Arrabbiata Pasta Sauce	4	3	0.2	0.2	568
Sainsbury's Taste the Difference Pomodoro & Chianti Sauce	4.2	1.4	0.2	0.5	42
Sainsbury's Fresh Red Pesto	4.4	38.6	6.3	1.23	403
Tesco Bolognaise Sauce	4.8	7.5	2.8	0.8	114
Tesco Tomato Sauce	4.9	1.8	0.2	0.5	51
Tesco Tomato & Basil Sauce	5	1.5	0.2	0.5	47
Tesco Chargrilled Vegetable Sauce	5.1	1.1	0.2	0.6	52
Tesco Tomato & Garlic Sauce	5.1	1.5	0.2	0.5	46
Waitrose Essential Tomato & Chilli Sauce	5.1	4.8	0.6	0.73	77
Asda Italian Mediterranean Vegetable Sauce	5.2	0.6	0.1	0.4	35
Waitrose Tomato Sauce with Pepperoni & Chilli	5.2	7.7	2.3	0.73	110
Sainsbury's Pomodoro Sauce SO Organic	5.3	2.1	0.3	0.5	51
Waitrose Essential Tomato & Basil Sauce	5.4	4.9	0.7	0.78	79
Waitrose Chargrilled Vegetable Sauce	5.4	4.6	0.7	0.83	75

Pasta: Fresh Sauces

Product	Sugar	Fat	Sat	Salt	Cals
			per 100g		
Tesco Finest Arrabbiata Sauce	5.5	4.1	0.5	0.5	68
Asda Italian Tomato & Mascarpone Sauce	5.6	7.4	3.1	0.5	104
Tesco Arrabbiata Sauce	5.7	0.5	0.2	0.2	43
Asda Italian Tomato & Basil Sauce	5.7	3.2	0.3	0.4	60
Sainsbury's Tomato & Smoked Bacon Sauce	6	1.3	0.2	0.5	53
Asda Italian Arrabbiata Sauce	6	3.8	0.5	0.4	70
Asda Italian Tomato & Smoked Bacon Sauce	6	0.5	0.2	0.6	54
Waitrose Cherry Tomato & Basil Sauce	6	6.7	1	0.73	97
Asda Italian Tomato & Garlic Sauce	6.1	1.1	0.1	0.4	52
Waitrose Red Chilli Pesto with Tomato	6.4	28.7	3.7	1.43	309
Pacino's Tomato & Basil Sauce	6.5	1.8	0.1	0.48	52
Sainsbury's Mediterranean Vegetable Sauce	6.9	2.5	0.4	0.3	62
Sainsbury's Tomato & Basil Sauce	6.9	2.5	0.4	0.3	58
Tesco Finest Pomodorini Sauce	7.4	6.9	0.9	0.7	103
Sainsbury's Arrabbiata Sauce	7.5	2.7	0.4	0.33	66

Ready Meals

Many of these products have added sugar, some as you can see more than most. Follow the 100g rule but beware of the product size. Look at the list of ingredients, if sugar is listed at the top beware.

Indian

To help you make the best choices, products are listed starting with the least sugar first.

Product	Sugar	Fat	Sat	Salt	Cals
			per 100g		
Asda Mushroom Rice	0.2	3.1	0.3	0.4	199
Asda Chosen by You Pilau Rice	0.3	3.6	0.3	0.4	203
Tesco Pilau Rice	0.3	3	0.3	0.5	155
Asda Chosen by You Chicken Tikka Pakoras with Raita	0.4	14	2.6	0.9	238
Sainsbury's Pilau Rice	0.5	2	0.2	0.39	168
Sainsbury's Three Colour Pilau Rice	0.5	1.8	0.1	0.4	164
Asda Chosen by You Hot Chicken Tikka Masala, Rice & Bombay Potato	0.6	3.4	1.7	0.6	118
Asda Chosen by You Mixed Samosa Selection	0.6	13.5	1.9	0.9	257
Asda Indian Takeaway Poppadoms	0.6	34.8	16.1	3.1	532
Asda Rice Tricolour	0.6	2.5	0.3	0.3	154
Morrisons Kitchen Pilau Rice	0.6	1.1	0.2	0.3	127
Tesco Takeaway Pilau Rice	0.6	2	0.2	0.5	143
Waitrose Pilau Rice	0.6	3.2	0.3	0.4	172
Sainsbury's Mushroom Pilau Rice	0.7	3.1	0.2	0.45	146
Asda Boiled Rice	0.8	3.5	0.5	trace	197
Tesco Indian Poppadoms	0.8	29.7	2.6	3.7	500
Asda Chicken Tikka & Rice	0.9	5.4	1.9	0.5	162
Asda Saag Aloo	0.9	6.2	0.6	0.5	100
Waitrose Mini Poppadoms	0.9	29.7	2.5	4.1	496
Tesco Takeaway Egg Fried Rice	1	3.7	0.4	0.2	154
Asda Chosen by You Chicken Pakora Selection	1.2	10.4	2.1	0.9	218
Sainsbury's Chicken Korma & Rice, Be Good To Yourself	1.2	1.5	0.4	0.28	100
Sainsbury's Tadka Daal	1.2	4.3	0.9	0.81	110
Sainsbury's Garlic & Coriander Naan Bread, Taste the Difference	1.3	12	2.6	0.65	313

Product	Sugar	Fat	Sat	Salt	Cals
			per 100g		
Waitrose Spinach & Carrot Pilau Rice	1.3	2.8	0.2	0.32	125
Asda Chosen by You Indian Sharing Feast	1.4	11	0.9	0.7	233
Asda Good & Counted Chicken Tikka Masala with Pilau Rice	1.4	1.8	0.8	0.33	97
Tesco Big Night In Indian Tarka Dahl	1.4	6.8	1.7	0.4	143
Tesco Finest Jalfrezi With Pilau Rice	1.4	2.9	0.4	0.4	127
Weight Watchers Chicken Tikka	1.4	1.7	0.3	0.4	90
Asda Smart Price Chicken Curry & Rice	1.5	1.5	0.8	0.6	76
Sainsbury's Chicken Madras & Pilau Rice (hot & aromatic)	1.5	6.5	1.5	0.53	166
Sainsbury's My Goodness! Keralan Cod & Lime Rice	1.5	1.8	1.1	0.44	92
Sainsbury's South Indian Coconut Chicken, Taste the Difference	1.5	6.2	2.6	0.39	166
Sainsbury's Beetroot & Green Chilli Samosa, Taste the Difference	1.6	19	1.3	0.3	197
Sainsbury's Chicken Samosas (medium & spicy)	1.6	10	1	0.92	237
Sainsbury's Lamb Rogan Josh & Pilau Rice (warm & aromatic)	1.6	5.3	0.8	0.47	165
Waitrose Spinach Dal	1.6	2.9	0.7	0.54	95
Asda Chosen by You Chefs Kerala Beef & Black Pepper Sauce	1.7	9.2	4.6	0.4	157
Asda Chosen by You Hot Chicken Tikka Masala	1.7	2.3	1	0.58	89
Asda Indian Chicken Korma & Rice	1.7	6.3	2.9	0.5	161
Asda Chosen by You Vegetarian Chicken Style Balti & Rice	1.7	5	0.4	0.5	125
Asda Chicken Madras	1.8	5.5	3.4	0.3	105
Sainsbury's Chapatti	1.8	4.2	0.3	0.53	279
Waitrose Indian Mushroom Rice	1.8	5.2	1.8	0.43	162
Waitrose Tarka Dal	1.8	4	0.3	0.41	114
Morrisons Kitchen Plain Naans	1.9	11.7	3.6	0.8	323
Morrisons NuMe Chicken Tikka & Pilau Rice	1.9	2.2	0.8	0.3	105
Sainsbury's Chicken Balti & Pilau Rice (medium & aromatic)	1.9	5	0.5	0.57	153
Sainsbury's Chicken Jalfrezi & Pilau Rice (spicy & vibrant)	1.9	5.9	0.5	0.56	156
Sainsbury's Plain Naan	1.9	8.9	2.2	0.75	306
Tesco Lamb Rogan Josh And Pilau Rice	1.9	3.9	0.7	0.5	120
Asda Bombay Potatoes	2	5.1	0.4	0.5	103
Asda Chicken Jalfrezi & Rice	2	3.8	0.4	0.4	125

RM: Indian

Product	Sugar	Fat	Sat	Salt	Cals
			per 100g		
Sainsbury's Chicken Tikka Biryani	2	4.6	0.9	0.55	156
Sainsbury's Vegetable Samosa, Basics	2	10.3	0.8	0.63	228
Tesco Big Night In Indian Saag Aloo	2	8.4	3.4	0.8	132
Asda Indian Takeaway Garlic & Coriander Naans	2.1	6.9	0.5	0.8	286
Asda Lamb Rogan Josh	2.1	5.4	1.7	0.3	101
Morrisons Kitchen Takeaway Chicken Tikka Biryani	2.1	5.3	2	0.45	152
Sainsbury's Aloo Saag (mild & delicate)	2.1	6.4	1.5	0.43	100
Sainsbury's Chicken Tikka Biryani, Be Good To Yourself	2.1	1	0.1	0.33	84
Sainsbury's Vegetable Samosas	2.1	11.7	0.8	0.83	231
Tesco Big Night In Indian Chicken Biryani	2.1	5.4	0.5	0.7	183
Tesco Chicken Korma And Pilau Rice	2.1	7.1	2.4	0.5	162
Tesco Finest Lamb Rogan Josh With Pilau Rice	2.1	4.7	0.9	0.4	144
Asda Chosen by You Mini Vegetable Samosas	2.2	13.3	1.8	0.7	261
Charlie Bigham's Chicken Korma	2.2	8.2	4.6	0.7	152
Linda McCartney Chana Masala Vegetable Cakes	2.2	12.3	4	0.58	235
Sainsbury's Kashmiri Chicken Korma, Taste the Difference	2.2	5	1.6	0.48	158
Tesco Chicken Korma	2.2	10.3	6.1	0.6	164
Asda Chosen by You Scorching Hot Chicken Vindaloo with Pilau Rice	2.3	3	0.3	0.4	121
Asda Thai Chicken Curry with Rice	2.3	2.3	1.4	0.4	105
Sainsbury's Chicken Jalfrezi, Taste the Difference	2.3	4.5	0.9	0.58	147
Sainsbury's Garlic & Coriander Naan	2.3	4.1	0.3	0.76	266
Tesco Everyday Value Chicken Curry	2.3	5.9	2.5	0.4	146
Tesco Finest Beef Madras With Pilau Rice	2.3	5.3	2.2	0.5	156
Asda Chosen by You Large Poppadoms	2.4	16.5	1.5	3.2	423
Sainsbury's Bombay Potato (medium & spicy)	2.4	5.3	0.3	0.58	95
Tesco Finest Light Malaysian Chicken Curry	2.4	2.2	1.2	0.6	100
Tesco Finest Prawn Tikka With Pilau Rice	2.4	4.5	1.3	0.6	139
Waitrose Indian Chicken Moilee	2.4	8.7	5.4	0.42	143
Waitrose Indian Chicken Shashlik	2.4	6.2	2	0.28	134
Waitrose Vegetarian Indian Spiced Bhaji Burgers	2.4	11.8	2.1	0.77	230

Product	Sugar	Fat	Sat per 100g	Salt	Cals
Asda Chosen by You Indian Sharing Feast	2.5	13.9	1.1	0.8	266
Asda Indian Takeaway Plain Naans 2	2.5	7.5	0.5	0.7	283
Charlie Bigham's Chicken Tikka Masala	2.5	9.3	5.1	0.6	165
Morrisons Kitchen Vegetable Samosas	2.5	14.8	1.7	0.9	280
Sainsbury's Chicken Phal & Rice	2.5	4.3	0.4	0.45	140
Tesco Chicken Jalfrezi And Pilau Rice	2.5	3.5	0.4	0.5	120
Tesco Finest Light Chicken Tikka W/Rice And Lime	2.5	4	0.5	0.6	126
Waitrose Bombay Potatoes	2.5	3.6	0.3	0.62	83
Asda Chicken Bhuna	2.6	5.8	0.5	0.3	113
Asda Chosen by You Chefs Special Bengali Lamb Bhuna	2.6	7.2	1	0.2	120
Asda Shish Kebabs	2.6	12	4.3	1.4	213
Sainsbury's Chicken Jalfrezi & Rice, Be Good To Yourself	2.6	2.1	0.4	0.37	106
Sainsbury's Poppadom	2.6	24.7	1.6	3.25	417
Sainsbury's Royal Chicken Biryani, Taste the Difference	2.6	5.5	1.1	0.4	147
Tesco Big Night In Chicken Jalfrezi And Pilau Rice	2.6	3.6	0.4	0.5	121
Tesco Big Night In Indian Chicken Korma And Pilau Rice	2.6	7.6	2.5	0.5	158
Tesco Big Night In Indian Lamb Rogan Josh And Pilau Rice	2.6	4	0.6	0.5	119
Tesco Chicken Hot Tikka And Pilau Rice	2.6	6.1	2.3	0.5	145
Tesco Tikka And Korma Meal	2.6	8.4	2	0.6	188
Waitrose LoveLife Calorie Ctrl Chicken Korma & Pilau Rice	2.6	1.4	0.5	0.35	105
Asda Beef Madras	2.7	6.1	3.4	0.3	116
Asda Chicken Jalfrezi	2.7	4	0.5	0.4	97
Asda Chosen by You Chicken Tikka Bites	2.7	3.1	1.1	0.8	167
Asda Tandoori Chicken Masala & Pilau Rice	2.7	4.3	0.6	0.4	129
Sainsbury's Tandoori Spiced Chicken Biryani, Taste The Difference	2.7	1.5	0.4	0.38	125
Tesco Naan Bread	2.7	8.6	2.4	0.9	306
Tesco Chicken Tikka Masala And Pilau Rice	2.7	6.8	2.2	0.5	161
Tesco Finest Chicken Korma With Pilau Rice	2.7	8	2.7	0.5	182
Tesco Finest Chicken Tikka Masala With Pilau Rice	2.7	5.4	1.3	0.4	156
Tesco Healthy Living Chicken Tikka And Rice	2.7	2.1	1.1	0.4	106

RM: Indian

Product	Sugar	Fat	Sat	Salt	Cals
			per 100g		
Asda Chicken Balti	2.8	3.4	0.4	0.6	85
Asda Chosen by You Mini Bhaji & Pakora Feast	2.8	11.1	0.8	0.6	238
Asda Chosen by You Chicken Tikka Skewers	2.8	2.7	0.9	0.68	152
Morrisons Kitchen Chicken Madras & Pilau Rice	2.8	4.6	1.9	0.4	144
Sainsbury's Chicken Tikka Masala & Rice, Be Good To Yourself	2.8	1.9	0.4	0.22	109
Tesco Chicken Jalfrezi	2.8	3.4	0.3	0.6	97
Waitrose Plain Parathas	2.8	24.9	3.5	0.83	439
Waitrose Vegetable Samosas	2.8	11.4	0.9	0.89	223
Sainsbury's Channa Masala (medium & earthy)	2.8	6.4	1	0.75	114
Morrisons Kitchen Vegetarian Paneer Jalfrezi	2.9	5.9	2	0.4	132
Tesco Big Night In Indian Vegetable Balti And Pilau Rice	2.9	5.3	1.1	0.7	137
Waitrose Aloo Gobi Saag	2.9	4.4	0.9	0.43	77
Asda Chosen by You Fresh Tastes Kitchen Tikka Masala & Rice	2.9	2.9	1	0.4	99
Asda Chosen by You Malaysian Chicken Curry	2.9	3.3	2.2	0.3	109
Asda Chosen by You Chicken Korma	3	8	4.3	0.5	140
Asda Good & Balanced Tandoori Chicken with Basmati Rice	3	2.9	0.4	0.33	122
Morrisons Kitchen Chicken Bhuna & Pilau Rice	3	3.1	0.5	0.4	125
Morrisons Kitchen Takeaway Tarka Dal	3	6.3	2.4	0.43	135
Sainsbury's Garlic & Chilli Chicken (medium & spicy)	3	5.2	0.4	0.61	121
Sainsbury's Prawn Biryani, Be Good To Yourself	3	1	0.3	0.36	76
Waitrose Indian Lamb Kofta Curry	3	9.4	4.4	0.62	131
Tesco Takeaway Hot Indian Meal	3.05	5.45	1.3	0.65	164
Asda Mini Satay	3.1	17.5	4.5	1.2	263
Asda Raita	3.1	23.4	2.1	0.3	232
Morrisons Kitchen Chicken Rogan Josh & Pilau Rice	3.1	2.6	0.4	0.43	123
Morrisons Kitchen Indian Chicken Jalfrezi & Rice	3.1	3.9	0.5	0.35	131
Sainsbury's King Prawn Makhani & Rice (mild & creamy)	3.1	7.5	2.6	0.65	174
Tesco Big Night In Indian Vegetable Samosas	3.1	11.6	0.9	0.6	232
Asda Buttery Chicken Masala	3.2	10.1	5.2	0.6	152
Morrisons Kitchen Takeaway Tandoori Chicken Sizzler	3.2	6.6	0.9	0.79	119

Product	Sugar	Fat	Sat	Salt	Cals
			per 100g		
Tesco Big Night In Chicken Tikka Masala And Pilau Rice	3.2	7.3	2.3	0.5	156
Morrisons Kitchen Chicken Dopiaza & Pilau Rice	3.3	3.1	0.4	0.32	132
Morrisons Kitchen Chicken Saag Masala	3.3	5.3	1.1	0.66	104
Morrisons Kitchen Takeaway Indian Chicken Balti	3.3	4.3	0.5	0.63	90
Morrisons Take Away Bag Tikka Masala	3.3	4.8	2.1	0.54	153
Sainsbury's Chicken Madras	3.3	7.4	2.4	0.54	133
Tesco Vegetable Samosas	3.3	12.6	1	0.6	247
Tesco Chicken Tikka Masala, Rice And Potato	3.3	6.5	2.2	0.6	137
Tesco Takeaway Chicken Madras	3.3	7.6	2.3	0.8	125
Waitrose Chicken Biryani	3.3	4.9	0.8	0.48	150
Waitrose LoveLife Calorie Ctrl Chicken Tikka Masala with Pilau Rice	3.3	1.3	0.5	0.41	111
Morrisons Kitchen Chicken Tandoori Pilau Rice	3.4	4.4	0.6	0.55	137
Morrisons Kitchen Chicken Tikka Skewers	3.4	17	4.6	1.5	267
Morrisons Kitchen Meal Chicken Tikka & Jalfrezi	3.4	4.2	1.1	0.54	139
Morrisons Kitchen Takeaway Indian Chicken Madras	3.4	7.7	3.8	0.65	130
Sainsbury's Onion Bhaji	3.4	11.9	1	1.33	253
Waitrose Chicken Madras	3.4	5.7	2.7	0.5	121
Asda Scorching Hot Chicken Vindaloo	3.5	3.2	0.4	0.4	92
Sainsbury's Chicken Tikka Masala & Rice, Taste the Difference	3.5	5.1	2.2	0.53	153
Sainsbury's Mushroom & Pea Masala	3.5	4.9	0.6	0.69	88
Sainsbury's Saag Paneer	3.5	10.9	4.7	0.33	147
Tesco Chicken Tandoori, Rice And Bombay Potatos	3.5	7.5	2.4	0.7	148
Waitrose Indian Aubergine Masala	3.5	4.7	1.3	0.56	82
Waitrose Indian Chef's Specials Tikka Pastries	3.5	7.3	1.5	0.6	223
Tesco Indian Vegetable Tikka And Rice	3.5	4.3	1.8	0.4	121
Asda Chicken Dopiaza	3.6	5.9	0.6	0.5	117
Sainsbury's Chicken Balti (medium & aromatic)	3.6	5.6	0.5	0.65	116
Sainsbury's Vegetable Biryani	3.6	4.8	0.8	0.45	127
Tesco Finest Chicken Pathia With Pilau Rice	3.6	4	0.5	0.3	147
Morrisons Kitchen Aloo Gobi Saag	3.7	3.9	0.3	0.73	82

RM: Indian

Product	Sugar	Fat	Sat	Salt	Cals
			per 100g		
Morrisons Kitchen Lamb Rogan Josh	3.7	4	0.8	0.53	94
Sainsbury's Lamb Rogan Josh (warm & aromatic)	3.7	7.2	1.8	0.53	151
Tesco Chicken Vindaloo	3.7	3.2	0.5	0.5	106
Tesco Takeaway Chicken Tikka Balti	3.7	3.4	0.4	0.7	82
Waitrose Lamb Rogan Josh	3.7	7.4	1.4	0.56	129
Asda Chosen by You Sizzler Tandoori Chicken	3.8	4.7	0.8	0.58	115
Morrisons Kitchen Bombay Potatoes	3.8	4.1	0.3	0.53	99
Sainsbury's Coriander & Mint Raita (cool & refreshing)	3.8	4.1	0.9	0.38	87
Tesco Takeaway Chicken Jalfrezi	3.8	4	0.4	0.7	84
Waitrose Plain Tandoori Naan Breads	3.8	2.3	0.7	1.59	258
Waitrose Chicken Saag Masala	3.8	5.4	1.5	0.47	121
Waitrose Indian Mini Plain Naans	3.8	2.3	0.7	1.59	258
Waitrose Indian Chilli Chicken	3.8	3.7	0.6	0.5	103
Morrisons Kitchen Chicken Tikka & Pilau Rice	3.9	5.7	2.1	0.47	144
Tesco Big Night In Mini Onion Naan	3.9	9.2	2.2	0.8	290
Tesco Bombay Potatoes	3.9	3.9	0.3	0.7	87
Tesco Takeaway Bombay Potatoes	3.9	3.9	0.3	0.7	87
Tesco Takeaway Vegetable Curry	3.9	3.4	0.7	0.5	68
Sainsbury's Vegetable Jalfrezi	4	4.5	0.3	0.5	78
Tesco Chicken Balti	4	5.4	0.6	0.5	116
Tesco Chicken Madras	4	6.7	2.8	0.5	125
Tesco Chicken Tikka Masala	4	8.9	3.5	0.6	145
Tesco Lamb Rogan Josh	4	4.4	0.8	0.5	98
Waitrose Chicken Tikka Masala with Pilau Rice	4	7.7	3.4	0.63	169
Asda Chicken Tikka Masala	4.1	5	2.1	0.6	116
Asda Chosen by You Chicken Tikka Masala	4.1	5	2.1	0.56	116
Morrisons Kitchen Chicken Pasanda & Pilau Rice	4.1	3.9	1	0.39	141
Morrisons Kitchen Indian Chicken Tikka Masala & Pilau Rice	4.1	5.2	1.9	0.48	149
Tesco Onion Bhajis	4.1	18.4	1.4	0.8	271
Tesco Big Night In Indian Onion Bhajis	4.1	18.4	1.4	0.8	271

Product	Sugar	Fat	Sat per 100g	Salt	Cals
Tesco Takeaway Onion Bhajis	4.1	18.4	1.4	0.8	271
Tesco Takeaway Chicken Korma	4.1	12	5.1	0.6	170
Waitrose Vegetable Korma	4.1	7.9	3.9	0.77	109
Waitrose Chicken Jalfrezi	4.1	3.6	0.6	0.48	105
Morrisons Kitchen Takeaway Lamb Bhuna	4.2	4.3	0.9	0.43	96
Sainsbury's Chicken Korma & Rice (mild & creamy)	4.2	5.2	2	0.5	154
Tesco Takeaway Vegetable Samosas	4.2	11	0.9	0.9	235
Waitrose Indian Garlic Chicken	4.2	6.6	2	0.61	131
Asda Chosen by You Vegetable Pakoras	4.3	14.1	1	0.9	252
Morrisons Kitchen Chicken Korma & Pilau Rice	4.3	7.1	4.1	0.43	152
Waitrose Chicken Korma & Pilau Rice	4.4	7.1	3.5	0.56	154
Waitrose Garlic & Coriander Naan Bread	4.4	2.7	0.8	1.61	264
Morrisons Kitchen Indian Chicken Korma & Pilau Rice	4.5	6.5	3.7	0.34	159
Morrisons Kitchen Takeaway Indian Paneer Masala	4.5	13.3	6.8	0.57	180
Sainsbury's Mini Onion Bahjia, Taste the Difference	4.5	13.5	1	0.88	246
Waitrose Chicken Korma	4.5	10	5.2	0.59	160
Waitrose Indian Smoky Masala Chicken	4.5	7.5	2.6	0.62	144
Morrisons Kitchen Chicken Jalfrezi	4.6	4.9	0.5	0.58	109
Sainsbury's Chicken Balti Topped Naan, Taste the Difference	4.6	6.3	1.4	0.55	194
Tesco Big Night In Indian Bombay Potatoes	4.6	2.4	0.2	0.7	75
Morrisons Kitchen Chicken Dopiaza	4.7	4.5	0.5	0.63	107
Sainsbury's Chicken Jalfrezi (spicy & vibrant)	4.8	6.2	0.7	0.59	127
Tesco Hot Chicken Tikka Masala	4.8	8.7	3.8	0.5	145
Sainsbury's Chicken Tikka Masala With Rice	4.9	5.5	1.7	0.58	161
Sainsbury's Hot Chicken Vindaloo (hot & fiery)	4.9	4.6	0.5	0.66	119
Waitrose Indian Chef's Special Ginger Chicken	4.9	4.8	1.9	0.55	114
Morrisons Kitchen Chicken Korma	5	11.2	7.1	0.48	168
Sainsbury's Butter Chicken (mild & rich)	5	8.4	4.5	0.74	144
Tesco Takeaway Chicken Tikka Masala	5	6.3	2	0.6	120
Tesco Takeaway Hot Chicken Tikka	5	6.3	2	0.6	120

RM: Indian

Product	Sugar	Fat	Sat per 100g	Salt	Cals
Asda Chosen by You Onion Bhajis	5.1	13.3	0.9	0.5	256
Asda Vegetable Jalfrezi	5.1	6	0.4	0.4	86
Sainsbury's Chicken Korma (mild & creamy)	5.1	6.9	3.1	0.55	147
Tesco Takeaway Lamb Rogan Josh	5.1	7.3	1	0.6	119
Tesco Vegetable Masala	5.1	5	2.7	0.4	90
Waitrose Indian Kashmiri Chicken	5.1	8.4	3.9	0.54	149
Asda Chosen by You Chicken Tandoori Masala	5.2	5	0.7	0.4	115
Waitrose Indian Snack selection	5.2	14.4	1.2	1	250
Waitrose Indian Vegetable Masala	5.2	6.5	3.3	0.5	95
Waitrose Prawn Mango Masala	5.2	5.9	2.4	0.56	104
Morrisons Kitchen Chicken Tikka Masala	5.4	9	4.3	0.63	142
Morrisons Kitchen Takeaway Onion Bhajis	5.4	17.8	1.4	0.93	283
Tesco Butter Chicken	5.4	14.1	8.5	0.5	200
Waitrose Onion Bhajis	5.6	12.8	1	1.05	240
Asda Chosen by You Chefs Special Spicy Paneer Tikka Masala	5.7	10.6	6.2	0.4	155
Tesco Prawn Tikka Masala	5.7	7.1	2.4	0.9	118
Morrisons Kitchen Takeaway Hot Chicken Tikka	5.8	8.2	3.2	0.66	138
Waitrose Chicken Tikka Masala	5.8	10.3	4.7	0.63	174
Tesco Takeaway Butter Chicken	6	6.6	3	0.7	119
Sainsbury's King Prawn Masala (medium & fruity)	6.1	5.2	2.3	0.5	113
Morrisons Kitchen Raita	6.5	6.6	4.6	0.5	110
Asda Indian Takeaway Peshwari Naans	6.6	8.2	2.7	0.7	282
Morrisons Kitchen Chicken Makhani	6.7	8.1	4.2	0.68	142
Sainsbury's Chicken Tikka Masala	6.8	7.7	2.7	0.65	158
Waitrose Peshwari Naan	7.6	6.8	3.7	1.25	278
Asda Tomato & Onion Dip	8.9	0.3	trace	0.5	46
Sainsbury's Sweet Potato & Red Onion Bhaji	9.5	11.8	0.9	1.26	249
Tesco Mini Indian Selection	10	54.2	4.4	2.3	850
Sainsbury's Peshwari Naan	11.2	8.6	3.8	0.5	301
Sainsbury's Red Onion & Courgette Bhajia, Taste the Difference	13	12.5	1.2	0.95	248

Product	Sugar	Fat	Sat	Salt	Cals
			per 100g		
Sainsbury's Spicy Butternut Squash Samosa, Taste the Difference	18.4	10	2.9	1.28	250
Waitrose Indian Dip Duo	37.2	2.3	0.2	0.75	182
Asda Indian Dip Trio	42.9	4.7	1.9	3.3	218
Morrisons Kitchen Mango Chutney	43.8	0.3	0.1	2.2	221
Asda Mango Chutney	52.6	0.5	0.2	2.2	218
Sainsbury's Mango Chutney (mild & fruity)	52.6	0.7	0.2	2.42	271

Ready Meals

Many of these products have added sugar, some as you can see more than most. Follow the 100g rule but beware of the product size. Look at the list of ingredients, if sugar is listed at the top beware.

Italian

To help you make the best choices, products are listed starting with the least sugar first.

Product	Sugar	Fat	Sat per 100g	Salt	Cals
Waitrose Spaghetti Bolognese	0.1	4.4	1.6	0.4	124
Tesco Finest Crab Rocket And Chilli Linguine	0.1	10.4	1.5	0.4	206
Waitrose Mushroom Risotto	0.2	4.6	2.5	0.44	124
Tesco Finest King Prawn Spaghetti	0.3	5.7	2.9	0.4	140
Tesco Finest Smoked Haddock Risotto	0.3	3.4	2	0.6	116
Tesco Finest Chicken Pancetta And Mozzarella	0.5	5.4	2.2	0.5	155
Menu from Waitrose Creamy Mushroom Risotto	0.7	6.2	2.1	0.53	162
Morrisons Kitchen Macaroni Cheese & Bacon Bake	0.7	4.4	2.4	0.5	163
Tesco Finest Spaghetti Carbonara	0.7	9	4	0.6	177
Asda Italian Spicy Chicken Pasta	0.71	0.83	0.09	0.11	35
Menu from Waitrose Creamy Chicken & Asparagus Risotto	0.8	3.8	1.3	0.48	141
Morrisons Kitchen Italian Ham & Mushroom Tagliatelle	0.8	5.3	2.9	0.6	134
Tesco Finest Steak Ragu Pappardelle	0.8	4.2	1.7	0.4	140
Asda Extra Special King Prawn Linguine	0.9	3.1	1.9	0.5	98
Sainsbury's Mushroom Risotto	0.9	5.8	2.9	0.6	130
Tesco Italian Tuna Pasta Bake	0.9	5.8	2.5	0.5	141
Waitrose Spaghetti Carbonara	0.9	7	2.9	0.53	162
Morrisons Signature Ham & Mushroom Tagliatelle	1	6.2	3.4	0.4	149
Sainsbury's Macaroni Cheese, Basics	1	5.8	2.8	0.58	143
Tesco Finest Spinach Pinenut Pasta	1	12.9	2.2	1	240
Tesco Italian Macaroni Cheese Pasta	1	8	4.1	0.5	183
Waitrose Spicy Fusilli with Sausage	1	5.2	1.9	0.45	166
Asda Chicken & Bacon Pasta Bake	1.1	6.5	3.6	0.5	167
Asda Italian Macaroni Cheese	1.1	7.8	4.5	0.5	174

RM: Italian

Product	Sugar	Fat	Sat per 100g	Salt	Cals
Kirsty's Beef Lasagne	1.1	2.1	1.2	0.4	88
Morrisons Kitchen Italian Macaroni Cheese	1.1	6.8	3.9	0.4	161
Morrisons Kitchen Italian Spaghetti Carbonara	1.1	6.2	3.6	0.4	121
Sainsbury's Bacon & Leek Pasta Bake	1.1	4.7	2.4	0.4	124
Sainsbury's Ham & Mushroom Tagliatelle, Be Good To Yourself	1.1	1.3	0.5	0.38	86
Tesco Healthy Living Chicken And Bacon Pasta	1.1	2	1.2	0.3	123
Waitrose Mushroom and Spinach Linguine	1.1	7.4	3.7	0.36	143
Tesco Finest Chicken And Bacon Pasta Bake	1.1	8.5	3.6	0.5	180
Sainsbury's Tagliatelle Carbonara, Taste the Difference	1.2	10.4	5.3	0.78	199
Tesco Family Favourites Carbonara Pasta	1.2	2.9	1.5	0.5	125
Waitrose Bacon and Pea Risotto	1.2	6.3	3.1	0.51	147
Asda Fresh Tastes Chicken & Mushroom Risotto	1.3	2.2	1	0.5	104
Sainsbury's Lamb & Rosemary Tagliatelle, Taste the Difference	1.3	2.9	0.9	0.43	103
Tesco Healthy Living Spaghetti Bolognese	1.3	1.7	0.6	0.4	113
Waitrose Ham and Mushroom Tagliatelle	1.3	6.1	3.2	0.5	139
Waitrose Macaroni Cheese	1.3	8.7	4.5	0.6	193
Asda Chosen by You Vegetarian Mushroom Risotto	1.3	4.2	2.5	0.5	92
Morrisons Kitchen Italian Bolognese Pasta Bake	1.4	4	2.2	0.4	144
Sainsbury's Italian Macaroni & Bacon Melt	1.4	8.2	4.6	0.58	171
Sainsbury's Macaroni Cheese	1.4	5.5	3.3	0.43	142
Sainsbury's Seafood Spaghetti, Taste the Difference	1.4	2.2	0.4	0.53	116
Tesco Italian Spaghetti Carbonara	1.4	8.4	4.3	0.6	169
Tesco Italian Spicy Beef And Jalapeno Melt	1.4	6.8	3.5	0.5	157
Asda Beef Bolognese Pasta Bake	1.5	5.5	2.9	0.5	135
Asda Good & Counted Spaghetti Carbonara	1.5	2	1	0.48	97
Asda Ham & Mushroom Tagliatelle	1.5	4.2	2.4	0.5	129
Asda Smart Price Spaghetti Carbonara	1.5	3.4	2.2	0.6	88
Morrisons Kitchen Italian Spaghetti Bolognese	1.5	2.6	1.3	0.3	106
Morrisons Savers Macaroni Cheese	1.5	7.8	5.2	0.5	163
Sainsbury's Bistro Mushroom & Spinach Risotto, Taste the Difference	1.5	6.3	3.2	0.45	136

Product	Sugar	Fat	Sat	Salt	Cals
			per 100g		
Tesco Finest Meatball Pasta	1.5	9.6	2.8	0.5	194
Tesco Italian Chicken And Bacon Pasta Bake	1.5	6.9	4	0.6	169
Tesco Italian Ham And Mushroom Tagliatelle	1.5	5.6	3.2	0.6	136
Tesco Italian Spaghetti Bolognese	1.5	4.2	1.9	0.3	119
Asda Chicken & Mushroom Tagliatelle	1.6	5.1	2.8	0.4	135
Asda Italian Spaghetti Carbonara	1.6	8.3	4.4	0.6	167
Morrisons Kitchen Bolognese Pasta Melt	1.6	6.1	3	0.6	137
Sainsbury's Bolognese Pasta Bake, Basics	1.6	2.9	1.1	0.45	104
Sainsbury's Mushroom & Butternut Squash Risotto, Taste the Difference	1.6	5.7	1.3	0.53	133
Tesco Finest Traditional Lasagne	1.6	6.8	3.2	0.5	140
Waitrose Chicken Tagliatelle	1.6	7.8	2.9	0.46	167
Asda Chosen by You Three Cheese & Tomato Pasta Bake	1.7	7.4	4.4	0.5	165
Asda Spaghetti Bolognese	1.7	5.9	2.6	0.5	133
Sainsbury's My Goodness! Chicken & Mascarpone Pasta	1.7	1.7	0.7	0.29	97
Tesco Everyday Value Spaghetti Bolognese	1.7	4.2	1.8	0.4	110
Asda King Prawn Linguine	1.8	3.1	0.4	0.5	95
Asda Smart Price Macaroni Cheese	1.8	5.7	3.2	0.4	122
Morrisons Kitchen Italian Chicken & Bacon Pasta Bake	1.8	7.6	4.2	0.4	171
Morrisons Kitchen Vegetarian Vegetable Pasta Bake	1.8	3.4	1.9	0.4	101
Sainsbury's Chicken & Bacon Pasta Bake	1.8	6.1	3.1	0.75	139
Sainsbury's Ham & Mushroom Tagliatelle	1.8	5.7	2.9	0.5	136
Tesco Italian Beef Lasagne	1.8	7.6	3.9	0.5	143
Waitrose LoveLife Calorie Ctrl Mushroom Risotto	1.8	2.5	1.4	0.56	100
Waitrose Spinach Cannelloni	1.8	7.1	3.1	0.35	119
Asda Extra Special Four Cheese Macaroni	1.9	9.3	5.7	0.5	188
Asda Good & Counted Tomato & Mascarpone Pasta Bake	1.9	2.7	1.2	0.22	100
Asda Pasta Bake Pepperoni	1.9	5.8	2.9	0.6	161
Sainsbury's Spaghetti Bolognese, Taste the Difference	1.9	7.6	2.2	0.25	188
Sainsbury's Spaghetti Carbonara	1.9	7.8	3.8	0.6	164
Waitrose Cajun Chicken Tagliatelle	1.9	4	1.3	0.45	121

RM: Italian

Product	Sugar	Fat	Sat	Salt	Cals
			per 100g		
Waitrose Rigatoni and Aubergine	1.9	6.8	1.4	0.55	137
Asda Italian Beef Cannelloni	2	5.4	3.1	0.6	127
Asda Italian Chicken Tagliatelle	2	2.9	0.3	0.3	116
Asda Meatball Pasta Bake	2	4.4	1.5	0.5	131
Tesco Italian Beef Lasagne	2	7.5	4.1	0.5	145
Asda Chicken and Mushroom Lasagna	2.1	5.4	2.8	0.4	126
Asda Chosen by Kids Pasta Bolognese	2.1	3.2	1.5	0.3	150
Asda Extra Special Spaghetti Bolognese	2.1	6.1	2.5	0.6	138
Tesco Finest Macaroni Cheese	2.1	8.7	5	0.6	208
Asda Chilli Beef Pasta Bake	2.2	5.4	2.9	0.5	156
Charlie Bigham's Lasagne	2.2	8.5	4	0.5	162
Asda Italian Tuna Pasta Bake	2.3	5.1	2.3	0.5	148
Morrisons Kitchen Meat Feast Pasta Melt	2.3	4.4	1.6	0.6	181
Tesco Everyday Value Lasagne	2.3	7.1	3.3	0.5	140
Tesco Finest Spaghetti Bolognese	2.3	9.2	3.2	0.5	177
Tesco Italian Beef Cannelloni	2.3	8.1	4	0.6	149
Asda Meat Feast Pasta Bake	2.4	4.9	1.4	0.4	132
Morrisons Kitchen Italian Penne Bolognese Bake	2.4	7.3	3.8	0.5	169
Morrisons Kitchen King Prawn Linguini	2.4	3	0.4	0.4	106
Tesco Italian Vegetable Lasagne	2.4	5.8	2.4	0.4	109
Waitrose LoveLife Calorie Ctrl Butternut Squash Risotto	2.4	1.7	0.5	0.36	95
Asda Spaghetti Meatballs	2.5	5.1	1.2	0.5	132
Sainsbury's Beef Lasagne, Basics	2.5	3.1	1.2	0.55	87
Sainsbury's Lasagne, Basics	2.5	3.3	1.4	0.5	95
Tesco Italian Spaghetti And Meatballs	2.5	6.2	1.9	0.5	136
Waitrose Beef Cannelloni	2.5	7.9	4	0.55	138
Waitrose World Caf_ Mozzarella & Pecorino Arancini	2.5	15.3	4.9	0.88	314
Weight Watchers Bolognese Al Forno	2.5	2.2	1.1	0.4	93
Asda Smart Price Spaghetti Bolognese	2.6	2.8	1.2	0.5	84
Morrisons Kitchen Cheese Feast Pasta Melt	2.6	6.1	2.9	0.3	161

Product	Sugar	Fat	Sat per 100g	Salt	Cals
Morrisons Kitchen Italian Chicken & Ham Pasta Bake	2.6	3.4	1.1	0.3	134
Morrisons Savers Spaghetti Bolognese	2.6	3.7	1.7	0.6	120
Sainsbury's My Goodness! Chilli Prawn Linguine Pasta	2.6	2.2	0.2	0.47	107
Sainsbury's Spaghetti Bolognese, Basics	2.6	1.8	0.8	0.49	92
Sainsbury's Tuna Pasta Bake	2.6	6.2	3.7	0.43	154
Tesco Italian Tomato And Mozzarella Pasta Bake	2.6	5.3	1.9	0.4	148
Waitrose Beef Lasagne	2.6	6.1	2.9	0.45	130
Sainsbury's My Goodness! Prawns With Orzo Pasta	2.6	2.2	0.4	0.54	99
Asda Italian Beef Lasagne	2.7	7.9	4.1	0.4	152
Menu from Waitrose Beef Lasagne	2.7	7.3	3.7	0.37	143
Sainsbury's Penne Bolognese Bake	2.7	7.9	3.6	0.53	158
Sainsbury's Sausage Ragu Pasta Bake	2.7	3.7	1.6	0.35	125
Tesco Family Favourites Chicken And Tomato Pasta	2.7	3.2	0.7	0.4	136
Tesco Italian Chicken Arrabbiata	2.7	2.4	0.4	0.4	123
Tesco Italian Pepperoni Pasta Bake	2.7	8.1	3.5	0.5	178
Waitrose Chicken Arrabiata	2.7	4	0.6	0.38	160
Sainsbury's My Goodness! Silky Butternut Squash Risotto	2.7	1.5	0.2	0.41	95
Asda Chicken Pasta in White Wine Sauce	2.8	2.7	1.2	0.5	94
Asda Smart Price Lasagne	2.8	4.1	2.2	0.5	93
Morrisons Kitchen Italian King Prawn Linguine	2.8	1.5	0.3	0.4	98
Morrisons Kitchen Italian Lasagne	2.8	4.8	2.2	0.4	120
Morrisons Kitchen Italian Vegetable Lasagne	2.8	2.9	0.8	0.4	84
Morrisons NuMe Lasagne	2.8	2.9	1.4	0.4	101
Morrisons NuMe Spaghetti & Meatballs	2.8	4.8	2.2	0.4	89
Morrisons Savers Beef Lasagne	2.8	5.3	2.3	0.5	122
Morrisons Signature Aberdeen Angus Lasagne	2.8	7.8	3.5	0.6	151
Sainsbury's Spaghetti Meatballs	2.8	6.4	1.6	0.4	130
Tesco Family Favourites Lasagne	2.8	3.4	1.6	0.5	110
Waitrose LoveLife Calorie Ctrl Beef & Pork Meatballs with Spaghetti	2.8	3.2	1.1	0.45	107
Asda Chosen by Kids Cheese & Creamy Tomato Pasta	2.9	2.9	1.8	0.3	123

RM: Italian

Product	Sugar	Fat	Sat	Salt	Cals
			per 100g		
Asda Good & Balanced Italian Chicken & Tomato Wholemeal Pasta	2.9	3.1	0.5	0.38	141
Asda Good & Counted Beef Lasagne	2.9	2.3	1.3	0.28	95
Asda Smart Price Pasta Bake Bolognese	2.9	5.7	3.1	0.5	133
Waitrose LoveLife Calorie Ctrl Roasted Vegetable Lasagne	2.9	1.9	0.5	0.32	82
Asda Good & Counted Spinach & Ricotta Cannelloni	3	2.6	1.6	0.35	89
Sainsbury's Beef Lasagne, Be Good To Yourself	3	2.6	1.3	0.45	104
Waitrose Four Cheese Ravioli	3	6.9	2.9	0.43	144
Asda Chosen by You Fresh Tastes King Prawn Linguine	3	1.9	0.4	0.38	92
Quorn Classic Lasagne	3	3.3	1.5	0.5	92
Asda Chosen by You Pepper & Courgette Lasagne	3	3.2	2	0.5	93
Asda Fresh Tastes Kitchen Italian Chicken Pasta	3.1	3.1	0.6	0.5	125
Morrisons Kitchen Hot 'N' Spicy Meatballs	3.1	13	6	0.7	201
Sainsbury's Ham & Mushroom Pasta Melt	3.1	7.8	2.4	0.55	177
Waitrose Vegetable Lasagne	3.1	5.4	2.7	0.53	109
Morrisons Kitchen Spaghetti & Meatballs	3.2	3.5	1	0.3	114
Sainsbury's Beef Lasagne	3.2	9	4.4	0.53	162
Asda Chosen by You Vegetarian Spinach & Ricotta Cannelloni	3.2	7.7	4.8	0.6	146
Morrisons Kitchen Italian Tuna Pasta Bake	3.3	5.2	2	0.4	140
Sainsbury's Meat Feast Pasta Bake	3.3	4.8	1.7	0.58	141
Morrisons Kitchen Italian Chicken Risotto	3.4	4.3	1.9	0.4	108
Waitrose Spaghetti and Meatballs	3.4	6.6	1.4	0.52	127
Morrisons Kitchen Beef Cannelloni	3.5	4	1.9	0.5	114
Sainsbury's Lasagne, Taste the Difference	3.5	7.6	3.6	0.58	154
Sainsbury's Spinach & Ricotta Cannelloni, Be Good To Yourself	3.5	2.5	1.4	0.45	85
Asda Lasagne Goat's Cheese & Butternut Squash	3.5	5.2	2.8	0.5	118
Sainsbury's Family Penne Bolognese Bake	3.6	10	4.5	0.5	172
Sainsbury's Family Sausage Pasta Bake	3.6	4.6	1.4	0.43	144
Sainsbury's Lasagne Al Forno, Slow Cooked Beef, Taste the Difference	3.6	8.1	3.9	0.63	171
Sainsbury's Sausage Pasta Bake	3.6	3.7	1.2	0.43	129
Sainsbury's Spaghetti Bolognese	3.6	6.2	2.8	0.53	132

Product	Sugar	Fat	Sat	Salt	Cals
			per 100g		
Waitrose Penne with Tomato and Mozzarella	3.6	6.2	1.6	0.3	156
Morrisons Kitchen Meatballs in Tomato Sauce	3.7	9.8	3.1	0.9	154
Heston from Waitrose Lasagne	3.8	10	3.7	0.63	194
Morrisons Kitchen Italian Chicken Tagliatelle	3.8	2.9	0.4	0.6	126
Asda Chosen by You Spicy Pork Arrabiata	4	2.5	0.8	0.4	110
Sainsbury's Family Beef Lasagne	4	8.6	4.1	0.53	148
Tesco Finest Lasagne Al Forno	4	10	4.1	0.6	183
Waitrose Beef Ravioli	4	3.5	0.8	0.39	125
Sainsbury's My Goodness! Mediterranean Vegetable Risotto	4	1.7	0.3	0.37	90
Charlie Bigham's Meatballs Al Forno	4.1	10	2.6	1.18	164
Morrisons Kitchen Penne Mozzarella	4.1	3.9	1	0.3	145
Sainsbury's Chicken Lasagne	4.1	4.8	2.4	0.44	125
Waitrose LoveLife Roasted Vegetable Pasta	4.2	3.2	0.9	0.24	116
Morrisons Kitchen Italian Four Cheese Ravioli	4.3	5.1	1.7	0.6	125
Sainsbury's Al Forno Lasagne, Taste the Difference	4.3	8.3	3.8	0.63	149
Sainsbury's Vegetable Lasagne	4.3	5.2	2.6	0.64	111
Sainsbury's Vegetable Lasagne, Be Good To Yourself	4.4	2.2	0.9	0.43	83
Sainsbury's Spinach & Riccotta Cannelloni	4.6	7.5	3.9	0.53	132
Sainsbury's Tomato & Smokey Bacon Pasta	4.6	2.8	0.9	0.38	92
Sainsbury's Beef Cannelloni	4.8	7.2	3.2	0.6	137
Tesco Italian Bbq Chicken Pasta	5.1	2.3	0.9	0.4	147
Tesco Butternut Squash Spinach Feta Lasagne	6	6.2	2.4	0.5	132

Ready Meals

Many of these products have added sugar, some as you can see more than most. Follow the 100g rule but beware of the product size. Look at the list of ingredients, if sugar is listed at the top beware.

Caribbean, Mexican & USA

To help you make the best choices, products are listed starting with the least sugar first.

Product	Sugar	Fat	Sat per 100g	Salt	Cals
Morrisons Kitchen Tex Mex Southern Fried Chicken Wings	0.2	14.8	3.1	0.8	241
Sainsbury's Stuffed Cheesy Nachos	0.5	24.2	10.6	1.19	354
Asda Good & Counted Chicken Enchiladas	0.5	2.2	0.4	0.4	101
Tesco Chicken Fajitas	0.5	4	1.5	0.7	135
Morrisons Kitchen Tex Mex Southern Fried-Style Chicken	0.8	10.8	2.8	0.8	242
Tesco Bbq Beef Short Rib	1	15.1	6.9	0.5	218
Asda Mexican Selection	1.3	8.7	1.9	0.7	259
Charlie Bigham's Chilli Con Carne	1.4	5.3	1.6	0.5	131
Morrisons Kitchen Tex Mex Southern Fried-Style	1.4	10.8	5.7	1	248
Tesco Tex Mex Spicy Beef Burrito	1.4	4.6	1.8	0.5	177
Tesco Chilli Con Carne And Rice	1.4	2.4	0.5	0.4	116
Asda Chosen by You Vegetarian Meat Free Chilli Burrito	1.4	2.7	1.3	0.6	124
Sainsbury's Cheese & Chive Onion Skins with Soured Cream & Chive Dip	1.5	14	7.7	0.53	229
Waitrose Vegetable Chilli with Rice	1.5	1.3	0.1	0.14	101
Waitrose World Caf_ Chilli Beef Burritos	1.5	6.3	2.7	0.85	195
Asda Chosen by You Spicy Three Bean Enchiladas	1.5	3.9	1.6	0.5	124
Morrisons Kitchen Tex Mex Chilli Con Carne & Rice	1.7	2.3	0.9	0.3	97
Morrisons Kitchen Mexican Chicken	1.8	7.2	2	0.8	171
Morrisons Kitchen Sticky Chilli Chicken Wings	1.8	13.2	3.1	0.6	225
Morrisons Mac & Cheese Bites	1.9	15.6	13.1	0.6	313
Morrisons Kitchen Tex Mex Chilli Beef Burrito	1.9	10	3.7	0.6	197
Sainsbury's Chilli With Coriander Rice, Taste the Difference	2	2.8	1	0.44	122
Asda Extra Special Spicy Chilli Steak & Rice	2	2.5	1	0.5	133
Asda Chicken Wings Hot & Spicy	2	11.7	3.1	0.7	193

RM: Caribbean, Mexico & USA

Product	Sugar	Fat	Sat	Salt	Cals
			per 100g		
Asda Jalapeno Bites	2	17.6	4.5	1.4	287
Asda Good & Counted Chicken Nacho Bake with Potato Wedges	2.1	2	0.5	0.38	92
Asda Good & Counted Beef Chilli & Rice	2.1	2.1	1	0.38	95
Morrisons Kitchen Chilli Con Carne	2.3	5.1	2.3	0.3	129
Morrisons Kitchen Tex Mex Loaded Chilli Wedges	2.3	6.1	2.3	0.5	131
Morrisons Kitchen Smokin' Mexican-Style Chicken	2.3	3.5	1.1	0.5	123
Tesco Chicken Enchiladas	2.3	9	4.2	0.9	184
Morrisons Kitchen Tex Mex Chicken Fajita Kit	2.4	5.2	1.8	0.6	149
Asda Good & Counted Turkey Meatballs with Mexican Herb Rice	2.4	2.9	0.5	0.4	93
Waitrose LoveLife Beef & Barbecue Beans	2.4	1.7	0.6	0.25	92
Heston from Waitrose Chilli Con Carne	2.4	9.6	4.8	0.49	153
Waitrose Chilli Con Carne with Rice	2.4	5.2	2	0.53	142
Morrisons NuMe Chilli Con Carne with Rice	2.5	2.1	0.9	0.3	112
Morrisons Kitchen Tex Mex Spicy Chicken Enchilada	2.5	5.9	2.6	1	146
Waitrose Chicken Enchiladas	2.6	7.5	2.5	0.47	173
Sainsbury's Chilli Con Carne, Be Good To Yourself	2.7	1.8	0.8	0.41	94
Morrisons Kitchen Habanero Chicken Burrito	2.7	4.9	1.8	0.6	162
Tesco Levi Roots Hot Chilli Beef	2.7	4.1	1.1	0.7	132
Asda Chosen by You South Carolina Chicken & Spicy Potatoes	2.7	4	1.6	0.56	111
Asda Spicy Cajun Chicken	2.8	1.2	0.3	0.4	96
Sainsbury's My Goodness! BBQ Chicken & Sweetcorn Rice	2.8	1.7	0.2	0.4	112
Sainsbury's Beef Burrito	2.9	7.2	2.6	0.58	196
Sainsbury's Beef Chilli & Rice	2.9	4.9	1.9	0.13	146
Asda Chosen by You Sizzler Fajita Chicken	2.9	4	0.4	0.78	103
Morrisons Kitchen Hot & Spicy Chicken Wings	3	13.1	3.9	0.6	228
Asda Good & Counted Ham Hock with Root Mash	3	2.3	1.3	0.43	70
Morrisons Kitchen Salt & Chilli Rack Of Ribs	3.1	17.3	6.5	1.17	257
Sainsbury's Mexican Chicken & Chorizo Rice	3.2	4	0.9	0.58	135
Sainsbury's Beef Chilli Taco Bowl	3.4	8.2	3	0.45	191
Waitrose LoveLife Beef & Pulled Pork Meatballs	3.4	3.3	1	0.38	127

Product	Sugar	Fat	Sat	Salt	Cals
			per 100g		
Sainsbury's Jambalaya, Be Good To Yourself	3.5	1.7	0.2	0.42	103
Morrisons Kitchen Vegetarian Enchiladas	3.5	9.6	3.9	0.8	193
Tesco Three Bean Chilli And Rice	3.5	2.6	0.2	0.3	127
Bol Mexican Sweet Potato Chilli	3.6	1.6	0.2	0.36	86
Sainsbury's Pulled Pork Burrito	3.7	4	1.3	0.51	164
Morrisons Kitchen BBQ Chicken & Rice	3.9	0.6	0.1	0.3	106
Morrisons Kitchen Pizza Dippers	4	15.2	5.4	1.1	268
Sainsbury's Hot & Spicy Chicken Fajita	4.1	6.6	1.6	0.6	173
Sainsbury's Spicy 3 Bean Enchilada	4.1	4.1	1.3	0.46	143
Sainsbury's Mexican Chicken Enchiladas	4.3	5.7	2.2	0.62	150
Waitrose Chicken & Prawn Jambalaya	4.5	4.8	0.7	0.57	140
Sainsbury's Mild Chicken Fajita	4.6	6.8	1.6	0.54	177
Tesco Americana Chipotle Chilli Rack Of Ribs	4.7	15	6.1	0.3	225
Sainsbury's BBQ Chicken Wings	5.1	10.8	2.3	0.41	199
Morrisons Kitchen Ultimate Beef Ribs	5.2	17.2	8.3	0.8	247
Asda Chosen by You Fresh Tastes Tex Mex Pork & Rice	5.2	1.5	0.5	0.3	96
Waitrose World Café Barbecue Pulled Pork	5.2	5.2	1.3	0.62	129
Tesco Levi Roots Pasta Chicken	5.3	3.6	0.6	0.4	123
Morrisons Jalapeno Bites	5.6	14.4	5.8	0.8	268
Sainsbury's Sweetcorn Fritters	6.1	13	1.2	0.92	249
Morrisons Kitchen BBQ Pulled Pork & Potato	6.3	3	0.5	0.5	113
Morrisons Kitchen Chilli Pulled Beef Brisket	6.4	4.6	1.6	0.6	177
Morrisons Kitchen Tex Mex Red Hot Texan Wings	6.6	10.7	2.8	0.8	219
Sainsbury's Plain Cornbread	6.7	8.1	3	1.02	299
Morrisons Kitchen BBQ Pulled Pork Shoulder	6.8	14.8	5.1	0.28	241
Asda Sticky BBQ Ribs	7	13	4.9	0.95	231
Asda Chosen by You World Favourites Mexican Salsa Chicken	7.5	4.7	0.8	0.4	144
Sainsbury's Love Vegetable Smoky Mexican Bean Burger	8.3	6.9	0.6	0.85	212
Morrisons Kitchen Tex Mex Slow-Cooked Smoky BBQ Ribs	8.4	12	4.7	0.4	223
Tesco Hickory BBQ Pulled Pork	8.5	7.1	2.6	0.7	163

RM: Caribbean, Mexico & USA

Product	Sugar	Fat	Sat per 100g	Salt	Cals
Morrisons Kitchen Pulled Pork Calzones	9.7	13	1.3	0.9	269
Tesco Rack Of Ribs	10.3	13.7	5.4	0.5	240
Morrisons Kitchen Sweet Potato Fritters & Dip	10.5	13.9	1.4	0.9	258
Morrisons Kitchen Bourbon Baby Back Ribs	12.9	8.5	3.3	0.5	197
Tesco Mini Sticky Bbq Ribs	14.6	13.1	5.1	0.6	251

Ready Meals

Many of these products have added sugar, some as you can see more than most. Follow the 100g rule but beware of the product size. Look at the list of ingredients, if sugar is listed at the top beware.

Mediterranean

To help you make the best choices, products are listed starting with the least sugar first.

Product	Sugar	Fat	Sat	Salt	Cals
			per 100g		
Floristan Spanish Potato Omelette	0.8	9	1.6	1.1	153
Sainsbury's Paella, Taste the Difference	1	4.3	1	0.55	135
Morrisons Kitchen Tapas Spanish Tortilla	1	7.5	1.2	0.6	139
Menu from Waitrose Smoky Paella	1.2	3.5	1	0.55	125
Tesco Finest Chicken And Chorizo Paella	1.4	3.6	0.9	0.6	134
Waitrose Love Life Piri Piri Chicken	1.4	1.6	0.2	0.17	105
Asda Chosen by You Mediterranean Spanish Tapas Platter	1.5	8	2.7	0.9	150
Weight Watchers Spanish Chicken	1.6	2.4	0.5	0.5	87
Morrisons Kitchen Piri Piri Chicken	1.6	2.8	0.5	0.5	122
Morrisons Kitchen Chorizo Paella	1.7	8.5	2.3	0.8	187
Waitrose Chicken & Chorizo Paella	1.8	4.3	0.9	0.46	133
Waitrose Piri Piri Chicken	1.9	3.1	0.3	0.23	111
Morrisons Kitchen Bistro Lamb Moussaka	2	10.9	4.6	0.6	167
Waitrose Love Life Smoky Chorizo Chicken	2	4.7	1.1	0.41	120
Waitrose Red Pepper & Chorizo Tortilla Slices	2	9.2	3.8	0.67	160
Bol Sri Lankan Lentil Sambar	2	2.9	1.9	0.37	77
Waitrose World Café Tortilla	2.1	12	6.1	0.7	174
Asda Chicken & King Prawn Paella	2.1	1.4	0.5	0.4	98
Charlie Bigham's Moussaka	2.2	7.4	2.8	0.34	121
Morrisons Kitchen Chicken Chorizo Paella	2.2	2.5	0.6	0.5	111
Morrisons Kitchen Tapas Spiced Lamb Empanadas	2.2	14	3.3	0.5	270
Tesco Finest Spanish Chicken With Chorizo	2.2	4.8	0.9	0.6	119
Tesco Finest Light Chicken And King Prawn Paella	2.2	4.3	0.6	0.7	148
Waitrose World Café Patatas Bravas	2.2	9.1	0.9	0.51	160

Product	Sugar	Fat	Sat	Salt	Cals
			per 100g		
Kirsty's Spanish Chicken With Rice	2.3	2.7	0.5	0.4	98
Asda Chosen by You Mediterranean Chicken & Patatas Bravas Bake	2.3	3.2	0.4	0.68	100
Asda Extra Special Oven-Roasted Meatballs & Paprika Spiced Potatoes	2.3	6.7	2	0.5	157
Charlie Bigham's Paella	2.5	5.1	0.9	0.9	107
Waitrose Goan Fish Curry	2.5	13.3	8.1	0.42	179
Sainsbury's Vegetarian Catalan Bean Casserole	2.5	0.8	0.1	0.48	79
Sainsbury's My Goodness! Chicken & Prawn Paella	2.6	2.7	0.7	0.33	114
Sainsbury's Chicken & Mushroom Marsala, Taste the Difference	2.7	3.3	1.1	0.53	109
Tesco Finest Light Chicken Piri Piri	2.8	3.6	0.4	0.7	123
Asda Good & Counted Chicken & King Prawn Paella	2.8	1.7	0.5	0.43	94
Asda Chosen by You World Favourites Piri Piri Chicken Traybake	2.8	6.6	1.5	0.65	124
Waitrose Chicken Patatas Bravas	2.8	6.7	0.9	0.4	142
Sainsbury's Bistro Cod & Chorizo Potato Bravas, Taste the Difference	2.9	4.8	1	0.61	123
Morrisons Kitchen Moroccan Chicken	2.9	3.6	0.7	0.5	123
Waitrose Love Life Calorie Controlled Lamb Moussaka	2.9	2.5	1.4	0.4	85
Asda Classic Moussaka	2.9	4.7	2.4	0.4	115
Morrisons Kitchen Tapas Tomato & Mozzarella Arrancini	3	9.9	2.4	0.5	237
Morrisons Kitchen Tapas Chorizo & Green Bean Fritters	3	12.1	2.3	1.2	218
Asda Good & Balanced Moroccan Lamb Meatballs with Cous Cous	3	3.5	1	0.28	121
Asda Piri Piri Chicken & Rice	3	0.7	0.2	0.4	95
Morrisons Kitchen Tapas Garlic Ciabatta Bites	3.2	16.1	10.1	1	359
Tesco Finest Moussaka	3.2	11.2	3.8	0.6	162
Asda Chosen by You Chicken Prawn & Chorizo Paella	3.2	3.8	1	0.6	122
Asda Chosen by You Mediterranean Chicken & Chorizo Paella	3.3	3.3	1	0.6	117
Waitrose Beef Moussaka	3.3	12.1	3.8	0.55	182
Waitrose Love Life Middle Eastern Spiced Duck	3.3	3.2	0.5	0.41	142
Tesco Finest Paella	3.4	4.2	0.6	0.6	136
Tesco Finest Moroccan Spiced Lamb Meatball	3.4	8.1	3.3	0.5	150
Waitrose Menu Spicy Piri Piri Chicken	3.4	4.4	0.6	0.6	130
Asda Chicken & Chorizo Paella	3.5	3.6	1.1	0.6	127

RM: Mediterranean

Product	Sugar	Fat	Sat	Salt	Cals
			per 100g		
Waitrose Vegetable Moussaka	3.5	11.2	3.3	0.58	163
Sainsbury's My Goodness! Spanish Chicken with Patatas Bravas	3.6	3.6	0.6	0.36	94
Waitrose Menu Lamb Moussaka	3.7	12.6	5.7	0.6	192
Waitrose Chicken Tagine	3.8	4	0.8	0.61	134
Waitrose Mediterranean Vegetable Gratin	3.8	4.6	0.9	0.55	83
Morrisons Kitchen Piri Piri Chicken & Spicy Rice	3.9	2.2	0.2	0.4	109
Morrisons Kitchen Patatas Bravas	3.9	3.8	0.7	0.5	108
Asda Chosen by You Sizzler Piri Piri Chicken	3.9	6.7	0.7	0.4	135
Waitrose World Café Chorizo in Red Wine	3.9	14.1	3.8	0.66	180
Asda Fresh Tastes Spanish Chicken & Chorizo with Rice	3.9	2.5	0.5	0.5	100
Sainsbury's Moussaka, Taste the Difference	4	10.3	5.7	0.63	191
Sainsbury's Piri Piri Chicken, Taste the Difference	4	3	0.5	0.73	102
Morrisons Kitchen Tapas Spanish Ham & Manchego Croquetas	4	10.8	2.2	0.6	241
Morrisons Kitchen Vegetarian Mousakka	4	5	2	0.5	104
Morrisons Kitchen Tapas Spanish Ham & Manchego Croquettes	4	10.8	2.2	0.6	241
Asda Fresh Tastes Cantonese Chicken Noodles	4	1	0.1	0.3	88
Sainsbury's Paprika Beef, Taste the Difference Bistro	4.5	3.2	0.7	0.55	111
Sainsbury's Vegetarian Moroccan Sweet Potato Croquettes	4.5	10.4	1.8	0.62	228
Sainsbury's Catalan Chicken, Taste the Difference Bistro	4.6	2.6	0.6	0.58	89
Sainsbury's Mediterranean Chicken & Pasta, Taste The Difference	4.6	3.8	0.9	0.49	136
Waitrose World Café Serrano Ham & Manchego Croquettes	4.8	18	4.3	0.88	305
Asda Piri Piri Mini Pork Ribs	5.2	16.9	6.5	0.9	262
Sainsbury's My Goodness! Savoury Cous Cous	5.5	2.8	0.5	0.35	124
Tesco Vegetable Moussaka	5.6	8.5	3.1	0.5	143
Sainsbury's My Goodness! Persian Chicken Salad	8.9	2.7	0.7	0.55	139

Ready Meals

Many of these products have added sugar, some as you can see more than most. Follow the 100g rule but beware of the product size. Look at the list of ingredients, if sugar is listed at the top beware.

Asian

To help you make the best choices, products are listed starting with the least sugar first.

Product	Sugar	Fat	Sat per 100g	Salt	Cals
Tesco Takeaway Sticky Jasmine Rice	<0.1	0.2	0.1	0	126
Asda Oriental Snacks	0.2	11	0.8	0.8	242
Tesco Takeaway Vegetable Chow Mein	0.3	1.5	0.2	0.5	96
Waitrose Asian Fusion Coconut Rice	0.3	4.6	2.6	0.19	181
Waitrose Asian Fusion Siu Mai	0.3	6	1.7	0.83	159
Asda Chinese Takeaway Szechaun Meal	0.5	3.3	0.4	0.48	169
Asda Chosen by You Chicken Fried Rice	0.5	2.8	0.3	0.58	173
Asda Chosen by You Chilli Noodles	0.5	4.7	1	0.13	122
Asda Chosen by You Egg Fried Rice	0.5	3.3	0.4	0.49	169
Asda Chosen by You Special Fried Rice	0.5	3.5	0.6	0.6	164
Asda Chosen by You Thai Jasmine Rice	0.5	1.3	0.1	0.22	155
Asda Feast Beef in Black Bean, Chicken Curry, Sweet & Sour Chicken	0.5	3.3	0.4	0.48	169
Sainsbury's Egg Fried Rice	0.5	6.5	0.8	0.51	177
Sainsbury's Special Fried Rice	0.5	5.4	0.7	0.55	164
Asda Chosen by You Vegetable Spring Rolls	0.6	8.6	0.6	0.8	216
Asda Chosen by You Crispy Shredded Duck Snack	0.6	16	4.4	0.88	254
Waitrose Egg Fried Rice	0.6	4.4	0.7	0.48	159
Morrisons Kitchen Chinese Egg Fried Rice	0.7	4.3	0.6	0.33	156
Sainsbury's Chilli & Coconut Prawn Curry & Rice	0.7	3.7	2.2	0.48	119
Tesco Healthy Living Chicken Chow Mein	0.8	1.1	0.3	0.3	85
Waitrose Special Fried Rice	0.8	5.2	0.6	0.48	164
Tesco Ken Hom Green Thai Chicken Curry And Rice	0.9	4.3	1.9	0.7	142
Asda Chinese Crispy Half Duck Pancakes	1	15.4	4.2	1.2	282
Sainsbury's Chinese Chicken Curry & Rice	1	2.4	0.5	0.43	132

Product	Sugar	Fat	Sat	Salt	Cals
			per 100g		
Tesco Takeaway Egg Fried Rice	1	3.7	0.4	0.2	154
Sainsbury's Thai Green Curry & Rice	1.1	6.6	3.8	0.58	151
Weight Watchers Red Thai Chicken Curry	1.1	1.9	0.9	0.4	90
Asda Chosen by You Chicken Singapore Noodles	1.2	5.3	0.8	0.5	137
Waitrose Love Life Red Thai Chicken Curry	1.2	1.3	1	0.35	95
Sainsbury's Asian Beef Rendang	1.3	6.1	1.4	0.35	142
Sainsbury's Thai Red Curry & Rice, Be Good To Yourself	1.3	1.6	0.8	0.38	87
Tesco Ken Hom Egg Fried Rice	1.3	4.3	0.5	0.2	185
Tesco Ken Hom Chicken Chow Mein	1.4	2.8	0.4	0.6	128
Waitrose Love Life Calorie Controlled Green Thai Chicken Curry	1.4	2.2	1.1	0.36	92
Weight Watchers Chicken Katsu Curry	1.4	1.7	0.6	0.45	97
Asda Chosen by You Chef's Special Singapore Noodles	1.5	7.9	1.1	0.6	154
Asda Chosen by You Chicken in Black Bean Sauce Meal	1.5	2.5	0.3	0.6	96
Sainsbury's Singapore Noodles	1.5	7.8	0.7	0.63	159
Asda Chosen by You Chefs Special Japanese Katsu Curry	1.6	8	1.4	0.88	215
Morrisons Kitchen Thai Green Chicken & Sticky Rice	1.6	3.8	2	0.28	123
Sainsbury's Beef In Black Bean & Rice	1.6	4.7	0.6	0.68	130
Sainsbury's Chicken Chow Mein	1.6	4.7	0.4	0.78	124
Sainsbury's My Goodness! Green Thai Noodle Soup	1.6	2.3	0.9	0.42	64
Sainsbury's My Goodness! Zingy Tom Yum Prawn Noodle Soup	1.6	2.3	0.8	0.4	72
Sainsbury's Coconut Chicken Curry & Noodles	1.7	4.4	2.9	0.64	136
Tesco Big Night In Chinese Chicken Chow Mein	1.7	2	0.3	0.6	107
Tesco Big Night In Thai Green Chicken Curry And Rice	1.7	5.2	2	0.5	163
Tesco Ken Hom Red Thai Chicken Curry And Rice	1.7	3.9	1.6	0.5	139
Waitrose Asian Fusion Prawn Dumplings	1.7	1.6	0.4	0.81	137
Morrisons Kitchen Oriental Special Chicken Fried Rice	1.8	3.8	0.5	0.35	143
Sainsbury's My Goodness! Thai Green Chicken Curry & Rice	1.8	2.4	1.4	0.31	97
Tesco Big Night In Thai Red Chicken Curry And Rice	1.9	4.7	2.5	0.4	157
Tesco Takeaway Singapore Noodles	1.9	5.5	0.8	0.6	162
Asda Chicken Chow Mein	2	0.7	0.4	0.4	78

RM: Asian

Product	Sugar	Fat	Sat per 100g	Salt	Cals
Asda Chosen by You Chicken Spring Roll Selection	2	13	1.5	0.83	260
Asda Chosen by You Thai Selection Pack	2	13	1.5	0.63	246
Asda Chosen by You Thai Vegetable Snack Selection	2	13	1.5	0.63	246
Sainsbury's My Goodness! Katsu Chicken Curry & Lemongrass Rice	2	2.7	0.9	0.44	121
Asda Chosen by You Chicken Chow Mein	2.1	3.2	0.5	0.63	102
Asda Chosen by You Prawn Toast	2.1	26	2.1	1.3	355
Bol Japanese Miso Soba	2.1	1.1	0.2	0.72	63
Sainsbury's Thai Red Curry & Rice	2.1	6.1	3.3	0.54	148
Asda Chosen by You Chicken Rolls	2.2	13	0.9	0.8	258
Asda Chosen by You Chicken Spring Rolls	2.2	13	0.9	0.83	258
Asda Chosen by You Fresh Tastes Korean Chicken with Udon Noodles	2.2	0.8	0.2	0.55	75
Asda Chosen by You Salt & Chilli Chicken Wings Snack	2.2	14	3.4	0.9	237
Asda Good & Counted Chicken Chow Mein	2.2	0.8	0.2	0.43	82
Morrisons Kitchen Thai Green Chicken Curry	2.2	6.4	3.6	0.6	142
Sainsbury's Malay Chicken Curry & Rice	2.2	6	1.4	0.55	131
Tesco Takeaway Chicken Satay	2.2	6.1	1.7	0.5	112
Asda Chosen by You Chef's Special King Prawns & Chicken	2.3	3.7	0.4	0.88	92
Asda Chosen by You Chefs Special Thai Beef Massaman Curry	2.3	5.8	2.2	0.76	123
Asda Chosen by You Thai Chicken Spring Rolls	2.3	13	1.7	0.83	265
Morrisons Kitchen Oriental Chinese Chicken Curry & Egg Fried Rice	2.3	6.1	1.8	0.44	143
Morrisons NuMe Red Thai Curry	2.3	1.8	1.3	0.4	107
Tesco Takeaway Green Thai Chicken Curry	2.3	6.2	3.1	0.9	105
Asda Chosen by You Chinese Snack Platter	2.4	15	1	0.8	272
Asda Chosen by You Thai Green Curry	2.4	4.6	1.7	0.63	100
Sainsbury's Asian Miso Chicken	2.4	3.9	0.6	0.45	120
Sainsbury's Korean BBQ Chicken Curry	2.4	3.4	0.7	0.6	135
Sainsbury's My Goodness! Chicken & Prawn Singapore Noodles	2.4	3.4	1.6	0.4	107
Tesco Big Night In Chinese Chicken Curry And Egg Fried Rice	2.4	3.8	1.1	0.6	127
Tesco Big Night Time In Beef Blackbean And Egg Fried Rice	2.4	2.6	0.4	0.6	127
Tesco Finest Light Malaysian Chicken Curry	2.4	2.2	1.2	0.6	100

Product	Sugar	Fat	Sat per 100g	Salt	Cals
Tesco Healthy Living Sweet And Sour Chicken	2.4	1.7	0.3	0.3	111
Waitrose Chicken Chow Mein	2.4	3	0.4	0.71	98
Asda Chosen by You Fresh Tastes Kitchen Chinese Chicken Curry & Rice	2.4	2.2	1	0.38	88
Asda Chosen by You Chinese Special Curry	2.5	4	1.9	0.43	105
Tesco Ken Hom Kung Po Chicken And Rice	2.5	4.6	0.7	0.5	145
Waitrose Love Life Chicken Katsu Curry & Jasmine Rice	2.5	3.2	1.5	0.44	153
Asda Chosen by You Chinese Chicken Curry	2.6	4.4	2	0.4	94
Asda Good & Balanced Lemon Chicken & Wild Rice	2.6	1.6	0.2	0.3	105
Morrisons Kitchen Chilli Garlic Chicken & Egg Fried Rice	2.6	3.8	0.5	0.51	125
Morrisons Kitchen Oriental Chicken Chow Mein	2.6	2.9	0.5	1.05	122
Sainsbury's My Goodness! Chinese Chicken Chow Mein	2.6	1.4	0.2	0.39	82
Tesco Ken Hom Sweet & Sour Chicken And Rice	2.6	2.9	0.5	0.5	136
Asda Chosen by You Char Sui Pork & Prawn Rice	2.6	0.7	0.2	0.4	93
Asda Good & Balanced Oriental Pork with Rice & Lentils	2.7	2.6	0.6	0.4	117
Bol Thai Coconut Curry	2.7	3.4	1.5	0.47	83
Sainsbury's Chicken Chow Mein, Be Good To Yourself	2.7	2.4	0.4	0.42	91
Tesco Ken Hom Chicken And Blackbean With Egg Fried Rice	2.7	4.4	0.6	0.5	146
Morrisons Kitchen Takeaway Oriental Special Fried Rice	2.8	5.1	0.8	0.51	154
Sainsbury's Chicken & Chilli Spring Rolls	2.8	14.3	1.9	0.57	264
Sainsbury's Chinese Chicken Curry & Rice, Be Good To Yourself	2.8	1.5	0.5	0.43	109
Sainsbury's My Goodness! Red Thai Vegetable Curry & Rice	2.8	3.1	1.3	0.46	111
Sainsbury's Shanghai Beef	2.8	2.2	0.3	0.54	119
Tesco Chicken Red Curry With Jasmine Rice	2.8	5.1	2.8	0.6	143
Asda Chosen by You Chicken & Mushrooms	2.9	5.6	0.7	0.88	111
Asda Chosen by You Japanese Teriyaki Chicken with Rice	2.9	0.8	0.2	0.6	114
Asda Chosen by You Malaysian Chicken Penang	2.9	3.2	1.7	0.82	84
Asda Chosen by You Vegetable Chow Mein	2.9	4.6	0.5	0.68	110
Asda Chosen by You Vegetable Rolls	2.9	12	0.8	0.7	241
Morrisons Kitchen Chicken in Black Bean Sauce	2.9	4.4	0.6	0.67	135
Asda Chosen by You Red Thai King Prawn Curry & Noodles	3	1.5	0.9	0.4	72

RM: Asian

Product	Sugar	Fat	Sat per 100g	Salt	Cals
Sainsbury's Chicken & Prawn Yaki Udon Noodles	3	4.6	0.8	0.58	133
Tesco Ken Hom Chinese Chicken Curry And Rice	3	5.4	1.2	0.6	153
Asda Fresh Tastes Red Thai Chicken Curry	3	2.1	1.4	0.4	119
Asda Fresh Tastes Sweet Chilli Beef Noodles	3	1.1	0.2	0.3	84
Asda Chosen by You Chicken & Sweetcorn Soup	3.1	0.5	0.1	0.5	52
Morrisons Kitchen Red Thai Vegetable Curry	3.1	2.7	1.1	0.2	90
Morrisons Kitchen Takeaway Oriental Special Chow Mein	3.1	3.1	0.8	0.93	122
Sainsbury's Satay Chicken & Udon Noodles, Taste The Difference	3.1	3.5	0.4	0.38	115
Tesco Takeaway Chinese Chicken Curry	3.1	4.4	2.1	0.6	101
Waitrose Asian Fusion Spicy Chicken Dumpling	3.1	3.2	0.4	0.89	158
Asda Mini Chicken Satay	3.2	12.3	2.8	1.3	210
Sainsbury's My Goodness! Laksa Chicken Noodle Soup	3.2	2.3	1.2	0.48	86
Sainsbury's Vegetable Spring Rolls	3.2	11.8	1.6	0.63	212
Waitrose Prawn Toasts	3.2	16.3	1.8	0.57	268
Waitrose Singapore Noodles	3.2	2	0.4	0.63	117
Asda Thai Chicken Noodles	3.2	1.6	0.8	0.4	91
Tesco Finest Light Thai Prawn Noodles	3.3	2.1	0.3	0.9	90
Morrisons Kitchen Vegetable Spring Rolls	3.4	12.1	0.9	0.56	224
Asda Chosen by You Duck Spring Rolls	3.4	15	1.5	1.1	293
Tesco Ken Hom Crispy Aromatic Half Duck	3.4	10.1	2.9	1	241
Waitrose Oriental Egg Noodles	3.4	5.5	0.7	0.62	147
Waitrose Asian Fusion Beef Rendang	3.5	9.6	2.2	0.39	152
Waitrose Asian Fusion Chicken Pad Thai	3.5	7.7	1.4	0.35	171
Waitrose 10 Chinese Pancakes	3.6	5.4	0.4	0.03	311
Waitrose Asian Fusion Malay Chicken	3.6	9.9	4.6	0.7	140
Asda Chosen by You Chicken & Cashew	3.7	8	1.2	0.88	144
Asda Chosen by You Thai Red Curry	3.7	4.1	1.8	0.58	103
Tesco Big Night In Chinese 6 Mini Vegetable Roll	3.7	11.8	5	0.4	244
Tesco Takeaway Black Bean Beef	3.7	4.5	0.7	0.8	96
Sainsbury's Chicken Pad Thai, Taste the Difference	3.8	3	0.6	0.4	122

Product	Sugar	Fat	Sat	Salt	Cals
			per 100g		
Sainsbury's Sweet Chilli Chicken, Be Good To Yourself	3.8	1.4	0.1	0.31	96
Tesco Ken Hom Chicken And Cashew With Egg Fried Rice	3.8	6.1	0.8	0.6	183
Bol Limited Edition Noodles	3.9	1.6	0.4	0.25	73
Tesco Ken Hom Meal For 2	3.9	10.8	2	1.02	254
Waitrose Oriental Black Pepper Chicken Sizzler	3.9	5.9	1.4	0.46	128
Asda Chosen by You Thai Chicken Pad Thai	4	5.6	1.2	0.6	148
Sainsbury's Chicken & Mushroom	4	2.8	0.3	0.93	90
Tesco Takeaway Red Thai Chicken Curry	4	6.8	3	0.7	121
Sainsbury's Prawn Spring Rolls	4.1	7.1	1	1.33	209
Waitrose Green Thai Chicken Curry	4.1	8.2	3.8	0.61	132
Waitrose Oriental Chicken with Chilli Bean Sauce	4.1	3.9	0.6	0.78	92
Asda Chosen by You Fresh Tastes Char Sui Pork Noodles	4.1	1.3	0.5	0.48	79
Sainsbury's Asian Teriyaki Salmon	4.2	5.7	0.7	0.45	138
Sainsbury's My Goodness! Hoisin Duck Noodle Soup	4.2	2.5	0.3	0.44	87
Asda Fresh Tastes Singapore Chicken Noodles	4.2	1.5	0.1	0.6	83
Asda Chilli Chicken Noodles	4.3	0.8	0.1	0.3	76
Morrisons Kitchen Chicken Satay Skewers	4.3	15.2	4.1	1.3	242
Morrisons Kitchen Chinese Chicken Noodles	4.3	3.2	0.6	0.8	119
Morrisons Kitchen Singapore Chicken Noodles	4.3	3.2	0.6	0.8	119
Asda Fresh Tastes Kitchen Teriyaki Chicken Noodles	4.3	0.6	0.1	0.4	94
Tesco Takeaway Thai Meal	4.35	8.05	2.13	0.9	205
Waitrose Asian Fusion Butternut Squash Curry	4.4	11.1	6.7	0.35	134
Asda Chosen by You Chef's Special Beef in Black Bean Sauce	4.5	6.2	1.3	0.88	128
Morrisons Kitchen Takeaway Chinese Chicken Curry	4.5	8.4	4.4	0.6	134
Morrisons Kitchen Takeaway Oriental Chicken & Mushroom	4.5	3	0.4	0.78	88
Sainsbury's Crispy Seaweed	4.5	60.3	3.4	0.7	607
Sainsbury's Duck Spring Rolls	4.5	15.1	2.3	0.74	280
Sainsbury's Hoisin Slow Cooked Duck Noodles	4.5	5.3	0.7	0.53	133
Waitrose Asian Fusion Chicken Penang	4.5	11.3	7.6	0.93	167
Asda Sticky Asian Chicken Noodles	4.5	0.6	0.1	0.3	69

RM: Asian

Product	Sugar	Fat	Sat	Salt	Cals
			per 100g		
Waitrose Beef in Black Bean Sauce	4.7	5.8	1.2	0.88	114
Morrisons Kitchen Meal Sweet & Sour and Chicken	4.8	5.5	1.5	0.64	149
Morrisons NuMe Sweet & Sour Chicken & Rice	4.8	1.5	0.2	0.5	121
Waitrose Asian Fusion Chicken Massaman Curry	4.8	11	6	0.58	176
Waitrose Oriental Kung Po Chicken	4.8	3.4	0.5	0.63	100
Sainsbury's Firecracker King Prawns & Rice	4.9	1.9	0.2	0.55	95
Sainsbury's Vegetable Spring Rolls, Basics	4.9	9.5	0.8	0.79	224
Tesco Ken Hom's Vegetable Spring Rolls	4.9	10.3	4.4	0.8	232
Waitrose Red Thai Chicken Curry	4.9	5.9	4.3	0.6	118
Morrisons Kitchen Takeaway Oriental Beef & Black Bean	5.1	4.1	1.3	0.83	102
Asda Chosen by You Chinese Chicken Skewers Snack	5.2	2.2	0.8	0.6	153
Asda Chosen by You Sweet Chilli Chicken Pieces	5.2	2.3	0.9	0.8	165
Waitrose Asian Chicken & Prawn Laksa	5.2	5.2	3	0.65	133
Morrisons Kitchen Chinese Barbecue Pork with Egg Fried Rice	5.3	4.6	0.7	0.69	139
Morrisons Kitchen Takeaway Black Pepper Chicken	5.3	3.3	0.4	0.77	100
Sainsbury's My Goodness! Chilli Chicken Noodles	5.3	1.5	0.2	0.36	87
Asda Chicken Skewers with Peanut Dip	5.4	14.4	3.7	1.3	243
Asda Chosen by You Kung Po Chicken	5.5	3.4	0.4	0.4	113
Waitrose Asian Fusion Prawn Krapow	5.5	2.5	0.2	0.55	115
Waitrose Oriental Snack Selection	5.5	12	1.1	0.41	283
Waitrose Duck Spring Rolls	5.8	12.9	1.9	0.64	249
Morrisons Kitchen Duck Spring Rolls	5.9	12.6	1.1	0.9	259
Tesco Ken Hom Crispy Sweet And Sour Chicken	5.9	9.9	3.8	1.1	191
Tesco Big Night Time In Sweet And Sour Chicken	6.1	2.3	0.4	0.6	143
Tesco Takeaway Chinese Meal	6.25	8.35	3.27	0.9	211
Waitrose Asian Fusion Battered Hake	6.6	8.5	0.9	0.55	160
Tesco Ken Hom Crispy Sweet And Sour Pork	6.7	7.1	0.7	1.3	179
Tesco Prawn Crackers	6.8	33.2	3.4	2.2	550
Morrisons Kitchen Half Crispy Aromatic Duck	6.9	8	1.7	0.8	282
Sainsbury's Crispy Chicken With Sweet Chilli Sauce	6.9	7	0.7	0.31	176

Product	Sugar	Fat	Sat per 100g	Salt	Cals
Asda Chinese Takeaway Prawn Crackers	7	31.3	11.3	2.2	530
Asda Prawn Crackers	7	31.3	3.1	2.2	530
Morrisons Kitchen Sweet & Sour Chicken & Rice	7.1	3.4	0.5	0.39	137
Sainsbury's Prawn Toasts	7.1	24.1	2.1	1.02	351
Waitrose Oriental Soy & Ginger Chicken Wings	7.1	11.3	3	0.98	217
Waitrose Crispy Seaweed	7.3	64.9	5.2	0.33	654
Sainsbury's Crispy Chicken With Lemon Sauce	7.4	6	0.7	0.3	107
Tesco Everyday Value Sweet And Sour Chicken	7.4	1.4	0.3	0.7	120
Asda Chosen by You Sweet & Sour Chicken	7.6	1	0.2	0.7	95
Waitrose Oriental Chicken with Satay Sauce	7.7	11.1	3.3	0.44	184
Asda Chosen by You Chef's Special Thai Fire Cracker Chicken	7.8	3.7	0.8	0.9	107
Tesco Chicken Chow Mein With Noodles	7.8	2.8	0.6	0.4	150
Waitrose Vegetable Spring Rolls	8	12	1.1	0.48	249
Asda Smart Price Sweet & Sour Chicken with Rice	8.2	1	0.2	0.5	97
Sainsbury's Prawn Crackers	8.2	30.9	2.7	2.4	530
Waitrose Chicken with Cashew Nuts	8.2	5.6	0.8	0.88	131
Morrisons Kitchen Sticky Mini Ribs	8.5	12.7	4.9	0.7	216
Morrisons Kitchen Hoisin Duck Noodles	8.7	3.9	0.6	0.9	144
Waitrose Sweet & Sour Chicken with Rice	8.9	1	0.1	0.18	130
Waitrose Half Aromatic Crispy Duck	9.1	11.6	3.4	0.81	247
Morrisons Kitchen Aromatic Shredded Duck Kit	9.2	8.7	2	1	243
Asda Chosen by You Peking Pork Mini Ribs	9.5	15	5.7	0.55	264
Asda Chinese Takeaway Thai Crackers	10	31	14	1.7	530
Sainsbury's Crispy Sweet & Sour Chicken With Rice	10.3	3.9	0.4	0.57	182
Morrisons Kitchen Takeaway Sweet & Sour Chicken	10.4	2.3	0.4	0.38	120
Tesco Ken Hom Crispy Chilli Prawns	10.4	11.1	3.2	1	224
Waitrose Sweet & Sour Chicken in Batter	10.4	4.2	0.5	0.63	154
Morrisons Kitchen Sweet Chilli Chicken Noodles	10.5	0.5	0.1	0.4	121
Tesco Chicken Pad Thai With Noodles	10.8	6.5	2.4	0.4	195
Waitrose Oriental Mandarin Chicken Sizzler	10.8	6.4	1.4	0.47	153

RM: Asian

Product	Sugar	Fat	Sat	Salt	Cals
			per 100g		
Asda Chosen by You Sweet Chilli Chicken Noodles	11	1.6	0.3	0.43	121
Tesco Ken Hom Crispy Chilli Beef	11	14.7	1.2	1.3	271
Sainsbury's Duck In Plum Sauce With Egg Fried Rice	11.1	4.8	0.8	0.55	170
Waitrose Lemon Chicken in Batter	11.2	3.1	0.4	0.4	148
Morrisons Kitchen Crispy Sweet & Sour Chicken	11.5	7.2	2.6	0.93	190
Sainsbury's Mini Spare Ribs	11.7	13.4	5.3	0.45	226
Sainsbury's Sweet & Sour Chicken With Rice	11.8	3.2	0.3	0.38	159
Tesco Ken Hom's Aromatic Duck And Pancakes	11.8	8.6	2	1.3	244
Waitrose Mini Spare Ribs	11.9	12.3	5	0.65	241
Asda Chosen by You Chef's Special Lemon Chicken	12	6.3	0.9	0.33	206
Asda Chosen by You Chef's Special Sweet & Sour Chicken	12	4.5	2	0.43	170
Waitrose Sweet & Sour Chicken	12	2.8	0.4	0.5	122
Waitrose Asian Fusion Char Siu Buns	12.2	6.5	1.5	0.91	236
Sainsbury's Shredded Peking Duck	12.9	4.4	1	1.09	190
Tesco Takeaway Sweet & Sour Chicken	12.9	1.8	0.2	0.4	103
Morrisons Crispy Sweet Chilli Chicken	14.7	7.6	2.7	0.93	211
Sainsbury's Crispy Chilli King Prawns	15	8.6	0.9	1.08	211
Sainsbury's Crispy Sweet & Sour Chicken	15.8	3.2	0.3	0.58	169
Sainsbury's Duck In Plum Sauce	15.9	2.9	0.7	0.44	145
Waitrose Oriental Crispy Rrawns	16.9	11.5	1.2	0.61	253
Morrisons Kitchen Crispy Lemon Chicken	17.6	5.1	2.3	0.61	196
Waitrose Oriental Crispy Beef	17.7	15.4	1.4	0.83	324
Asda Chosen by You Chef's Special Crispy Chilli Beef	19	6.6	1.2	0.85	283
Morrisons Kitchen Sweet Chilli Sauce	42.1	0.1	trace	0.3	269
Morrisons Kitchen Hoisin Sauce	42.7	0.3	0.1	1.7	234
Asda Hoisin Dip	46.3	0.6	0.2	1.9	232
Asda Chinese Dip Trio	50	0.5	0.1	0.91	232
Asda Sweet Chilli Dip	50	0.5	0.1	0.9	232

Ready Meals

Many of these products have added sugar, some as you can see more than most. Follow the 100g rule but beware of the product size. Look at the list of ingredients, if sugar is listed at the top beware.

Traditional

To help you make the best choices, products are listed starting with the least sugar first.

Product	Sugar	Fat	Sat per 100g	Salt	Cals
Asda Filled Yorkshire Pudding with Roast Beef	0.1	3.7	1	0.6	130
Morrisons Kitchen Liver & Bacon with Mash	0.1	3.7	1.4	0.5	103
Morrisons Parmentier Potato & Bacon	0.1	11.2	1.4	0.3	191
Asda Cheesy Jacket Potatoes	0.2	4.5	3.1	0.3	130
Asda Chosen by You Classic Favourites Chicken Wrapped in Bacon	0.2	9.6	4.8	0.8	189
Asda Chosen by You Classic Favourites Ham & Mushroom Chicken	0.2	4.3	2.4	0.6	120
Morrisons Kitchen Chicken Casserole	0.2	5.9	1.7	0.4	129
Tesco Finest Chicken Kiev	0.2	5.9	0.9	0.5	175
Asda Chosen by You Classic Favourites Chicken Kiev	0.3	11	5.7	0.2	204
Morrisons Kitchen Parmentier Potatoes	0.3	7.2	3.5	0.3	193
Morrisons Kitchen Roast Potatoes	0.3	3.2	0.2	0.4	146
Morrisons Kitchen Sausage & Mash	0.3	5.3	1.9	0.6	107
Morrisons Signature Skin On Chunky Chips	0.3	8.2	2.4	0.4	212
Waitrose Menu Crunchy Topped Fish Pie	0.3	4.7	2.5	0.63	112
Weight Watchers Cottage Pie	0.3	2.4	1.2	0.4	89
Morrisons Signature Coq Au Vin	0.3	9	2.4	0.6	148
Asda Chosen by You Classic Chicken Breasts in Red Wine Sauce	0.4	0.9	0.2	0.6	70
Asda Chosen by You Classic Favourites Cod Pie	0.4	2.9	1.8	0.5	90
Asda Chosen by You Classic Favourites Gammon & Cheese	0.4	5.4	2.9	1.7	139
Morrisons Kitchen Cheesy Mashed Potato	0.4	6.6	4.3	0.4	139
Morrisons Savers Cottage Pie	0.4	3.9	1.8	0.5	108
Tesco Everyday Value Cottage Pie	0.4	1.3	0.4	0.4	73
Waitrose Beef Stroganoff	0.4	4.3	1.9	0.39	126
Waitrose Chicken in Red Wine	0.4	3.1	1.1	0.45	84

Product	Sugar	Fat	Sat	Salt	Cals
			per 100g		
Asda Chosen by You Classic Favourites Cod with Cheese Sauce	0.5	2.9	1.8	0.5	91
Asda Chosen by You World Favourites Lime & Coriander Chicken	0.5	10.7	1.1	0.4	178
Asda Cottage Pie	0.5	5.1	2.4	0.4	109
Asda Cumberland Pie	0.5	5.1	2.6	0.4	114
Asda Extra Special Cheddar Mash	0.5	6.6	4.4	0.4	126
Asda Shepherds Pie	0.5	4.4	2.2	0.4	97
Morrisons Kitchen Braised Beef & Mash	0.5	3.6	1.5	0.5	98
Morrisons Kitchen Slow-Cooked Beef Brisket with Gravy	0.5	2.6	1.3	0.5	106
Sainsbury's Buttery Potato Mash	0.5	3.4	2.3	0.33	97
Sainsbury's Classic Buttery Mash Side	0.5	3.4	2.3	0.33	97
Sainsbury's Ready to Roast Mini Jackets & Roasted Garlic Butter	0.5	5.3	3.1	0.05	121
Tesco Everyday Value Sausage And Mash	0.5	3.8	1	0.6	101
Waitrose Love Life Calorie Controlled Fish Pie	0.5	1.9	1	0.33	87
Asda Chosen by Kids Roast Chicken Dinner	0.6	2.4	0.6	0.4	92
Asda Hunter's Chicken	0.6	2	0.6	0.4	121
Heston from Waitrose Fish Pie	0.6	3.5	1.3	0.56	105
Morrisons Kitchen Chicken & Mushroom Cumberland Pie	0.6	6.3	3.9	0.5	125
Morrisons Kitchen Fisherman's Pie	0.6	4.4	2.4	0.6	116
Sainsbury's Chicken & Mushroom Pie, Be Good To Yourself	0.6	2.1	0.9	0.32	92
Sainsbury's Luxury Fish Pie, Taste the Difference	0.6	4.3	2.4	0.58	116
Sainsbury's Prepared Baby Potatoes With Seasoned Butter	0.6	0.8	0.4	0.15	80
Tesco Everyday Value Fishermans Pie	0.6	2.2	1.2	0.5	81
Waitrose Braised Steak with Mashed Potato	0.6	2.9	1.6	0.41	96
Waitrose Menu Chicken Tarragon	0.6	6.5	3.4	0.78	144
Waitrose Fisherman's Pie	0.6	5.9	3.5	0.62	127
Asda Cheesy Mash	0.7	6.9	4.5	0.5	125
Heston from Waitrose Cauliflower Macaroni Cheese	0.7	10.1	5	0.38	189
Morrisons Kitchen Beef Rib with Gravy	0.7	8.4	4.3	0.6	151
Morrisons Kitchen Cabbage & Onion Mashed Potato	0.7	5.8	3.7	0.4	106
Morrisons Kitchen Mini Roast Chicken Dinner	0.7	7.2	2.6	0.9	160

RM: Traditional

Product	Sugar	Fat	Sat (per 100g)	Salt	Cals
Morrisons Kitchen Smoky Chicken & Bacon Parcels	0.7	13.5	6.8	0.9	237
Morrisons Signature Smoked Haddock & King Prawn Fish Pie	0.7	8	4	0.7	152
Sainsbury's Fish Pie, Taste the Difference	0.7	4.1	2.3	0.62	111
Sainsbury's Steak & Ale Puff Pastry Pie	0.7	13.6	6	0.48	253
Tesco Fish Pie	0.7	3	1.8	0.3	92
Morrisons Signature British Steak Diane	0.7	4.2	2	0.5	113
Tesco Breaded Mushrooms With Garlic And Onion	0.7	33	2.5	0.5	350
Asda Chosen by You Classic Favourites Peppercorn Chicken	0.8	2.7	1.2	0.4	106
Asda Classic Sausage & Mash	0.8	5.1	2	0.6	107
Asda Smart Price Sausage and Mash	0.8	5.2	2.1	0.5	109
Morrisons Mini Classics Haddock & Parsley Sauce	0.8	3.9	2.6	0.4	100
Morrisons NuMe Chicken Dinner	0.8	1.8	0.5	0.3	78
Morrisons Signature Cottage Pie with Real Ale Gravy	0.8	2.9	1.7	0.5	96
Sainsbury's Chicken With Cheese & Bacon Sauce	0.8	7.4	4.1	0.78	166
Sainsbury's Classic Cumberland Fish Pie	0.8	4.7	2.6	0.64	121
Sainsbury's Steak Puff Pastry Pie	0.8	16.4	6.9	0.63	280
Tesco Finest Aberdeen Angus Cottage Pie	0.8	5.3	2.5	0.7	113
Tesco Finest Beef Stroganoff With Rice	0.8	6.6	3.8	0.6	153
Tesco Finest Creamed Spinach	0.8	8.5	4.5	0.6	103
Tesco Roast Beef Dinner	0.8	2.4	0.5	0.4	105
Waitrose Cottage Pie	0.8	5	2.5	0.56	117
Asda Smart Price Fish Pie	0.9	4.1	2.5	0.6	93
Morrisons Cottage Pie	0.9	4.9	2.5	0.6	110
Morrisons Mini Classics Braised Steak & Mash	0.9	2.5	1.3	0.6	87
Sainsbury's British Classic Cottage Pie	0.9	4.1	2.2	0.45	90
Sainsbury's Classic Cottage Pie	0.9	4.1	2.2	0.45	90
Sainsbury's Fish Pie, Be Good To Yourself	0.9	2.1	0.9	0.44	90
Tesco Beef Casserole And Dumplings	0.9	5.6	2.4	0.5	141
Tesco Finest Cod And Crab Bake	0.9	3	1.4	0.4	86
Waitrose Beef Goulash	0.9	3.8	0.6	0.46	101

Product	Sugar	Fat	Sat	Salt	Cals
			per 100g		
Waitrose Love Life Calorie Controlled Cottage Pie	0.9	2	0.9	0.46	82
Morrisons Signature Rump Steak Stroganoff & Rice	0.9	5.4	2.9	0.7	132
Morrisons Signature King Prawn & Slow Roasted Tomato	0.9	4.3	1.8	0.6	108
Asda Extra Special Mustard Mash	1	6.1	4.1	0.7	105
Morrisons Kitchen Beef Casserole	1	6.2	2.5	0.5	132
Morrisons Mini Classics Beef Casserole & Dumplings	1	5.3	2.3	0.5	124
Sainsbury's Classic Chicken Hotpot	1	2.1	0.4	0.35	87
Sainsbury's Cottage Pie, Taste the Difference	1	6.9	4.1	0.63	150
Sainsbury's Fish & Chips	1	7.4	0.7	0.3	208
Tesco Cottage Pie	1	3.6	1	0.5	94
Tesco Finest Shepherds Pie	1	4.9	2.3	0.5	121
Tesco Shepherds Pie	1	2.3	1	0.4	81
Waitrose Love Life Beef & Red Wine Casserole	1	1.6	0.7	0.46	90
Morrisons Cumberland Pie	1.1	5.9	3	0.6	120
Morrisons Kitchen Cauliflower Cheese	1.1	4.1	2.4	0.3	74
Morrisons Kitchen Chicken In White Wine Sauce	1.1	5	1.2	0.3	121
Morrisons Kitchen Cottage Pie	1.1	4.8	2.5	0.6	108
Morrisons Kitchen Cumberland Pie	1.1	7.8	4	0.6	140
Morrisons Kitchen Minced Beef Hotpot	1.1	3.1	1	0.7	107
Sainsbury's Chicken & White Wine Cream Sauce, Taste the Difference	1.1	5.3	2.7	0.43	119
Sainsbury's British Classic Braised Steak	1.1	4.5	2.3	0.61	121
Sainsbury's Cottage Pie, Basics	1.1	3	1.6	0.45	79
Sainsbury's Crispy Potato Slices	1.1	9.7	0.7	0.38	190
Sainsbury's Fish Pie, Basics	1.1	2.8	1.3	0.58	89
Sainsbury's Maris Piper Potato Mash, Taste the Difference	1.1	8.3	5.5	0.7	136
Sainsbury's Mashed Potato	1.1	1.4	1	0.25	69
Sainsbury's Ready To Roast Diced Pots, Garlic, Herbs & Rosemary Butter	1.1	2	1.1	0.3	104
Sainsbury's Steak Deep Filled Shortcrust Pastry Pie	1.1	18.5	7.3	0.55	327
Sainsbury's Top Crust Steak Pie, Taste the Difference	1.1	10	6	0.63	188
Tesco Chicken Roast Dinner	1.1	2.9	0.6	0.5	93

RM: Traditional

Product	Sugar	Fat	Sat per 100g	Salt	Cals
Tesco Family Favourites Cottage Pie	1.1	1.1	0.5	0.3	74
Tesco Sausage And Mash	1.1	7.4	3.3	0.6	132
Waitrose Chicken Forestiere	1.1	2.1	0.7	0.45	81
Waitrose Cumberland Pie	1.1	5.5	3	0.53	126
Sainsbury's Green Vegetable Risotto Kiev	1.1	11.2	3.4	0.58	234
Asda Chosen by You Classic Favourites Chicken En Croute	1.2	16	5.6	0.6	272
Asda Potato Gratin	1.2	4	2.4	0.6	89
Menu from Waitrose Chicken Forestiere	1.2	4.1	2	0.62	128
Morrisons Kitchen Chicken with Leeks, Bacon & Roast Potatoes	1.2	4.9	1.5	0.6	120
Morrisons Kitchen Steak & Ale with Cheesy Mash	1.2	4	2.2	0.6	105
Morrisons Signature Maris Piper Dauphinoise Potatoes	1.2	11.9	7.5	0.3	177
Sainsbury's Carrot & Swede Mash	1.2	2.5	1.6	0.48	62
Sainsbury's Classic Toad In The Hole	1.2	15.1	5.6	0.76	262
Sainsbury's Shepherds Pie, Basics	1.2	2.6	1.5	0.55	75
Sainsbury's Steak & Ale, Taste the Difference	1.2	8.8	3.6	0.87	183
Sainsbury's Yorkshire Top Chicken Dinner, Be Good To Yourself	1.2	1.6	0.4	0.35	89
Tesco Finest Beef In Peppercorn Sauce	1.2	7	3.9	0.3	130
Tesco Finest Steak Diane	1.2	9.4	4.1	0.3	157
Waitrose Chicken with Cheese and Bacon	1.2	4.3	1.9	0.42	100
Waitrose Love Life Calorie Ctrl Pulled Ham Hock in Mustard Sauce	1.2	2.7	1.2	0.6	84
Waitrose Potato Gratin	1.2	4.3	2.7	0.33	113
Waitrose Shepherd's Pie	1.2	7	4	0.5	130
Tesco Mushroom Stroganoff And Rice	1.2	3.5	2.3	0.3	113
Asda Chosen by You Classic Favourites Chicken Mini Roasts	1.3	5.2	1.7	0.7	131
Asda Classic Minced Beef Hot Pot	1.3	4.9	2.1	0.5	102
Asda Extra Special Chilli Crab Bucatini	1.3	5.7	0.8	0.33	166
Asda Smart Price Minced Beef & Dumplings	1.3	5.7	2.9	0.4	126
Morrisons Kitchen Creamed Cabbage & Spring Greens	1.3	4.6	3	0.4	66
Morrisons NuMe Braised Beef with Mash	1.3	2.2	1.2	0.2	78
Morrisons NuMe Cumberland Pie	1.3	1.6	0.8	0.3	77

Product	Sugar	Fat	Sat per 100g	Salt	Cals
Sainsbury's Braised Beef & Mash, Be Good To Yourself	1.3	1.2	0.4	0.46	81
Sainsbury's British Classic Bangers & Mash	1.3	6.2	2.9	0.82	133
Sainsbury's Classic Liver & Bacon With Mash	1.3	4.5	2.3	0.66	112
Sainsbury's Classic Shepherds Pie	1.3	3.4	1.9	0.55	95
Tesco Turkey Roast Dinner	1.3	4.3	1.3	0.5	104
Waitrose Beef Gratin	1.3	6.9	2.6	0.45	157
Waitrose Chicken Hotpot	1.3	3.1	0.4	0.4	84
Asda Chicken Leek & Bacon Bake	1.4	3.6	1.8	0.6	115
Asda Classic Chicken Hotpot	1.4	1.4	0.8	0.6	73
Asda Good & Counted Cottage Pie	1.4	2.3	1.2	0.4	93
Asda Minced Beef Hot Pot	1.4	4.9	2.3	0.5	103
Charlie Bigham's Cottage Pie	1.4	9	3.9	0.58	155
Menu from Waitrose Cottage Pie	1.4	6.7	3.3	0.52	140
Morrisons Kitchen Corned Beef Hash	1.4	3.3	1.3	0.5	123
Waitrose Bubble & Squeak	1.4	2.3	1.7	0.47	78
Waitrose Roast Chicken Pie	1.4	16.5	7.6	0.6	289
Asda Creamy Chicken & Bacon Bake	1.5	3.6	1.8	0.6	125
Charlie Bigham's Fish Pie	1.5	7.4	4	0.7	133
Morrisons Kitchen Shepherd's Pie	1.5	4	2.3	0.5	100
Sainsbury's Carrot & Swede Potato Mash	1.5	1.7	1.1	0.32	55
Sainsbury's Sausages & Mash, Basics	1.5	3.9	1.4	0.53	98
Sainsbury's Shepherds Pie, Be Good To Yourself	1.5	1.8	0.9	0.35	82
Tesco Cumberland Pie	1.5	5.3	2.6	0.5	125
Tesco Minced Beef Hot Pot	1.5	4.6	2.5	0.3	128
Sainsbury's Love Vegetable Bubble & Squeak Meat Free Sausages	1.5	21.2	4.4	0.68	313
Asda Buffalo Chicken Wings	1.6	12.1	2.7	0.8	200
Menu from Waitrose Beef Strogonoff	1.6	9.7	6.1	0.53	154
Sainsbury's Potato Croquettes	1.6	10.3	1.1	0.54	214
Sainsbury's Rumbledethumps	1.6	5.8	3.7	0.48	82
Tesco Braised Beef And Mash	1.6	3.9	1.9	0.6	97

RM: Traditional

Product	Sugar	Fat	Sat	Salt	Cals
			per 100g		
Tesco Healthy Living Cottage Pie	1.6	2.4	1.2	0.3	82
Tesco Liver Bacon And Mash	1.6	3.1	0.6	0.4	111
Waitrose Jacket Potato with Cheese	1.6	5.5	3.6	0.37	137
Waitrose Sausage & Mash	1.6	5.3	1.8	0.61	113
Waitrose Spinach Mornay	1.6	8.4	4.8	0.59	113
Asda Extra Special Creamy Mash	1.7	6.4	4.2	0.8	117
Asda Smart Price Cottage Pie	1.7	4.3	2.4	0.6	89
Waitrose Smoked Fish Gratin	1.7	5.4	2.2	0.55	123
Waitrose Steak Pie	1.7	17.5	6.8	0.64	296
Sainsbury's Liver & Mash, Basics	1.8	2.5	1.2	0.45	83
Tesco Healthy Living Baked Potatoes With Cheese	1.8	2.9	1.9	0.2	100
Waitrose Chicken Provençal	1.8	1.8	0.2	0.38	66
Waitrose Cod Fillet in Parsley Sauce	1.8	2.2	1	0.4	78
Quorn Cottage Pie	1.8	2.5	0.8	0.5	89
Sainsbury's British Classic Minced Beef Hotpot	1.9	4.9	2.2	0.49	127
Sainsbury's Chicken Casserole, Be Good To Yourself	1.9	1.3	0.1	0.42	69
Tesco Finest Beef Wellington	1.9	13.8	8.3	0.2	289
Tesco Finest Chicken Chasseur	1.9	2.6	0.5	0.3	104
Tesco Finest Chicken With Lemon And Herb Butter	1.9	8.3	3.6	0.6	209
Sainsbury's Bistro Chicken with Red Wine Sauce, Taste the Difference	1.9	4	1	0.25	101
Sainsbury's Steak Au Poivre, Taste the Difference	1.9	5.2	2.7	0.65	128
Morrisons Kitchen Cod In Parsley Sauce	2	2.3	1.2	0.2	91
Morrisons Kitchen Peas, Green Beans & Broccoli	2	3	1.9	trace	67
Morrisons Kitchen Slow-Cooked Lamb Shank with Mint Gravy	2	9.4	4.2	0.4	174
Sainsbury's Chicken & Madeira Wine, Be Good To Yourself	2	1.6	0.5	0.38	96
Sainsbury's Classic Sausage & Mash Yorkshire	2	7.5	2.5	0.65	157
Sainsbury's Minced Beef Casserole, Be Good To Yourself	2	1.6	0.8	0.41	77
Waitrose Ham Hock in Cider & Mustard Sauce	2	2.9	1.2	0.63	89
Waitrose Steak & Kidney Puddings	2	12.6	6.8	0.75	233
Sainsbury's Beef Stroganoff & Herb Rice, Taste the Difference	2	4.1	2	0.38	148

Product	Sugar	Fat	Sat	Salt	Cals
			per 100g		
Sainsbury's Love Vegetable Mushroom & Spinach Meat Free Burger	2	14.6	1.4	0.63	254
Morrisons Kitchen Vegetable Medley	2.1	0.4	0.1	0.2	52
Morrisons Signature Shepherd's Pie with Leeks	2.1	4.4	1.9	0.6	116
Sainsbury's Cheese & Potato Bake	2.1	5	3.1	0.73	94
Sainsbury's Classic Cumberland Pie	2.1	5.7	2.9	0.72	128
Tesco Finest Beef Chianti And Rosemary Potatoes	2.1	3.9	0.7	0.5	103
Tesco Finest Potato Dauphinoise	2.1	11.9	8	0.5	174
Tesco Healthy Living Braised Beef And Mash	2.1	1.5	0.6	0.4	75
Tesco Healthy Living Chicken Potatoes And Vegetables	2.1	0.8	0.3	0.3	69
Waitrose Lamb Hotpot	2.1	6	2.2	0.42	131
Asda Extra Special Beef Bourguignon	2.1	3.7	1.6	0.6	115
Asda Chosen by You Classic Favourites Chicken Bacon & Leek Traybake	2.2	7.4	2.7	0.65	144
Menu from Waitrose Slow-Cooked Beef Bourguignon	2.2	4.1	1.3	0.56	117
Sainsbury's Beef Stew	2.2	6.1	3.4	0.72	154
Sainsbury's British Classic Chicken Casserole	2.2	5.5	2.2	0.71	129
Sainsbury's Ham Hock & Sweet Potato Mash, Be Good To Yourself	2.2	2	0.7	0.38	77
Sainsbury's My Goodness! Classic Roast Chicken Dinner	2.2	1.5	0.3	0.27	81
Sainsbury's Roast Chicken Dinner	2.2	3	0.8	0.46	111
Sainsbury's Roast Potatoes, Taste the Difference	2.2	3.6	1	0.33	112
Tesco Finest Cumberland Sausage And Mash	2.2	8.7	3.5	0.5	143
Tesco Finest Slow Cooked Beef With Potatoes	2.2	3.4	1.2	0.4	122
Waitrose Yorkshire with Sausage and Mash	2.2	8.3	2	0.59	173
Asda Fresh Tastes Roast Chicken Dinner	2.2	1.8	0.5	0.4	85
Waitrose Indian Lemon & Coriander Hake	2.2	3.7	0.6	0.6	107
Asda Garlic Mushrooms	2.3	11.2	1	0.4	195
Asda Good & Counted Chicken in Peppercorn Sauce	2.3	1.8	0.9	0.5	81
Asda Steak & Ale with Mash	2.3	1.5	0.8	0.5	80
Morrisons Kitchen Chicken Dinner	2.3	3.4	0.3	0.4	103
Morrisons Kitchen Minced Lamb Hotpot	2.3	2.9	1	0.6	94
Sainsbury's British Classic Beef Dinner	2.3	3.1	1.1	0.38	122

RM: Traditional

Product	Sugar	Fat	Sat per 100g	Salt	Cals
Tesco Finest Beef Madras With Pilau Rice	2.3	5.3	2.2	0.5	156
Tesco Finest Ham Hock And Potato Gratin	2.3	9	4.7	0.9	160
Tesco Finest Lancashire Hotpot	2.3	3.7	1.2	0.4	116
Tesco Finest Roast Chicken And Pancetta Bake	2.3	9.6	3.4	0.6	174
Waitrose Beef Casserole	2.3	3.8	2	0.61	129
Waitrose Haddock in Cheese Sauce	2.3	2.7	1.6	0.52	83
Sainsbury's Bistro Minty Lamb Casserole with Baby Potatoes, TtD	2.3	2.6	1.2	0.43	76
Asda Beef Stew & Dumplings	2.4	4	2	0.5	117
Morrisons Kitchen Minced Beef & Potatoes	2.4	1.1	0.5	0.3	63
Sainsbury's Green Vegetable Selection	2.4	2.1	1.1	0.15	58
Sainsbury's Luxury Shepherds Pie, Taste the Difference	2.4	5	2.6	0.44	119
Sainsbury's Tomato & Basil Chicken, Be Good To Yourself	2.4	2	0.2	0.38	95
Waitrose Liver & Bacon	2.4	3.6	1.2	0.46	101
Tesco Mushroom And Ale Potato Topped Pie	2.4	3.2	1.4	0.4	85
Asda Chosen by You Classic Favourites Minted Lamb Loin Chops	2.5	22.2	9.9	0.4	311
Morrisons Kitchen Slow-Cooked Lamb Shank in a Red Wine	2.5	8.9	4	0.6	168
Morrisons Signature Beef Bourguignon	2.5	2.8	1.1	0.5	84
Tesco Chicken And Bacon Pie	2.5	5	2.9	0.5	116
Tesco Chicken And Mushroom Hotpot	2.5	6.5	2	0.3	135
Waitrose Roast Beef Dinner	2.6	6.1	0.42	0.42	170
Asda Chosen by You Vegetarian Chicken Style Casserole & Dumplings	2.6	3.8	1.6	0.4	105
Waitrose Vegetarian Mushroom & Spinach Filo Parcel	2.6	10.9	5.4	0.66	213
Asda Extra Special Green Vegetable Medley	2.7	4.5	2.8	0.3	72
Sainsbury's Classic Lamb Dinner	2.7	3.3	1.3	0.33	107
Tesco Family Favourites Beef Casserole	2.7	3.9	1	0.6	98
Tesco Family Favourites Chicken And Vegetable Casserole	2.7	3.9	1	0.6	98
Tesco Finest Baby Potatoes With Minted Peas	2.7	4.4	2.9	0.3	107
Tesco Finest Chicken Potato Topped Pie	2.7	8.4	4.4	0.7	142
Tesco Finest Chunky Chips	2.7	3.5	0.3	0.8	167
Tesco Finest Creamy Fish Pie	2.7	8.4	4.4	0.7	142

Product	Sugar	Fat	Sat	Salt	Cals
			per 100g		
Tesco Healthy Living Sausage And Mash	2.7	2.7	1.2	0.4	104
Tesco Liver And Bacon	2.7	4	1.1	0.5	121
Sainsbury's Bistro Beef Bourguignon, Taste the Difference Bistro	2.7	3.8	1.2	0.53	137
Linda McCartney Lentil Cottage Pie	2.7	2.6	1	0.4	94
Asda Vegetable Medley Side	2.8	4.3	2.7	0.9	71
Menu from Waitrose Rich Beef Casserole	2.8	5.6	2.7	0.54	158
Sainsbury's Roast Potatoes	2.8	2.1	0.3	0.37	120
Tesco Finest Beef In Chianti	2.8	2.8	0.6	0.6	113
Waitrose Leek Gratin	2.8	10.1	6.2	0.85	143
Waitrose Menu Lamb Shanks	2.8	6.6	2.9	0.75	144
Morrisons Kitchen Beef & Ale	2.9	3.4	1.6	0.5	92
Sainsbury's Bistro Creamy Ham Hock & Chicken Pie, Taste the Difference	2.9	7.6	3.9	0.38	135
Sainsbury's British Classic Lancashire Hotpot	2.9	3.8	1.4	0.45	107
Sainsbury's Chicken & White Wine Puff Pastry Pie	2.9	14.9	6.5	0.65	267
Sainsbury's Classic Minced Beef Cobbler	2.9	8.2	4.4	0.79	171
Sainsbury's Creamy Basil Chicken & Potatoes, Taste the Difference Bistro	2.9	6	2	0.58	115
Sainsbury's Haddock & Prawn Dauphinoise Taste the Difference	2.9	7.1	3	0.58	153
Sainsbury's Rustic Chips, Taste the Difference	2.9	2.4	0.4	0.65	144
Tesco Finest Pulled Beef And Sweet Onion Mash	2.9	6.6	3.2	0.5	142
Tesco Finest Light Tomato And Olive Chicken	2.9	2.5	0.5	0.4	76
Sainsbury's Classic Minced Lamb Hotpot	3	6.7	2.7	0.6	129
Morrisons Kitchen Chicken En Croute	3	16.8	9.4	0.7	281
Menu from Waitrose Succulent Pork Meatballs	3.1	14.2	3.3	0.64	191
Sainsbury's Chicken In Vintage Cider, Taste the Difference Bistro	3.1	4.6	1	0.38	125
Tesco Finest Chicken Leek And Bacon Filo Pie	3.1	13.9	7	0.7	242
Tesco Finest Roast Potatoes With Goose Fat	3.1	6.8	1.4	0.3	158
Tesco Finest Rosemary Roasted Potatoes	3.1	1.7	0.3	0.5	102
Asda Chosen by You Fresh Tastes Ham Hock with Potatoes	3.2	2.5	1	0.4	71
Asda Liver & Onions	3.2	2.4	1	0.3	98
Kirsty's Cottage Pie Sweet Potato Mash	3.2	1.4	0.6	0.4	75

RM: Traditional

Product	Sugar	Fat	Sat	Salt	Cals
			per 100g		
Sainsbury's Lamb Shanks, Taste the Difference	3.2	6.4	1.3	0.54	144
Sainsbury's Vegetable Selection With Herb Butter	3.2	3.2	2.1	0.34	74
Asda Vegetarian Carrot & Lentil Cottage Pie	3.2	2.1	0.7	0.5	89
Sainsbury's My Goodness! Spicy Pulled Pork & Sweet Potato Mash	3.3	2.3	0.4	0.44	83
Tesco Finest Root Vegetable Mash	3.3	4.8	3.2	0.4	91
Morrisons Kitchen Chicken Kievs	3.3	11.2	5.8	0.6	236
Morrisons Kitchen Chicken, Cheese & Bacon	3.4	6.8	4.1	0.5	170
Tesco Finest Cauliflower Cheese	3.4	8.2	5.5	0.5	124
Tesco Finest Pork Belly With Apple	3.4	15	5.6	0.6	200
Morrisons Kitchen Chunky Chips	3.5	6	0.5	0.1	153
Morrisons Kitchen Fresh Ideas Cheesy Chicken with Ham	3.5	5.4	3.4	0.4	155
Sainsbury's Parmentier Potatoes	3.5	7.5	2.3	0.58	197
Asda Fiery Hot Onion Rings	3.6	14.1	1.5	0.7	255
Waitrose Love Life Cal Ctrl Chicken, Madeira Wine & Porcini Mushrooms	3.6	2	0.6	0.41	88
Asda Baby Potatoes with Butter & Herbs	3.8	1.2	0.5	0.1	80
Asda Chosen by You Sizzler Steak Diane	4	6.2	1.5	0.4	135
Morrisons Kitchen Hunters Chicken	4.1	5.3	2.8	0.7	171
Waitrose Mild & Creamy Fruity Chicken with Rice	4.1	4.4	2.2	0.18	152
Waitrose World Caf_ Pork & Beef Meatballs	4.5	13.4	3	0.54	200
Asda Chosen by You Vegetarian Aubergine & Mozzarella Bake	4.7	3.1	1.5	0.5	69
Heston from Waitrose Confit Duck	4.9	6.2	1.3	0.46	138
Morrisons NuMe Hunter's Chicken with Wedges	5	2.3	0.6	0.3	111
Morrisons Kitchen Carrot & Swede Mashed Potato	5.1	2	1.2	0.4	70
Waitrose Vegetarian Aubergine & Feta Burgers	5.1	12.7	1.9	0.64	235
Asda Chosen by You Fresh Tastes Smoky BBQ Chicken & Rice	5.3	1.2	0.2	0.39	115
Tesco Finest Lamb Shanks With Roasted Vegetables	5.3	4.9	1.8	0.7	115
Asda Chosen by You Lamb Meatballs with Fruity Chickpea Rice	5.4	3.3	1.1	0.33	108
Waitrose Vegetarian Aubergine, Pepper & Cheese Parcels	5.4	11.8	5.7	0.68	213
Asda Chosen by You Firecracker Chicken & Rice	5.5	1.8	0.5	0.4	99
Morrisons Kitchen Sweet Potato & Pumpkin Seed Croquettes	5.5	9.7	1.5	0.3	218

Product	Sugar	Fat	Sat	Salt	Cals
			per 100g		
Sainsbury's Vegetarian Cottage Pie	5.6	3.3	1.4	0.63	102
Asda Extra Special Tender Lamb Shanks with Mint Sauce	5.7	7.2	2.9	0.4	157
Morrisons Kitchen Vegetarian Naked Bean Burger	5.7	6.5	0.5	0.3	167
Waitrose Chicken with Spring Onion & Ginger	6	4.4	0.5	0.73	102
Sainsbury's Chicken & Spinach Filo Pie, Taste the Difference	6.2	5.5	2.9	0.38	135
Waitrose Duck à la Orange	6.2	5.4	1.4	0.61	140
Waitrose Butter Chicken	6.4	11.9	6	0.57	190
Morrisons Kitchen Gammon & Pineapple	7.7	1.4	0.5	1.3	116
Morrisons Signature Lamb Shoulder Honey & Balsamic	8.3	22.4	11.4	0.4	319
Asda Chosen by You Classic Favourites Gammon & Pineapple	8.4	1.6	0.6	1.3	112
Asda Chosen by You World Favourites Tomato & Chilli Chicken	8.5	4.7	0.5	0.4	156
Morrisons Kitchen BBQ Pork Shanks	8.9	5.6	2	0.5	176
Asda Chosen by You World Favourites Mango Chicken	9.8	1.9	0.5	0.4	126
Asda Chosen by You Classic Favourites Hunters Chicken Traybake	13	6.4	2.4	0.4	173

Cooking Sauces

I was delighted to find that some cooking sauces don't contain added sugar. This list shows the sugar content but make sure you check the ingredients list to find out if it's natural (from tomatoes for example), or added.

Indian

To help you make the best choices, products are listed starting with the least sugar first.

Product	Sugar	Fat	Sat	Salt	Cals
		per 100g / 100ml			
Waitrose Essential Reduced Fat Coconut Milk	0.8	6	5.5	0.05	61
Morrisons Canned Reduced Fat Coconut Milk	1	7.6	5.3	0.1	77
Patak's Madras Spice Paste	1.6	24.9	1.8	4.89	296
Sharwood's Lime Pickle	1.6	5.5	1.2	10.8	88
Waitrose Cooks' Ingredients Oorganic Coconut Milk	1.7	18	16.6	0.08	180
The Spice Tailor Spiced Spinach Curry Sauce	1.9	9.4	2.6	1.7	116
Morrisons Chilli Cheese Sauce	1.9	8.5	1.6	0.8	105
Morrisons Canned Coconut Milk	2	17.3	15.9	0.1	172
Sainsbury's Raita Dipping Sauce	2.1	10.2	0.8	0.75	129
Asda Chosen by You Fruity Biryani Oven Bake Sauce	2.1	5.8	1.3	0.7	108
Waitrose Essential Coconut Milk	2.3	18	16.6	0.13	188
Tesco Healthy Living Vegetable Rogan Josh Cooking Sauce	2.5	0.5	0	0.4	31
Tesco Saag Aloo	2.6	6.8	1.6	0.9	94
Loyd Grossman Madras Sauce	2.7	8.9	1.6	0.71	114
Waitrose Essential Coconut Cream	2.7	21	19.4	0.15	219
Loyd Grossman Bhuna Curry Sayce	2.8	7.2	0.7	0.76	98
Tesco Spicy Lime Pickle	2.9	12.2	0.8	7.1	168
The Spice Tailor Mangalore Herb Curry Sauce	2.9	12.1	3.8	1.9	155
Asda Chosen by You Balti Cooking Sauce	2.9	2.6	0.2	0.6	53
Patak's Saag Masala Sauce	3	5	0.9	0.81	79
Spice Tailor Keralan Coconut Sauce	3	19.1	13.1	1.1	215
Sainsbury's Butter Chicken Cooking Sauce	3	8.4	5.3	0.5	107
Morrisons Beef Madras	3.1	4.1	0.8	0.6	96
Tesco Balti Mild Sauce	3.2	1.7	0.1	0.6	48

Cooking Sauces: Indian

Product	Sugar	Fat	Sat	Salt	Cals
	per 100g / 100ml				
Asda Chosen by You Madras Cooking Sauce	3.2	3.4	0.8	0.4	60
Patak's Mild Curry Paste	3.3	24.7	1.8	3.58	306
Sharwood's Madras Sauce	3.3	4.4	1.1	0.85	75
Geeta's Madras Paste	3.3	7.8	1.8	1.2	104
Patak's Madras Sauce	3.5	5.3	0.4	0.73	86
Waitrose Half Fat Jalfrezi Sauce	3.5	7.3	0.5	0.63	102
Asda Chosen by You Butter Chicken Cooking Sauce	3.5	9.4	4.6	0.75	112
Asda Good & Counted Tikka Cooking Sauce	3.6	2.2	0.4	0.6	57
Patak's Bhuna Sauce	3.8	5.6	0.4	0.72	85
Patak's Biriyani Oven Bake Sauce	3.8	5.3	0.4	0.72	80
Patak's Vindaloo Sauce	3.9	6.3	0.5	0.71	90
Sharwood's Butter Chicken Curry Sauce	3.9	7.5	2.7	0.78	102
Asda Chosen by You Tikka Masala	3.9	3.5	1.7	0.5	70
Patak's Dopiaza Sauce	4	5.1	0.4	0.72	81
Geeta's Korma Paste	4	7.4	1.7	1.2	99
Geeta's Tikka Paste	4	5.7	0.4	1.3	82
Waitrose Korma Cooking Sauce	4	19.9	9.7	0.65	214
Patak's Spice Sensations Balti Sauce	4.1	5.7	0.4	0.77	86
Sharwood's Jalfrezi Sauce	4.1	5.5	0.4	0.95	82
Sainsbury's Korma Sauce	4.1	9.2	5.6	0.52	123
Tesco Butter Chicken Sauce	4.1	9.9	5	0.7	126
Tesco Jalfrezi Sauce	4.1	6.9	0.6	1.3	95
Waitrose Balti Curry Paste	4.1	17.1	1.1	2.17	219
Asda Chosen by You Rogan Josh	4.1	4.7	0.7	0.6	84
Asda Chosen by You Curry Cooking Sauce	4.1	8.6	3.5	0.7	118
Asda Chosen by You Jalfrezi Cooking Sauce	4.1	2.4	0.2	0.3	49
Patak's Bailti Sauce	4.2	5.3	0.4	0.76	84
Patak's Tandoori Spice Marinade	4.2	2.7	0.3	6.07	99
Sharwood's Balti Sauce	4.2	5.8	0.8	0.83	86
Sharwood's Rogan Josh Sauce	4.2	4.8	0.5	0.68	75

Cooking Sauces: Indian

Product	Sugar	Fat	Sat	Salt	Cals
			per 100g / 100ml		
Morrisons Raita	4.2	1.5	0.9	0.8	53
Homepride Curry Cooking Sauce	4.3	1.7	0.5	1	51
Sainsbury's Balti Cooking Sauce	4.3	1.6	<.1	0.47	49
Sainsbury's Korma Light Sauce	4.4	5.1	3.5	0.47	88
Tesco Finest Jalfrezi Cooking Sauce	4.4	3.9	1.1	0.6	72
Asda Smart Price Mild Curry Cooking Sauce	4.4	3.6	1.4	1	74
Patak's Rogan Josh Sauce	4.5	3.3	0.2	0.72	68
Patak's Spice Sensations Jalfrei Sauce	4.5	6.2	0.4	0.77	94
Sharwood's Bhuna Sauce	4.5	4.5	0.4	0.88	76
Tesco Finest Madras Cooking Sauce	4.5	6	1.6	0.7	93
Waitrose Half Fat Biryani Sauce	4.5	4	0.3	0.7	69
Sainsbury's Madras Sauce	4.6	4.9	0.8	0.53	85
Tesco Madras Cooking Sauce	4.6	5.8	0.5	0.8	88
Morrisons Madras Sauce	4.6	5.9	0.7	0.8	91
Asda Chosen by You Madras	4.6	5.8	0.4	0.68	102
Asda Chosen by You Rogan Josh Cooking Sauce	4.6	3	0.3	0.5	54
Asda Chosen by You Dopiaza Cooking Sauce	4.6	3.6	0.2	0.5	72
Asda Chosen by You Raita	4.6	19.7	1.6	0.9	214
Sainsbury's Rogan Josh Cooking Sauce	4.7	3.8	0.3	0.54	70
Asda Chosen by You Balti	4.7	3.8	0.5	0.73	76
Asda Chosen by You Bhuna Cooking Sauce	4.8	2.8	0.3	0.6	57
Sharwood's Dopiaza Sauce	4.9	7	0.6	0.8	99
Spice Tailor Punjabi Tomato Sauce	4.9	8.4	1	1	122
Tesco Rogan Josh Cooking Sauce	4.9	4.2	0.3	0.7	75
Waitrose Rogan Josh Curry Paste	4.9	21.2	1.3	2.48	249
Patak's Butter Chicken Curry Sauce	5	10.5	4.1	0.72	133
Sharwood's Spicy Tikka Masala Sauce	5	6.5	3.3	0.7	103
Seeds of Change Organic Balti Sauce	5.1	4.1	0.5	0.81	78
Tesco Healthy Living Tikka Masala Cooking Sauce	5.1	2.5	1.1	0.5	62
The Spice Tailor Punjabi Tomato Curry Sauce	5.1	9.3	1	1.7	130

Cooking Sauces: Indian

Product	Sugar	Fat	Sat	Salt	Cals
Morrisons Massaman Curry Paste	5.1	4.2	1	1.9	85
Spice Tailor Rogan Josh Sauce	5.2	13.4	2.2	1.2	189
Tesco Hot Tikka Masala Cooking Sauce	5.2	7	2.2	0.7	110
The Spice Tailor Rustic Rogan Josh Sauce	5.2	13.4	2.2	1.2	169
Morrisons Rogan Josh Sauce	5.2	5.4	0.4	0.8	88
Morrisons NuMe Bhuna Sauce	5.2	1.2	0.1	0.8	48
Sainsbury's Curry Sauce, Basics	5.3	2.2	0.2	0.7	62
Meena's Tangy Rogan Josh Sauce	5.4	6.2	1.6	0.37	90
Patak's Pasanda Sauce	5.4	8	3.1	0.7	122
Seeds of Change Organic Jalfrezi Sauce	5.4	7.2	2.7	0.82	110
Seeds of Change Organic Korma Sauce	5.4	10.2	5.9	0.78	140
Spice Tailor Southern Pepper Sauce	5.4	13	1.5	2.2	167
Uncle Ben's Medium Curry Sauce	5.4	4.5	1.9	0.8	88
The Spice Tailor Southern Pepper Curry Sauce	5.4	13	1.5	2.2	167
Asda Free From Tikka Masala Sauce	5.4	6.4	4.2	0.7	96
Loyd Grossman Jalfrezi Sauce	5.5	5.9	1.7	0.76	91
Morrisons Balti Sauce	5.5	3.6	0.3	0.7	69
Sainsbury's Jalfrezi Sauce	5.6	2.3	0.4	0.57	59
Tesco Tikka Masala Cooking Sauce	5.6	7.9	2.3	0.7	125
Seeds of Change Organic Tikka Masala Sauce	5.7	8.4	2.4	0.81	118
Sharwood's Tikka Masala Saag Sauce	5.7	6	3.4	0.85	100
Sainsbury's Creamy Coconut Stir Through Sauce	5.7	9.4	6.8	0.88	133
Tesco Finest Balti Cooking Sauce	5.8	3.8	0.3	0.5	76
Homepride Curry Cooking Sauce	5.9	2.5	0.8	1	69
Tesco Finest Royal Korma	5.9	8.3	5.2	0.6	124
Morrisons NuMe Tikka Sauce	6	2.4	0.7	0.8	68
Morrisons Jalfrezi Sauce	6	3.8	0.3	0.7	74
Patak's Spice Sensations Korma Sauce	6.1	9.8	5.8	0.76	155
Tesco Tarka Dahl	6.1	3.8	0.7	0.7	85
Sainsbury's Balti Paste	6.2	8.1	0.6	1.75	147

Cooking Sauces: Indian

Product	Sugar	Fat	Sat	Salt	Cals
			per 100g / 100ml		
Asda Chosen by You Dopiaza	6.2	3.2	0.2	0.68	77
Loyd Grossman Balti Curry Sauce	6.3	6.7	0.5	0.84	103
Sharwood's Tikka Masala Creamy Sauce	6.3	6.6	3.9	0.83	108
Spice Tailor Korma Curry Sauce	6.3	16.8	9.1	1.2	206
Sainsbury's Bhuna Cooking Sauce	6.3	0.7	<.1	0.47	46
The Spice Tailor Delicate Korma Curry Sauce	6.3	16.8	9.1	1.2	206
Waitrose Onion Base for Curry	6.3	9.3	0.6	0.1	138
Asda Chosen by You Korma Cooking Sauce	6.3	6.5	3.7	0.7	104
Morrisons Korma Sauce	6.4	12.1	7.7	0.8	158
Loyd Grossman Rogan Josh Sauce	6.5	8.7	1.9	0.68	127
Patak's Raita Dip	6.5	1.8	1	1	65
Uncle Ben's Korma Sauce	6.6	5.9	4.2	0.81	107
Tesco Korma Cooking Sauce	6.6	9.3	7.4	0.8	134
Meena's Tikka Masala Sauce	6.7	7.9	2.3	0.75	117
Patak's Korma Sauce	6.7	12.7	7.3	0.72	163
Sainsbury's Biriyani Cooking Sauce	6.7	4.3	1.2	0.62	89
Waitrose Half Fat Korma Sauce	6.7	7.3	3	0.63	109
Patak's Rogan Josh Paste	6.8	20.1	1.5	3.33	261
Patak's Balti Paste	6.9	21.4	1.5	4.75	289
Tesco Tikka Curry Paste	7	8.3	2.4	1	145
Asda Chosen by You Tikka Masala Cooking Sauce	7	3.5	1.3	0.6	77
Meena's Creamy Korma Sauce	7.1	14.5	8	0.75	182
Patak's Spice Sensations Tikka Masala Sauce	7.1	6.9	2.3	0.79	122
Tesco Sauce for Bombay Potatoes	7.1	6.8	0.5	0.7	109
Tesco Vindaloo Cooking Sauce	7.1	3.9	0.3	0.7	85
Meena's Spicy Jelfrezi Sauce	7.2	6.2	1.3	0.62	102
Asda Chosen by You Korma	7.3	7	5.1	0.68	122
Tesco Finest Tikka Masala	7.4	6.3	1.9	0.6	113
Sharwood's Korma Sauce	7.6	7.7	5.5	0.74	125
Spice Tailor Tikka Masala Sauce	7.6	11.2	4.1	1.6	152

Cooking Sauces: Indian

Product	Sugar	Fat	Sat	Salt	Cals
			per 100g / 100ml		
Sainsbury's Jalfrezi Stir Through Sauce	7.6	2.9	1.4	0.95	80
The Spice Tailor Original Tikka Masala Sauce	7.6	11.2	4.1	1.6	152
Waitrose Keralan Curry Paste	7.6	16.7	8.6	2.83	227
Tesco Biriyani Cooking Sauce	7.7	6.7	1.4	0.7	115
Waitrose Tikka Half Fat Sauce	7.7	7.4	1.5	0.65	111
Waitrose Tikka Curry Paste	7.7	23.6	4.4	2.23	279
Sainsbury's Madras Paste	7.9	6.3	0.6	1.14	120
Waitrose Tikka Cooking Sauce	7.9	14.3	3.9	0.57	183
Waitrose Sauce Makhani	8	19.8	8.6	0.68	227
Patak's Jalfrezi Paste	8.1	26.9	4.3	3.32	323
Loyd Grossman Korma Sauce	8.9	8.3	5.8	0.72	128
Loyd Grossman Tikka Massala Sauce	9	10.6	3.7	0.83	147
Patak's Korma Paste	9.9	15.4	1.6	4.76	227
Waitrose Pasanda Cooking Sauce	10.7	16.6	6.6	0.63	222
Waitrose Korma Curry Paste	10.7	22.8	10.1	3	305
Tesco Korma Curry Paste	10.9	13	5.3	1.6	220
Waitrose Makhani Curry Paste	11.1	17	3.6	2.98	237
Patak's Tikka Masala Paste	11.3	22.7	1.6	4.73	307
Sainsbury's Korma Paste	11.4	17.9	5.2	1.68	244
Asda Chosen by You Onion & Mint Dip	16	<0.5	<0.1	0.45	81
Tesco Tomato, Onion & Mint Dip	17.9	0.3	0.1	0.6	89
Patak's Brinjal (Aubergine) Pickle	33.4	24.8	1.7	4	381
Tesco Mango & Kashmiri Chilli Dip	41.3	0.3	0.1	1	186
Waitrose Mango Chutney	43.7	trace	trace	0.3	261
Sharwood's Mango Chutney	44.7	<1	<1	2.9	240
Tesco Finest Mango Chutney	48.5	0.7	0.2	2.8	270
Sainsbury's Mango Chutney Dipping Sauce	49	<.5	<1	2.47	231
Sharwood's Mango Chutney & Kashmiri Chilli	49.8	<1	<1	2.9	234
Waitrose Hot & Spicy Mango Chutney	50.4	0.3	0.2	1.83	233
Sainsbury's Mango Chutney	51.8	0.8	0.1	3	248

Cooking Sauces: Indian

Product	Sugar	Fat	Sat	Salt	Cals
			per 100g / 100ml		
Morrisons Mango Chutney	53.1	0.2	0.2	2.8	216
Tesco Mango Chutney	54.2	0.3	0.1	2.5	242
Geeta's Mango Chutney	57.2	0.2	trace	2	253
Tesco Spicy Mango Chutney	58.8	0.6	0.1	2.5	250

Cooking Sauces

I was delighted to find that some cooking sauces don't contain added sugar. This list shows the sugar content but make sure you check the ingredients list to find out if it's natural (from tomatoes for example), or added.

Mexican & Moroccan

To help you make the best choices, products are listed starting with the least sugar first.

Product	Sugar	Fat	Sat	Salt	Cals
			per 100g / 100ml		
Al'fez Natural Tahini	0	60	10	0.43	686
Old El Paso Burrito Dinner Kit	2.8	3.2	1.1	1.16	186
Santa Maria Enchilada Sauce	3	3.4	1.8	1.5	57
Al'fez Harissa Paste	3.2	11.2	0.9	2.02	190
Loyd Grossman Classic Chilli Sauce	3.5	3	0.3	0.82	69
Old El Paso Stand N Stuff Taco Kit	3.5	14.4	1.2	1.86	303
Santa Maria Smoked Paprika Medium Chilli Sauce	3.7	1	0.2	0.56	76
Asda Chosen by You Mexican Style Classic Medium Salsa	3.7	0.3	0.1	0.45	28
Asda Smart Price Chilli Con Carne Cooking Sauce	3.7	9	3.7	0.7	110
Old El Paso Crispy Chicken Fajita Kit	3.9	3.6	1.3	1.47	241
Tesco Mexican Mild Salsa Dip	3.9	0.2	0.1	1	30
Al'Fez Paprika & Coriander Stir Fry	4	4.6	0.3	0.2	343
Old El Paso Nacho Kit	4	8.1	0.7	0.97	226
Old El Paso One Pan Rice Chilli & Garli	4.1	1.1	0.2	2.64	207
Tesco Hot Salsa	4.1	0.2	0.1	1.2	34
Santa Maria Fajita Kit Medium	4.3	4.6	2.1	4	230
Asda Chosen by You Mexican Style Cheesy Enchilada Cooking Sauce	4.5	6.4	1.7	0.5	96
Asda Chosen by You Mexican Style Hot-Hot-Hot Chilli	4.7	0.9	0.1	0.5	60
Santa Maria Fajita Kit Smoky BBQ	4.8	9	5	2.9	265
Old El Paso Squeexy Chunky Salsa	5	0.5	0	1.38	44
Asda Chosen by You Mexican Style No Bean Chilli Cooking Sauce	5	0.7	0.1	0.7	50
Asda Chosen by You Hot Chilli Cooking Sauce	5.1	0.6	0.1	0.7	69
Old El Paso Thick 'N' Chunky Salsa, Hot	5.2	0.5	0	1.18	39
Asda Chosen by You Mexican Style Smoky Barbecue Fajita Sauce	5.3	1.3	0.2	0.5	61

Cooking Sauces: Mexican & Moroccan

Product	Sugar	Fat	Sat	Salt	Cals
			per 100g / 100ml		
Santa Maria Enchilada Kit	5.4	3.5	1.5	2.4	235
Uncle Ben's Chilli Sauce, Medium	5.4	0.4	0.1	0.7	58
Asda Chosen by You Fajita Cooking Sauce	5.7	2.1	0.2	0.5	64
Asda Chosen by You Mild Chilli Cooking Sauce	5.7	0.5	0.1	0.7	58
Asda Chosen by You Mexican Style Classic Fajita	5.9	1.1	0.1	0.7	59
Old El Paso Fajita Kit, Tomato & Pepper	6	4	1.4	1.9	229
Santa Maria Salsa, Medium	6	0.4	0.2	1.5	46
Sainsbury's Chilli Cooking Sauce, Light	6	0.7	0.1	0.56	71
Asda Gluten Free Chilli Cooking Sauce	6	0.4	0.1	0.6	68
Sainsbury's Chilli Cooking Sauce, Hot	6.1	1.8	0.2	0.58	78
Homepride Chilli Cooking Sauce	6.2	0.5	<.1	0.71	58
Santa Maria Habanero Chilli Con Carne Sauce	6.2	0.7	0.1	1.3	78
Morrisons Fajita Cooking Sauce	6.5	2.2	0.4	0.6	64
Old El Paso Quesadilla Kit	6.7	3.4	1.1	2.25	224
Sainsbury's Chilli Cooking Sauce, Medium	6.7	1.6	0.2	0.61	77
Santa Maria Fajita Seasoning & Sauce	6.9	1.5	0.1	1.5	63
Tesco Hot Chilli Sauce	7	0.4	0.1	0.6	59
Tesco Chilli Sauce Mild	7.1	0.4	0.1	0.5	63
Old El Paso Stand N Stuff Soft Taco Smoky BBQ Kit	7.2	4.2	1.6	2.44	213
Seeds of Change Organic Chilli Sauce	7.2	1.4	0.3	0.78	75
Al'fez Apricot & Chilli Stir Fry	10.3	7	0.93	0.52	533
Al-fez Apricot & Coriander Tagine Pour Sauce	13	5.1	0.5	1	536
Al'fez Moroccan Meatball Sauce	14	5.5	0.4	0.34	489
Old El Paso Chilli Spice Mix, Mild	21	4.2	0.4	22.8	280
Old El Paso Squeezy Red Jalapeno Relish	22.1	0.5	0	0.41	133

Cooking Sauces

I was delighted to find that some cooking sauces don't contain added sugar. This list shows the sugar content but make sure you check the ingredients list to find out if it's natural (from tomatoes for example), or added.

Asian

To help you make the best choices, products are listed starting with the least sugar first.

Product	Sugar	Fat	Sat	Salt	Cals
	per 100g / 100ml				
Yutaka Organic Tamari Soy Sauce	0.2	0.1	0.6	13.5	67
Kikkoman Soy Sauce Naturally Brewed	0.6	0	0	16.9	77
Amoy Reduced Fat Coconut Milk	1.4	10	8.9	trace	101
Tukata Shaoxing Rice Wine	1.8	0.5	0.1	<1	27
Amoy Rich/Creamy Coconut Milk	2.1	17.5	14.4	trace	172
Asda Chosen by You Thai Green Cooking Sauce	2.7	11	7.3	0.3	130
Sharwoods Chinese Curry Sauce	2.9	1.6	0.2	0.98	47
Morrisons Chinese Curry Cooking Sauce	2.9	3.5	1.4	0.8	75
Asda Chosen by You Red Thai Cooking Sauce	3	6.7	4.7	0.7	95
Waitrose Cooks' Ingredients Green Thai Paste	3.2	5.3	0.5	2.65	91
Sainsbury's Chinese Chip Shop Cooking Sauce	3.3	3.4	1.4	0.8	75
Blue Dragon Thai Green Curry Paste	3.7	8.6	0.8	1.3	128
Asda Chosen by You Chinese Curry Cooking Sauce	3.7	3.1	1.3	1.1	71
Tesco Healthy Living Black Bean Cooking Sauce	3.8	0.9	0.1	0.5	46
Waitrose Cooks' Ingredients Red Thai Paste	3.8	9.1	0.8	1.02	131
Asda Chosen by You Chinese Curry Cooking Sauce	3.8	4	1.7	0.65	78
Tesco Green Thai Curry Cooking Sauce	4.1	11.2	7.6	0.8	137
Yuzu Seasoning Sauce	4.3	0.5	0.1	<1	33
Blue Dragon Thai Red Curry Paste	4.4	16	1.5	3.2	206
Sharwoods Thai Red Curry Cooking Sauce	4.4	6	5.2	0.7	95
Sainsbury's Thai Green Curry Paste	4.7	8.3	3.1	1.75	132
Asda Good & Counted Sweet and Sour Cooking Sauce	4.7	0.1	0	0.6	34
Amoy Red Chilli Stir Fry Soy Sauce	4.9	trace	trace	14.8	28
Loyd Grossman Thai Red Curry Sauce	4.9	7.3	6.6	0.7	107

Cooking Sauces: Asian

Product	Sugar	Fat	Sat	Salt	Cals
		per 100g / 100ml			
Blue Dragon Thai Green Curry Sauce	5	6.4	3.2	0.92	100
Tesco Red Thai Curry Cooking Sauce	5.1	10.2	7.4	0.7	133
Loyd Grossman Thai Green Curry Sauce	5.2	7.7	7	0.75	110
Sainsbury's Lime & Coconut Curry Cooking Sauce	5.2	9.2	4.9	0.75	133
Tesco Finest Green Thai Curry Sauce	5.3	2.6	2.2	0.8	60
Tesco Thai Stir Fry Paste	5.3	8.3	0.5	4.5	126
Tesco Miso Paste	5.5	7.5	1.2	11.6	162
Morrisons Mild Chilli Cooking Sauce	5.6	0.4	0.1	0.7	56
Tesco Thai Green Curry Paste	5.8	13.8	2.2	4.2	174
Morrisons Hot Chilli Cooking Sauce	5.8	0.2	0.1	0.6	57
Sainsbury's Thai Basil Paste	5.9	16.9	1	3.95	202
Blue Dragon Fish Sauce	6.3	<1	<1	26.2	57
Tesco Finest Red Thai Curry Sauce	6.6	8.8	4.5	0.7	123
Tesco Finest Rendang Cooking Sauce	6.6	4.3	3.7	1	85
Blue Dragon Thai Red Curry Sauce	6.7	6.8	4.7	1.01	112
Tesco Thai Red Curry Paste	6.7	10.2	1.4	4.1	152
Blue Dragon Creamed Coconut	6.9	63.6	57.1	0.1	666
Tesco Finest Massaman Sauce	7	17.5	10.1	0.6	209
Sharwoods Thai Green Curry Cooking Sauce	7	6.6	5.9	0.73	107
Waitrose Cooks' Ingredients Laksa Paste	7	7.7	0.7	3.33	135
Asda Chosen by You Thai Red Curry Paste	7	10.5	4.4	3.9	142
Morrisons Red Thai Curry Paste	7.1	0.1	0	2.6	69
Tesco Black Bean Cooking Sauce	7.5	3.1	0.3	0.7	84
Sainsbury's Black Bean Cooking Sauce	7.8	1.5	<1	0.64	76
Amoy Lemongrass & Lime Stir Fry Soy Sauce	7.9	trace	trace	13.5	41
Sharwoods Stir Fry Black Bean Sauce	7.9	1.3	0.4	1.6	67
Asda Smart Price Sweet & Sour Sauce	8.1	0.1	0	0.6	52
Yutaka Japanese Wasabi Paste	8.18	9.2	1.85	5.4	256
Tesco Black Pepper & Garlic Glaze	8.2	0.5	0.1	1.4	58
Sharwoods Stir Fry Spicy Tomato Szechuan	8.3	0.3	0.2	1.2	57

Cooking Sauces: Asian

Product	Sugar	Fat	Sat	Salt	Cals
			per 100g / 100ml		
Asda Chosen by You Satay Stir-Fry Sauce	8.3	3.1	0.5	1.6	91
Thai Taste Green Curry Paste	8.5	0.7	0.2	9	106
Asda Chosen by You Nasi Goreng Stir-Fry Sauce	8.5	1.4	0.2	1.4	69
Tesco Chinese Style Curry Sauce	8.6	0.4	0	0.8	60
Sainsbury's Sweet & Sour, Basics	8.7	<.5	<.1	0.59	55
Tesco Healthy Living Sweet & Sour Cooking Sauce	8.7	0.7	0.1	0.5	54
Uncle Bens Sweet & Sour Light Sauce	8.8	0.1	0	0.42	56
Sainsbury's Fragrant Thai Base	8.8	11.8	0.7	4.8	175
Sainsbury's Pad Thai Stir Fry Sauce	8.8	10.6	2.2	1.78	156
Tesco Yellow Thai Curry Paste	9	10.8	1.7	4.3	174
Sainsbury's Tom Yum Soup Paste	9.4	12.6	0.9	4.35	177
Asda Chosen by You Thai Green Curry Paste	9.4	9.6	3.9	4	149
Sainsbury's Miso Soup Paste	9.7	1.8	0.3	4.25	82
Morrisons Green Thai Curry Paste	9.7	0.1	0.1	2.6	72
Thai Taste Red Curry Paste	9.9	1.6	0.3	9	137
Asda Chosen by You Oyster Stir-Fry Sauce	10	0	0	2.5	62
Waitrose Cooks' Ingredients Black Bean Sauce	10.5	0	0	4.3	69
Tesco Cha Cha Chicken Glaze	10.8	2.5	2.2	1.4	84
Blue Dragon Light Soy Sauce	11	0	0	11.4	51
Sainsbury's Soy Sauce Reduced Salt	11.2	<.5	<.1	8.71	55
Sharwoods Hoi Sin & Five Spices Sauce	11.2	1.8	0.2	0.95	81
Tesco Hot & Sour Paste	11.4	0.5	<.1	1.4	81
Asda Chosen by You Black Bean Cooking Sauce	11.6	1.8	0.3	1	84
Sharwoods Chow Mein Stir Fry Sauce	11.7	0.3	<.1	1.6	66
Yutaka Miso Paste, Organic	11.7	1	10.9	10.9	5.9
Sainsbury's Umami Paste	11.8	8	2.2	7.75	152
Waitrose Cooks' Ingredients Dark Soya Sauce	11.8	0	0	14.1	58
Waitrose Cooks' Ingredients Light Soya Sauce	12	0	0	18.7	53
Asda Chosen by You Hoisin Stir-Fry Sauce	12.1	0.3	0.1	1.3	77
Sharwoods Stir Fry Sweet Chilli & Lemon Grass Sauce	12.4	0.4	0.1	1.4	73

Product	Sugar	Fat	Sat	Salt	Cals
			per 100g / 100ml		
Asda Chosen by You Lemon & Ginger Cooking Sauce	12.4	0.1	0	0.7	78
Blue Dragon Szechuan Tomato Stir Fry Sauce	12.5	3	0.2	1.38	98
Blue Dragon Reduced Salt Soy Sauce	12.5	0	0	12.25	59
Tesco Satay Stir Fry Sauce	12.6	16.9	8	1.4	233
Sainsbury's Satay Dipping Sauce	12.7	8.9	4.6	1.39	168
Uncle Bens Cantonese Sauce	12.7	0.2	0.1	0.83	78
Asda Chosen by You Chow Mein Stir-Fry Sauce	12.7	1.1	0.2	1.3	84
Blue Dragon Kung Po Stir Fry Sauce	12.9	1.1	0.2	1.5	93
Sainsbury's Massaman Curry Paste	13	6.4	2	1.5	149
Tesco Everyday Value Sweet & Sour Sauce	13	0.1	0	0.7	87
Amoy Stir Fry Pad Thai Sauce	13.1	4.8	1.3	1.8	125
Morrisons Black Bean Stir Fry Sauce	13.1	1.5	0.1	1.6	112
Morrisons Sweet & Sour Sauce	13.2	0.1	0.1	0.7	72
Asda Chosen by You Pad Thai Stir Fry Sauce	13.2	1.1	0.2	1.5	87
Asda Chosen by You Sweet & Sour Cooking Sauce	13.3	0.1	0	0.6	75
Sainsbury's Sweet & Sour Sauce Light	13.8	<.5	<.1	0.63	81
Sharwoods Szechuan Sweet Chilli & Red Pepper Sauce	13.8	0.2	trace	0.69	74
Amoy Stir Fry Rich Hoi Sin Sauce	13.9	2.6	0.4	2	109
Amoy Stir Fry Teriyaki & Sesame Seeds	14.1	2.4	0.3	1	105
Asda Chosen by You Sweet & Sour Cooking Sauce	14.1	0.2	0	0.6	75
Asda Chosen by You Cantonese Cooking Sauce	15.3	1.3	0.1	0.8	96
Sainsbury's Light Soy Sauce	15.4	0	0	11.48	69
Asda Chosen by You Gluten Free Sweet & Sour Cooking Sauce	15.4	0.3	0.1	0.5	77
Sainsbury's Chinese BBQ Oven Bake Sauce	15.6	2.2	0.2	1.4	127
Sainsbury's Chow Mein Stir Fry Sauce	15.8	1.3	0.3	1.43	100
Sainsbury's Satay Stir Fry Sauce	16	8.2	1.9	1.63	168
Asda Chosen by You Hot Chilli Sauce	16	<0.5	<0.1	1.2	92
Sharwoods Stir Fry Hoi Sin & Spring Onion Sauce	16.1	1	0.1	1.5	98
Amoy Stir Fry Chow Mein Sauce	16.2	5.7	0.8	2	145
Tesco Szechuan Sweet Chilli Sauce	16.2	0.4	0.1	0.7	84

Cooking Sauces: Asian

Product	Sugar	Fat	Sat	Salt	Cals
	per 100g / 100ml				
Uncle Bens Sweet & Sour Sauce	16.2	0.2	0	0.43	85
Waitrose Cooks' Ingredients Oyster Sauce	16.4	0	0	4.73	98
Blue Dragon Chow Mein Stir Fry Sauce	16.5	0.9	0.1	1.5	103
Uncle Bens Sweet & Sour Extra Pineapple Sauce	16.5	0.2	0	0.43	86
Waitrose Essential Sweet & Sour Sauce	16.6	1.2	0.7	0.73	96
Sainsbury's Szechuan Stir Fry Sauce	16.9	3.5	0.2	1.73	113
Nem Vietnamese Pho Kit	17	0.5	0.1	6.8	281
Asda Chosen by You Oyster Sauce	17	<0.5	<0.1	4.8	90
Tesco Finest Black Bean Cooking Sauce	17.4	2.1	0.4	0.7	114
Tesco Finest Sweet & Sour Cooking Sauce	17.7	0.3	0.1	0.8	100
Asda Chosen by You Sweet Chilli Sauce	18	<0.5	<0.1	1.1	101
Tesco Korean Bulgogi Cooking Sauce	18.1	1.2	0.2	0.7	105
Asda Chosen by You Sweet & Sour Stir-Fry Sauce	18.5	0	0	0.7	98
Blue Dragon Soy Infusions Sweet Chilli Soy Sauce	18.8	0.1	<1	8	120
Tesco Hot & Spicy Sweet & Sour Sauce	18.9	0.7	0.1	0.8	105
Uncle Bens Sweet Chilli Sauce	19.1	0.3	0	0.75	106
Blue Dragon Yellow Bean & Cashew Nut Stir Fry Sauce	19.2	3.8	0.6	1.63	149
Tesco Sweet & Sour Sauce	19.4	0.7	0.1	0.7	105
Blue Dragon Restaurant Specials Sweet & Sour Battered Chicken	19.6	0.1	0	1.5	150
Sharwoods Szechuan Kung Po Sauce	19.9	1.1	0.2	0.8	120
Blue Dragon Black Bean Stir Fry	20.1	1.6	0.2	1.5	124
Sainsbury's Sweet & Sour Cooking Sauce	20.1	0.6	0.2	0.72	108
Tesco Hoi Sin Stir Fry Sauce	20.1	4.9	0.7	1.5	145
Homepride Sweet & Sour Cooking Sauce	20.3	<.5	<.1	0.8	103
Sainsbury's Oyster & Spring Onion Stir Fry Sauce	20.3	0.3	0.1	1.75	109
Sainsbury's Sticky Soy & Ginger Oven Bake	20.5	2.2	<.1	1.33	143
Asda Chosen by You Dark Soy Sauce	20.5	0	0	15	92
Blue Dragon Soy Infusions Five Spice Soy Sauce	20.8	0.3	0.2	7.8	105
Tesco Kung Po Sauce	20.8	1.4	0.2	0.6	118
Seeds of Change Sweet & Sour Sauce	20.9	0.1	0	0.57	101

Product	Sugar	Fat	Sat	Salt	Cals
			per 100g / 100ml		
Blue Dragon Dark Soy Sauce	21.3	0	0	16.7	90
Sainsbury's Hoisin & Garlic Stir Fry Sauce	21.8	1.9	0.3	1.88	144
Sainsbury's Sweet Chilli Cooking Sauce	22	0.6	0.1	0.58	116
Sainsbury's Peking Lemon Cooking Sauce	22.6	<.5	<.1	0.7	113
Sainsbury's Sweet & Sour Sauce with Extra Pineapple	22.7	<.5	0.2	0.7	116
Sharwoods Sweet & Sour Cooking Sauce	22.7	0.6	trace	0.78	113
Tesco Pai Thai Stir Fry Sauce	22.8	9.8	1.7	1.5	202
Blue Dragon Sweet & Sour Stir Fry Sauce	23.1	0.1	0	1.3	120
Asda Chosen by You Sweet Chilli & Garlic Stir-Fry Sauce	23.1	0.1	trace	1.3	114
Sainsbury's Dark Soy Sauce	23.2	0	0	12.6	117
Sainsbury's Spicy Sweet & Sour Cooking Sauce	23.5	0.7	<.1	0.59	125
Sharwoods Stir Fry Sweet & Sour Sauce	24.3	0.2	<.1	1.3	113
Blue Dragon Oyster & Spring Onion Stir Fry Sauce	24.5	0.1	0	1.8	121
Blue Dragon Hoi Sin & Garlic Stir Fry Sauce	24.9	1.4	0.1	1.8	141
Blue Dragon Restaurant Specials Cantonese Stir Fry Sauce	25.6	0.6	0.1	1.43	133
Sharwoods Real Oyster Sauce	27	0.1	0.1	5.7	129
Sainsbury's Sweet & Sour Stir Fry Sauce	27.4	0.6	0.1	0.2	153
Amoy Sticky Glaze Sweet Soy	27.4	2.5	0.3	1.3	186
Morrisons Sweet & Sour Stir Fry Sauce	27.9	trace	trace	0.3	136
Blue Dragon Sweet Chilli & Garlic Stir Fry Sauce	28.3	0.1	trace	1.25	118
Amoy Stir Fry Tangy Sweet & Sour Sauce	29	0.8	0.1	1.3	144
Sainsbury's Hoisin Dipping Sauce	29.6	<.5	<.1	1.71	176
Blue Dragon Peking Lemon Stir Fry Sauce	30.1	0.7	trace	0.34	134
Tesco Ketjap Manis Soy Sauce	30.7	0.1	0	5.6	139
Blue Dragon Double Plum Dipping Sauce	32	0.2	0	0.5	306
Blue Dragon Mango Chilli Dipping Sauce	32.3	0.1	<.1	2.8	165
Sharwoods Hoisin Marinade Sauce	33.9	1.3	0.1	2.8	171
Amoy Sticky Glaze Chinese BBQ	35.4	2.6	0.3	1.3	187
Sainsbury's Sweet Chilli & Ginger Stir Fry Sauce	35.9	0.2	0.1	1.63	174
Asda Chosen by You Pad Thai Cooking Paste	36.4	0.1	0.1	4.1	171

Cooking Sauces: Asian

Product	Sugar	Fat	Sat	Salt	Cals
		per 100g / 100ml			
Blue Dragon Chilli & Ginger Dipping Sauce	38.3	0.1	0	3	188
Sainsbury's Sweet Chilli Sauce	38.6	<.5	<.1	1.27	195
Sainsbury's Plum Dipping Sauce	38.7	<.5	<.1	1.21	182
Yutaka Japanese Mirin	42.1	<.5	<.1	<.1	218
Tesco Sweet Chilli Dipping Sauce	42.4	0.2	0.1	1.7	213
Morrisons Sweet Chilli Dipping Sauce	43.8	2.1	0.7	2.8	212
Sharwoods Plum Sauce	45	0.1	0.1	2.7	201
Morrisons Sweet Chilli Stir Fry Sauce	46.1	trace	trace	1.5	223
Waitrose Cooks' Ingredients Hoisin sauce	46.5	1.7	0.3	4.07	231
Gressingham Plum & Hoisin Sauce	49	0.9	0	0.9	221
Blue Dragon Rich Hoisin Dipping Sauce	49.7	2.6	1.4	4.3	275
Sharwoods Mango Chutney Chilli	49.8	<.1	<.1	2.9	234
Waitrose Teriyaki Sauce	50.7	0	0	4.78	220
Blue Dragon Sweet Chilli Dipping Sauce	54.7	0.7	<.1	4.3	230

Cooking Sauces

I was delighted to find that some cooking sauces don't contain added sugar. This list shows the sugar content but make sure you check the ingredients list to find out if it's natural (from tomatoes for example), or added.

Traditional

To help you make the best choices, products are listed starting with the least sugar first.

Product	Sugar	Fat	Sat	Salt	Cals
	per 100g / 100ml				
Loyd Grossman Parmesan & Cheddar	0.9	11	4.3	0.72	129
Loyd Grossman Beef Bourguignon	1	2.6	0.6	0.74	58
Loyd Grossman Coq Au Vin	1.1	2.7	0.7	0.74	60
Loyd Grossman White Wine & Parsley	1.4	9.3	3.2	0.73	111
Loyd Grossman Creamy Leek & Bacon	1.5	9.5	3.1	0.74	117
Asda Chosen by You Beef & Ale Slow Cook Sauce	1.6	0.1	0	0.6	30
Asda Chosen by You Creamy Mushroom Pour Over Sauce	1.6	11	4.2	0.7	127
Asda Chosen by You Peppercorn Pour Over Sauce	1.6	7.5	4.4	0.8	98
Chicken Tonight Mushroom Sauce	1.7	5.9	1.6	0.84	33
Sainsbury's Creamy Cheese & Bacon Potato Bake	1.7	10.9	2.8	0.57	134
Loyd Grossman Creamy Peppercorn	1.7	7.8	2.3	0.73	103
Sainsbury's Beef & Ale Casserole Cooking Sauce	1.8	<.5	<.1	0.65	31
Loyd Grossman Creamy Mustard	1.8	9.9	3.1	0.73	122
Morrisons White Wine Sauce	1.8	8.5	1.9	0.7	104
Asda Chosen by You White Wine & Cream Cooking Sauce	2	5.3	1.2	0.7	73
Sainsbury's Dauphinoise Potato Bake	2.1	14.1	2.3	0.72	154
Morrisons Beef In Ale Cook Sauce	2.1	0.3	0.1	0.7	33
Homepride Lemon & Herb Cooking Sauce	2.2	6.9	3.5	0.83	91
Chicken Tonight French Wine Sauce	2.3	7.6	1.4	0.8	91
Loyd Grossman Beef & Ale	2.3	1.3	0.1	0.66	47
Homepride White Wine & Cream Cooking Sauce	2.4	4.5	0.6	1.08	90
Asda Chosen by You Stroganoff Cooking Sauce	2.4	4.5	0.9	0.7	70
Asda Chosen by You Creamy Garlic Pour Over Sauce	2.5	11	3.1	0.5	127
Homepride Roast Chicken Sauce	2.7	<.5	<.5	0.88	37

Cooking Sauces: Traditional

Product	Sugar	Fat	Sat	Salt	Cals
	per 100g / 100ml				
Sainsbury's Creamy White Wine Cooking Sauce	2.9	6.5	2.3	0.75	91
Asda Chosen by You Dauphinoise Potato Bake Cooking Sauce	2.9	15	2.7	0.6	164
Chicken Tonight Red Wine Sauce	3	3	0.4	0.65	51
Tesco Creamy Leek & Bacon Sauce for Chicken	3.1	8.2	2.4	0.8	113
Asda Chosen by You Creamy Mushroom Cooking Sauce	3.1	8.1	1.9	0.7	104
Asda Chosen by You Cider & Apple Pour Over Sauce	3.1	6.1	1.2	0.6	89
Morrisons Cheese & Bacon Sauce	3.3	8.1	2.3	0.7	116
Loyd Grossman Creamy Cider & Apple	3.4	9.3	3.1	0.74	117
Loyd Grossman Chicken & Chorizo	3.5	6.1	1.2	0.7	102
Loyd Grossman Chicken Cacciatore	3.5	5	0.6	0.72	86
Sainsbury's Spanish Chicken	3.7	1.6	0.6	0.6	48
Loyd Grossman Beef Provencal	3.9	3.6	0.4	0.74	73
Asda Chosen by You Sausage Casserole Cooking Sauce	4	<0.5	<0.1	0.7	67
Tesco Mushroom & Ale Sauce	4.2	0.3	0.1	0.6	43
Asda Chosen by You Spanish Chicken Cooking Sauce	4.3	0.8	<0.1	0.6	42
Homepride Red Wine Cooking Sauce	4.4	0.5	0.1	0.95	50
Sainsbury's Sausage Casserole Cooking Sauce	4.5	0.1	0.1	0.59	42
Loyd Grossman Stroganoff	4.5	9	2.9	0.65	123
Tesco Butternut Squash & Sage Risotto Bake	4.7	4.4	3.1	0.8	72
Morrisons Dauphinoise Sauce	4.7	10.3	1.5	0.7	127
Tesco Sausage Casserole	5.2	0.3	0.1	0.7	48
Morrisons Honey & Mustard Sauce	5.3	4.4	1.3	0.6	81
Chicken Tonight Spanish Chicken	5.5	0.9	0.1	0.77	43
Homepride Peri Peri	5.9	0.6	<.5	0.81	42
Loyd Grossman Moroccan Tagine	6	5.5	0.8	0.73	106
Homepride Beef & Ale Casserole Cooking Sauce	6.4	<.5	<1	0.55	50
Homepride Meat Ball Sauce	7.5	0.7	0.1	0.72	56
Homepride Barbecue Cooking Sauce	8.6	1.5	0.1	1.03	77
Sainsbury's Honey & Mustard Cooking Sauce	8.7	4.2	1	0.68	96
Asda Chosen by You Honey & Mustard Cooking Sauce	8.9	7.5	1	0.7	122

Cooking Sauces: Traditional

Product	Sugar	Fat	Sat	Salt	Cals
		per 100g / 100ml			
Chicken Tonight Honey & Mustard	9.9	5.4	0.8	1.2	104
Asda Smoky Chilli & Garlic Paste	13.7	9.3	0.6	1.5	168
Sainsbury's Hunters Chicken	15.4	<.5	<.1	0.52	89
Tesco Hunters Chicken	16.4	0.2	0	0.6	91
Uncle Bens Lemon Chicken Sauce	17.7	0.4	0.1	0.81	97
Tesco Lemon & Ginger Cooking Sauce	18.7	0.2	0	0.7	96
Morrisons Hunters Chicken	20.8	0.2	0.1	0.7	101
Morrisons Lemon Chicken Cooking Sauce	23.1	0.6	0.1	0.7	110

Cooking Sauces

I was delighted to find that some cooking sauces don't contain added sugar. This list shows the sugar content but make sure you check the ingredients list to find out if it's natural (from tomatoes for example), or added.

Italian

To help you make the best choices, products are listed starting with the least sugar first.

Product	Sugar	Fat	Sat	Salt	Cals
		per 100g / 100ml			
Tesco Carbonara Sauce	<.1	10	4	0.9	129
Sainsbury's Lasagna Sauce Cheesy White	<.5	11.4	4.8	0.83	138
Sainsbury's Lasagna Sauce Creamy White	<.5	9.2	3.1	0.78	109
Sainsbury's Pasta Sauce Carbonara	<.5	9.7	3.7	0.83	127
Sainsbury's Pasta Sauce Four Cheeses	<.5	13	4.8	0.83	156
Sainsbury's Pasta Sauce, Alla Genovese, Taste the Difference	<.5	41.8	8.5	2	406
Asda Chosen by You Carbonara Pasta Sauce	<0.5	12	3.1	0.5	135
Morrisons Carbonara Sauce	0	7.5	2.7	0.8	90
Tesco White Lasagna Pasta Sauce	0.1	8.5	3	0.7	107
Tesco Reduced Fat Green Pesto	0.4	19.4	2.8	1.4	194
Morrisons Green Pesto	0.4	39.3	6.2	1	389
Morrisons White Lasagne Sauce	0.4	11.5	4.9	0.8	132
Waitrose Pesto Alla Genovese	0.4	46.1	10	1.5	445
Asda Chosen by You Reduced Fat Green Pesto	0.4	18.1	2.7	1.3	199
Waitrose Green Basil Pesto	0.5	46.9	9.6	1.5	452
Waitrose Essential Bechamel Pasta Sauce	0.6	10.1	1.6	0.5	111
Homepride Pasta Bake Cheese & Bacon	0.7	5.3	1	0.73	74
Morrisons Spinach & Ricotta Sauce	0.7	8.6	3.1	0.8	105
Loyd Grossman Lasagna Creamy White Sauce	0.8	9.3	3.4	0.59	112
Sacla Coriander Pesto	0.8	40.7	5.5	2.5	399
Morrisons Savers Pasta Sauce	0.9	0.5	0.1	0.6	37
Sainsbury's Green Pesto	1	34.8	5.5	2	346
Dolmio Stir In Pasta Sauce Creamy Carbonara	1.4	10.8	6.7	1.3	131
Homepride Chicken Supreme Cooking Sauce	1.5	11.5	2	0.98	124

Cooking Sauces: Italian

Product	Sugar	Fat	Sat	Salt	Cals
			per 100g / 100ml		
Sainsbury's Creamy Bacon & Leek Pasta Bake Sauce	1.7	8.6	2.5	0.62	115
Sainsbury's Creamy Mushroom Pasta Bake	1.7	6.2	3.7	0.74	83
Asda Smart Price Bolognese Pasta Sauce	1.7	0.9	0.1	0.7	40
Sainsbury's Pasta Sauce, Basics	1.8	0.6	<.1	0.57	34
Sainsbury's Sun Dried Tomato Paste	1.9	43.6	5	2	414
Asda Chosen by You Cheese & Bacon Pasta Bake	2	6.4	1.4	0.5	91
Sainsbury's Pasta Bake Sauce Macaroni Cheese	2.1	10.9	2.5	0.65	131
Tesco Finest Pesto Alla Genovese	2.2	30.2	6.2	1.6	311
Morrisons Sundried Tomato Paste	2.2	31.1	3.8	1.7	311
Waitrose Creamy Asparagus Pasta Sauce	2.2	33.2	4.8	0.5	322
Asda Chosen by You Green Pesto	2.2	29.7	4	1.6	368
Dolmio Lasagne Cheese Sauce	2.3	8.1	3.3	0.77	102
Tesco Everyday Value Pasta Sauce	2.3	0.7	0.1	0.6	33
Waitrose Cooks' Ingredients Bechamel Pasta Sauce	2.3	8.5	5.9	0.67	108
Sainsbury's Spinach & Ricotta Pesto	2.4	31.4	4.2	1.5	320
Morrisons Red Pesto	2.5	25.8	4.1	1.2	269
Waitrose Carbonara	2.5	18.2	10.6	0.53	206
Dolmio Pasta Bake Sauce Carbonara	2.6	10.6	3.3	0.8	123
Tesco Classic Green Pesto	2.6	31.9	4.7	2	331
Tesco Green Pesto	2.6	31.9	4.7	2	331
Homepride Chassuer Cooking Sauce	2.7	1.1	<.1	0.53	43
Sacla Stir In Olive & Tomato	2.7	18.7	2.4	0.9	192
Dolmio Lasagna Kit	2.8	2.8	1.6	0.49	105
Sainsbury's Passata, Basics	3	<.5	<.1	0.36	22
Weight Watchers Tomato & Basil Sauce	3	<.5	<.1	0.6	36
Dolmio Lasagna Sauce Creamy Light	3.2	6.3	2.3	0.76	86
Sacla Basil Pesto	3.2	48.2	6.8	2.9	477
Morrisons NuMe Tomato Pasta Sauce	3.2	0.1	0.1	0.4	27
Waitrose Essential Creamy Tomato Pasta Bake	3.2	3.6	2.4	0.5	60
Sainsbury's Roasted Red Pepper Pesto	3.3	25.4	3.5	1.5	266

Cooking Sauces: Italian

Product	Sugar	Fat	Sat	Salt	Cals
	per 100g / 100ml				
Waitrose Tomato & Mascarpone Pasta Sauce	3.3	7.6	3.6	0.7	89
Dolmio Lasagna Creamy White Sauce	3.4	7.5	2.9	0.77	98
Dolmio Lasagna White Sauce	3.4	7.5	2.9	0.77	98
Sainsbury's Bolognaise Pasta Sauce, Taste the Difference	3.4	4	0.7	0.98	62
Sainsbury's Pesto, Red	3.4	31.4	4.4	1.5	327
Barilla Puttanesca Sauce	3.5	3	0.4	0.9	52
Barilla Ricotta Sauce	3.5	5.8	1.6	1.4	84
Waitrose Puttanesca Pasta Sauce	3.5	5.2	0.9	1	73
Sainsbury's Lemon Pesto	3.6	30.5	3.9	1.5	312
Tesco Goodness Pasta Sauce	3.6	1.7	0.2	0.2	51
Asda Chosen by You Tomato & Basil Pizza Topper	3.6	3.1	0.2	0.8	73
Asda Chosen by You Red Lasagne Sauce	3.6	0.7	<0.1	0.7	39
Sainsbury's Chilli Pesto	3.7	25.4	3.1	1.5	260
Weight Watchers Bolognaise Sauce	3.7	0.5	0.1	0.6	38
Barilla Mediterranean Vegetable Sauce	3.8	4	0.5	1	62
Waitrose Essential Tomato & Mushroom Pasta Sauce	3.8	0.7	0.2	0.5	35
Asda Chosen by You Tuna & Sweetcorn Pasta Bake	3.8	1.6	0.7	0.53	69
Waitrose Suggo Alla Bolognese Pasta Sauce	3.9	3.8	0.6	0.5	63
Asda Chosen by You Smooth Bolognese Pasta Sauce	3.9	0.7	0.2	0.73	43
Sacla Chargrilled Aubergine Pesto	4	34.9	4.1	2	353
Barilla Bolognese Sauce	4	4	0.4	1.05	68
Asda Extra Special Genovese Basil Pesto	4	39	74	1.3	635
Sacla Stir In Tomato & Mascarpone	4.1	14.4	8.5	1	161
Asda Chosen by You Meatballs Pasta Sauce	4.1	<0.5	<0.1	0.68	38
Asda Good & Counted Bolognese Pasta Sauce	4.1	0.3	0.1	0.6	27
Dolmio Bolognese Sauce Low Fat	4.2	0.1	0	0.8	33
Homepride Shepherds Pie Cooking Sauce	4.2	<.5	<.1	1.1	40
Sainsbury's Pasta Sauce, Tomato & Herb, Light	4.2	0.3	0.1	0.59	28
Morrisons Just For Kids Pasta Sauce	4.2	1.4	0.1	0.2	48
Asda Extra Special Tomato & Chilli Pasta Sauce	4.2	3.5	0.5	0.48	63

Cooking Sauces: Italian

Product	Sugar	Fat	Sat	Salt	Cals
		per 100g / 100ml			
Dolmio Lasagna Kit Original	4.3	3.5	2.1	0.51	118
Dolmio Stir In Pasta Sauce Smoked Bacon & Tomato	4.3	5.6	1.6	1.32	100
Homepride Curry Cooking Sauce	4.3	1.7	0.5	1	51
Waitrose Arrabbita Pasta Sauce	4.3	4.5	0.7	0.7	72
Dolmio Lasagna Sauce Light	4.4	0.2	0	0.82	39
Sainsbury's Pasta Bake Sauce Spicy Pepperoni	4.4	7.2	1.1	0.68	99
Weight Watchers Spicy Tomato Sauce	4.4	0.6	0.1	0.4	39
Morrisons Tomato & Mushroom Pasta Sauce	4.4	0.5	0.1	0.6	38
Asda Chosen by You Tomato & Mushroom Pasta Sauce	4.4	0.7	0.1	0.6	32
Sainsbury's Pasta Sauce Pancetta & Red Wine, Taste the Difference	4.5	5.5	1.5	1.25	83
Barilla Arrabbiata Sauce	4.5	3.1	0.3	1	58
Waitrose Tomato & Sun-Dried Tomato	4.5	1.9	0.3	1	53
Asda Chosen by You Italian Passata	4.5	0.1	trace	trace	28
Waitrose Essential Tomato & Chilli Pasta Sauce	4.6	0.8	0.2	0.5	37
Waitrose Essential Tomato, Onion & Garlic Pasta Sauce	4.6	0.2	0.1	0.5	35
Homepride Pasta Bake Creamy Tuna	4.7	5.6	0.7	1	86
Loyd Grossman Pasta Sauce, Tomato & Wild Mushroom	4.7	3.4	0.4	0.83	61
Sainsbury's Stir In Red Onion & Blue Cheese Pasta Sauce	4.7	6.4	1.1	0.87	96
Sainsbury's Stir In Sweet Pepper Pasta Sauce	4.7	5.8	0.5	1.09	86
Tesco Tomato & Chilli Pesto	4.7	38.9	5.1	1.2	399
Morrisons Creamy Tomato Pasta Sauce	4.7	8.7	2.2	0.3	112
Waitrose Essential Tomato & Basil Pasta Sauce	4.7	1	0.2	0.5	41
Waitrose Roasted Pepper & Almond Pesto	4.7	19.6	3.9	1.5	223
Asda Chosen by You Spicy Tomato Pasta Sauce	4.7	0.7	0.1	0.7	32
Loyd Grossman Pasta Sauce, Tomato & Basil	4.8	3.4	0.4	0.83	61
Loyd Grossman Pasta Sauce, Tomato & Chilli	4.8	3.4	0.4	0.82	60
Waitrose Essential Lasagne Pasta Sauce	4.8	1.3	0.2	0.7	47
Homepride Sausage Casserole Cooking Sauce	4.9	<.5	<.1	1.05	40
Sacla Sun Dried Tomato	4.9	29.3	4.2	2.9	312
Sainsbury's Creamy Tomato Pasta Bake	4.9	8.8	2	0.65	115

Cooking Sauces: Italian

Product	Sugar	Fat	Sat	Salt	Cals
		per 100g / 100ml			
Morrisons Spicy Tomato & Pepperoni Pasta Bake	4.9	4.9	1.5	0.5	82
Sacla Whole Cherry Tomato & Parmesan Pasta Sauce	5	11.5	2	1	150
Barilla Olive Sauce	5	4.5	0.5	1.87	72
Asda Chosen by You Italian Passata with Garlic	5	<0.5	<0.1	0.13	41
Asda Chosen by You Red Pesto	5	27.7	3.7	1.1	299
Asda Extra Special Tomato & Pancetta Pasta Sauce	5	6.7	2.3	0.58	102
Asda Extra Special Tomato & Olive Pasta Sauce	5	8.4	1.2	1.1	113
Homepride Pasta Bake Spicy Tomato Pepperoni	5.1	3.8	0.9	0.97	81
Loyd Grossman Pasta Sauce, Smoky Bacon	5.1	4.8	0.9	0.83	81
Sainsbury's Pasta Sauce, Puttanesca Taste the Difference	5.1	9.4	1.6	1.3	118
Tesco Pasta Bake Spicy Pepperoni	5.1	5.5	0.9	0.7	85
Loyd Grossman Bolognaise Sauce	5.2	2.5	0.3	0.82	55
Sacla Roasted Pepper Pesto	5.2	21	3.1	1.5	239
Sacla Whole Cherry Tomato & Chilli Pasta Sauce	5.2	11.5	1.4	1	147
Waitrose Tomato Pesto	5.2	22.3	3.6	1.5	263
Loyd Grossman Pasta Sauce, Tomato & Sweet Red Petter	5.3	5.3	0.7	0.83	78
Sacla Whole Cherry Tomato & Basil Pasta Sauce	5.3	10.4	1.2	1	127
Morrisons Tomato & Chorizo Stir In Sauce	5.3	4.4	0.7	1	80
Morrisons Tomato & Basil Stir In Sauce	5.3	4.8	0.4	0.8	76
Asda Chosen by You Spicy Tomato & Pepperoni Pasta Bake	5.3	5.9	0.3	0.7	92
Dolmio Lasagna Kit Extra Onion & Bacon	5.4	3.5	2	0.64	131
Tesco Classic Red Pesto	5.4	40.8	5.6	1.2	419
Tesco Finest Salami Fennel & Chianti Pasta Sauce	5.4	7.2	1.7	0.6	112
Barilla Napoletana Sauce	5.4	4	0.5	0.97	69
Morrisons Hot and Spicy Meatball Sauce	5.4	1.6	0.1	0.4	44
Homepride Pasta Bake Creamy Tomato & Herb	5.5	7.5	0.8	0.97	106
Morrisons Bolognese Sauce	5.5	0.5	0.1	0.7	39
Asda Chosen by You Tomato & Garlic Pasta Sauce	5.5	1	0.2	0.7	41
Asda Chosen by You Tomato & Basil Stir-In Pasta Sauce	5.5	3	0.3	0.98	67
Loyd Grossman Lasagna Tomato Sauce	5.6	3.4	<.5	0.71	70

Cooking Sauces: Italian

Product	Sugar	Fat	Sat	Salt	Cals
			per 100g / 100ml		
Morrisons Tomato & Garlic Pasta Sauce	5.6	0.4	0.1	0.7	40
Asda Chosen by You Creamy Tomato Pasta Bake	5.6	12.2	3.3	0.7	144
Dolmio Pasta Bake Sauce Roast Mediterranean Vegetable	5.7	1.2	0.2	0.82	49
Dolmio Stir In Pasta Sauce Sun Dried Tomato Light	5.7	3.9	0.6	1.39	88
Seeds of Change Organic Cherry Tomato & Parmesan Sauce	5.7	2.9	1	0.65	59
Cook Italian Tomato & Pecorino Pasta Sauce	5.7	5.7	1.7	0.5	102
Morrisons Creamy Tomato Pasta Bake	5.7	6.6	1.6	0.6	94
Morrisons Red Lasagne Sauce	5.7	0.3	0.1	0.6	35
Morrisons Signature Tomato & Mascarpone Sauce	5.7	9.6	2.9	0.8	127
Morrisons Tomato & Garlic Stir In Sauce	5.7	5.6	0.5	1	89
Dolmio Pasta Bake Creamy Tomato	5.8	5.3	1.8	0.8	89
Dolmio Stir In Pasta Sauce Roasted Vegetable	5.8	6.6	0.9	1.31	107
Tesco Finest Puttanesca	5.8	9.4	1.1	1.5	123
Morrisons Signature Sweet & Spicy Arrabbiata Sauce	5.8	4.7	0.8	0.6	82
Waitrose Vine-Ripened Tomato Salsa	5.8	3.7	0.3	0.57	67
Dolmio Bolognese Sauce Original	5.9	0.6	0.1	0.8	44
Dolmio Meatballs Pasta Sauce Tomato & Basil	5.9	0.1	0	0.56	34
Homepride Peri Peri Cooking Sauce	5.9	0.6	<.5	0.81	42
Loyd Grossman Pasta Sauce, Seasonal Sauce	5.9	5.5	0.7	0.83	83
Sainsbury's Pasta Sauce, Cherry Tomato & Chilli, Taste the Difference	5.9	5.6	0.9	1.08	88
Sainsbury's Stir In Red Pepper & Goats Cheese Pasta Sauce	5.9	7.5	1.2	1.49	106
Tesco Finest Tomato & Pancetta Sauce	5.9	6.1	1.9	0.8	104
Dolmio Tomato & Chilli Meatball Sauce	6	0.1	0	0.57	36
Homepride Mediterranean Chicken	6	1.5	0.2	0.82	51
Sainsbury's Pasta Sauce, Tomato & Chilli	6	<.5	<.1	0.8	45
Sainsbury's Stir In Sundried Tomato & Olive Pasta Sauce	6	7.6	0.7	1.74	107
Sainsbury's Stir In Tomato & Basil Pasta Sauce	6	4.7	0.5	1.23	79
Sainsbury's Stir In Tomato & Roasted Garlic Pasta Sweet	6	5.1	0.5	0.64	95
Tesco Pasta Bake Creamy Tomato & Herb	6	9.9	2.5	0.7	128
Dolmio Stir In Pasta Sauce Sweet Pepper	6.1	6.2	0.8	1.25	103

Cooking Sauces: Italian

Product	Sugar	Fat	Sat	Salt	Cals
			per 100g / 100ml		
Barilla Basilico Sauce	6.1	2.7	0.4	1	61
Asda Chosen by You Tomato & Chunky Vegetable Pasta Sauce	6.1	0.7	0.1	0.7	39
Asda Chosen by You Gluten Free Bolognese Sauce	6.1	1.5	0.1	0.6	49
Asda Extra Special Bolognese Pasta Sauce	6.1	3.7	0.5	0.53	71
Dolmio Bolognese Sauce Extra Mushroom	6.2	0.1	0	0.8	37
Homepride Chilli Cooking Sauce	6.2	0.5	<.1	0.71	58
Homepride Pasta Bake Tomato Garlic & Chilli	6.2	6.6	0.6	0.9	104
Sainsbury's Pasta Sauce, Sicilian Tasta the Difference	6.2	5.3	0.9	0.95	85
Tesco Finest Sundried Tomato Pesto Rosso	6.2	35	6	1.8	375
Dolmio Stir In Pasta Sauce Sun Dried Tomato	6.3	8.3	1.1	1.41	127
Loyd Grossman Pasta Sauce Roasted Garlic & Tomato	6.3	3.2	0.4	0.82	76
Sacla Stir In Tomato & Garlic Sauce	6.3	15.7	1.9	2	190
Sainsbury's Pasta Sauce, Tomato Muschroom & Basil	6.3	0.8	0.1	0.69	43
Dolmio Stir In Pasta Sauce Garlic & Tomato	6.4	6.1	0.8	1.4	109
Tesco Chunky Vegetable Pasta Sauce	6.4	1	0.1	0.8	47
Cook Italian Bolognaise Sauce	6.4	1.8	0.3	0.5	50
Morrisons Signature Tomato & Basil Sauce	6.4	4.4	0.7	0.6	83
Dolmio Bolognese Extra Basil	6.5	0.6	0.1	0.7	42
Dolmio Bolognese Sauce Extra Spicy	6.5	0.4	0.1	0.8	41
Dolmio Pasta Bake Sauce Tomato & Cheese	6.5	1.5	0.9	0.78	56
Dolmio Stir In Pasta Sauce Spicy Pepperoni & Tomato	6.5	11.4	3	1.48	156
Seeds of Change Stir Through Sundried Tomato Pasta Sauce	6.5	13.3	1.8	1.15	159
Sainsbury's Tomato & Basil Pizza Sauce Topper	6.5	1.3	<.1	0.63	53
Tesco Sweet Pepper Pasta Sauce	6.5	8.4	0.7	1	120
Cook Italian Tomato & Pancetta Pasta Sauce	6.5	3.3	1	0.74	75
Dolmio Bolognese Sauce Extra Mediterranean Vegetable	6.6	0.6	0.1	0.79	43
Dolmio Bolognese Sauce Extra Onion & Garlic	6.6	0.5	0.1	0.8	42
Sacla Chilli Pesto	6.6	30.9	3.7	1.5	330
Sacla Truffle Pesto	6.6	56.7	10.5	2.5	628
Sainsbury's Pasta Sauce Tomato & Mascarpone, Taste the Difference	6.6	8.7	4.7	0.57	122

Cooking Sauces: Italian

Product	Sugar	Fat	Sat	Salt	Cals
		per 100g / 100ml			
Cook Italian Tomato Basil Garlic Pasta Sauce	6.6	2.6	0.4	0.6	76
Morrisons Tomato & Herb Pizza Topper	6.6	2.8	0.2	0.8	67
Dolmio Lasagna Sauce Onion & Garlic	6.7	0.2	0	0.83	49
Dolmio Stir In Pasta Sauce Tomato & Chilli	6.7	6	0.8	1.47	103
Sainsbury's Pasta Sauce, Onion & Garlic	6.7	0.1	0.1	0.63	41
Cook Italian Tomato & Red Pepper Pasta Sauce	6.7	2	0.4	0.53	58
Tesco Finest Tomato & Chilli Sauce	6.8	6.8	0.8	0.5	107
Asda Chosen by You Bolognese Pasta Sauce	6.8	0.5	0.1	0.8	42
Seeds of Change Organic Tomato & Basil Sauce	6.9	2.9	0.4	0.65	63
Sainsbury's Pasta Sauce, Chunky Vegetable	6.9	0.9	0.2	0.61	48
Tesco Tomato Mascarpone Pasta Sauce	6.9	5.8	2.8	0.8	97
Waitrose Roasted Red Pepper & Chorizo Sauce	6.9	22.5	3.1	1.5	250
Dolmio Bolognese Extra Pepper Sauce	7	0.5	0.1	0.8	44
Sainsbury's Pasta Sauce, Tomato & Herb	7	1	0.1	0.67	51
Sainsbury's Tomato & Herb Pasta Sauce	7	1	0.1	0.67	51
Tesco Tomato & Basil Sauce for Meatballs	7	1.1	0.2	0.6	50
Dolmio Stir In Pasta Sauce Tomato & Basil	7.1	6.2	0.8	1.4	108
Seeds of Change Organic Bolognaise Sauce	7.1	1	0.2	0.65	46
Sainsbury's Stir In Chargrilled Vegetable Pasta Sauce	7.1	4.7	0.4	0.94	89
Tesco Finest Tomato Mascarpone Pasta Sauce	7.1	12.7	5.3	0.7	164
Tesco Tomato & Chilli Sauce for Meatballs	7.1	1.8	0.3	0.7	56
Asda Chosen by You Pepper & Parmesan Pasta Sauce	7.1	3.8	1	1	80
Seeds of Change Organic Tomato & Chilli Sauce	7.2	2.2	0.3	0.66	57
Tesco Mushroom Pasta Sauce	7.2	1.1	0.2	0.8	53
Tesco Red Lasagna Pasta Sauce	7.2	1	0.1	0.8	55
Asda Chosen by You Chilli Cheese Pasta Bake	7.2	4.9	0.7	0.43	103
Asda Extra Special Tomato & Mascarpone Pasta Sauce	7.3	11	5.1	0.63	148
Cook Italian Tomato & Chilli Pasta Sauce	7.4	2	0.4	0.53	60
Asda Chosen by You Tomato & Chilli Stir-In Pasta Sauce	7.4	1.9	0.2	1.4	61
Asda Chosen By Kids Tasty Tomato Pasta Sauce	7.4	1.4	0.2	0.2	57

Cooking Sauces: Italian

Product	Sugar	Fat	Sat	Salt	Cals
			per 100g / 100ml		
Morrisons Tomato & Chilli Pasta Sauce	7.5	0.4	0.1	0.5	49
Tesco Tomato & Chilli Pasta Sauce	7.7	0.7	0.1	0.7	54
Tesco Onion & Garlic Pasta Sauce	7.8	0.7	0.1	0.7	51
Tesco Spicy Pepper Pasta Sauce	8	1	0.1	0.8	56
Asda Extra Special Tomato & Garlic Pasta Sauce	8	4.8	0.8	0.6	90
Sainsbury's Stir In Roasted Tomato & Chilli Pasta Sauce	8.1	4.5	0.4	1.35	85
Tesco Bolognaise Sauce	8.4	0.7	0.1	0.8	51
Tesco Bologanise Sauce, Spicy	8.5	0.3	0.1	0.8	45
Morrisons Bolognese Sauce	9.2	0.4	0.1	0.7	49
Tesco Finest Sun Dried Tomato Garlic & Basil Sauce	9.4	8.6	1	0.8	129
Asda Chosen by You Ricotta & Red Pepper Pesto	10.2	19.6	3	1.5	256
Sainsbury's Pasta Sauce, Sweet Pepper	11.3	1.1	0.2	0.84	65
Sainsbury's BBQ Pizza Sauce Topper	19.5	<.5	<.1	0.64	110
Asda Extra Special Sun-Dried Tomato Pesto	34	33	6	1.1	629

Savoury Biscuits

The sugar is relatively low compared to other snacks.
The ones containing seeds are even better for you.

To help you make the best choices, products are listed starting with the least sugar first.

Product	Sugar	Fat	Sat	Salt	Cals
			per 100g		
Ardens Pesto Bakes	<.1	12.1	1.5	2	442
Sainsbury's Cheddar Cheese Crispies, Taste the Difference	<.5	40.6	27	2	581
Sainsbury's Low Fat Rice Cake, Be Good To Yourself	<.5	2.9	0.7	0.02	388
Morrisons Cheese Crispies	0.1	39.4	21.9	1.8	576
Sainsbury's Cheddar & Black Pepper Bites, Taste the Difference	0.2	34	21.7	1.3	541
Clearspring Corn Cakes Organic	0.2	3.4	0.5	0.3	380
Waitrose All Butter Gouda Ovals	0.2	34.8	21	1.9	550
Sainsbury's Cheddar Cheese Bites, Taste the Difference	0.3	34.2	22.1	1.35	543
Kallo Rice Cakes Multigrain Buckwheat Super-Seeds Gluten Free	0.4	2.9	0.8	trace	377
Rude Health Corn Thins	0.4	0.9	0.1	0.7	373
Morrisons Lightly Salted Rice Cakes	0.4	2.6	0.9	0.6	381
Morrisons Rough Scottish Oatcakes	0.4	20	8	1	456
Morrisons Salt and Vinegar Rice Cakes	0.4	2.8	0.7	2.1	389
Asda Chosen by You Cheese Crackers	0.4	23	12.3	2.8	499
Asda Gluten Free Lightly Salted Rice Cakes	0.4	2.6	0.9	0.2	381
Asda Good & Counted Salt & Vinegar Rice Cakes	0.4	2.8	0.7	2	389
Kallo Rice Cakes Wholegrain Lightly Salted	0.5	5.2	0.9	0.3	399
Mrs Crimble's Gluten Free Cheese Bites	0.5	14.1	7.6	3	439
Kallo Corn Cakes Gluten Free	0.6	1.9	0.3	0.3	379
Nairn's Cheese Oatcakes	0.6	26.6	12	2.8	473
Nairn's Organic Oatcake	0.6	16.7	4.2	1.6	441
Sainsbury's Sea Salt & Black Pepper Crackers, Taste the Difference	0.6	24.8	16.8	1.3	497
Rude Health Brown Rice Thins	0.6	1.9	0.6	0.05	379
Dietary Special Gluten Free Pretzels	0.7	21	9.8	3.5	483

Savoury Biscuits

Product	Sugar	Fat	Sat	Salt	Cals
			per 100g		
Tesco Scottish Rough Oat Cakes	0.7	18.4	7.4	2	448
Waitrose Love Life Fine Oatcakes	0.7	23.5	2.5	1.21	488
Dietary Specials Gluten & Wheat Free Salted Rice Cakes	0.7	3.2	0.6	0.3	384
Marmite Rice Cakes	0.8	2.5	0.6	2	391
Sainsbury's Rough Oatcakes	0.8	18.7	4.4	1.8	454
Tesco Finest All Butter Cheese Straws	0.8	38.1	23.8	2	566
Nairn's Fine Oatcakes	0.9	19.9	8.6	1.67	462
Tesco Cheese Bites	0.9	31.2	17	2	535
Morrisons Signature All Butter Pastry Pesto Hearts	0.9	27.7	17.1	1.5	509
Waitrose Love Life Rough Oatcakes	0.9	18.9	1.9	1.5	451
Waitrose Love Llife Seeded Oatcakes	0.9	22.9	2.7	1.24	470
Asda Rough Oatcake's	0.9	17.8	1.8	1.5	440
Jacob's Cornish Wafer	1	28.8	13.8	0.83	527
Sainsbury's Black Onion Seed Cracker, Taste the Difference	1	25.8	16.4	1.21	508
Sainsbury's Corn Thins	1	1.8	0.4	1.23	368
Nairn's Cheese Oatcakes, Gluten Free	1	25.7	9.2	2.07	498
Crosta & Mollica Crostini Chilli	1	14.1	6.4	2.4	484
Stockan's Original Thin Oatcakes	1	22.7	6.7	1.5	481
Ryvita Crackers Black Pepper	1.1	2.9	0.4	0.89	384
Ryvita Crackers Golden Rye	1.1	2.9	0.4	0.87	384
Asda Extra Special All-Butter Gouda Biscuits	1.1	44.9	29.8	1.8	599
Asda Cracked Black Pepper Oatcakes	1.1	17.4	1.5	1.2	442
Kallo Rice Cakes Wholegrain Sesame Seed	1.2	5.3	0.9	trace	369
Sainsbury's Butter Puffs Biscuits	1.2	25	11.9	0.94	488
Ardens Garlic & Parsley	1.2	30.5	17.9	2.4	530
Tesco Lightly Salted Rice Cakes	1.2	3.1	0.7	0.3	382
Nairn's Rough Oatcake	1.3	17.3	4	1.53	431
Dr Karg Organic Seeded Crispbread, 3 Grains & 3 Seeds	1.4	21.2	3.5	1.7	465
Jacob's Cream Cracker	1.4	13.5	6.2	1.3	440
Jacob's Savours Salt & Black Pepper	1.4	16.6	7.5	1.4	465

Savoury Biscuits

Product	Sugar	Fat	Sat per 100g	Salt	Cals
Ryvita Cheese Crackerbread	1.4	3.7	0.6	1.32	386
Sainsbury's Cream Crackers	1.4	13.4	6.1	1.25	436
Nairn's Cheese Snackers	1.4	15.9	7.1	1.83	447
Tesco Cream Crackers	1.4	13.4	6.1	1.2	440
Waitrose Essential Cream Crackers	1.4	13.6	6.2	1.2	442
Waitrose Cheddar Cheese Nibbles	1.4	37.5	24.9	1.66	562
Asda Chosen by You Cream Crackers	1.4	13.6	6.2	1.2	442
Ryvita The Original Crispbread	1.5	2.8	0.4	1.05	378
Sainsbury's Mini High Bake Water Biscuits	1.5	6.5	0.6	1.3	427
Sainsbury's Parmesan & Basil Flatbread	1.5	13.2	4	1.2	440
Amaizin Corn Chips Gluten Free	1.5	21.5	2.2	0.8	480
Tesco Rice Cakes BBQ Flavour	1.5	5.9	0.8	1.4	393
Waitrose Plain Grissini Breadsticks	1.5	6.4	1	1.46	404
Carr's Table Water Biscuits Black Pepper	1.6	7.6	3.3	1.5	417
Carr's Water Biscuits	1.6	7.7	3.3	1.5	417
Finn Crisp Original Crispbread	1.6	2.6	0.3	1.6	339
Jacob's Cream Crackers High Fibre	1.6	18.3	6.1	1.7	463
Sainsbury's Reduced Fat Cream Crackers, Be Good To Yourself	1.6	6.1	2.8	1.34	397
Snack a Jacks Salt & Vinegar	1.6	5.7	0.9	3.5	386
Nairn's Herb & Seeded Oatcakes	1.6	21.9	7.8	1.63	490
Jacob's Cheeselets Sharing	1.6	25.6	8.6	2.5	499
Asda Extra Special Rustic Cracker Collection	1.6	10.3	0.8	2.5	400
Crosta & Mollica Torines Breadsticks	1.7	6.1	2.5	2.3	390
Morrisons Dark Rye Crispbreads	1.7	2.9	0.5	0.9	340
Asda Good & Counted Original Rye Crispbread	1.7	2.8	0.5	0.6	350
Dr Karg Organic Emmental Crispbreads	1.8	20.9	5.5	2	456
Ryvita Cheddar & Pepper Thins Bites	1.8	19	6	1.98	422
Ryvita Pepper Crackerbread	1.8	3.6	0.5	1.46	385
Sainsbury's Water Biscuits	1.8	7.1	3	1.12	412
Tesco Garlic Cracker	1.8	23.6	1.8	1.1	511

Product	Sugar	Fat	Sat per 100g	Salt	Cals
Tesco High Baked Water Biscuits	1.8	7.2	3	1.1	415
Tesco Sesame Breadsticks	1.8	12.7	2	1.5	439
Waitrose Essential High Bake Water Biscuits	1.8	7.2	3	1.13	415
Asda Chosen by You Water Biscuits	1.8	7.2	3	1.1	416
Sainsbury's 5 Seed Flatbread, Taste the Difference	1.9	17.6	58.7	2.2	456
Sainsbury's Breadsticks Toasted Wheat Bran	1.9	7	1.2	2.13	393
Ryvita Crispbread Sesame Seed	2	7	1.1	0.86	373
Sainsbury's Multiseed Flatbread	2	21.6	2.6	0.95	478
Llamas Steak Baked Bites	2	19	2	1.3	450
Waitrose Oat and Chive Biscuits for Cheese	2	22.4	13.2	2.05	483
Asda Gluten Free Crackerbreads	2	1	0.3	1.3	385
Asda Good & Counted Sesame Seed Crispbread	2	7	1	0.9	365
Sainsbury's Poppy & Sesame Biscuits	2.1	23	9.4	1.84	488
Waitrose Sesame Seed Grissini Breadsticks	2.1	11.1	1.8	1.16	423
Fortt's Original Bath Oliver Biscuits	2.2	13.8	7.7	1.2	433
Tesco Multiseed Flatbread	2.2	14.7	1.3	1.5	440
Tesco Pizza Shapes	2.2	23.6	2.1	1.3	507
Tesco Rice Cakes Salt & Vinegar	2.2	5.7	0.8	1.5	392
Asda Chosen by You Tomato & Cheese Cracker Bites	2.2	23.6	2.1	1.3	507
Asda Good & Counted Multigrain Crispbread	2.2	4.8	0.7	0.9	366
Doria Doriano Italian Crackers	2.3	14	8.8	2.5	443
Finn Crisp Original Rye	2.3	2.7	1	0.6	350
Doria Doriano Cracker	2.3	14	8.8	2.5	443
Tesco Salt & Pepper Cracker	2.3	19.8	1.6	1.3	489
Ryvita Mediterranean Herb Crispbread	2.4	1.6	0.3	0.98	401
Ryvita Thins Mature Cheddar & Pepper	2.4	9.8	5.8	2.18	418
Asda Chosen by You Sesame Italian Breadsticks	2.4	19.3	2.9	1.2	469
Asda Extra Special All Butter Green Olive Twists	2.4	36.1	20.8	2	555
Rakusen's 99% Fat Free Herb & Onion Crackers	2.5	1	0.2	2	360
Ryvita Black Pepper Crispbread	2.5	1.6	0.2	0.56	344

Savoury Biscuits

Product	Sugar	Fat	Sat	Salt	Cals
			per 100g		
Sainsbury's Melba Toast	2.5	2.4	1.1	2	374
Weight Watchers Oat & Wheat Crackers	2.5	1.5	0.3	1.8	368
Tesco Finest Extra Mature Cheddar Oat Nibbles	2.5	36.9	21.6	1.4	563
Jacob's Flatbreads Multi Grain	2.6	6.8	2.9	1.1	411
Jacob's Krackawheat	2.6	18.7	9.4	1.6	465
Ryvita Crispbread Sunflower & Oat	2.6	9	0.7	0.76	384
Ryvita Sunflower & Oat Crisp Bread	2.6	9	0.7	0.76	384
Tesco Finest Tomato & Sweet Chilli Oatcakes	2.6	18.7	7.4	2.4	442
Morrisons Water Biscuits	2.6	6.8	3	1.2	408
Sainsbury's Oatcakes Highland	2.7	17.6	5	1.23	446
Snack a Jacks Sweet Chilli	2.7	7.5	0.8	2.25	415
Dietary Special Gluten Free Breadsticks	2.7	6.3	3.5	2	402
Peppa Pig Breadsticks Cheddar Cheese	2.7	11.5	3	1.3	432
Waitrose Nigella Seed Biscuits for Cheese	2.7	24.6	16.2	2.4	490
Waitrose Seeded Wheat Biscuits for Cheese	2.7	22	14.3	1.75	482
Jacob's Flatbreads Mixed Seeds	2.8	9.6	3.3	1.1	423
Jacob's Savours Thins, Sour Cream & Chive	2.8	21.3	16.5	1.8	485
Tesco Finest Black Olive Grissini Rubata	2.8	13.2	2.7	1.8	436
Tesco Italian Original Breadstick	2.8	7.9	1.4	1.8	414
Tesco Sesame & Poppy Thins	2.8	23	9.1	1.8	482
Morrisons Wholegrain Melba Toast	2.8	7.6	2.8	1.6	396
Waitrose Essential Poppy & Sesame Seed Thins	2.8	23	9.1	1.82	482
Asda Good & Counted Caramel Rice Cakes	2.8	2.4	0.6	0.3	369
Rakusen's Matzos Crackers	2.9	0.8	0.2	0.02	382
Ryvita Original	2.9	1.7	0.3	0.5	350
Ryvita Thins Multi Seed	2.9	14.1	3.3	1.54	434
Sainsbury's Salt & Pepper Crackers	2.9	21	1.8	1.2	485
Tesco Original Mini Breadsticks	2.9	7.7	1.4	1.8	412
Morrisons Salt/Pepper Crackers	2.9	21.3	1.8	1.2	485
Asda Chosen by You Chosen by You Salt & Pepper Crackers	2.9	21.3	1.8	1.2	485

Savoury Biscuits

Product	Sugar	Fat	Sat	Salt	Cals
			per 100g		
Asda Garlic Crackers	2.9	22.4	1.9	1.3	489
Asda Chosen by You Breadsticks	2.9	7.9	1.4	1.5	413
Asda Extra Special Italian Black Olive Breadsticks	2.9	9.9	1.4	1.9	427
Ryvita Dark Rye	3	1.2	0.2	0.74	342
Ryvita Hint of Chilli Crispbread	3	1.9	0.3	0.57	349
Sainsbury's Caramelised Onion Cheese Nibbles, Taste the Difference	3	35.1	22.2	1.27	550
Sainsbury's Grissini Bread Sticks, Sesame Seed	3	11	1.9	1.6	417
Sainsbury's Grissini Bread Sticks	3	7.8	1.2	1.88	408
Ardens Gruyere & Spinach Twist	3	22	14	2.3	480
Waitrose Sun Dried Tomato Bites	3	34.2	21.9	1.81	545
Asda Perfect for Cheese Cracker Selection	3	21	9.7	1.2	481
Ryvita Minis Salt & Vinegar	3.1	10.2	1	2.13	387
Sainsbury's Mini Breadsticks	3.1	8	1.3	1.83	400
Dietary Special Gluten Free Herb & Onion Crackers	3.1	13	5.4	1.3	410
Ardens Cheddar & Spring Onion Bites	3.1	29	15.9	2.4	535
Waitrose LoveLife Calorie Controlled Plain Breadsticks	3.1	1.4	0.6	0.5	383
Asda Extra Special All Butter Parmesan & Garlic Mini Twists	3.1	25.9	16.7	1.6	496
Jacob's Flatbreads Salt & Pepper	3.2	8.6	3.1	1.1	419
Sainsbury's All Butter Parmesan Twists, Taste the Difference	3.2	25.3	17	1.83	487
Tesco Mini Breadsticks	3.2	7.7	1.1	1.3	401
Morrisons NuMe Melba Toast	3.2	2.4	1.3	1.7	384
Morrisons Rye Crispbreads	3.2	2.9	0.8	1	353
Waitrose Mini Breadsticks	3.2	7.7	1.1	1.25	401
Asda Chosen by You Melba Toasts	3.2	2.4	1.3	1.7	384
Sainsbury's Multigrain Melba Toast	3.3	5.9	1.3	2	393
Tesco Finest Italian Flatbread	3.3	13.4	2.1	1.8	439
Waitrose Chive & Onion Twists	3.3	22.4	15	1.9	484
Asda Chosen by You Party Nibbles Cheese Twists	3.3	30	18	1.5	530
Sainsbury's Gruyere Poppy Seed Twists, Taste the Difference	3.4	28	18.1	1.9	514
Sainsbury's Olive Oil Crostini, Taste the Difference	3.4	7.5	1.4	1.7	410

Savoury Biscuits

Product	Sugar	Fat	Sat	Salt	Cals
			per 100g		
Asda Extra Special Italian Olive Oil Crostini	3.4	6.4	1.1	1.8	390
Sainsbury's Cheese Topped Straws, Taste the Difference	3.5	26	15.3	2.36	497
Asda Extra Special Italian Breadsticks	3.5	11	1.6	1.7	427
Sainsbury's Cheese Mini Twists	3.6	26.2	15.2	1.75	500
Sainsbury's Sunflower & Pumpkin Oatcakes, SO Organic	3.6	26.4	8.4	0.98	500
Tesco Cheese Twists	3.6	26.2	15.2	1.8	500
Tesco Ham & Cheese Snackers	3.6	24	2.3	1.8	512
Tesco Mini Twist Cheese Cups	3.6	26.2	15.2	1.8	500
Tesco Multigrain Cracker	3.6	19.9	1.7	1.9	493
Morrisons Cheese Thins	3.6	31.1	15.3	1.7	529
Morrisons Signature Gruyere Twists	3.6	25.3	15.9	1.4	489
Waitrose All Butter Cheese Twists	3.6	25.3	16	1.4	490
Asda Chosen by You Ham & Cheese Cracker Bites	3.6	24	2.3	1.7	511
Asda Chosen by You Multigrain Crackers	3.6	19.9	1.7	1.9	493
Asda Extra Special All Butter Gruyère & Poppy Seed Twists	3.6	27.8	17.7	1.7	507
Ryvita Minis Sweet Chilli	3.7	7.4	0.71	0.98	376
Morrisons Italian Breadsticks	3.7	7.7	6.1	1.8	410
Morrisons Signature All Butter Cheddar Wafers	3.7	31	20.5	1.6	526
Jacob's Savours Cheese Thins	3.8	21.7	16	1.3	480
Kingsmill Mini Toast Salt & Vinegar	3.8	10.7	1	2	425
Asda Chosen by You Tomato & Basil Melba Toasts	3.8	2.6	1.4	2.3	373
Sainsbury's Cheese Twists	4	28.5	15.5	1.9	511
Snack Org Teriyaki Rice Crackers	4	3.5	0.8	0.9	400
Tesco Finest Gruyeye & Poppy Seed Twists	4	28.6	19.5	1.6	505
Asda Seeded Oatcake's	4.1	18.8	2.2	1.3	441
Ryvita Sun Dried Tomato & Herb Thins	4.2	5.9	1	2	405
Tesco Sun Dried Tomato & Olive Breadsticks	4.2	15.8	1.2	1.4	455
Asda Chosen by You Sundried Tomato & Black Olive Breadsticks	4.2	15.8	1.2	1.4	454
Tesco Chive & Onion Twists	4.3	24.4	15.5	1.8	489
Asda Extra Special Biscuits for Cheese	4.4	12.6	1.1	1.3	396

Product	Sugar	Fat	Sat	Salt	Cals
			per 100g		
Asda Chosen by You Mini Chive & Onion Twists	4.4	23	14.3	2	487
Mrs Crimble's Gluten Free Cheese Crackers	4.5	14.2	9	3.5	439
Nairn's Caramelised Onion Oaty Bakes	4.5	17.4	1.7	2.03	455
Fiery Jalapeno Wafers	4.5	30	18.3	3.45	478
Snack a Jacks Jumbo Cheese	4.5	2.5	1	1.5	384
Waitrose Duchy Originals Organic Rosemary & Thyme Oaten Biscuits	4.6	21.5	10.9	1.25	467
Kallo Rice Cakes Chilli	4.7	25	0.6	1.6	369
Ryvita Crispbread Pumpkin & Oat	4.8	7.2	1.3	0.61	370
Tesco Cheese Thins	4.8	32.3	16	2	527
Tesco Wheat Cracker	4.8	19.5	1.7	2.2	490
Waitrose Essential Cheese Thins	4.8	32.3	16	1.98	527
Asda Chosen by You Cheese Thins	4.8	32.3	16	2	527
Cathedral City Baked Bites Mini Biscuits	4.9	26	10.1	2.15	495
Ryvita Crispbread Multigrain	4.9	7.2	1.3	0.61	370
Ryvita Sweet Onion Crispbread	5.1	1.4	0.2	0.69	356
Sunbites Cheddar & Onion Pitta Bread Crisps	5.1	16.8	1.6	1.49	461
Sunbites Roasted Red Pepper & Chilli Pitta Chips	5.2	16.9	1.6	1.48	461
Tesco Crackerbread	5.2	3.5	0.7	1.6	380
Asda Chosen by You Crispbread	5.2	3.5	0.7	1.6	380
Tesco Finest Smoked Apple Oatcakes	5.3	18.6	7.6	2.1	442
Jacob's Crispy Baked Cheddars Crispy Bacon	5.4	31.8	15.7	1.6	531
McVitie's Cheddars	5.5	31.4	15.5	1.6	529
Sainsbury's Chive & Onion Mini Twists	5.5	25.4	14.1	1.93	497
Jacob's Crispbreads Mixed Seed	5.7	16.8	6.5	1	451
Asda Chosen by You Biscuits for Cheese	5.7	18.4	8.3	1.4	466
Jacob's Crispbreads Chive	5.8	14.3	6.4	1.1	440
Ritz Breaks Rosemary & Olive Oil Crackers	5.9	18.5	7.7	2.42	465
Jacob's Crispbreads Mixed Grain	6	14	6.3	1.1	438
Tesco Mini Twist Salted Cups	6	26.8	18.3	1.6	501
Dietary Specials Gluten & Wheat Free Crispbread	6	1.7	0.3	1.4	380

Savoury Biscuits

Product	Sugar	Fat	Sat	Salt	Cals
			per 100g		
Sainsbury's Cheese Mini Crackers	6.2	16.7	1.9	1.38	461
Jacob's Choice Grain Savoury Biscuits	6.4	13.7	7	2	428
Pagen Golden Wheat Krisprolls	6.5	6.5	2.2	1.5	390
Snack a Jacks Sour Cream & Chive	6.5	7.6	0.9	2.75	416
Sainsbury's Snack Crackers	6.6	17.3	5.7	1.38	461
Kingsmill Mini Toast Mature Cheddar	6.6	9.6	0.9	1.23	423
Sainsbury's BBQ Mini Crackers	6.7	19.6	2	1.38	472
Carr's Melts	6.9	21.7	15.1	2.5	476
Ryvita Wholegrain Crackerbread	6.9	3.9	0.5	1.13	379
Sainsbury's Harvest Grain Crackers	7.1	18.1	7.9	1.52	461
Sainsbury's Pizza Mini Crackers	7.1	15.9	1.7	1.38	454
Morrisons Tuck Ins	7.1	17.3	4.1	1.3	450
Tuc Crackers	7.3	28.3	13	2.4	511
Milton's Garlic & Herb Crackers	7.3	15.4	1.1	1.5	405
Tesco Snackers	7.3	21.5	5.2	2.1	488
Milton's Multigrain Crackers	7.5	16.6	1.2	1.5	414
Sunbites Cracker Tomato & Red Pepper Cracker & Dip	7.9	8.8	0.7	1.34	245
Carr's Melts, Cheese	8	22.9	16.2	2.2	493
Sainsbury's Piri Piri Flatbread	8	7.2	1.1	1.3	410
Kallo Rice & Corn Cakes Wholegrain Smoked Paprika	8.1	2.3	0.7	1.7	367
Sainsbury's Scalloped Rosemary Crackers	8.2	20	2	1.7	485
Morrisons Rosemary Crackers	8.2	20.2	2	1.7	485
Asda Chosen by You Seeded Crackers 6 Snack Packs	8.2	17.3	5.8	0.5	481
Asda Chosen by You Chosen by You Rosemary Crackers	8.2	20.2	2	1.7	486
Asda Chosen by You Cracker Bites	8.2	19.5	6.2	1.8	481
Tuc Crackers Savoury Sandwich	8.3	29.4	10.8	1.4	520
Morrisons Cheese & Chive Crackers	8.3	19.1	1.9	1.5	478
Ryvita Flatbread Sweet Chilli Thins	8.9	5.7	0.9	1.68	405
Jacob's Oddities Bacon	9.1	14.7	1.4	1.6	446
Ritz Breaks Original Crackers	9.1	18	8.5	2.23	460

Savoury Biscuits

Product	Sugar	Fat	Sat	Salt	Cals
			per 100g		
Tesco Dutch Crisp Bakes	9.2	5.3	1.9	0.7	397
Jacob's Savours Sweet Chilli Thins	9.5	21.7	16.6	2	488
Jacob's Oddities Salt & Vinegar	9.9	14.6	1.4	1.9	443
Jacob's Oddities Cheese	10	15	1.7	1.3	445
Waitrose Duchy Originals Organic Original Oaten Biscuits	10.5	17.6	8.5	1.25	453
Tesco Sweet Chilli Mini Bruschetta	11.3	10.8	0.9	1.7	423
Asda Chosen by You Sweet Chilli Brushetta	11.3	10.8	0.9	1.7	423
Sainsbury's Crispbakes	11.4	2.7	1.1	0.75	391
Sunbites Lightly Salted Multigrain Crackers	12	17	1.3	1.36	459
Asda Chosen by You Crispbakes	12	3.3	1.4	0.8	385
Morrisons NuMe Crispbakes	12.1	3.6	1.2	0.8	382
Waitrose Malted Wheat Biscuits for Cheese	12.3	23.8	15.3	1.8	500
Tesco Everyday Value Multigrain Crackers	12.9	18	1.4	2	446
Sunbites Onion & Rosemary Multigrain Crackers	13	17	1.5	1.45	459
Sainsbury's Snack Crackers, Basics	13.7	20.2	9.4	1.9	475
Sunbites Cream Cheese & Chive Multigrain Crackers	14	17	1.6	1.5	458
Sunbites Multigrain Sweet Chilli Crackers	14	17	1.3	1.41	456
Kallo Rice & Corn Cakes Blueberry & Vanilla	14.4	2.1	0.6	trace	377
Asda Chosen by You Cheese Bites	16	31.2	16	1.7	530
Nairn's Astro Bites	17.4	16.9	7.4	0.9	450
Tesco French Toast	18	11.7	5	0.4	440
Morrisons French Toast	18.6	10	4.8	0.4	430
Ryvita Crispbread Fruit Crunch	19.6	5.4	0.7	0.03	358
Kallo Rice & Corn Cakes Caramel	22.2	1.9	0.5	trace	377
Sunbites Multigrain Cracker Onion & Chutney Dip	22.2	8.4	0.8	1.04	294
Tesco Rice Cakes Milk Chocolate	23.2	21.4	13	0.1	480
Kallo Organic Dark Chocolate Ricecakes	23.4	24.1	14.6	trace	488
Kallo Yoghurt & Muesli Thin Rice Cake	25.8	23	12.8	0.1	491
Tesco Rice Cakes Caramel Flavour	25.9	3.9	0.6	<.01	397
Kallo Organic Milk Chocolate Thin Rice Cakes	27	23	14.3	trace	495

Savoury Biscuits

Product	Sugar	Fat	Sat per 100g	Salt	Cals
Asda Gluten Free Belgian Milk Chocolate Rice Cakes	27.9	21.3	13.3	0.1	489
Snack a Jacks Caramel	28	2.1	0.4	0.5	392
Snack a Jacks Jumbo Chocolate Chip	30	7	3.5	0.05	414
Sainsbury's Dark Chocolate Corn Thins	33	21	13	0.75	476
Kallo Milk Chocolate & Caramel Thin Rice Cake	37.6	21.8	13.5	0.1	485

Salad Dressings

Olive oil; plain and flavoured, are fantastic salad dressings.
Use balsamic vinegar sparingly and choose carefully
as many contain added sugar.

To help you make the best choices, products are listed starting with the least sugar first.

Product	Sugar	Fat	Sat	Salt	Cals
	per 100g / 100ml				
Aspall White Wine Vinegar	<.4	trace	trace	0.3	23
Sainsbury's Greek Kalamata Extra Virgin Olive Oil, Taste the Difference	<.5	91.4	13.3	<.01	823
Sainsbury's Puglian Extra Virgin Olive Oil, Taste the Difference	<.5	91.4	13.1	<.01	823
Sainsbury's Sicilian Extra Virgin Olive Oil, Taste the Difference	<.5	93	13	<.01	837
Sainsbury's Toscana Extra Virgin Olive Oil, Taste the Difference	<.5	91.4	13.1	<.01	823
Sainsbury's Umbrian Extra Virgin Olive Oil, Taste the Difference	<.5	91.4	13.1	<.01	823
San Leandro Extra Virgin Olive Oil	0	91.6	12.8	0	824
Aspall Cyder Vinegar	0	0	0	0	18
Cardini Original Caesar Dressing	0.3	65.9	5.2	2.1	608
Newman's Own Olive Oil & Vinegar Salad Dressing	0.3	53.8	6.24	2.24	490
Newman's Own Italian Dressing	0.3	53.8	6.24	2.24	490
Morrisons Sherry Vinegar	0.3	0	0	0.1	4
Newman's Own Caesar Dressing	0.6	59.5	4.6	2.33	553
Aspall Red Wine Vinegar	0.6	0	0	0	22
Morrisons White Wine Vinegar	0.6	0	0	trace	4
Morrisons Red Wine Vinegar	0.6	0	0	trace	4
Cardini Caesar Low Fat Salad Dressing	2	45.2	3.8	2.1	429
Hellman's Caesar Dressing	2.2	33	4.7	1.6	326
Pizza Express Olive Oil Dressing	2.7	44.2	6.1	2.4	422
Tesco Caesar Dressing	2.7	40.9	3	1.5	393
Sainsbury's Blue Cheese Dressing, Be Good to Yourself	2.9	1.6	0.7	1.23	53
Waitrose Half-Fat Olive Oil Dressing	3	25.6	3.9	1.58	253
French's Ranch Dressing	3.1	27.7	2.3	1.32	276
Waitrose Essential French Dressing	3.1	15.1	1.1	2.13	229

Salad Dressings

Product	Sugar	Fat	Sat	Salt	Cals
		per 100g / 100ml			
French's Blue Cheese Dressing	3.2	34.2	3.7	1.5	335
Morrisons Caesar Salad Dressing	3.4	30.3	2.4	1.7	310
Waitrose Olive Oil Dressing	3.4	52.6	7.9	1.6	502
Sainsbury's Caesar Dressing, Be Good to Yourself	3.5	2.9	0.4	1.25	64
Waitrose Love Life You Count Citrus Zest Vinaigrette	3.5	0.2	0	0.13	44
Sainsbury's Caesar Dressing	3.7	45.5	3.3	1.58	439
Tesco Garlic & Herb Dressing	3.8	23.7	1.6	1	251
Morrisons NuMe Garlic & Herb Dressing	3.8	2.3	0.2	1.5	61
Waitrose Lemongrass, Ginger & Lime Dressing	3.8	58.2	5.6	1.6	552
Asda Extra Special Caeser Salad Dressing	3.8	47	5	1.3	459
Asda Chosen by You French Dressing	4.2	35.7	2.8	1	340
Asda Good & Counted Caeser Dressing	4.4	1.4	0.7	1.3	61
Waitrose Love Life You Count Carrot, Ginger & Chilli Vinaigrette	4.5	0.3	0.1	0.5	46
Pizza Express Dressing Light	4.6	30.3	4.2	2.2	298
Newman's Own Honey & Mustard Dressing	4.8	31.4	2.8	2.1	339
Sainsbury's Thousand Island Dressing, Be Good to Yourself	4.8	2.8	0.3	1.5	61
Tesco Healthy Living Caesar Dressing	4.8	1.6	0.6	1	65
Newman's Own Ranch Dressing	4.9	41.7	3.1	2.29	417
Morrisons NuMe Caesar Dressing	4.9	2.4	1.2	1.7	62
Newman's Own Blue Cheese Dressing	5.3	53.3	3.8	1.75	512
Tesco Finest Caesar Dressing	5.7	47.6	4.2	1.5	470
Newman's Own Balsamic Dressing	5.8	38.2	5.3	1.3	372
Sainsbury's Sweet Balsamic Dressing, Be Good to Yourself	5.8	<.5	<.1	0.75	61
Pizza Express Caesar Light Dressing	6.1	34.2	3.5	2.3	348
Tesco Finest French Dressing	6.5	34.7	2.5	1.5	350
Waitrose Essential Thousand Island Dressing	6.5	53.5	4.1	1.98	520
Sainsbury's Cracked Black Pepper Dressing	6.8	36.6	4.7	1.68	361
Hellman's French Dressing	6.9	26	2.1	1.8	280
Morrisons NuMe Lemon & Herb Dressing	6.9	1.9	0.1	0.5	49
Waitrose Blue Cheese Dressing	6.9	61.2	5.3	3.65	598

Salad Dressings

Product	Sugar	Fat	Sat	Salt	Cals
		per 100g / 100ml			
Pizza Express Basil Pesto Dressing	7.1	45.2	3.9	2.3	445
Morrisons NuMe Reduced Fat French Dressing	7.5	4.1	0.3	1.7	82
Waitrose Essential Italian Dressing	7.5	39.8	2.8	2.2	402
Morrisons NuMe Thousand Island Dressing	7.6	2.6	0.2	1.5	75
Asda Good & Counted Vinaigrette Dressing	7.8	1.1	0.3	1.5	55
Hellman's Garlic & Herb Dressing	8	17	3.9	1.7	205
Asda Chosen by You Garlic & Herb Dressing	8	16.1	1.1	1	193
Morrisons Honey & Mustard Dressing	8.1	20.5	1.4	1.5	241
Asda Chosen by You Creamy Caesar Dressing	8.1	17.9	1.6	1.5	213
Morrisons NuMe Blue Cheese Dressing	8.2	2.8	1.7	1.6	90
Morrisons French Salad Dressing	8.2	20.8	1.4	1.8	244
Waitrose Love Life You Count Fat Free Raspberry Vinaigrette	8.3	0.5	0.1	0.14	62
Newman's Own French Dressing	8.5	54.1	5	2.1	530
Sainsbury's Soy Chilli & Ginger Dressing, Taste the Difference	8.9	8.9	0.7	1.42	135
Morrisons Fine Herb Dressing	9	0.1	0	1.6	44
Waitrose Half-Fat Caesar Dressing	9	22.8	3.2	1.55	259
Waitrose Caesar Dressing	9	49	5.8	1.55	494
Morrisons NuMe Soy Chilli/Ginger Dressing	9.1	0.5	0.1	1.6	55
Sainsbury's French Dressing	9.3	23.9	1.4	1.1	263
Sainsbury's Harissa Dressing, Taste the Difference	9.3	8.6	1.1	1.01	128
Sainsbury's Red Pepper & Chilli Dressing, Be Good to Yourself	9.3	<.5	0.1	0.72	52
Waitrose Dressing Piri Piri	9.3	46.7	4.1	1.5	484
Asda Good & Counted Lemon & Pepper Dressing	9.6	0.7	0.1	0.75	46
Sainsbury's French Dressing, Be Good to Yourself	10	2.4	0.3	1.08	70
Tesco French Style Dressing	10.5	15.5	1.2	1.3	199
Sainsbury's Honey & Mustard Dressing, Be Good to Yourself	10.7	1.3	0.4	0.68	78
Pizza Express Tomato & Chilli Dressing	10.8	50.7	5.4	1.7	505
Hellman's Balsamic Vinaigrette	11	2.7	0.4	1.6	75
Hellman's Fat Free Vinaigrette	11	<.5	<.1	0.85	48
Hellman's Honey & Mustard Dressing	11	14	1.6	1.6	186

Salad Dressings

Product	Sugar	Fat	Sat	Salt	Cals
		per 100g / 100ml			
Tesco Healthy Living Moroccan Dressing	11.2	3.2	0.4	1	95
Tesco Thousand Island Dressing	11.3	17.6	1.8	1.3	245
Waitrose Dressing Mango & Chilli	11.3	44.9	3.2	1.1	462
Sainsbury's French Vinaigrette, Taste the Difference	11.4	43.6	2.7	1.03	450
Sainsbury's Mango & Chilli Dressing	11.7	20.1	2	0.68	232
Hellman's Thousand Island Dressing	12	20	3	1.8	238
Mary Berry Caesar Dressing	12	56.8	7.8	1.3	575
Asda Good & Counted Honey & Mustard Dressing	12	0.7	0.4	1.3	62
Morrisons NuMe Honey & Mustard Dressing	12.2	3.1	0.3	1.7	102
Tesco Healthy Living Balsamic Dressing	12.5	1.7	0.2	0.3	91
Asda Extra Special French Vinaigrette	13	28	1.7	1.1	319
Pizza Express Sicilian Lemon, Garlic & Chilli Dressing	13.1	29.6	3.9	1.7	328
Tesco Healthy Living French Dressing	13.2	2	0.5	0.8	89
Sainsbury's Balsamic Dressing, Taste the Difference	14	30	1.8	1.02	338
Asda Good & Counted Italian Dressing	14	0.5	0.1	0.75	63
Pizza Express Olive Oil & Balsamic Dressing	14.6	39.4	5.6	3.1	417
Sainsbury's Balsamic Dressing	15.2	4.9	0.4	1	124
Sainsbury's Balsamic Vinegar Of Modena 1 Leaf	15.3	<.5	<.1	0.05	90
Waitrose Honey & Mustard Dressing	15.3	39.4	4	1.15	433
Waitrose Essential Low Fat Vinaigrette	15.8	1.2	0.1	1.6	83
Sainsbury's Honey & Mustard Dressing	15.9	9.2	1.4	1.4	159
Tesco Healthy Living Three Citrus Dressing	16.1	3.2	0.2	1	113
Newman's Own Santa Cruz Chilli & Lime Dressing	16.7	6.9	0.5	0.54	158
Newman's Own Chilli & Lime Dressing	16.7	6.9	0.5	0.54	158
Pizza Express Honey & Mustard Dressing	16.9	39.3	2.7	2.2	435
Asda Chosen by You Thousand Island Dressing	17.3	12	0.7	0.8	189
Sainsbury's Balsamic Vinegar	18	<.5	<.1	0.03	88
Asda Extra Special Balsamic Vinaigrette	18	6.6	0.6	1.3	276
Tesco Finest Balsamic Dressing	18.1	33.5	5.6	1	381
Tesco Honey & Mustard Dressing	18.2	15.2	1	1.1	220

Salad Dressings

Product	Sugar	Fat	Sat	Salt	Cals
		per 100g / 100ml			
Tesco Balsamic Dressing	21.1	4.6	0.3	1.1	132
Tesco Healthy Living Honey & Mustard Dressing	21.1	3.4	0.8	1	129
Mary Berry Light Salad Dressing	21.9	21.9	2.6	1.3	309
Morrisons Balsamic Vinegar	22	0	0	trace	114
Tesco Healthy Living Sweet Chilli Dressing	22.5	0.3	0.1	0.8	99
Mary Berry Lemon & Thyme Sauce	22.6	34.3	4.5	2.4	409
Tesco Finest Honey & 3 Mustard Dressing	24.1	30.2	3.6	2	387
Sainsbury's Balsamic Vinegar, SO Organic	25.6	<.5	<.1	0.07	127
Asda Chosen by You Balsamic Dressing	26.1	4	0.2	0.8	144
Mary Berry Salad Dressing	26.1	43.9	5.2	1.3	507
Napolina Balsamic Vinegar	27.8	0	0	<.01	134
Asda Chosen by You Honey & Mustard Dressing	28.4	5.4	1	0.8	168
Sainsbury's Balsamic Vinegar Of Modena 1 Leaf, Taste the Difference	32.5	<.5	<.1	0.04	160
De Nigris Italian Herbs White Wine Vinegar	32.5	0	0	1.5	146
De Nigris Roasted Garlic White Wine Vinegar	32.5	0	0	1.5	146
Tesco Finest Vinaigrette Dressing	34.9	34.9	2.8	1.3	380
Asda Extra Special Balsamic Vinegar	45.5	0	0	trace	194

Soups: Fresh

Most of the soups listed in all forms contain sugar, there are a few exceptions.

As in other categories, check the label to see if the sugar content is coming from natural sugar or is added to bring out the taste. Tinned and packet instant will contain a lot less nutrients than fresh.

To help you make the best choices, products are listed starting with the least sugar first.

Product	Sugar	Fat	Sat	Salt	Cals
		per 100g / 100ml			
Morrisons Kitchen Chicken & Vegetable Broth	0.1	1.5	0.3	0.5	44
Tesco Creamy Chicken Soup	0.3	1.7	0.9	0.6	45
Asda Chicken & Mushroom Soup	0.3	3.8	2.5	0.6	62
Tesco Finest Chicken Chardonnay Wine & Tarragon Soup	0.4	3.2	1.9	0.6	57
Morrisons Kitchen Creamy Vegetabe Soup	0.4	1	0.6	0.5	37
Sainsbury's Mushroom Soup	<.5	1.5	0.6	0.5	33
Asda Chosen by You Broccoli & Stilton Soup	<.5	4.4	1.7	0.4	60
Tesco Chicken & Mushroom Soup	0.5	1.3	0.6	0.6	41
Morrisons Kitchen Carrot & Coriander Soup	0.5	2.9	1.2	0.4	42
Morrisons Signature Petit Pois & Wiltshire Ham Soup	0.5	2.4	0.8	0.3	48
Sainsbury's Broccoli & Stilton Soup	0.6	4.2	2.8	0.38	59
Morrisons Kitchen Pea & Crème Fraiche Soup	0.6	0.8	0	0.4	38
Morrisons Kitchen Chicken, Rice & Mushroom Soup	0.6	2.4	0.9	0.5	58
Morrisons Kitchen Butternut Squash Soup	0.7	1.5	0.6	0.4	25
Morrisons Signature Italian Tomato, Basil & Mascarpone Soup	0.7	4.3	2.3	0.4	55
Tesco Finest Chestnut Mushroom & Madeira Soup	0.8	4.1	2.4	0.4	67
New Covent Garden Wild Mushroom Soup	0.9	1.4	0.8	0.55	27
Sainsbury's Lentil Dahl Soup	0.9	2.7	1.8	0.4	84
Glorious! Sicily Tomato & Balsamic Soup	0.9	1	0.5	0.4	30
Morrisons Signature Moroccan-Spiced Chicken Tagine Soup	1	2.9	0.7	0.3	65
Waitrose Broccoli & Stilton Soup	1	2.8	1.2	0.48	42
New Covent Garden British Chicken Soup	1.1	5.8	2.3	0.75	85
Tesco Macaroni Pasta Pot	1.1	5.6	3	0.7	157
Asda Chicken Noodle Soup	1.1	0.4	0.1	0.6	33

Product	Sugar	Fat	Sat	Salt	Cals
	per 100g / 100ml				
Glorious! Louisiana Voo Doo Soup	1.2	2.6	0.7	0.4	60
Tesco Finest Pork Goulash Soup	1.2	1.1	0.1	0.4	46
Morrisons Kitchen Potato & Leek Soup	1.2	2.3	0.9	0.4	46
Morrisons Signature Lamb Mulligatawny Soup	1.2	3.8	2.3	0.2	75
Waitrose Leek & Potato Soup	1.2	1.9	1.2	0.4	42
Sainsbury's Leek & Potato Soup	1.3	1.8	1.2	0.48	45
Tesco Noodle Pot Chicken Chow Mein	1.3	3	0.4	0.6	130
Asda Hearty Vegetable Soup	1.3	2.1	0.1	0.5	54
Asda Chicken & Vegetable Broth	1.3	1.6	0.8	0.5	46
Asda Chosen by You Chicken & Sweetcorn Soup	1.3	<.5	<.1	0.6	40
Waitrose Chicken & Vegetable Broth	1.3	1.7	0.3	0.55	45
Yorkshire Provender Roast Chicken Soup with Vegetables	1.3	1.4	0.7	0.3	39
Sainsbury's Chicken & Vegetable Broth	1.4	0.8	0.2	0.43	36
Asda Leek & Potato Soup	1.4	2.3	0.6	0.5	47
Yorkshire Provender Cauliflower Cheese Soup with Ham	1.4	4.7	2.9	0.7	73
Tesco Beef Chilli Rice Pot	1.5	2.1	0.5	0.4	129
Tesco Broccoli & Stilton Soup	1.5	3.4	1.8	0.4	57
Tesco Ham Hock, Leek & Potato Soup	1.5	1.8	0.5	0.6	50
Asda Chicken Curry Soup	1.5	2.2	0.5	0.5	66
Waitrose Love Life Calorie Spinach & Crème Fraiche & Herb Soup	1.5	2	1.3	0.5	33
Sainsbury's My Goodness! Green Thai Noodle Soup	1.6	2.3	0.9	0.42	64
Sainsbury's My Goodness! Zingy Tom Yum Prawn Noodle Soup	1.6	2.3	0.8	0.4	72
Tesco Pasta Pot Carbonara	1.6	3.3	1.6	0.4	137
New Covent Garden Potato & Leek Soup	1.7	2.2	1.3	0.68	53
Innocent Malaysian Laksa Noodles	1.7	1.6	1	0.44	81
Morrisons Kitchen Broccoli & Stilton Soup	1.7	3.3	1.6	0.5	60
Glorious! San Antonio Fiesta Soup	1.8	0.5	0.2	0.4	33
Asda Bacon & Lentil Soup	1.8	1.4	0.3	0.6	59
Asda Extra Special Italian Vine Ripened Tomato & Lentil Soup	1.8	3.4	0.7	0.4	77
Waitrose Burmese Chicken Soup	1.8	4.2	3.5	0.5	101

Soups: Fresh

Product	Sugar	Fat	Sat	Salt	Cals
		per 100g / 100ml			
Yorkshire Pea, Spinach & Coriander Soup	1.8	2.8	1.8	0.6	54
Sainsbury's Chicken & Sweetcorn Soup	1.9	1.7	1	0.5	54
Tesco Bolognaise Pasta Pot	1.9	2.9	1	0.6	136
Morrisons Kitchen Chicken & Sweetcorn Soup	1.9	0.5	0	0.4	56
Asda Red Thai Chicken Soup	1.9	3.2	1.9	0.5	59
Waitrose Love Life Italian Bean Soup	1.9	2	0.2	0.35	42
Glorious! Heart of West Africa, Chicken & Peanut Soup	2	3.7	1.8	0.4	73
Innocent Noodle Pot, Japanese Ramen	2	0.6	0.1	0.59	72
New Covent Garden Souper Greens & Pesto Skinny Soup	2	1.2	0.3	0.28	36
Innocent Japanese Noodles Pot	2	0.6	0.1	0.59	72
Innocent Singapore Noodles	2	1.7	0.3	0.32	71
New Covent Garden Skinny Souper Greens Italian Pesto Soup	2	1.2	0.3	0.28	36
Tesco Finest British Chicken Mulligatawny Soup	2	3.3	1.8	0.3	79
Asda Extra Special British Chicken Tagine Soup	2	3.2	1.2	0.5	67
Waitrose Keralan Spiced Chicken Soup	2	6.5	4.7	0.57	99
Waitrose Love Life Pea, Edamame & Chilli Soup	2	2.3	1.1	0.54	52
Waitrose Love Life Mexican Chicken Soup	2	3.1	0.6	0.23	71
New Covent Garden Thai Red Chicken Soup	2.1	3.3	2.5	0.75	59
Sainsbury's Creamy Vegetable Soup	2.1	1.3	0.6	0.43	36
Sainsbury's Thai Green Chicken Soup	2.1	3.8	3.1	0.43	68
Tesco Chicken & Sweetcorn Soup	2.1	2.3	0.8	0.5	58
Asda Mexican Chilli Beef Soup	2.1	2.4	0.8	0.3	70
Waitrose Gazpacho Soup	2.1	2.2	0.3	0.4	36
Yorkshire Provender Rustic Vegetable & Ham Soup with Lentils	2.1	2.8	0.5	0.5	53
Sainsbury's Green Vegetable Primevara Soup, Taste the Difference	2.2	0.7	0.4	0.38	46
Tesco Finest Sri Lankan Chicken Soup	2.2	3.5	2.5	0.3	62
Tesco Pea & Asparagus Soup	2.2	2.1	0.5	0.5	43
Waitrose Pea & Mint Soup with Leek	2.2	1.7	0.7	0.45	44
Tesco Finest Red Thai Chicken Soup	2.3	4.4	3.2	0.5	79
Asda Chosen by You Super Greens Soup	2.3	1.4	0.2	0.5	62

Product	Sugar	Fat	Sat	Salt	Cals
			per 100g / 100ml		
Waitrose Love Life Red Lentil & Chilli Soup	2.3	1.8	0.1	0.35	48
Yorkshire Provender Tomato & Red Pepper Soup	2.3	3.2	1.3	0.65	50
Sainsbury's Tomato, Lentil & Red Pepper Soup	2.4	1.2	<.1	0.45	59
Innocent Indian Lentil Sambar Vegetable Pot	2.4	2.9	1.7	0.41	86
Tesco Leek & Potato Soup	2.4	2.9	1.8	0.6	66
Waitrose Green Thai Chicken Soup	2.4	5.4	3.3	0.5	81
Waitrose Chunky Vegetable Soup	2.4	1.8	1.1	0.5	44
New Covent Garden Minestrone with Pancetta Soup	2.5	1.9	0.6	0.48	51
Tesco Chicken Tikka Masala Rice Pot	2.5	4.7	1.3	0.5	152
Tesco Mexican Chilli Bean Soup	2.5	1.1	0.2	0.5	49
Asda Pea & Ham Soup	2.5	2.6	0.3	0.3	59
New Covent Garden Pea & Mint Soup	2.6	1.4	0.8	0.45	49
Tesco Tomato Vegetable & Lentil Soup Pot	2.6	1	0.1	0.5	50
Waitrose Pea & Ham Soup	2.6	3.3	0.8	0.56	69
Glorious! Skinnylicious New England in Autumn, Butternut Squash Soup	2.7	0.9	trace	0.5	34
Glorious! New England in Autumn	2.7	0.9	trace	0.5	34
New Covent Garden Pulled Pork & Bean Soup	2.7	0.9	0.3	0.38	37
Sainsbury's Butternut Risotto Meal Soup	2.7	1.6	0.9	0.42	54
Glorious! New England In Autumn Soup	2.7	0.9	trace	0.5	34
Tesco Finest Pea & Wiltshire Cured Ham Soup	2.7	2.4	1.4	0.5	64
Waitrose Thai Parsnip Soup	2.7	4.1	2.6	0.2	59
Innocent Noodle Pot, Vietnamese Curry	2.8	2.4	1.1	0.42	93
New Covent Garden Vegetable & Supergrain Soup	2.8	1.5	0.1	0.48	49
Sainsbury's Petits Pois & Ham Soup, Taste the Difference	2.8	2.4	1.4	0.4	64
Innocent Vietnamese Noodles Pot	2.8	2.4	1.1	0.42	93
Tesco Tomato & Mascarpone Pasta Soup	2.8	4.1	1.4	0.6	133
Glorious! Skinnylicious Thai Tuk Tuks, Carrot & Lemongrass Soup	2.9	1.7	1.5	0.6	40
Glorious! Thai Tuk-Tuks & Tumeric	2.9	1.7	1.5	0.6	40
New Covent Garden Skinny Goan Spiced Chicken Soup	2.9	0.4	0.1	0.28	44
Sainsbury's Carrot & Coriander Soup	2.9	1.4	0.5	0.45	32

Soups: Fresh

Product	Sugar	Fat	Sat	Salt	Cals
			per 100g / 100ml		
Sainsbury's Sweet Potato Coconut & Chilli Soup, Taste the Difference	2.9	1.7	0.7	0.37	46
Glorious! Thai Tuk Tuks & Turmeric	2.9	1.7	1.5	0.6	40
New Covent Garden Skinny Spiced Chicken & Lentils Soup	2.9	0.4	0.1	0.28	44
Asda Creamy Butternut Squash Soup	2.9	3.9	1.2	0.5	55
Glorious! Skinnylicious Goa Express, Tomato & Lentil Soup	3	1.3	0.1	0.5	50
Glorious! Timeless Tuscany Chicken & Orzo Soup	3	0.4	trace	0.6	40
New Covent Garden Vegetable Soup	3	1.1	0.6	0.43	38
Sainsbury's Butternut Squash Soup	3	1.8	<.1	0.43	41
Tesco Finest Vine Ripened Tomato & Lentil Soup	3	1.6	0.1	0.4	74
Asda Red Pepper & Wensleydale Soup	3	2.1	1	0.3	51
Yorkshire Provender Smoky Pulled Pork Soup with Beans	3	2.6	0.6	0.6	76
New Covent Garden Skinny Tomato, Vegetable & Lentil Soup	3.1	0.8	0.1	0.28	44
Tesco Butternut Squash Soup	3.1	2.1	0.7	0.5	42
Asda Carrot & Coriander Soup	3.1	2.5	0.6	0.4	39
New Covent Garden Carrot & Coriander Soup	3.2	1.5	0.9	0.45	36
Sainsbury's My Goodness! Laksa Chicken Noodle Soup	3.2	2.3	1.2	0.48	86
Waitrose Minestrone Soup	3.2	1.5	0.2	0.5	47
Waitrose Love Life Mediterranean Vegetable Soup	3.2	1.2	0.2	0.45	32
Morrisons Kitchen Minestrone Soup	3.3	2.3	0.3	0.5	56
Tesco Finest Butter Bean & Catalan Chorizo Soup	3.4	2.3	0.8	0.2	63
Morrisons Kitchen Tomato & Roasted Vegetable Soup	3.4	2.3	0.3	0.5	49
Asda Piri Piri Chicken Soup	3.4	1	0.2	0.2	40
Waitrose Carrot & Coriander Soup	3.4	2.6	1.7	0.43	43
Waitrose Chicken Jambalaya	3.4	1.3	0.2	0.5	49
Innocent Seasonal Vegetable Pot	3.5	2	0.8	0.47	76
Tesco Finest Sweet Potato Coconut & Chili Soup	3.5	4	2.9	0.3	65
Waitrose Butternut Squash & Tarragon Soup	3.5	2.2	1.4	0.57	43
Tesco Finest Moroccan Chicken Soup	3.6	1.7	0.4	0.3	59
Tesco Minestrone Soup	3.6	1.1	0.1	0.3	50
Innocent Vegetable Pot Caribbean Jerk Curry	3.7	2.4	1.3	0.46	77

Soups: Fresh

Product	Sugar	Fat	Sat	Salt	Cals
	per 100g / 100ml				
Tesco Carrot & Coriander Soup	3.7	2.8	1.1	0.4	48
Morrisons Kitchen Tomato & Basil Soup	3.7	1.3	0.4	0.4	40
Glorious! Singapore Fling	3.8	1.8	1.4	0.4	43
New Covent Garden Carrot & Butternut Squash Soup	3.8	1	0.6	0.53	28
Innocent Mexican Chipotle Chilli Vegetable Pot	3.8	1	0.1	0.45	75
Tesco Carrot & Butternut Squash Soup Pot	3.8	1.7	0.5	0.4	45
Tesco Moroccan Chicken Tagine Soup Pot	3.8	1.3	0.2	0.5	58
Tesco Rice Pot Chicken Paella	3.8	4.9	0.8	0.6	146
Asda Chunky Minestrone Soup	3.8	0.8	0.1	0.4	43
Waitrose Chicken & Chorizo Soup	3.8	1.6	0.4	0.48	47
Sainsbury's Chicken Balti Meal Soup	3.9	1.8	0.2	0.43	61
Innocent Indian Madras Vegetable Pot	3.9	2.5	1.5	0.4	86
Tesco Chicken Teriyaki Noodle Pot	3.9	1.6	0.2	0.7	105
Waitrose French Onion Soup	3.9	1.4	0.2	0.55	39
Sainsbury's Chorizo & Butterbean Soup, Taste the Difference	4	2	0.6	0.44	60
Sainsbury's Hungarian Beef Goulash Meal Soup	4.1	1.9	0.5	0.42	50
Tesco Noodle Pot Spicy BBQ Pork	4.1	2.6	0.4	0.7	125
New Covent Garden Slow Roast Tomato Soup	4.2	0.4	0.1	0.35	28
Sainsbury's Chicken Arrabiata Meal Soup	4.2	1.5	0.3	0.37	58
Sainsbury's My Goodness! Hoisin Duck Noodle Soup	4.2	2.5	0.3	0.44	87
New Covent Garden Roasted Tomato & Basil Soup	4.2	0.4	0.1	0.35	28
Tesco Sweet Chilli Chicken Noodle Pot	4.2	1.4	0.2	0.5	85
Tesco Tomato & Basil Soup	4.2	1.8	0.3	0.5	42
Sainsbury's Minestrone Soup	4.3	1.4	0.2	0.5	65
Sainsbury's Chantenay Carrot & Parsnip Soup, Taste the Difference	4.4	2.2	1.3	0.43	44
Sainsbury's French Onion Soup	4.4	1.1	0.4	0.5	42
Duchy Originals Organic Tomato, Thyme Soup & Cracked Black Pepper	4.5	1.9	0.6	0.53	47
New Covent Garden Lentil & Smoked Bacon Soup	4.6	1	0.2	0.46	51
Sainsbury's Jamaican Jerk Chicken Soup, Taste the Difference	4.6	1.4	0.3	0.33	62
Sainsbury's Mediterranean Veg & Balsamic Soup, Taste the Difference	4.6	1	0.2	0.29	36

Soups: Fresh

Product	Sugar	Fat	Sat	Salt	Cals
	per 100g / 100ml				
Sainsbury's Moroccan Spiced Chicken Soup, Taste the Difference	4.6	1.3	0.2	0.32	65
Waitrose Love Life Moroccan Chicken Soup	4.6	1.8	0.2	0.18	60
Sainsbury's Cream of Tomato Soup	4.8	2.2	0.9	0.4	52
Asda Creamy Tomato Soup	4.8	2	0.7	0.4	48
Asda Chosen by You Tomato & Basil Soup	4.9	1.1	<.1	0.3	35
Waitrose Tomato & Basil Soup	4.9	1.3	0.1	0.48	36
Tesco Finest Plum Tomato & Mascarpone Soup	5	2.2	1.2	0.3	54
Morrisons Kitchen Cream of Tomato Soup	5.1	2.1	0.5	0.5	62
Sainsbury's Tomato & Basil Soup	5.3	1.1	0.2	0.43	40
Tesco Rice Pot Sweet & Sour Chicken	5.5	1	0.2	0.2	113

Soups: Packet & Instant

Most of the soups listed in all forms contain sugar, there are a few exceptions. As in other categories, check the label to see if the sugar content is coming from natural sugar or is added to bring out the taste. Tinned and packet instant will contain a lot less nutrients than fresh.

To help you make the best choices, products are listed starting with the least sugar first.

Product	Sugar	Fat	Sat	Salt	Cals
		per 100g / 100ml			
Knorr Packet Soup Broccoli & Stilton	<0.5	3.2	2	0.6	45
Knorr Packet Soup Chicken Noodle	<0.5	<0.5	<0.1	0.53	20
Sainsbury's Chicken Noodle Cup Soup, Be Good To Yourself	<0.5	<0.5	<0.1	0.57	27
Sainsbury's Moroccan Cup Soup	<0.5	<0.5	<0.1	0.56	43
Batchelors Slim a Soup, Chicken & Leek	0.3	0.8	0.5	0.58	25
Tesco Healthy Living Asparagus Soup In A Mug	0.4	0.6	0.3	0.4	26
Tesco Chicken And Vegetable Soup In A Mug	0.5	1.6	0.8	0.6	43
Tesco Healthy Living Thai Chicken Soup In A Mug	0.5	0.7	0.4	0.4	27
Morrisons Creamy Chicken Simmer Soup	0.5	3.2	1.6	0.5	56
Asda Chosen by You Simmer Soup Chicken	0.5	3.4	2	0.7	58
Tesco Healthy Living Chicken Noodle Soup In A Mug	0.6	0.1	0.1	0.4	21
Morrisons Savers Chicken & Vegetable Cup Soup	0.6	0.8	0.4	0.5	35
Sainsbury's Indian Style Lentil Cup Soup	0.6	<0.5	<0.1	0.55	36
Asda Good & Counted Chicken Flavoured Noodle Soup in a Mug	0.7	0.1	trace	0.7	21
Knorr Packet Soup Spring Vegetable	0.7	<0.5	<0.1	0.6	16
Morrisons Mushroom Cup Soup	0.8	1.1	0.3	0.6	54
Asda Chosen By Kids Chicken & Veg Risotto in Slurpy Tomato Sauce	0.8	0.9	0.5	0.3	104
Waitrose Essential Chicken & Vegetable Soup in a Cup	0.8	1.6	0.8	0.56	38
Waitrose LoveLife Calorie Controlled Asparagus Soup in a Cup	0.8	0.7	0.4	0.5	27
Batchelors Cup a Soup Special, Chicken Noodle	0.8	0.5	0.1	0.53	37
Batchelors Cup a Soup, Chicken	0.8	2.1	1.3	0.53	40
Tesco Everyday Value Chicken And Vegetable Soup In A Mug	0.9	1	0.3	0.6	166
Tesco Mushroom Soup In A Mug	0.9	2.1	1.1	0.6	51
Tesco Roast Chicken Soup In A Mug	0.9	1.5	0.7	0.5	46

Soups: Packet & Instant

Product	Sugar	Fat	Sat	Salt	Cals
		per 100g / 100ml			
Morrisons Chicken Cup Soup	0.9	1.3	0.3	0.5	58
Morrisons Spring Vegetable Simmer Soup	0.9	0.2	trace	0.7	23
Morrisons Chicken Noodle Simmer Soup	0.9	0.1	trace	0.5	24
Asda Good & Counted Asparagus Soup	0.9	0.7	0.4	0.4	27
Tesco Healthy Living Lentil And Bacon Soup In A Mug	1	0.1	0.1	0.4	26
Waitrose Creamed Vegetable Soup in a Cup with Croutons	1	1	0.5	0.55	34
Waitrose Thick & Creamy Spicy Lentil Soup in a Cup	1	0.6	0.2	0.63	41
Batchelors Cup a Soup Original, Cream of Mushroom	1	2.5	1.4	0.58	47
Knorr Packet Soup Thick Vegetable	1	0.8	0.5	0.68	30
Sainsbury's Chicken & Tarragon Cup Soup	1	0.7	0.3	0.55	43
Morrisons Asparagus Cup Soup with Croutons	1.1	2.1	0.8	0.6	64
Morrisons Mulligatawny Cup Soup	1.1	0.2	trace	0.6	48
Waitrose Essential Mushroom Soup in a Cup with Croutons	1.1	2	1	0.53	50
Waitrose Thick & Creamy Mushroom & Madeira Soup in a Cup	1.1	1.4	0.8	0.57	46
Batchelors Cup a Soup, Chicken & Leek	1.1	1.6	0.9	0.55	37
Batchelors Cup a Soup, Chicken & Vegetable With Croutons	1.1	2.4	1.4	0.55	51
Sainsbury's Cream Of Chicken Cup Soup	1.1	0.8	0.4	0.58	38
Sainsbury's Tomato & Balsamic Cup Soup	1.1	<0.5	<0.1	0.53	40
Tesco Broccoli And Stilton Soup In A Mug	1.2	0.7	0.4	0.6	40
Tesco Healthy Living Leek And Potato Soup In A Mug	1.2	0.4	0.3	0.4	26
Tesco Red Thai Soup In A Mug	1.2	1.7	1.4	0.5	45
Waitrose Essential Asparagus Soup in a Cup	1.2	3	1.6	0.51	61
Waitrose Duchy Originals Organic British beef & Yorkshire ale soup	1.2	2.4	0.9	0.63	54
Ainsley Harriott Broccoli & Stilton Cup Soup	1.2	0.8	0.4	0.55	40
Ainsley Harriott Cream Of Garden Vegetable Cup Soup	1.2	1.5	0.8	0.77	39
Batchelors Cup a Soup, Broccoli & Cauliflower	1.2	2	1.4	0.53	42
Sainsbury's Asparagus Cup Soup	1.2	2.2	1.3	0.55	62
Sainsbury's Thai Style Chicken Cup Soup, Be Good To Yourself	1.2	0.6	0.3	0.54	30
Tesco Everyday Value Vegetable Soup In a Mug	1.3	0.7	0.4	0.6	31
Asda Smart Price Chicken & Vegetable Instant Soup	1.3	0.9	0.5	0.6	39

Soups: Packet & Instant

Product	Sugar	Fat	Sat	Salt	Cals
		per 100g / 100ml			
Asda Smart Price Vegetable Instant Soup	1.3	0.7	0.4	0.6	29
Batchelors Cup a Soup, Golden Vegetable	1.3	0.9	0.5	0.55	33
Tesco Vegetable Soup In a Mug	1.4	1.5	0.7	0.6	43
Asda Chosen by You Chicken Mug Soup	1.4	1.5	0.8	0.65	48
Asda Good & Counted Golden Vegetable Soup in a Mug	1.4	0.5	0.3	0.6	24
Waitrose Minestrone Soup in a Cup With Croutons and Noodles	1.4	0.2	trace	0.55	30
Waitrose LoveLife Calorie Ctrl Carrot & Corriander Soup in a Cup	1.4	0.8	0.4	0.55	29
Waitrose Thick & Creamy Pea & Mint Soup in a Cup	1.4	1	0.5	0.57	48
Ainsley Harriott Aromatic Thai Chicken & Lemongrass Cup Soup	1.4	1.1	0.9	0.63	41
Batchelors Cup a Soup Special, Cream of Vegetable	1.4	2.5	1.3	0.48	54
Sainsbury's Broccoli & Stilton Cup Soup	1.4	1.2	0.7	0.67	47
Sainsbury's Vegetable Cup Soup	1.4	1.1	0.6	0.6	56
Tesco Healthy Living Vegetable Soup In Mug	1.5	0.5	0.3	0.3	30
Morrisons Asparagus Simmer Soup	1.5	1.2	0.7	0.4	40
Waitrose Thick & Creamy Potato & Leek Soup in a Cup	1.5	1.1	0.7	0.6	45
Waitrose Love Life Mixed Bean & Chorizo Soup	1.5	4	1.1	0.55	74
Ainsley Harriott Cream Of Mushrooms Cup Soup	1.5	1.3	0.7	0.63	45
Batchelors Cup a Soup Original, Cream of Asparagus	1.5	2.5	1.5	0.55	53
Batchelors Cup a Soup, Creamy Potato & Leek	1.5	1.7	1	0.53	44
Sainsbury's Spiced Butternut Squash Cup Soup	1.5	0.8	0.5	0.56	50
Tesco Carrot And Lentil Soup In A Mug	1.6	0.4	0.2	0.5	37
Morrisons Golden Vegetable Cup Soup with Croutons	1.7	1.9	0.7	0.5	64
Asda Good & Balanced Butternut Squash Mug Soup	1.7	0.8	0.4	0.53	41
Ainsley Harriott Scottish Chicken & Leek Cup Soup	1.7	0.2	0.1	0.53	31
Ainsley Harriott Vegetable Chowder Cup Soup	1.7	1	0.5	0.85	41
Waitrose Duchy Originals Organic Spiced Vegetable Mulligatawny Soup	1.8	1.3	0.3	0.53	45
Batchelors Slim a Soup, Minestrone	1.8	0.6	0.3	0.58	29
Batchelors Cup a Soup Special, Minestrone	1.9	0.7	0.3	0.2	36
Sainsbury's Beef & Vegetable Soup	1.9	1.5	0.6	0.55	51
Waitrose LoveLife Calorie Ctrl Country Vegetable Soup in a Cup	2	0.5	0.3	0.57	29

Soups: Packet & Instant

Product	Sugar	Fat	Sat	Salt	Cals
		per 100g / 100ml			
Waitrose Organic Carrot, Red Lentil & Cumin Soup	2	1.8	1.1	0.5	45
Waitrose Love Life Chicken & Root Vegetable Soup	2	1.1	0.2	0.33	37
Sainsbury's Carrot & Coriander Cup Soup, Be Good To Yourself	2	<0.5	0.3	0.55	31
Asda Good & Counted Vegetable & Noodle Soup in a Mug	2.1	0.3	0.2	0.5	26
Asda Chosen by You Mushroom Mug Soup	2.1	1.2	0.6	0.75	47
Tesco Minestrone Soup In A Mug	2.2	0.4	0.2	0.6	36
Tesco Spiced Butternut Squash Cup Soup	2.2	1	0.5	0.6	40
Morrisons Minestrone Cup Soup with Croutons	2.2	0.7	0.3	0.6	42
Asda Chosen by You Simmer Soup Beef & Vegetable	2.2	0.5	0.1	0.73	44
Ainsley Harriott East Indian Mulligatawny Cup Soup	2.2	0.6	0.3	0.48	48
Waitrose Love Life Ham Hock & Split Pea Soup	2.4	1.2	0.2	0.4	45
Sainsbury's Minestrone Cup Soup	2.5	<0.5	<0.1	0.58	50
Batchelors Cup a Soup, Tomato & Basil	2.6	0.7	0.5	0.58	36
Morrisons French Onion Simmer Soup	2.8	0.2	0.1	0.6	25
Asda Chosen by You Golden Vegetable Mug	2.8	1.8	0.9	0.5	54
Batchelors Cup a Soup Special, Tomato & Vegetable	2.8	1	0.5	0.5	43
Waitrose Thick & Creamy Tomato Pepper & Herb Soup in a Cup	2.9	1	0.5	0.57	41
Tesco Sweet And Spicy Noodle Soup In A Mug	3	0.1	0.1	0.6	37
Waitrose Duchy Originals Organic Parsnip & Apple Soup	3	0.9	0.1	0.48	35
Asda Chosen by You Tomato & Basil Mug Soup	3.2	0.9	0.5	0.63	40
Ainsley Harriott Shropshire Pea Cup Soup	3.2	1.2	1	0.62	54
Sainsbury's Tomato & Basil Cup Soup, Be Good To Yourself	3.4	<0.5	<0.1	0.49	29
Waitrose Organic Red Pepper & Mediterranean Vegetable Soup	3.5	1.2	0.1	0.5	31
Waitrose Love Life Gazpacho Soup	3.5	1.5	0.2	0.33	39
Batchelors Cup a Soup, Tomato	3.5	0.8	0.4	0.5	35
Asda Chosen by You Classic Tomato Mug Soup	3.6	1	0.6	0.5	41
Asda Oven Baked Chilli & Garlic Croutons	3.6	12.3	1	1.1	439
Asda Chosen by You Oven Baked Black Olive Croutons	3.6	11.7	1.1	1.2	432
Tesco Tomato And Basil Soup In A Mug	3.9	0.2	0.1	0.5	36
Tesco Tomato Soup In A Mug	3.9	1.1	0.5	0.4	41

Soups: Packet & Instant

Product	Sugar	Fat	Sat	Salt	Cals
		per 100g / 100ml			
Waitrose Duchy Originals Organic Tomato & Rosemary Soup	4	1	0.2	0.45	32
Ainsley Harriott Szechuan Hot & Sour Cup Soup	4.4	<0.1	<0.1	0.72	30
Morrisons Tomato Cup Soup	4.6	1.2	0.7	0.6	54
Sainsbury's Black Pepper Soup Crouton	5.5	6.8	0.5	0.82	398
Sainsbury's Cream of Tomato Cup Soup	5.9	1	0.5	0.53	59
Sainsbury's Cream Of Tomato Soup	5.9	2.5	0.2	0.56	57
Asda Chosen by You Simmer Soup Oxtail	10.6	6.5	3.8	6.6	353

Soups: Tinned

Most of the soups listed in all forms contain sugar, there are a few exceptions.

As in other categories, check the label to see if the sugar content is coming from natural sugar or is added to bring out the taste. Tinned and packet instant will contain a lot less nutrients than fresh.

To help you make the best choices, products are listed starting with the least sugar first.

Product	Sugar	Fat	Sat	Salt	Cals
	per 100g / 100ml				
Sainsbury's Broccoli & Stilton Soup	<0.5	2	0.7	0.48	42
Sainsbury's Cream Of Chicken Soup	<0.5	3.6	0.7	0.5	59
Waitrose Essential Cream of Mushroom Soup	0.1	4.3	1	0.6	57
Waitrose Beef Consomme Soup	0.2	0.2	0.1	0.57	22
Tesco Cream Of Chicken Soup	0.3	3	0.5	0.5	48
Morrisons Cream of Mushroom Soup	0.4	2.7	0.6	0.4	52
Heinz Weight Watchers Chicken Noodle Soup	0.4	0.2	trace	0.6	17
Tesco Cream Of Mushroom Soup	0.5	3	0.6	0.6	50
Morrisons Chicken Soup	0.5	2.6	0.6	0.6	52
Asda Chosen by You Cream of Chicken Soup	0.5	3.1	0.6	0.5	54
Waitrose Essential Cream of Chicken Soup	0.5	4.9	1.2	0.5	68
Tesco Everyday Value Chicken Soup	0.6	2.4	0.5	0.5	42
Tesco Finest Roast Chicken Soup	0.6	2.6	1	0.5	62
Tesco Healthy Living Chicken And Sweetcorn Soup	0.6	0.3	0.2	0.5	37
Morrisons Savers Chicken Soup	0.6	2.4	0.5	0.5	42
Waitrose Chicken Consomme Soup	0.6	0.5	0.2	0.52	14
Heinz Classic Scotch Broth	0.6	0.6	0.3	0.6	39
Sainsbury's Mushroom Cup Soup	0.6	1.3	0.7	0.58	48
Asda Smart Price Chicken Soup	0.7	1.8	0.9	0.5	32
Waitrose Lentil & Smoked Bacon Soup	0.7	1.1	0.4	0.48	55
Baxters Favourites, Pea & Ham Soup	0.7	0.8	0.2	0.6	54
Heinz Squeeze & Stir Chicken & Vegetable Instant Soup	0.7	2.6	1.5	0.6	45
Sainsbury's Chicken & Mushroom Soup	0.7	4.1	0.8	0.49	70
Sainsbury's Wild Mushroom & Tarragon Soup, Taste the Difference	0.7	3	1	0.55	54

Product	Sugar	Fat	Sat	Salt	Cals
			per 100g / 100ml		
Morrisons Lentil & Bacon Soup	0.8	1.4	0.4	0.4	59
Morrisons NuMe Chickpea & Spinach Soup	0.8	0.07	0.1	0.4	44
Asda Chosen by You Lentil Soup with Carrots and Potatoes	0.8	0.3	0.1	0.5	49
Baxters Luxury, Beef Consomme Soup	0.8	0	0	0.7	17
Campbell's Condensed Cream Of Chicken Soup	0.8	6.8	0.8	1.15	96
Sainsbury's Scotch Broth Soup	0.8	1.1	0.4	0.58	45
Tesco Broccoli And Stilton Soup	0.9	2.6	1.2	0.6	50
Asda Chosen by You Oxtail Soup	0.9	1.7	0.7	0.58	44
Asda Chosen by You Chunky Chicken & Vegetable Soup	0.9	0.7	0.1	0.5	42
Asda Good & Counted Thai Chicken Soup	0.9	1.5	0.3	0.5	31
Waitrose Seafood Chowder Soup	0.9	2.8	0.8	0.53	58
Campbell's Condensed Cream of Mushroom Soup	0.9	6.7	0.8	1.15	89
Heinz Classic Potato & Leek Soup	0.9	1.5	0.1	0.6	46
Heinz Cream of Chicken Cup Soup	0.9	1.1	0.8	0.5	32
Sainsbury's Chicken Leek & Barley Soup	0.9	0.8	0.3	0.55	41
Sainsbury's Cream Of Mushroom Soup	0.9	3.7	0.6	0.6	54
Tesco Chicken And Mushroom Soup	1	4	0.4	0.5	65
Waitrose Scotch Broth Soup	1	0.8	0.4	0.57	44
Baxters Favourites, Highlanders Broth Soup	1	1.2	0.6	0.6	45
Sainsbury's Chunky Chicken Potato & Bacon Soup	1	1.9	1	0.53	57
Sainsbury's Cream of Chicken Soup, Basics	1	2.3	0.7	0.6	37
Morrisons Leek & Potato Soup	1.1	0.9	0.4	0.6	37
Asda Chosen by You Scotch Broth Soup	1.1	1.1	0.5	0.6	44
Baxters Favourites, Cream Of Chicken Soup	1.1	2.9	1.2	0.7	58
Baxters Favourites, Lentil & Bacon Soup	1.1	0.7	0.3	0.6	52
Baxters Favourites, Scotch Broth Soup	1.1	1.6	0.7	0.7	49
Heinz Big Soup Smokin Chicken & Bacon	1.1	2.6	2.6	0.7	65
Heinz Chicken Noodle Soup	1.1	0.3	0.1	0.7	31
Heinz Cream of Chicken Soup	1.1	2.7	0.4	0.6	48
Heinz Lentil & Bacon Soup	1.1	1.4	0.4	0.6	58

Soups: Tinned

Product	Sugar	Fat	Sat	Salt	Cals
			per 100g / 100ml		
Waitrose Essential Vegetable Soup	1.2	0.5	trace	0.55	52
Amy's Kitchen Gluten Free Lentil Soup	1.2	2	0.4	0.6	72
Heinz Cream of Chicken Soup	1.2	2.9	0.5	0.6	51
Sainsbury's Asian Chicken Noodle Soup	1.2	<0.5	0.2	0.43	33
Sainsbury's Curried Parsnip Soup	1.2	1.9	1.2	0.5	41
Sainsbury's Oxtail Soup	1.2	1	0.4	0.58	39
Sainsbury's Seafood Chowder Soup, Taste the Difference	1.2	2.8	0.8	0.55	57
Morrisons Oxtail Soup	1.3	1.4	0.7	0.5	43
Morrisons Chunky Chicken & Vegetable Soup	1.3	1.1	0.2	0.5	46
Asda Chosen by You Classic Leek & Potato Soup	1.3	0.9	0.5	0.55	40
Baxters Favourites, Chicken Broth Soup	1.3	0.3	0.1	0.6	35
Baxters Favourites, Royal Game Soup	1.3	0.2	0.1	0.6	38
Heinz Cream of Chicken Soup with Thai Spices	1.3	3.4	0.5	0.6	65
Sainsbury's Potato & Leek Simmer Soup	1.3	0.7	0.4	0.58	35
Sainsbury's Spring Vegetable Soup	1.3	<0.5	<0.1	0.58	32
Tesco Potato And Leek Soup	1.4	1.3	0.7	0.5	33
Baxters Vegetarian Garden Pea & Mint Soup	1.4	0.8	0.3	0.6	50
Heinz Big Soup Roast Chicken & Vegetable	1.4	1.2	0.2	0.5	55
Heinz Farmhouse Beef Broth	1.4	0.5	0.2	0.6	43
Heinz Lentil Soup	1.4	0.2	trace	0.6	48
Sainsbury's Chunky Lamb & Mint Soup	1.4	1.7	0.6	0.45	51
Sainsbury's Cream Of Asparagus Soup, Taste the Difference	1.4	3.2	2.1	0.48	54
Tesco Chunky Beef And Vegetable Soup	1.5	1.8	0.8	0.4	55
Tesco Healthy Living Lentil And Vegetable Soup	1.5	0.2	0.1	0.6	39
Tesco Oxtail Soup	1.5	1.2	0.6	0.6	48
Tesco Tuscan Bean Soup	1.5	0.9	0.2	0.4	70
Asda Chosen by You Minestrone Soup	1.5	0.5	trace	0.6	35
Asda Chosen by You Chunky Steak & Ale Soup	1.5	0.6	0.3	0.6	53
Asda Good & Balanced Chicken Curry Soup	1.5	1.3	0.4	0.25	58
Heinz Chicken & Mushroom Soup	1.5	2.8	0.4	0.7	49

Soups: Tinned

Product	Sugar	Fat	Sat	Salt	Cals
	per 100g / 100ml				
Heinz Weight Watchers Chicken Soup	1.5	0.8	0.1	0.7	31
Sainsbury's Chunky Beef & Dumplings Soup	1.5	1.8	0.8	0.4	54
Sainsbury's Chunky Beef & Vegetable Soup	1.5	1.8	0.8	0.4	54
Sainsbury's Chunky Chicken & Vegetable Soup	1.5	0.9	0.2	0.4	49
Tesco Finest Wild Mushroom Soup	1.6	2.2	1	0.6	181
Asda Good & Balanced Chickpea & Spinach Soup	1.6	1	0.1	0.28	51
Waitrose Essential Oxtail Soup	1.6	1	0.5	0.57	43
Waitrose Love Life Chunky Chicken & Vegetable Soup	1.6	0.8	0.2	0.48	50
Baxters Favourites, Cream Of Mushroom Soup	1.6	3.8	1.8	0.7	61
Heinz Big Soup Beef Broth	1.6	0.6	0.2	0.5	45
Heinz Big Soup Chicken & Leek	1.6	1.4	0.3	0.6	58
Heinz Chicken & Sweetcorn Soup	1.6	2.9	0.5	0.6	60
Heinz Weight Watchers Lentil & Carrot Soup	1.6	0.1	trace	0.6	29
Heinz Weight Watchers Vegetable Broth	1.6	0.2	trace	0.5	46
Sainsbury's Cream Of Vegetable Soup	1.6	2.6	0.7	0.55	48
Sainsbury's Thai Green Curry Soup	1.6	3.4	2.8	0.53	67
Sainsbury's Vegetable Soup, Be Good To Yourself	1.6	0.5	0.1	0.35	34
Morrisons Savers Vegetable Soup	1.7	0.5	0.1	0.5	39
Morrisons Chicken Curry Soup	1.7	1.8	0.6	0.5	61
Asda Chosen by You Thick Country Veg Soup	1.7	2.1	1.4	0.5	48
Asda Chosen by You Chunky Beef & Vegetable Soup	1.7	1	0.5	0.5	45
Waitrose Love Life Chunky Beef & Vegetable Soup	1.7	0.5	0.1	0.4	50
Baxters Favorites, Potato & Leek Soup	1.7	1.8	0.3	0.6	52
Baxters Favourites, Cock-a-Leekie Soup	1.7	0.6	0.2	0.6	31
Baxters Luxury, Cream Of Asparagus Soup	1.7	3.1	1.9	0.8	59
Sainsbury's Minestrone Soup	1.7	<0.5	<0.1	0.55	36
Tesco Chicken And Vegetable Meal Soup	1.8	0.9	0.2	0.5	50
Tesco Vegetable Soup	1.8	0.5	0.1	0.6	35
Baxters Favorites, Chicken & Vegetable Soup	1.8	0.5	0.1	0.7	41
Baxters Favourites, Minestrone Soup	1.8	0.6	0.2	0.6	42

Soups: Tinned

Product	Sugar	Fat	Sat	Salt	Cals
		per 100g / 100ml			
Baxters Luxury, Broccoli, Stilton & Bacon Soup	1.8	5	1.7	0.7	78
Heinz Big Soup, Chicken & Vegetable	1.8	0.7	0.2	0.5	50
Heinz Lentil with Indian Spices Soup	1.8	0.5	0.1	0.6	48
Heinz Minestrone Soup	1.8	0.2	trace	0.6	32
Heinz Oxtail Soup	1.8	0.5	0.2	0.6	39
Heinz Rich Beef Broth with Smokey Paprika	1.8	0.5	0.2	0.6	41
Sainsbury's Leek & Potato Soup	1.8	1.6	0.3	0.58	46
Sainsbury's Minestrone Simmer Soup	1.8	<0.5	<0.1	0.5	31
Sainsbury's Pea & Ham Soup	1.8	0.9	0.3	0.4	90
Tesco Muligatawny Soup	1.9	1.2	0.5	0.5	65
Morrisons Scotch Broth with Mutton, Onion, Carrot & Peas	1.9	2.1	0.7	0.4	52
Morrisons Minestrone Soup	1.9	0.3	0.1	0.5	34
Asda Chosen by You Chunky Chilli Beef Soup	1.9	1	0.4	0.6	53
Asda Good & Balanced Spicy Lentil, Chicken & Tomato Soup	1.9	0.5	0.1	0.23	63
Waitrose Carrot & Coriander Soup	1.9	0.4	0.1	0.53	23
Waitrose Love Life Vegetable, Bean & Buckwheat Soup	1.9	0.7	0.1	0.35	55
Morrisons Pea & Ham Soup	2	0.7	0.2	0.4	41
Morrisons Mulligatawny Soup	2	1.6	0.7	0.5	49
Asda Chosen by You Classic Pea & Ham Soup	2	0.7	0.2	0.43	41
Asda Smart Price Vegetable Soup	2	0.3	trace	0.5	36
Heinz Big Soup Angus Steak & Vegetable	2	1	0.4	0.5	53
Heinz Big Soup Fiery Chicken & Chorizo Soup	2	2.5	0.8	0.5	66
Heinz Oxtail Soup	2	0.5	0.2	0.6	41
Sainsbury's Mulligatawny Soup	2	0.9	0.4	0.48	53
Tesco Minestrone Soup	2.1	0.4	0.1	0.6	40
Morrisons Chunky Beef & Vegetable Soup	2.1	1	0.5	0.5	47
Asda Chosen by You Chunky Minted Lamb Hotpot Soup	2.1	1.5	0.6	0.5	59
Waitrose Spicy Parsnip Soup	2.1	0.8	0.4	0.35	37
Waitrose Cream of Petit Pois & Smoked Bacon Soup	2.1	3	1.8	0.57	61
Baxters Healthy, Lentil & Vegetable Soup	2.1	0.3	0	0.6	43

Product	Sugar	Fat	Sat	Salt	Cals
			per 100g / 100ml		
Baxters Hearty Broccoli Salmon and Watercress Soup	2.1	2.2	0.6	0.6	67
Baxters Hearty Spiced Red Lentil & Smoked Bacon Soup	2.1	1.7	0.8	0.5	68
Baxters Luxury, Mushroom Potage Soup	2.1	4.9	1.1	0.6	77
Baxters Vegetarian, Country Garden Soup	2.1	0.6	0.3	0.6	36
Heinz Big Soup Angus Steak & Potato	2.1	0.8	0.3	0.6	49
Sainsbury's Extra Thick Chunky Vegetable Soup	2.1	0.8	0.2	0.45	42
Tesco Everyday Value Vegetable Soup	2.2	0.5	0.1	0.5	43
Tesco Pea And Ham Soup	2.2	0.5	0.1	0.5	46
Asda Good & Counted Three Bean Soup	2.2	0.5	0.1	0.25	56
Baxters Hearty Beef & Vegetable Soup	2.2	0.5	0.1	0.6	47
Baxters Hearty Chicken & Black Eyed Pea Gumbo Soup	2.2	0.5	0.1	0.7	46
Heinz Cream of Mushroom Soup	2.2	2.8	0.4	0.7	53
Heinz Cream Of Mushroom With Wild Porcini Soup	2.2	2.7	0.4	0.6	51
Sainsbury's Chicken Korma Soup	2.2	3.9	2.5	0.58	77
Sainsbury's Tomato Red Pepper & Lentil Soup	2.2	<0.5	<0.1	0.5	51
Morrisons NuMe Mexican Chicken & Bean Soup	2.3	0.4	0.1	0.5	46
Waitrose Love Life Chunky Tomato, Bean & Pork Soup	2.3	1.6	0.3	0.43	61
Baxters Favourites, Oxtail Soup	2.3	1.2	0.2	0.7	49
Heinz Big Soup Simmerin Sausage & Vegetable	2.3	2.3	0.8	0.6	58
Heinz Big Soup, Beef & Vegetable	2.3	2.3	0.8	0.6	53
Sainsbury's Carrot & Coriander Soup	2.3	2.3	1.5	0.58	42
Sainsbury's Spicy Mexican Bean Soup	2.3	0.8	<0.1	0.5	61
Tesco Healthy Living Three Bean And Vegetable Soup	2.4	0.3	0.1	0.4	45
Morrisons NuMe Tomato & Three Bean Soup	2.4	0.9	0.3	0.5	58
Morrisons NuMe Carrot & Coriander Soup	2.4	1.1	0.5	0.4	42
Waitrose LoveLife Chunky Tuscan Bean Soup	2.4	0.5	0.1	0.43	50
Baxters Luxury, Lobster Bisque Soup	2.4	4.3	2.6	0.6	75
Sainsbury's Tomato & Spicy Lentil Soup, Be Good To Yourself	2.4	0.9	<0.1	0.38	58
Sainsbury's Tomato & Three Bean Soup, Be Good To Yourself	2.4	1.1	0	0.43	60
Morrisons Vegetable Soup	2.5	1	trace	0.5	42

Soups: Tinned

Product	Sugar	Fat	Sat	Salt	Cals
			per 100g / 100ml		
Morrisons Carrot & Parsnip Soup	2.5	1.8	0.9	0.5	41
Morrisons Chunky Chilli Beef Soup	2.5	1.1	0.5	0.6	62
Asda Chosen by You Classic Mulligatawny Soup	2.5	1	0.4	0.53	51
Heinz Big Soup, Minted Lamb Hot Pot	2.5	1.3	0.5	0.6	58
Sainsbury's Moroccan Spinach & Chickpea Soup, Be Good To Yourself	2.5	0.8	<0.1	0.43	47
Sainsbury's Vegetable Soup, Basics	2.5	<0.5	<0.1	0.48	42
Baxters Healthy, Minestrone Pasta Soup	2.6	0.2	<0.1	0.6	40
Baxters Hearty Chicken & Vegetable Soup	2.6	0.4	0.1	0.6	46
Heinz Big Soup, Lamb & Vegetable	2.6	1.3	0.5	0.6	61
Sainsbury's Butternut Squash & Red Pepper Soup	2.6	2.2	0.5	0.53	51
Waitrose Tomato & Red Pepper Soup	2.7	1.8	0.2	0.57	45
Baxters Carrot & Butterbean Soup	2.7	1.9	0.2	0.7	58
Baxters Hearty Butternut Squash & Sweet Potato with Chilli & Lime Soup	2.7	0.7	0.3	0.6	58
Heinz Vegetable Cup Soup	2.7	0.3	0.1	0.5	31
Baxters Hearty Country Vegetable Soup	2.8	0.6	0.3	0.6	48
Baxters Vegetarian Puy Lentil & Tomato Soup	2.8	0.3	0	0.6	59
Heinz Weight Watchers Tomato Soup	2.8	0.5	trace	0.6	26
Morrisons NuMe Pumpkin & Lentil Soup	2.9	1	0.6	0.5	48
Waitrose Love Life Chunky Minestrone Soup	2.9	0.7	0.1	0.43	38
Baxters Hearty Smoked Bacon and Three Bean Soup	2.9	0.7	0.2	0.6	52
Baxters Hearty Tomato and Chorizo Soup	2.9	1.1	0.1	0.6	57
Baxters Vegetarian, Italian Tomato & Basil Soup	2.9	0.9	0.2	0.9	43
Baxters Vegetarian, Spicy Parsnip Soup	2.9	2.5	1	0.8	54
Sainsbury's Tarka Dal Soup	2.9	1.7	1.2	0.58	70
Morrisons Chunky Vegetable Soup	3	0.6	trace	0.4	44
Waitrose Tomato & Basil Soup	3	0.3	0.1	0.5	26
Baxters Vegetarian, Mediterranean Tomato Soup	3	0.2	<0.1	0.6	32
Asda Chosen by You Classic Vegetable Soup	3.1	0.7	0.1	0.45	47
Baxters Favourites, French Onion Soup	3.1	0.6	0.3	0.6	33
Baxters Hearty Tuscan Style Bean, Bacon & Pecorino Soup	3.1	1	0.5	0.6	61

Product	Sugar	Fat	Sat	Salt	Cals
		per 100g / 100ml			
Sainsbury's Root Vegetable Soup, Be Good To Yourself	3.1	<0.5	<0.1	0.33	40
Heinz Vegetable Soup	3.2	0.8	0.1	0.7	47
Sainsbury's Chunky Butter Bean & Chorizo Soup	3.2	2.8	1.1	0.43	75
Baxters Carrot & Coriander Soup	3.3	1.4	0.4	0.8	42
Heinz Country Vegetable Big Soup	3.4	0.9	0.1	0.6	45
Tesco Chunky Beef Chilli Meal Soup	3.5	1.1	0.5	0.5	51
Baxters Luxury, Cullen Skink Soup	3.5	3.3	2	1.1	84
Sainsbury's Vegetable Soup	3.5	1.2	<0.1	0.5	49
Heinz Weight Watchers, Mediterranean Vegetable Soup	3.7	0.5	trace	0.5	34
Waitrose French Onion & Red Wine Soup	3.8	0.7	0.4	0.53	40
Sainsbury's Creamed Tomato Soup, Basics	3.8	1.7	0.1	0.48	39
Asda Smart Price Tomato Soup	4	1.9	0.1	0.6	47
Sainsbury's French Onion Soup	4	<0.5	0.3	0.58	36
Baxters Healthy, Spicy Tomato & Rice Soup	4.1	0.3	0.1	0.6	53
Heinz Classics, Carrot & Coriander Soup	4.1	1.6	0.2	0.6	41
Heinz Mulligatawny Soup	4.1	1.8	0.3	0.6	55
Heinz Weight Watchers Tomato & Basil Soup	4.1	0.6	0.1	0.5	26
Tesco Everyday Value Tomato Soup	4.2	1.9	0.2	0.6	48
Morrisons Savers Tomato Soup	4.2	1.9	0.2	0.6	48
Heinz Carrot & Coriander Soup with Moroccan Spice	4.2	1.9	0.2	0.6	49
Tesco Healthy Living Tomato Soup	4.4	0.5	0.1	0.5	33
Sainsbury's Tomato Soup, Be Good To Yourself	4.4	1.1	0.1	0.53	39
Heinz Cream of Tomato Cup Soup	4.5	0.6	0.1	0.5	36
Asda Chosen by You Slurpy Tomato Soup	4.6	3.6	0.5	0.25	68
Sainsbury's Italian Tomato & Mascarpone Soup, Taste the Difference	4.6	3.5	2	0.63	65
Tesco Finest Tomato And Mascarpone Soup	4.8	3	1.5	0.6	56
Heinz Tomato With Chilli Soup	4.8	3	0.2	0.6	58
Heinz Cream of Tomato Soup, Reduced Salt	4.9	3	0.2	0.5	58
Heinz Organic Tomato Soup	4.9	2.6	0.9	0.6	56
Heinz Cream of Tomato Soup	5	3	0.2	0.6	59

Soups: Tinned

Product	Sugar	Fat	Sat	Salt	Cals
		per 100g / 100ml			
Heinz Cream of Tomato Soup with Chorizo Soup	5	3	0.5	0.6	61
Heinz Limited Edition Cream Of Tomato Soup With A Hint Of Basil	5	3	0.2	0.6	59
Morrisons Cream of Tomato Soup	5.1	3.1	0.4	0.4	61
Heinz Cream of Tomato Soup with Mexican Spices	5.3	3	0.2	0.6	61
Morrisons Roast Red Pepper Soup	5.4	3	0.4	0.5	59
Baxters Favourites, Cream Of Tomato Soup	5.4	2.7	1	0.7	66
Sainsbury's Tomato & Basil Soup	5.4	2.8	0.2	0.43	57
Sainsbury's Tomato & Red Pepper Soup	5.7	1.5	1	0.48	49
Amy's Kitchen Gluten Free Chunky Tomato Soup	5.8	1.4	0.8	0.7	51
Tesco Cream Of Tomato Soup	5.9	2.5	0.2	0.6	57
Heinz Squeeze & Stir Tomato Instant Soup	6	2.9	0.2	0.6	58
Asda Chosen by You Classic Cream of Tomato Soup	6.3	2.8	0.2	0.58	62
Sainsbury's Freefrom Tomato & Basil Soup	6.4	1.5	0.2	0.5	48
Waitrose Essential Cream of Tomato Soup	7.1	4.3	1	0.5	79
Miso Tasty Spicy Aka Miso Soup	11.8	8.9	1.1	9.9	221
Miso Tasty Classic Shiro Miso Soup	11.9	9.1	1.1	9.9	222
Campbell's Condensed Cream Of Tomato Soup	14.4	6.7	0.8	1.15	159
Itsu Miso Soup Vegetarian	14.6	5.1	trace	9.5	167
Itsu Miso Soup Original	16.7	4.9	trace	10.3	175

Table Sauces

You may be surprised to see how good mayonnaise fares on this list.

Many people have been led to believe full fat mayonnaise is off the menu, but it's the reduced fat mayo you need to change. Mustard varies depending on the type, some are very high.

To help you make the best choices, products are listed starting with the least sugar first.

Product	Sugar	Fat	Sat	Salt	Cals
	per 100g / 100ml				
Tabasco Pepper Sauce	<.1	0.7	0.2	1.8	16
Grey Poupon Dijon Mustard	<.5	11	0.7	5.8	150
Colman's Fresh Garden Mint Concentrate	<.5	0.5	<.1	5.3	46
Cholula Original Hot Sauce	0	0.9	0	5	19
Geo Watkins Mushroom Ketchup	0.1	0.2	0	13.3	13
Gran Luchito Smoked Chilli Mayonnaise	0.2	81.1	5.3	1.4	838
Delouis Mayonnaise	0.3	81	10.2	1.7	741
Tesco Finest Red Onion Chutney	0.3	0.3	0	0.5	246
Frank's Buffalo Wings Sauce	0.6	1.5	0.2	7	25
Tesco Sandwich Pickle	0.6	0.6	0.1	2.1	85
Asda Chosen by You BBQ USA Chilli Cheese Sauce	0.6	9.7	2.6	0.9	124
Frank's Red Hot Chilli & Lime Sauce	0.7	0.8	0.1	9.2	23
French's Classic Yellow Mustard	1	4.1	0.3	3	73
Tesco Dijon Mustard	1	12	1.5	6	162
Sainsbury's Mayonnaise	1	73.2	5.2	0.9	677
Maille Mustard Mayonnaise	1	77	9	1.2	700
Morrisons Garlic Mayonnaise	1.2	26.9	2.3	1.3	275
Hellman's Real Mayonnaise	1.3	79	6.2	1.5	721
Asda Chosen by You BBQ Peppercorn Steak Sauce	1.4	11.3	4	0.8	124
Tesco Mayonnaise	1.4	74	5.1	1.3	680
Morrisons Mayonnaise	1.4	74.8	5.3	1	687
Hellman's Mayonnaise Olive Oil	1.5	66	5.7	1.2	592
Tesco French Mayonnaise	1.5	69.5	4.6	1.3	635
Morrisons Squeezy Mayonnaise	1.5	74.8	5.4	1	687

Table Sauces

Product	Sugar	Fat	Sat	Salt	Cals
			per 100g / 100ml		
GBK Blue Cheese Mayonnaise	1.6	31.2	4.1	2.5	328
Morrisons Garlic Sauce	1.8	27.8	1.8	0.8	270
Waitrose Mayonnaise with Olive Oil	1.8	75.9	5.4	0.83	699
Asda Chosen by You Mayonnaise	1.8	77	5.8	1.1	707
Tesco Organic Mayonnaise	1.8	75.8	7.2	1	705
Morrisons Chilli Cheese Sauce	1.9	8.5	1.6	0.8	105
Asda Chosen by You Dijon Mustard	1.9	11.7	1.3	5.3	154
Maille Dijon Original Mustard	1.9	11	0.6	5.7	150
Sainsbury's French Style Mayonnaise	2	69.5	6.7	1.17	642
Simply Delicious Organic Mayonnaise	2	74.2	9.1	2	680
Morrisons Dijon Mustard	2.1	11.4	0.8	5.4	157
Waitrose Organic Mayonnaise	2.1	76.8	7.6	0.88	715
Asda Chosen by You Coarse Grain French Mustard	2.2	8.6	0.7	3.8	129
Tesco Finest Wholegrain Mustard	2.2	11.7	0.5	2.8	190
Hellman's Garlic Mayonnaise	2.2	27	2.7	1.7	267
Morrisons Savers Mayonnaise	2.2	26.9	2.2	1.8	285
Waitrose Essential Wholegrain Mustard	2.3	9.9	0.7	4.25	166
Waitrose Essential Mayonnaise	2.3	73	4.9	1.1	685
Tesco Finest Dijon Mustard	2.3	10.8	2.9	5.5	149
Hellman's Lemon Mayonnaise	2.3	27	2.6	1.7	270
Hellman's Light Mayonnaise	2.3	26	2.6	1.7	165
Sainsbury's Mayonnaise, SO Organic	2.3	73.8	8.3	0.83	695
Waitrose Wholegrain Mustard Mayonnaise	2.4	73.1	4.8	1	676
Asda Mild French Mustard	2.4	5.6	0.2	2.5	107
Asda Extra Special Tewkesbury Mustard	2.5	10.8	0.8	2.2	152
Sainsbury's Dijon Mustard	2.5	12	0.6	6	168
Sainsbury's Mayonnaise, Taste the Difference	2.5	78.3	5.5	1.17	722
Tesco Light Mayonnaise	2.5	26	2.9	1.3	264
Tesco Reduced Calorie Mayonnaise	2.5	26	2.9	1.3	264
Waitrose Duchy Originals Organic Wholegrain Mustard With Honey	2.6	9.2	0.6	1.35	171

Table Sauces

Product	Sugar	Fat	Sat	Salt	Cals
	per 100g / 100ml				
Asda Chosen by You Mustard Squeezy Mayonnaise	2.6	27.5	2.3	1.2	284
Sainsbury's Peri Peri Sauce	2.7	3.1	0.2	2.13	52
Waitrose Essential Dijon Mustard	2.7	11.5	0.6	6.5	159
Sainsbury's Horseradish Mustard	2.7	7.1	0.4	3.37	128
Tesco Wholegrain Mustard	2.7	12.3	1.4	3	188
Sainsbury's Mayonnaise Light	2.7	27.5	2.4	1.45	279
Tesco Finest Roast Garlic Cracked Black Pepper Mayonnaise	2.7	77.5	5	0.9	715
Morrisons Light Mayonnaise	2.7	27.1	2.2	1.8	276
Sainsbury's Dark French Mustard	2.8	4.9	0.2	3.58	120
Farrington's Mellow Yellow Mayonnaise	2.8	70.2	4.5	1.5	659
Waitrose Essential English Mustard	2.9	12.7	0.7	5.05	187
Sainsbury's Mayonnaise, Be Good to Yourself	2.9	4.5	0.6	1.45	90
Heinz Mayonnaise	2.9	71.5	5.4	1.1	660
Heinz Lively & Fruity Hot Pepper	3	0.2	trace	1.5	39
Morrisons Sweet Chilli Mayo	3	27.3	2.2	1.2	285
Sainsbury's Hollandaise Sauce	3	53.1	3.9	1.58	504
Asda Chosen by You Chilli Squeezy Mayonnaise	3.1	26.4	2.2	1.2	273
Asda Chosen by You Hot Chilli Sauce for Subs	3.2	1.5	0.3	1.1	52
Hellman's Chilli Mayonnaise	3.4	27	2.6	1.9	275
Asda Extra Special Aioli Sauce	3.6	44	5.1	1.6	480
Sainsbury's Nacho Cheese Dipping Sauce	3.7	17	1.9	0.92	193
Sainsbury's Bernaise Sauce	3.7	37.4	2.5	1.4	372
Sainsbury's Creamy Garlic Sauce	3.8	29	2.1	0.83	296
Sainsbury's Hot Pepper Sauce	3.8	<.5	<.1	1.66	26
Sainsbury's Seafood Sauce, Taste the Difference	3.8	64.1	4.5	0.83	598
GBK Harissa Mayonnaise	3.8	25	2.2	1.8	267
Waitrose Tewkesbury Mustard	4	9.5	1.4	2.73	149
Asda Chosen by You Garlic Squeezy Mayonnaise	4	26.3	2.2	1.2	276
Hellman's Caramelised Onion Mayonnaise	4	27	2.6	1.4	274
Hellman's Pepper Squeezy Mayonnaise	4	27	2.5	1.4	270

Table Sauces

Product	Sugar	Fat	Sat	Salt	Cals
	per 100g / 100ml				
Hellman's Lighter than Light Mayonnaise	4.1	2.9	0.7	1.7	70
Heinz Flamin Cajun Sauce	4.2	53.2	3.9	1.6	515
Morrisons Raita	4.2	1.5	0.9	0.8	53
Sainsbury's Garlic Mayonnaise, Taste the Difference	4.2	68.3	5.4	0.98	654
Tiger Tiger May-O Original	4.3	45.6	5.4	1	440
Heinz Hot & Zingy Peri Peri Sauce	4.5	3.1	0.4	1.3	70
Waitrose Essential Half Fat Mayonnaise	4.5	31.5	2.1	0.95	331
Waitrose Essential French Mustard	4.5	4.4	0.5	3.75	100
Sainsbury's French Style Mayonnaise 50% Less Fat	4.5	31.7	2.7	1.78	323
Tesco Garlic Mayonnaise	4.5	29.2	4.5	1.6	311
Morrisons Burger Sauce	4.7	16.1	1.3	1.3	197
Asda Smart Price Mayonnaise	4.7	25.5	1.8	1.2	276
Sainsbury's Salsa Dipping Sauce	4.8	<.5	<.1	0.87	33
Tesco Finest Bearnaise Sauce	4.8	60.4	4.8	1.6	575
GBK Smoked Chilli Mayonnaise	4.8	23.3	1.7	2.4	252
Waitrose Hollandaise Sauce	4.9	54.2	6.9	1.75	521
Asda Chosen by You Ranch Sauce for Subs	5.1	16.9	1.5	0.9	198
Asda Extra Special Horseradish Sauce	5.1	24	3.1	0.9	261
Waitrose Duchy Originals Organic Wholegrain Mustard & Ruby Ale	5.2	4	0.2	1.49	130
Sainsbury's Mayonnaise, Basics	5.2	25.6	2.4	1.78	280
Tesco Everyday Value Mayonnaise	5.2	25.6	2.4	1.8	280
Asda Smart Price Mint Sauce	5.2	0.3	0.1	1.4	39
Waitrose Garlic Mayonnaise	5.3	69.8	5.4	1	659
Tesco French Mustard	5.4	7.6	0.4	2.8	141
Tesco Mayonnaise with Chilli	5.4	29.4	2.4	1.7	311
Maille Bernaise Sauce	5.5	47	4.1	1.7	459
Morrisons Tandoori Marinade	5.5	6	0.5	1	100
Nando's Garlic Peri Peri Sauce	5.7	3.4	0.4	5.5	59
Nando's Peri Peri Marinade Medium	5.7	2.1	0.2	2.25	61
Sainsbury's Fresh Mint Sauce	5.7	<.5	<.1	2.38	50

Table Sauces

Product	Sugar	Fat	Sat	Salt	Cals
		per 100g / 100ml			
Sainsbury's Tartare Sauce, SO Organic	5.7	50.8	6.3	2.25	485
Haywards Piccalilli	5.8	0.7	0.1	1.5	51
Asda Smart Price English Mustard	5.9	7.7	1.9	5.3	157
Maille Tartare Sauce	5.9	61	5.2	2	574
Colman's Hot Garlic Chilli Sauce	6	26	2	1.7	270
Maille Wholegrain Mustard	6	10	0.4	5.2	176
Grey Poupon Old Style Mustard	6	10	0.4	5.2	176
Wahaca Chilli De Arbol	6.1	1.2	0.2	1.2	67
Morrisons Piri Piri Marinade	6.1	2.5	0.2	0.5	61
Morrisons NuMe Mayonnaise Squeezy	6.1	10.8	1.1	1.8	156
Morrisons Savers Mint Sauce	6.1	0.1	0	1.4	35
Nando's Lemon & Herb Peri Peri Sauce	6.2	3.8	0.4	1.75	64
Tesco Finest Hollandaise Sauce	6.2	63	5.5	1.8	600
Nando's Hot Peri Peri Sauce	6.3	3.8	0.4	7	75
Waitrose Lemon Mayonnaise	6.4	69.5	4.7	1.02	661
Nando's Wild Herb Peri Peri Sauce	6.5	3.8	0.4	5.5	66
Waitrose Essential Mustard Piccalilli	6.6	0.8	trace	2.33	56
Asda Chosen by You Hot English Mustard	6.6	10.8	2.6	5	179
Colman's Horseradish Sauce	6.7	6.4	0.6	0.92	108
Asda Chosen by You Lighter Squeezy Mayonnaise	6.7	5	0.7	1.8	102
Morrisons Wholegrain Mustard	6.8	12.6	0.8	2.9	225
Tesco Healthy Living Mayonnaise	6.8	5.3	0.6	1.5	96
Colman's Original English Mustard Powder	6.9	42	2.3	0.02	560
Colman's Chunky Burger Sauce	7	21	1.5	1.9	230
Nando's Lemon & Lime Marinade	7	5.9	0.6	1.5	99
Sainsbury's Creamy Dill Dressing, Taste the Difference	7	33.8	2	1.1	336
Sainsbury's Wholegrain Mustard	7	12	1	3.3	216
Maille Hollandaise Sauce	7	49	6.5	2.7	482
Sainsbury's Burger Sauce	7.1	28	2.2	1.01	299
Coleman's Wholegrain Mustard	7.1	7.8	0.4	3	162

Table Sauces

Product	Sugar	Fat	Sat	Salt	Cals
		per 100g / 100ml			
Morrisons Squeezy Light Salad Cream	7.1	12.6	1.6	1	165
Wahaca Chipotle	7.2	0.8	0.3	0.9	54
French's Tex-Mex Chipotle Dressing	7.2	15.06	1.08	1.17	171
Colman's Hot Dog Squeezy Mustard	7.2	5.3	0.3	2	113
Tesco Sweet Burger Sauce	7.2	11.1	0.8	0.8	142
Sainsbury's Wholegrain Mustard & Chilli	7.3	12.1	0.8	3.18	219
Maille Dijonnaise Sauce	7.4	41	3.6	2.9	413
Tesco Mustard Mayonnaise	7.4	43.5	4.7	1.6	450
Tesco Finest Tartare Sauce	7.5	31.5	3.4	2.2	324
Asda Chosen by You Light Mayonnaise	7.6	30	2.5	1.7	342
Nando's Medium Peri Peri Sauce	7.7	3.7	0.4	6.25	69
Cardini Red Jalapeno Dressing	7.7	41.4	3.6	1.5	414
Waitrose Essential sweet piccalilli	7.8	0.5	trace	2.36	65
Asda Chosen by You Garlic Ketchup	8	34	3.2	0.9	346
Nem Vit Dipping Sauce	8.2	0.2	trace	4.5	205
Heinz Salad Cream Extra Light	8.2	7.1	0.8	1.7	138
Wahaca Habanero	8.3	2	0.3	1.1	67
Tesco Everyday Value Salad Cream	8.4	8.7	0.8	1.3	139
Sainsbury's Salad Cream, Be Good to Yourself	9.2	14.1	1.1	0.9	183
Sainsbury's Salad Cream, Basics	9.3	9	0.7	1.1	137
Tesco Mustard Piccalilli	9.4	0.6	0.1	1.4	69
Sainsbury's Piccalilli, Taste the Difference	9.5	0.8	13.8	1	64
Tesco Healthy Living Salad Cream	9.5	7.9	0.8	1.2	132
Tesco Everyday Value Mint Sauce	9.5	0.2	0.1	1	53
Waitrose Cooks' Ingredients Hot Chilli Sauce	9.8	1.6	0.2	1.3	68
Heinz Horseradish Sauce	9.8	17.7	1.9	1.8	231
Waitrose Essential Seafood Sauce	10	50.6	3.7	1.3	503
Asda Smart Price Salad Cream	10.1	25.9	2	1.6	291
Heinz Salad Cream Light	10.1	16.3	1.4	1.7	218
Geeta's Lime & Chilli Chutney	10.1	0.3	trace	0.9	50

Table Sauces

Product	Sugar	Fat	Sat	Salt	Cals
			per 100g / 100ml		
Morrisons Savers Salad Cream	10.2	8.5	0.8	1	135
Asda Extra Special Tartare Sauce	10.6	48.7	3.8	4.3	490
Waitrose Essential Reduced Fat Seafood Sauce	10.7	34.4	2.5	1.75	365
Heinz Tartare Sauce	10.8	28.3	2.1	2.2	312
Heinz Garlic Sauce	11	36	3.3	1.5	398
Sainsbury's Wholegrain Mustard & Honey	11	11	0.6	3.3	220
Geeta's Mango & Chilli Chutney	11	trace	trace	0.4	49
Sainsbury's Mint Sauce, Taste the Difference	11	<.5	<.1	0.75	59
Heinz Tomato Ketchup 50% Less Sugars	11.4	0.1	trace	1.3	64
Nando's Perinaise	11.4	21.8	1.5	1	259
Geeta's Mango Chutney	11.4	trace	trace	0.4	51
Waitrose Piccalilli	11.5	1.9	0.4	1.75	81
Morrisons Reduced Sugar & Salt Tomato Ketchup	11.6	0.2	trace	0.3	67
Asda Chosen by You Squeezy Mint Sauce	11.6	0.2	0	1.5	55
Tesco English Mustard	11.8	10.2	1.4	7.3	183
Asda Chosen by You Honey & Mustard Sauce for Subs	11.9	13.4	1.3	1.2	190
Tesco Tartare Sauce	12.1	25.8	2	3.3	312
Waitrose Essential Hot Horseradish Sauce	12.1	17.7	1.3	1.65	234
Morrisons American Hot Dog Mustard	12.2	4.3	0.5	1.7	117
Sainsbury's Creamy Horseradish Sauce, Taste the Difference	12.2	36	3.2	0.97	391
Tabasco Sauce & Marinade Peppery Deep South Creole	12.3	6.1	0.6	1.11	129
Sainsbury's Tomato Ketchup, Reduced Salt	12.4	<.5	<.1	0.49	68
Asda Chosen by You Squeezy Piccalilli	12.4	0.6	0	1.6	78
Asda Chosen by You Tartare Sauce	12.4	45.8	3.1	3.1	472
Asda Chosen by You Spiced Fruit Chutney	12.5	6.3	1.5	1.2	118
Sainsbury's Satay Dipping Sauce	12.7	8.9	4.6	1.39	168
Tesco Sweet Piccalilli	12.7	0.5	0.1	1.2	75
Sainsbury's Tartare Sauce	12.7	23.7	1.6	3.05	281
Morrisons Piccalilli	12.9	1.6	0.4	1.4	94
Asda Smart Price Brown Sauce	12.9	0.1	0.1	1.04	87

Table Sauces

Product	Sugar	Fat	Sat	Salt	Cals
	per 100g / 100ml				
Colman's Original English Mustard	13	12	0.7	8.5	195
Hellman's Salad Cream	13	26	2.1	1.8	292
Morrisons Tartare Sauce	13	21.1	1.6	3	267
Tesco Finest Horseradish Sauce	13.1	26.5	3	1.9	323
Sainsbury's Piccalilli	13.2	0.7	<.1	1.17	76
Morrisons Squeezy Salad Cream	13.2	19.9	2.8	1.1	251
Morrisons English Mustard	13.3	10.4	0.6	7.3	205
Tesco Everyday Value Brown Sauce	13.4	0.1	<.1	1.2	81
Sainsbury's English Mustard	13.5	9.8	0.5	8.25	191
Morrisons Squeezy Brown Sauce	13.7	0.2	0	1.3	90
Waitrose Essential tartare sauce	13.9	32.8	2.6	2.35	361
Eat 17 Chorizo Jam	14	14	4	2.1	344
Newman's Own Fiery Bourbon BBQ Sauce	14.1	3.9	0.3	1	118
Asda Extra Special Spicy Marie Rose Sauce with Brandy	14.1	47.4	4	1.2	498
Waitrose Essential Creamed Horseradish Sauce	14.1	28.5	4.5	1.45	341
Asda Chosen by You Mustard Piccalilli	14.2	0.3	0.1	1	78
Asda Chosen by You Onion Chutney	14.2	0.4	0.1	1.1	107
Morrisons Savers English Mustard	14.3	8.3	0.5	8.3	188
Asda Extra Special Mint Sauce	14.3	0.5	0	1.2	74
Tesco Everyday Value Horseradish Sauce	14.4	19.7	1.4	1.8	246
Asda Chosen by You Light Salad Cream	14.8	8.3	0.6	1.7	156
Heinz Mint Sauce	14.8	1	0.1	1.6	81
Sainsbury's Brown Sauce, Reduced Salt & Sugar	15	<.5	<.1	0.73	86
Colman's Sauce Mix Tartare Sauce	15	24	2.1	3.2	291
Tesco Finest British Piccalilli	15.1	0.7	0.2	2.5	83
Tesco Hot Horseradish	15.1	16.9	1.2	2.1	233
Waitrose Essential Brown Sauce	15.2	0.3	0	0.85	103
HP Reduced Salt Brown Sauce	15.4	0.1	trace	0.9	86
Morrisons Seafood Sauce	15.5	48.3	3.2	1.3	511
Asda Chosen by You Brown Sauce	15.7	0.2	0.1	1.1	102

Table Sauces

Product	Sugar	Fat	Sat	Salt	Cals
			per 100g / 100ml		
GBK Habanero Relish	15.7	0	0	1.8	98
Frank's Red Hot Sriracha	15.8	0.7	0.1	6.1	90
Tabasco Chipotle & Bourbon Sauce	15.8	0	0	1.33	86
Sainsbury's English Mustard, Basics	15.8	7.5	0.5	8.1	193
Asda Chosen by You Light Seafood Sauce	15.8	15.8	1.3	1.7	227
Colman's Fiery BBQ Chilli Sauce	16	<.5	<.5	1.5	95
Tesco Finest Marie Rose Sauce	16	51.5	5.5	1.5	536
Sainsbury's Horseradish Sauce	16.1	8	0.5	1.97	168
Asda Chosen by You Seafood Sauce	16.2	22.8	1.9	1.7	290
Sainsbury's Mint Sauce	16.2	<.5	<.1	0.78	94
Tesco Finest British Mint Sauce	16.2	0.6	0.2	0.5	80
Waitrose Essential Bramley Apple Sauce	16.4	0	0	0.18	80
Asda Chosen by You Salad Cream	16.6	26.2	2.1	1.6	315
Sainsbury's Mint Sauce, SO Organic	16.6	<.5	<.1	0.73	81
Tesco Brown Sauce	16.7	0.1	0.1	1	103
Sainsbury's American Style Mustard	16.8	5	0.7	2.75	160
Tesco Reduced Fat Seafood Sauce	16.8	24.6	2	1.5	305
Asda Chosen by You Smoky BBQ Marinade & Glaze	16.8	0.1	0	1.1	97
Tesco Seafood Sauce	16.9	52	3.8	1.5	543
Heinz Piccalilli Pickle	16.9	0.5	trace	2.3	99
Colman's Sweet Chilli Mango Sauce	17	<.5	<.5	1.2	90
Heinz Salad Cream	17	23.8	1.8	1.7	293
Asda Chosen by You Tomato Chutney	17.1	2.5	0.4	1.4	103
Morrisons Squeezy Sweetcorn Relish	17.2	1	0.1	0.9	122
Morrisons Tomato & Chilli Relish	17.2	0.7	0.1	0.5	91
Tesco Salad Cream	17.3	25.8	2.9	1.3	323
Tabasco Sauce & Marinade Sweet Chipotle & Cola	17.4	0.1	0	1.33	101
Tabasco Chipotle & Cola Sauce	17.4	0.1	0	1.33	101
Colman's Seafood Sauce	18	22	1.8	1.8	294
Branston Beetroot Pickle	18	0.6	0.2	0.8	106

Table Sauces

Product	Sugar	Fat	Sat	Salt	Cals
			per 100g / 100ml		
Waitrose Essential Salad Cream	18	24.2	2.8	1.15	307
Asda Chosen by You Sweet Onion Relish	18	0.2	0.1	0.9	86
Sainsbury's Brown Sauce, Basics	18.1	<.5	<.1	1.13	86
Morrisons Tomato Ketchup	18.1	0.2	trace	0.8	96
Asda Chosen by You Horseradish Sauce	18.1	9.5	1.1	4	170
Daddies Brown Sauce	18.4	trace	trace	2	108
Sainsbury's BBQ Sauce	18.4	<.5	<.1	1.31	150
Sainsbury's Dill Mustard Sauce	18.4	37.6	2.5	1.9	440
Sainsbury's Seafood Sauce	18.4	30	2	1.73	356
Daddies Tomato Ketchup	18.5	trace	trace	3.7	102
Tesco Mint Sauce	18.5	0.1	0	1.5	90
Tesco Sticky BBQ Marinade	18.6	0.4	0.1	1.1	107
Tesco American Style Mustard	18.7	4.6	0.7	2.6	155
GBK BBQ Relish	18.7	1.3	0.2	2.2	128
Tiger Tiger Gluten Free Tomato Ketchup	18.8	0.05	0.02	3	88
Waitrose Duchy Originals Organic Tomato Chutney	18.8	0.3	0	1.74	113
Tesco Sweet Curry Sauce	18.8	0.5	0	0.9	111
Branston Tomato Sauce	19	0	0	2.2	119
Hellman's Tomato Ketchup	19	<.5	<.1	1.7	84
Haywards Sweet Piccalilli	19	0.8	<.5	2.3	105
Waitrose Essential Tomato Ketchup	19	0.1	0	1.08	102
Asda Chosen by You BBQ Tennessee Bourbon Last Minute Marinade	19.3	0.3	0	1.1	91
Waitrose Essential Mint Sauce	19.4	0	0	0.38	98
Great British Sauce Co. Proper Tomato Sauce	19.6	<.1	<.05	2.09	124
French's Relish New York Pickle	19.7	<.1	<.1	0.66	92
Forces Sauces Brigadier Brown Sauce	19.9	0.5	<.1	1.4	112
Heinz Ploughmans Pickle	19.9	trace	trace	2.1	99
Sainsbury's Sweet Piccalilli	19.9	<.5	<.1	0.66	98
Sainsbury's Salad Cream	20	34	2.5	1.4	397
Tesco BBQ Sauce	20.6	0.2	0	0.8	120

Table Sauces

Product	Sugar	Fat	Sat	Salt	Cals
		per 100g / 100ml			
French's Mustard Sweet Yellow	20.7	4	0.3	2.9	161
Tesco Creamed Horseradish	20.7	10.2	1.7	4	197
Sainsbury's Sweet Pickle	20.9	<.5	<.1	2.38	104
Morrisons Chipotle Sauce	20.9	trace	trace	1.1	116
Asda Chosen by You Mint Sauce	20.9	1.5	0.4	1.8	104
Morrisons Onion Relish	21	0.4	0.1	0.8	102
Asda Chosen by You Bramley Apple Sauce	21	0.3	0.1	0.1	111
Sainsbury's Spicy Brown Sauce	21.2	0.5	0	1.25	129
Tabasco Fiery Habanero Sauce	21.2	3.2	0.3	0.61	150
Tesco Organic Tomato Ketchup	21.3	0.6	0.6	0.8	110
Sainsbury's Tomato Ketchup	21.6	<.5	<.1	1.05	99
Tesco Tomato Ketchup	21.7	0.3	0.2	1.8	105
Tesco Everyday Value Sweet Pickle	21.7	0.1	<.1	2.7	109
Morrisons Mint Sauce	21.7	0.4	0.2	1.6	101
Heinz Firecracker Sauce	22	0.9	trace	1.4	116
Old El Paso Red Jalapeno Relish	22.1	0.5	0	0.41	133
Morrisons BBQ Sauce	22.2	0.2	0.1	0.7	124
Asda Chosen by You Fiery Caribbean Style Hot Jerk Sauce	22.4	0.1	0	1.3	107
Asda Chosen by You Sweetcorn Relish	22.4	0.8	0.2	1.1	184
Heinz Mild Mustard Pickle	22.5	1.2	trace	2.1	124
Asda Chosen by You Tomato Ketchup	22.6	0.6	0.4	1.2	113
Heinz Curry Sauce Classic	23	0.3	trace	1.5	116
Sainsbury's Brown Sauce	23	<.5	<.1	1.3	125
HP Brown Sauce	23.1	0.1	trace	1.3	122
Morrisons Squeezy Burger Relish	23.1	0.5	0.1	0.7	106
Tesco Everyday Value Tomato Ketchup	23.2	0.2	<.1	0.8	137
Morrisons Bramley Apple Sauce	23.2	0.3	0.1	0.1	101
Tesco Finest Pepper Chutney with Paprika	23.2	1	0.2	1.3	118
French's Relish Texan Jalapeno	23.3	0.4	trace	1.8	107
Asda Chosen by You Sweet Piccalilli	23.3	0.2	0	1	114

Table Sauces

Product	Sugar	Fat	Sat	Salt	Cals
			per 100g / 100ml		
Heinz Tomato Ketchup Fiery Chilli	23.5	0.3	trace	1.8	117
Heinz Original Ketchup	23.7	0.1	0.1	2.2	103
Asda Chosen by You Bourbon BBQ Sauce	23.8	0	0	1.1	153
Tesco Caramelised Onion Chutney	23.8	0.2	<.1	0.7	140
Branston Original Pickle	24	<.5	0	4	112
Branston Relish Spicy Tomato with Chilli & Jalapeno	24	0.7	<.1	1.3	125
Asda Chosen by You Sweet Pickle	24	0.2	0.1	4.8	120
Asda Smart Price Sweet Pickle	24.3	0.2	0.1	0.9	127
Asda Chosen by You Burger Relish	24.5	0.7	0.2	0.7	114
Morrisons Tomato Chutney	24.6	0.9	0.1	1.3	117
Newman's Own Tangy Carolina BBQ Sauce	24.7	2.3	0.2	1.23	152
Tesco Everyday Value Apple Sauce	24.8	0.1	<.1	0.1	102
Sainsbury's Tomato Ketchup, Basics	24.9	<.5	<.1	0.8	112
Forces Sauces Corporal Ketchup Sauce	25	0.4	<.1	1.3	122
Asda Smart Price Apple Sauce	25	0	0	0	104
Colman's Classic Mint Sauce	25	<.5	<.1	2.7	131
Tesco Fruity Brown Sauce	25.2	0.1	<.1	1	145
Sainsbury's Ploughmans Plum Chutney	25.2	<.5	0.2	1	137
GBK House Relish	25.4	0.7	0.1	2.3	140
Sainsbury's Creamed Horseradish Sauce	25.4	14.3	1.9	2.9	253
HP Original Woodsmoke Barbecue Sauce	25.5	trace	trace	1.4	133
HP Fruity Sauce	25.6	trace	trace	1.5	135
Colman's Smoky BBQ Sauce	26	0.6	<.5	1.7	140
Colman's Bramley Apple Sauce	26	<.5	0	<.01	111
Asda Chosen by You Sandwich Pickle	26.4	0.1	0.1	1.9	126
Morrisons Creamed Horseradish	26.4	12.8	1.4	3.4	246
Cross & Blackwell Branston Rice & Fruity Sauce	27	<.5	<.5	0.89	144
Frank's Redhot Original Pepper Sauce	27	0	0	3	133
Branston Fruity Sauce	27	<.5	<.5	0.89	144
Frank's Red Hot Original Cayenne Pepper Sauce	27	0	0	3	133

Table Sauces

Product	Sugar	Fat	Sat	Salt	Cals
			per 100g / 100ml		
Morrisons Sandwich Pickle	27	1.5	0.3	2.6	144
Sainsbury's Chutney British Onion	27	0.6	0.2	1	142
Asda Extra Special English Bramley Apple Sauce with Cider	27	0.4	0.1	0.1	125
Sainsbury's Sweetcorn Relish	27	<.5	<.1	1.01	170
Colman's Cranberry Sauce	27	<.5	<.1	0.02	117
Eat 17 Bacon Jam	27	7.8	2.2	0.75	244
Asda Smart Price Tomato Ketchup	27.1	0.2	0.2	0.7	114
Asda Chosen by You Sweet Onion Sauce for Subs	27.1	0.3	0	0.8	141
Tesco Mustard & Dill Sauce	27.3	38.1	2.7	0.8	471
Heinz Speciality Tangy Sandwich Pickle	27.3	trace	trace	2.1	130
Morrisons Sweet Pickle	27.3	1.3	0.3	3	143
Sainsbury's Spicy BBQ Sauce	27.5	<.5	<.1	1.15	141
Asda Chosen by You BBQ Texas Fruity Last Minute Marinade	28.1	0.3	0	1.2	135
Heinz Sweet Chilli Tomato Pickle	28.2	0.1	trace	1.5	127
Guinness Sauce	28.3	0.1	0	1.1	156
Morrisons Onion Chutney	28.3	0.6	0.1	1.4	138
French's Relish Sweet Onion	28.6	0.3	trace	1	132
Heinz Barbecue Classic Sauce	28.7	0.1	trace	1.3	133
Heinz Tomato Ketchup Sweet Chilli	28.9	0.2	trace	1.8	133
Branston Small Chunk Pickle	29	0.8	0.3	3.9	159
Waitrose Apple Sauce with Kentish Cider	29	0	0	0.13	119
Tesco Original Pickle	29.2	0.1	<.1	3	133
Tesco Sweet Pickle	29.2	0.1	<.1	3	133
Asda Chosen by You Hot BBQ Sauce	29.2	0.2	0.1	1.1	161
Sainsbury's Tomato & Jalapeno Relish	29.2	<.5	<.1	2.03	136
Tesco Bramley Apple Sauce	29.3	0.1	<.1	0.1	131
Levi Roots Reggae Reggae Caribbean BBQ Sauce & Marinade	29.5	0.1	0	1.1	132
Sainsbury's Tomato Relish	30.4	<.5	<.1	1.51	135
Asda Chosen by You BBQ Ketchup	30.5	0.1	0	1	166
Baxters Tomato Chutney, Handmade	30.7	0.4	0	1.6	146

Table Sauces

Product	Sugar	Fat	Sat	Salt	Cals
			per 100g / 100ml		
Tiptree Ketchup	31	0	0	1.2	182
Tiptree Tomato Chutney	31	0	0	2	153
Sainsbury's Chutney Caramelised Onion, Taste the Difference	31.3	<.5	0.2	1.07	161
Morrisons Sweet Chilli Sauce	31.6	0.3	0.2	2.1	160
Sainsbury's Apple Sauce	31.8	<.5	<.1	0.03	134
Sainsbury's Bramley Apple Sauce	31.8	<.5	<.1	0.03	134
Sainsbury's Smooth Apple Sauce	31.8	<.5	<.1	0.03	134
Tesco Everyday Value Cranberry Sauce	31.9	0.3	<.1	0.1	169
Sainsbury's Chutney Apple & Pear, Taste the Difference	32	0.8	0.4	1.23	193
Baxters Victorian Chutney	32.2	0.3	0	2.2	151
Sainsbury's Soy & Ginger Dipping Sauce	32.3	<.5	<.1	0.93	179
Sainsbury's Onion Relish	32.4	<.5	<.1	1.01	153
Tesco Ploughmans Plum Chutney	32.5	0.4	0.1	0.7	154
Baxters Alberts Victorian Chutney	32.9	0.3	<.1	2.1	156
Ocean Spray Whole Cranberry Sauce	33	0	0	0	152
Branston Mediterranean Tomato Chutney	33.1	0.6	0.2	0.76	155
Ballymaloe Original Relish	33.1	trace	trace	1.4	161
Waitrose Essential Cranberry Sauce	33.3	0	0	trace	153
Tesco Tomato Chutney	33.7	0.1	<.1	1.2	173
Heinz BBQ Sauce Sweet & Spicy	34	0.2	<.1	1.2	154
Tesco Finest Brown Sauce	34	0.6	0.2	0.4	180
The English Provender Co, Moroccan Spiced Chutney	34.9	0.8	0.36	1.6	160
Branston Tomato & Red Pepper Relish	35	<.5	0	1.2	160
Tesco Finest Beetroot Relish	35.2	0.4	<.1	0.9	159
Great British Sauce Co. Smoky Barbecue Sauce	35.4	<.1	<.05	2.29	164
Branston Caramelised Onion Chutney	35.5	1.3	0.2	0.71	169
Jack Daniel's Steak Sauce	35.6	0.2	0	2.9	162
Jack Daniel's Original Barbacue Sauce	35.9	0.1	0	0.77	163
Sainsbury's Chutney Tomato & Chilli, Taste the Difference	36.2	3.8	0.7	1.25	198
Asda Extra Special Plum & Apple Chutney	36.2	0.3	0.1	0.9	165

Table Sauces

Product	Sugar	Fat	Sat	Salt	Cals
		per 100g / 100ml			
The English Provender Co, Plum & Bramley Apple Chutney	36.9	0.36	0.1	1	168
Sainsbury's Apple Sauce with Kentish Cider, Taste the Difference	37.3	<.5	<.1	0.25	153
Morrisons Mint Jelly	37.8	0.3	0.1	0.5	165
Jack Daniel's Smokey BBQ Sauce	38.2	0.1	0	0.76	173
Ocean Spray Cranberry & Apple Sauce	39	1.3	0.5	0.1	177
Tiptree BBQ Relish	39	0	0	1.6	194
Heinz Sticky Barbecue Sauce	39.2	0.1	trace	1.1	172
Asda Extra Special Tomato & Chilli Chutney	39.6	0.4	0.1	0.8	188
Asda Extra Special Redcurrant Sauce with Port	39.6	1.1	0.1	0.1	223
Waitrose Tomato Chutney	39.8	0.1	0.1	2.08	195
Tiptree Brown Sauce	40	0	0	1.4	191
Tesco Finest Tomato Ketchup	40.3	0.3	0.1	1	174
Tiptree BBQ Sauce	41	0.6	0.1	1.6	187
Sainsbury's Caramelised Onion Chutney, SO Organic	41.2	<.5	<.1	1	211
Sainsbury's Cranberry Sauce	41.3	<.5	<.1	0.13	170
The English Provender Co, Apple Pear & Fig Chutney	41.5	0.36	0.1	1.15	181
Morrisons Cranberry Sauce	41.7	2	0.7	0.3	207
Tesco Finest British Bramley Apple Sauce with Cider	41.8	0.3	0.1	0.1	179
Asda Extra Special Mango, Apple & Ginger Chutney	42.1	0.5	0.2	1	182
Waitrose Piri Piri Chutney	42.5	1	0.1	1.25	191
Waitrose Spicy Peach Chutney	43.3	0	0	1.23	217
Sharwood's Mango Chutney	44.7	<.1	<.1	2.9	240
Tiptree Chutney	45	0	0	0.8	248
Tesco Finest Mango Apricot & Coriander Chutney	45.8	0.4	<.1	1.1	200
Tesco Cranberry Sauce	46.9	0.4	0.1	0.1	198
Baxters Caramelised Onion Chutney	47.9	0.4	0.2	0.4	206
Waitrose Duchy Originals Organic Cranberry Sauce with Port	47.9	0.4	0.2	0.02	203
Tesco Finest Sweet Tomato & Piri Piri Chilli Chutney	48.1	2.4	0.3	1.2	224
Tesco Mint Jelly	48.7	0.3	0.1	0.6	232
Asda Extra Special Caramelised Onion Chutney	48.9	0.3	0.1	1	207

Table Sauces

Product	Sugar	Fat	Sat	Salt	Cals
			per 100g / 100ml		
Asda Extra Special Cranberry Sauce with Port	48.9	0.4	0.2	0.1	220
Waitrose Duchy Originals Organic Beetroot Relish	49.8	0.1	0	0.09	213
Sainsbury's Mango Chutney, Taste the Difference	50	<.5	<.1	2.63	263
Tiptree Ploughmans Plum Chutney	50	0	0	1.4	210
Sainsbury's Mango Chutney	50.5	<.5	<.1	2.73	255
Waitrose Rhubarb Chutney	50.6	0.4	0	0.25	219
Waitrose Apple & Walnut Chutney	51.3	2.6	0.9	1.08	251
Asda Chosen by You Cranberry Sauce	51.6	0.3	trace	trace	245
Sainsbury's Mint Jelly	51.8	<.5	<.1	0.58	238
Morrisons Redcurrant Jelly	52.1	0.4	0.1	0.1	270
Tesco Finest Victorian Plum Chutney	53.4	0.3	0.1	0.6	230
The English Provender Co, Hot Chilli & Red Pepper Chutney	54.3	0.3	0.1	1.45	239
Jack Daniel's Tennesse Honey Glaze	54.4	0.1	0	1.8	231
Sainsbury's Cranberry Sauce, Taste the Difference	54.7	<.5	<.1	<.01	235
The English Provender Co, Caramelised Onion Chutney	55.3	0.56	0.1	1.2	221
Asda Extra Special Redcurrant & Port Jelly	56.3	2.5	0.1	0.1	254
Tesco Finest Fig Chutney	56.4	1.7	0.4	0.6	274
Tesco Finest Cranberry Sauce	57.1	0.5	0.1	<.01	244
Asda Chosen by You Mango Chutney	57.2	0.7	0.4	2.5	239
Waitrose Duchy Originals Organic Onion Marmalade	57.6	2.4	0.5	0.05	262
Sainsbury's Redcurrant Jelly	58.9	<.5	<.1	0.15	260
Tiptree Red Onion Chutney	59	1.5	0.2	1	301
Waitrose Red Onion Chutney	59.1	0.3	0.1	0.39	242
Tesco Redcurrant Jelly	59.2	0.1	0.1	0.2	267
Waitrose Redcurrant Sauce with Ruby Port	59.6	0	0	0.03	249
Waitrose Onion Garlic Chutney	59.9	0.3	0.1	0.25	258
Tiptree Chilli Chutney	62	0	0	0	261
Sainsbury's Chilli Jam, Taste the Difference	62.9	1.4	0.6	0.13	273
Asda Chosen by You Redcurrant Jelly	63	0	0	0	253
Asda Chosen by You Mint Jelly	63.3	0.6	0.2	0.1	263

Table Sauces

Product	Sugar	Fat	Sat	Salt	Cals
		per 100g / 100ml			
Lingham's Chilli Sauce	66.7	6.7	1.3	1.5	380
Waitrose Essential Redcurrant Jelly	66.8	0.5	0.2	0.13	293
Tesco Finest Chilli Relish	67	0.7	0.2	0.1	306
Waitrose Essential Mint Jelly	69.3	0.5	0.1	0.03	293
Asda Extra Special Quince Jelly	69.8	0.4	0.1	0.1	293

Tinned Beans & Pasta

Many tinned products have sugar added, but there are definitely some better options out there. Look out for low sugar and salt options.

To help you make the best choices, products are listed starting with the least sugar first.

Product	Sugar	Fat	Sat	Salt	Cals
			per 100g		
Asda Chosen By Kids Chicken & Veg Risotto in Slurpy Tomato Sauce	0.8	0.9	0.5	0.3	104
Heinz Weight Watchers Spaghetti	1.2	0.2	trace	0.4	50
Tesco Goodness Macaroni Cheese	1.2	3	1.5	0.4	78
Tesco Macaroni Cheese In Sauce	1.3	3.9	1.2	1	95
Heinz Mini Meals Carbonara	1.4	1.4	0.5	0.6	65
Morrisons Bolognese Ravioli	1.4	1.3	0.4	0.5	79
Asda Chosen By Kids Kids Pasta & Meatballs in Tomato Sauce	1.4	1.3	0.5	0.3	89
Branston Macaroni Cheese	1.5	4	1.3	0.78	86
Heinz Macaroni Cheese	1.5	2.9	1.1	0.7	88
Asda Chosen By Kids Tuna Pasta & Veg in Tomato Sauce	1.5	0.9	0.4	0.7	73
Heinz Mini Meals Chicken & Sweetcorn Pasta	1.7	1.9	0.3	0.6	80
Morrisons Macaroni Cheese	1.7	3.4	1.2	0.8	89
Asda Chosen by You Macaroni Cheese	1.7	3.4	1.2	0.8	89
Asda Chosen By Kids Vegetable Ravioli in Tomato Sauce	1.7	1.5	0.5	0.4	78
Tesco Goodness Spaghetti Numbers	1.7	1.2	0.3	0.2	54
Heinz Fajita Beanz	1.8	0.8	0.1	0.5	79
Asda Chosen by You Pasta Shells Bolognese	1.8	1.9	0.8	0.8	76
Asda Chosen By Kids Beef Ravioli in Tomato Sauce	1.8	1.5	0.5	0.4	76
Tesco Goodness Beans With Sausages	1.8	3.3	1	0.3	110
Tesco Beef Ravioli In Tomato And Beef Sauce	1.9	2.7	0.6	0.5	90
Sainsbury's Macaroni Cheese	2	4.8	1.8	0.75	103
Asda Chosen By Kids Dinky Pork Sausages & Beans in Tomato Sauce	2.1	3.8	1.3	0.2	115
Tesco Everyday Value Macaroni Cheese	2.1	2.5	1.2	0.7	80
Asda Smart Price Macaroni Cheese	2.2	1.5	0.7	0.6	73
Tesco Goodness Pizza Tortellini	2.2	2.2	0.8	0.3	79

Product	Sugar	Fat	Sat	Salt	Cals
			per 100g		
Tesco Goodness Vegetable Ravioli	2.2	0.9	0.3	0.4	71
Heinz Baked Beanz Reduced Salt & Sugar	2.3	0.2	trace	0.4	67
Morrison Savers Spaghetti in Tomato Sauce	2.3	0.4	0.1	0.4	64
Asda Smart Price Ravioli	2.3	0.9	0.4	0.6	75
Heinz Spaghetti Bolognese	2.4	1.5	0.2	0.7	84
Heinz Vegetable Chilli Beanz	2.4	0.9	0.1	0.5	80
Asda Chosen by You Spaghetti Bolognese	2.4	1.8	0.8	0.6	76
Crosse & Blackwell 4 Kids Disney Planes Pasta Shapes	2.5	0.5	trace	0.35	50
Crosse & Blackwell 4 Kids Disney Princess Pasta & Sausages	2.5	2.7	0.8	0.5	86
Crosse & Blackwell 4 Kids Scoobydoo Pasta & Sausages	2.5	2.7	0.8	0.5	86
Crosse & Blackwell 4 Kids Sponge Bob Pasta Shapes	2.5	0.5	trace	0.35	50
Crosse & Blackwell 4 Kids Tom & Jerry with Sausages	2.5	2.7	0.8	0.5	86
Crosse & Blackwell 4 Kids Disney Princess Pasta Shapes	2.5	0.5	trace	0.35	50
Crosse & Blackwell 4 Kids Scooby Doo Pasta Shapes	2.5	0.5	trace	0.35	50
Crosse & Blackwell 4 Kids Winnie the Pooh Pasta Shapes	2.5	0.5	trace	0.35	50
Heinz Tuscan Beanz	2.5	1.7	0.2	0.6	91
Asda Chosen by You Reduced Sugar & Salt Baked Beans in Tom Sauce	2.5	0.4	0.1	0.3	74
Tesco Vegetarian Beans Sausages	2.7	2.2	0.3	0.8	91
Sainsbury's Pasta Cheese & Bacon	2.8	6.5	2.8	0.63	128
Asda Beef Ravioli in a Rich Tomato Sauce	2.8	2.6	1.3	0.6	90
Tesco Spaghetti Bolognese	2.8	3.8	1.2	0.9	94
Sainsbury's Baked Beans with Meatfree Sausages	2.9	2.1	0.2	0.7	91
Morrisons Spaghetti Loops with Sausages in Tomato Sauce	2.9	3.1	1.3	0.6	87
Branston Reduced Sugar & Salt Baked Beans	3	0.3	0.1	0.5	82
Morrisons NuMe Reduced Sugar Baked Beans in a Tasty Tom Sauce	3	0.4	trace	0.4	86
Crosse & Blackwell 4 Kids Sponge Bob Pasta & Meatballs	3.1	1.5	0.3	0.23	71
Heinz Mini Meals Tomato & Vegetable Shells	3.1	0.3	0.1	0.3	65
Heinz Ravioli	3.1	1.5	0.7	0.6	73
Asda Chosen by You Baked Beans & Jumbo Sausages In Tom Sauce	3.1	4.2	1.5	0.6	120
Sainsbury's Vegetable Ravioli in Tomato & Herb Sauce	3.2	1.3	0.2	0.58	81

Tinned Beans & Pasta

Product	Sugar	Fat	Sat	Salt	Cals
			per 100g		
Branston Bean Meals Lincolnshire Sausage	3.3	6	2.1	0.58	130
Morrisons Spaghetti in Tomato Sauce	3.3	0.3	trace	0.3	58
Asda Chosen by You Spaghetti Loops	3.3	0.3	0.1	0.3	58
Asda Smart Price Spaghetti Bolognese	3.3	1.1	0.4	0.7	64
Tesco Everyday Value Spaghetti Bolognese	3.3	1.7	0.4	0.6	73
Branston Spaghetti	3.4	0.1	trace	0.5	57
Branston Spaghetti Loops	3.4	0.1	trace	0.5	57
Sainsbury's Baked Beans Reduced Sugar & Salt	3.4	<.5	0.1	0.44	76
Asda Chosen by You Baked Beans & Veggie Sausages in Tom Sauce	3.4	1.9	0.2	0.5	114
Asda CbK Sweet & Sour Chicken Meatballs & Whole-wheat Spaghetti	3.4	0.6	0.1	0.1	78
Tesco Spaghetti Rings And Pork Sausages	3.4	3.6	1.3	0.7	94
Sainsbury's Spicy Tomato Pasta	3.5	<.5	0.2	0.63	59
Heinz Weight Watchers Baked Beans	3.5	0.2	trace	0.6	73
Asda CbK Veggie Sausages & Whole-wheat Spaghetti in Tom Sauce	3.5	3	0.3	0.4	87
Tesco Cheese Ravioli In Tomato Sauce	3.5	1.7	0.4	0.7	78
Hunger Orgran Gluten Free Spaghetti	3.6	0.3	0	1	62
Asda Chosen by You Baked Beans & Sausages In Tomato Sauce	3.6	2	0.7	0.5	104
Asda Chosen by You Spaghetti Loops in Tomato Sauce	3.6	trace	trace	0.3	60
Waitrose Essential Spaghetti Rings	3.7	0.2	trace	0.28	59
Morrisons Spaghetti Loops in Tomato Sauce	3.7	0.2	trace	0.3	58
Morrisons Spaghetti Bolognese	3.7	1.8	0.6	0.5	73
Asda Chosen By Kids Mild Chicken Curry with Brown Rice	3.7	4.2	1.5	0.8	115
Heinz Spaghetti Hoops	3.8	0.2	trace	0.4	53
Asda Chosen By Kids Spelly Spaghetti in Tomato Sauce	3.8	0.5	0.1	0.22	62
Tesco Healthy Living Baked Beans In Tomato Sauce	3.8	0.5	0.1	0.4	82
Tesco Spicy Fusilli In Tomato Sauce	3.8	1	0.2	0.5	62
Heinz Alphabetti Pasta Shapes in Tomato Sauce	3.9	0.3	trace	0.4	57
Heinz Numberetti Pasta Shapes	3.9	0.3	trace	0.4	56
Heinz Spaghetti & Sausages	3.9	2.6	1	0.7	82
Sainsbury's Spaghetti	3.9	<.5	<1	0.38	62

Tinned Beans & Pasta

Product	Sugar	Fat	Sat per 100g	Salt	Cals
Asda Chosen by You Spaghetti in Tomato Sauce	3.9	0.3	trace	0.5	66
Tesco Short Cut Spaghetti In Tomato Sauce	3.9	0.6	0.1	0.3	67
Heinz Baked Beanz with Pork Sausages	4	2.6	1	0.7	96
Heinz Bob the Builder Pasta Shapes	4	0.3	trace	0.4	56
Heinz Dora the Explora Pasta Shapes	4	0.3	trace	0.4	56
Heinz Hello Kitty Pasta Shapes	4	0.3	trace	0.4	55
Heinz Madagascar Pasta Shapes	4	0.3	trace	0.4	55
Heinz Moshi Monsters Pasta Shapes	4	0.3	trace	0.4	56
Heinz Peppa Pig Pasta Shapes	4	0.3	trace	0.4	56
Heinz Thomas the Tank Engine Pasta Shapes	4	0.3	trace	0.4	58
Sainsbury's Cheese & Tomato Ravioli	4	1	0.3	0.63	85
Sainsbury's Spaghetti Basics	4	<.5	<.1	0.5	50
Sainsbury's Vegetarian Spaghetti Bolognese	4	<.5	<.1	0.8	65
Waitrose Essential Baked Beans in Tomato Sauce	4	0.4	0.1	0.53	87
Morrisons Five Bean Mix in Tomato Sauce	4	0.5	trace	0.5	99
Tesco Everyday Value Spaghetti Hoops	4	0.3	0.1	0.3	50
Tesco Everyday Value Spaghetti In Tomato Sauce	4	0.3	0.1	0.6	48
Tesco Spaghetti Rings In Tomato Sauce	4	0.3	0.1	0.4	55
Branston Beef Ravioli	4.1	1.4	0.6	0.63	80
Asda Chosen by You Baked Beans	4.1	0.5	0.1	0.5	90
Asda Chosen by You Baked Beans In Tomato Sauce	4.1	0.5	0.1	0.5	90
Asda Smart Price Baked Beans & Sausages In Tomato Sauce	4.1	3.5	1.2	0.5	120
Asda Chosen by You Spaghetti Loops & Sausages in Tomato Sauce	4.1	3.3	1.2	0.6	98
Morrisons Baked Beans & Vegetarian Sausages in Tomato Sauce	4.2	2.3	0.2	0.6	103
Tesco Spaghetti Letters In Tomato Sauce	4.2	0.2	0.1	0.4	61
Tesco Spaghetti Rings	4.2	0.2	0.1	0.4	60
Heinz Angry Birds Pasta Shapes in Tomato Sauce	4.3	0.3	trace	0.4	56
Heinz Baked Beanz with Spicy Meatballs	4.3	2.4	0.7	0.7	84
Heinz Teenage Mutant Ninja Turtles Pasta Shapes	4.3	0.3	trace	0.4	56
Morrisons Baked Beans & Sausages in Tomato Sauce	4.3	3.3	1.3	0.6	113

Tinned Beans & Pasta

Product	Sugar	Fat	Sat	Salt	Cals
			per 100g		
Asda Smart Price Spaghetti Loops in Tomato Sauce	4.3	0.2	trace	0.3	60
Sainsbury's Spaghetti Bolognese	4.4	1.8	0.5	0.3	73
Tesco Baked Beans & Pork Sausages In Tom Sauce	4.4	3.8	1.4	0.7	115
Tesco Spaghetti Meatballs In Tomato Sauce	4.4	2.8	0.3	0.9	80
Morrisons Savers Baked Beans in Tomato Sauce	4.5	0.3	0.1	0.5	66
Asda Smart Price Baked Beans in Tomato Sauce	4.5	0.3	0	0.5	66
Tesco Everyday Value Baked Beans In Tomato Sauce	4.5	0.5	0.1	0.6	87
Tesco Everyday Value Beans And Sausages	4.5	3.5	1.4	0.5	114
Heinz Baked Beanz Cheddar Cheese	4.6	0.7	0.3	0.5	84
Branston Beans & Chilli Bits	4.7	0.5	0.3	0.53	88
Heinz Five Beans	4.7	0.2	trace	0.6	87
Morrisons Baked Beans	4.7	0.5	trace	0.6	90
Heinz Baked Beanz Tomato with Garlic & Herbs	4.8	0.2	trace	0.6	81
Sainsbury's Basics Baked Beans	4.8	0.5	0.1	0.53	77
Waitrose Organic Baked Beans	4.8	0.4	0.1	0.57	86
Branston Bean Meals Chorizo	4.9	2	1.2	0.6	100
Sainsbury's Baked Beans with Sausages	4.9	3.7	1.4	1.13	119
Waitrose Essential Short Cut Spaghetti in Tomato Sauce	4.9	0.2	0.1	0.44	65
Tesco Everyday Value Ravioli In Tomato Sauce	4.9	1.1	0.4	0.6	88
Heinz Baked Beanz	5	0.2	trace	0.6	79
Sainsbury's Baked Beans	5	0.6	0.1	0.71	85
Sainsbury's Ravioli	5	0.8	0.2	0.75	76
Morrisons Alphabet Pasta in Tomato Sauce	5	0.3	0.1	0.4	65
Heinz Baked Beanz Organic	5.1	0.2	trace	0.6	81
Asda Smart Price Spaghetti in Tomato Sauce	5.3	0.2	trace	0.3	64
Tesco Organic Baked Beans In Tomato Sauce	5.3	0.6	0.1	0.5	94
Tesco Baked Beans In Tomato Sauce	5.5	0.5	0.1	0.6	87
Tesco Long Cut Spaghetti In Tomato Sauce	5.6	0.2	0.1	0.3	69
Branston Baked Beans	5.7	0.4	0.2	0.89	85
Tesco Curried Baked Beans	5.7	0.6	0.1	0.6	95

Tinned Beans & Pasta

Product	Sugar	Fat	Sat per 100g	Salt	Cals
Sainsbury's Baked Beans Organic	5.8	<.5	<.1	0.7	95
Heinz Mini Meals Tomato & Pork Sausages	6	2.2	0.8	0.7	96
Heinz Beanz Barbecue	6.9	0.2	trace	0.6	88
Heinz Beanz Fiery Chilli	6.9	0.3	trace	0.6	91
Tesco Spaghetti In Tomato Sauce	7.8	0.6	0	1	135
Heinz Baked Beanz Curry	8.8	1.6	0.1	0.6	109

Yoghurts

Dairy products contain natural sugar in the form of lactose. This sugar is fine. What you need to be on the look for are flavoured and fruit varieties, as they all have sugar added to the fruit.

To help you make the best choices, products are listed starting with the least sugar first.

Product	Sugar	Fat	Sat	Salt	Cals
			per 100g		
Tesco Free From Natural Yoghurt	0.7	2.6	0.4	0.1	46
Alpro Yogurt Alternative Coconut	2.1	3	1.1	0.32	55
Alpro Yogurt Alternative Simply Plain	2.1	2.3	0.4	0.25	50
Alpro Yogurt Alternative Almond	2.2	2.8	0.4	0.25	54
Benecol Yogurt Drink Tropic Fruit & Soya	2.5	2.8	0.3	0.03	36
St Helen's Farm Goat's Milk Natural Yogurt	3.2	7.3	5	0.1	105
Tesco Cholesterol Reducing Blueberry Yoghurt Drink	3.2	1.5	0.1	0.1	49
Actimel Yogurt Drink 0.1% Fat Original	3.3	<.5	<.1	0.1	28
Tesco Healthy Living Natural Fromage Frais	3.3	0.2	0.1	0.1	46
Morrisons NuMe Fromage Frais	3.3	0.2	0.1	0.1	50
Onken Natural Yogurt	3.4	3.7	2.4	0.15	68
Tesco Cholesterol Reducing Strawberry Yogurt Drink	3.5	1.7	0.2	0.1	46
Liberte Greek Style 0% Fat Natural Yogurt	3.6	0.1	<.1	0.14	5
Actimel Yogurt Drink 0.1% Fat Strawberry	3.6	0.1	<.1	0.1	30
Liberte Greek Style 0% Fat Natural Yogurt	3.6	0.1	<.1	0.14	58
Tesco Cholesterol Reducting Apricot & Peach Yoghurt Drink	3.7	1.5	0.1	0.1	53
Waitrose Authenic Greek Natural Strained Yogurt	3.7	10.2	6.7	0.15	131
Fage Total Greek Natural Yogurt	3.8	5	3.6	0.1	96
Arla Skyr Natural	4	0.2	0.1	0.14	65
Fage Total 0% Fat Greek Natural Yogurt	4	0	0	0.1	57
Sainsbury's Fat Free Normandy Natural Fromage Frais	4.2	<.5	<.1	0.09	50
Sainsbury's Fat Free Fromage Frais, Be Good To Yourself	4.2	<.5	<.1	0.09	50
Onken Fat Free Natural Yogurt	4.3	0.1	0.1	0.2	46
Flora pro.activ Yogurt Drink Original	4.5	1.5	<.5	0.1	45

Yoghurts

Product	Sugar	Fat	Sat per 100g	Salt	Cals
Flora pro.activ Yogurt Drink Pomegranate & Raspberry	4.5	1.5	<.5	0.1	45
Flora pro.activ Yogurt Drink Strawberry	4.5	1.5	<.5	0.1	45
Tesco Finest Greek Yoghurt 2% Fat	4.5	2.1	1.6	0.3	73
Woodlands Sheep's Milk Yogurt	4.8	5.8	3.8	0.3	92
Asda Natural Set Yogurt	4.8	3.2	2.4	0.1	62
Asda Greek Style Natural Yogurt	4.9	9.4	6.7	0.2	125
Rachel's Organic Greek Style Natural Yogurt	5	9	5.6	0.1	116
Flora pro.activ Yogurt Drink Mango & Cherry	5	1.5	<.5	0.1	50
Asda Natural Fromage Frais	5	0.3	0.1	0.1	52
Weight Watchers Fat Free Berry Fruits Fromage Frais	5.1	0.2	<.1	0.12	50
Morrisons Greek Style Yogurt	5.1	10.4	6.4	0.2	131
Weight Watchers Fat Free Citrus Fruit Yogurt	5.2	0.1	<.1	0.26	46
Weight Watchers Fat Free Confectionary Yogurt	5.2	0.1	<.1	0.15	45
Sainsbury's Greek Style Fat Free Natural Yogurt	5.2	<.5	0.3	0.18	54
Tesco Fat Free Greek Style Yoghurt	5.3	0.4	0.3	0.2	55
Asda Chosen by You Fat Free Greek Style Yogurts	5.3	<.5	0.3	0.18	54
Asda Fat Free Greek Style Yogurt	5.3	0.4	0.3	0.2	54
Tesco 0% Fat Greek Style Yoghurt	5.3	0.4	0.3	0.2	55
Weight Watchers Fat Free Summer Fruits Fromage Frais	5.4	<.1	<.1	0.11	49
Tesco Greek Style Yoghurt	5.4	9.5	6.3	0.1	124
Waitrose Essential Greek Style Natural Yogurt	5.4	9.1	6.1	0.13	122
Tesco Finest 0% Fat Greek Yoghurt	5.5	0.3	0.2	0.3	62
Waitrose Authentic Greek Natural Fat Free Strained Yogurt	5.5	0.4	0.3	0.2	65
Yakult Light Yogurt Drink	5.6	0	0	0.04	42
Morrisons Savers Low Fat Natural Yogurt	5.6	1.7	1.1	0.1	58
Benecol Yogurt Drink Blueberry	5.7	1.9	0.1	trace	52
Benecol Plus Heart Vitamin Multifruit Yogurt Drink	6	1.9	0.1	0.02	54
Benecol Yogurt Drink Strawberry	6	1.9	0.1	0.1	53
Activia Low Fat Natural Yogurt	6.1	1.9	1.3	0.2	62
Irish Yogurt Creamier Live Yogurt	6.1	4.2	2.8	0.17	85

Product	Sugar	Fat	Sat per 100g	Salt	Cals
Benecol Plus Bone Health Strawberry Yogurt Drink	6.2	1.9	0.2	0.11	53
Arla Protein Blueberry	6.3	0.2	0.1	0.1	70
Arla Protein Strawberry	6.3	0.2	0.1	0.1	70
Arla Potein Raspberry	6.3	0.2	0.1	0.1	70
Shape Raspberry & Strawberry Yogurt	6.3	0.1	0	0.2	49
Asda Whole Milk Natural Yogurt	6.3	3.9	2.5	0.2	82
Yeo Valley Organic Greek Style Natural Yogurt	6.4	9.5	5.9	0.18	129
Sainsbury's Fat Free Natural Yogurt	6.4	<.5	0.2	0.18	48
Waitrose Essential Fat Free Natural Yogurt	6.4	0.3	0.1	0.18	50
Waitrose Duchy Organic Low Fat Natural Yogurt	6.4	1.4	1	0.18	61
Yeo Valley Organic Natural Yogurt	6.5	4.2	2.7	0.18	82
Weight Watchers Fat Free Dessert Recipe Yogurt	6.5	0.1	<.1	0.15	49
Sainsbury's Low Fat Natural Yogurt, SO Organic	6.5	1.3	0.8	0.2	59
Morrisons NuMe Fat Free Greek Style Yogurt	6.5	0.3	0.1	0.3	68
Benecol Yogurt Drink Peach & Apricot	6.6	2	0.2	0.01	56
Shape 0% Fat Apple & Rhubarb Crumble Yogurt	6.6	0.1	0	0.2	49
Tesco Natural Yoghurt	6.6	3.8	2.5	0.2	81
Waitrose Duchy Organic Thick & Creamy Natural Yoghurt	6.6	5.4	3.8	0.18	100
Tesco 0% Fat Natural Yoghurt	6.8	0.3	0.2	0.2	52
Waitrose Essential Low Fat Natural Yogurt	6.8	1.4	0.9	0.15	61
Benecol Yogurt Drink Light	6.9	1.9	0.1	0.1	57
Irish Yogurt Diet Fat Free, Apricot & Nectarine	6.9	0.2	<.1	0.28	51
Shape 0% Fat Blackberry & Cherry Yogurt	6.9	0.2	0.1	0.2	52
Tesco Low Fat Natural Yoghurt	6.9	1.4	0.9	0.2	61
Yeo Valley Organic 0% Greek Style Yogurt	7	0	0	0.15	63
Muller Light Raspberry & Cranberry Yogurt	7	0.1	0.1	0.3	51
Muller Light Vanilla Yogurt	7	0.1	0.1	0.2	51
Shape 0% Fat Peach & Apricot Yogurt	7	0.1	0	0.2	49
Shape Pineapple & Coconut Yogurt	7	0.1	0	0.2	52
Muller Light Orange & Chocolate Yogurt	7	0.5	0.3	0.2	55

Yoghurts

Product	Sugar	Fat	Sat	Salt	Cals
			per 100g		
Sainsbury's Low Fat Natural Yogurt, Basics	7	1.5	0.9	0.2	61
Tesco Low Fat Greek Style Yoghurt	7	3	2	0.2	77
Asda Fat Free Rhubarb & Vanilla Yogurt	7	<.5	<.1	0.15	56
Waitrose Essential Low Fat Greek Style Natural Yogurt	7	2.9	1.9	0.18	77
Muller Light Red Fruit Yogurt	7.1	0.1	0.1	0.3	51
Muller Light Toffee & Vanilla Yogurt	7.1	0.1	0.1	0.2	51
Muller Light Strawberry Yogurt	7.1	0.1	0.1	0.2	51
Muller Light Toffee Yogurt	7.1	0.1	0.1	0.2	51
Muller Light Turkish Delight	7.1	0.5	0.3	0.2	55
Muller Light Vanilla & Dark Chocolate Yogurt	7.1	0.5	0.3	0.2	54
Sainsbury's Greek Style Low Fat Yogurt	7.1	2.7	1.7	0.2	75
Arla Skyr Apple & Lingonberry	7.2	0.2	0.1	0.16	74
Arla Skyr Honey	7.2	0.1	0.1	0.13	73
Tesco Everyday Value Low Fat Natural Yoghurt	7.2	1.5	0.9	0.2	62
Waitrose Duchy Fat Free Natural Yogurt	7.2	0.2	0.1	0.18	52
Asda Chosen by You Red Cherry Fat Free Yogurts	7.3	<.5	<.1	0.15	58
Asda Fat Free Red Cherry Yogurt	7.3	<.5	<.1	0.15	58
Arla Skyr Strawberry	7.4	0.2	0.1	0.13	75
Tesco Healthy Living Red Fruits Yoghurt	7.4	0.2	0.2	0.2	53
Morrisons Low Fat Greek Style Yogurt	7.5	2.9	1.8	0.3	80
Asda Chosen by You Blueberry Fat Free Yogurts	7.5	<.5	<.1	0.15	59
Asda Fat Free Blueberry Yogurt	7.5	<.5	<.1	0.15	59
Activia 0% Fat Vanilla Yogurt	7.6	0.1	0	0.2	54
Muller Light Citrus Fruit Yogurt, Peach & Pineapple	7.6	0.1	0.1	0.2	53
Asda Fat Free Natural Yogurt	7.7	0.2	0	0.2	55
Arla Skyr Nordic Mixed Berry	7.8	0.2	0.1	0.08	76
Delamere Goats Yogurt with Honey	7.8	6.2	4.4	0.01	123
Asda Low Fat Natural Yogurt	7.9	1.4	1	0.2	65
Rachel's Organic Greek Style Low Fat Natural Yogurt	8	2.9	1.8	0.2	80
Tesco Healthy Living Peach, Mango & Passionfruit Yoghurt	8.2	0.2	0.1	0.2	57

Yoghurts

Product	Sugar	Fat	Sat per 100g	Salt	Cals
Arla Skyr Nordic Sour Cherry	8.3	0.2	0.1	0.02	79
Activia Lemon & Lime Yogurts	8.3	0.1	0	0.2	55
Asda Fat Free Greek Style Yogurt with Honey	8.4	0.3	0.2	0.2	66
Yeo Valley Organic 0% Fat Natural Yogurt	8.5	0	0	0.23	59
Activia 0% Fat Mixed Yellow Fruits Yogurt	8.5	0.1	0	0.2	54
Activia 0% Fat Forest Fruit Yogurt	8.6	0.1	0	0.2	56
Activia 0% Fat Mixed Red Fruits Yogurt	8.6	0.1	0	0.2	56
Activia 0% Fat Raspberry Yogurt	8.6	0.1	0	0.2	56
Asda Low Fat Strawberry Yogurt	8.6	1.3	0.9	0.1	74
Munch Bunch Strawberry & Yogurt, 30% less sugar	8.7	2.9	1.9	0.1	76
Rachel's Organic Greek Style Fat Free Natural Yogurt	8.7	0.1	0.1	0.2	60
Activia 0% Fat Peach Yogurt	8.7	0.1	0	0.2	56
Tesco 0% Fruit & Vegetable Greek Style Yoghurt	8.7	0.2	0.1	0.2	66
Muller Light Greek Style Coconut Yogurt	8.9	0.5	0.4	0.2	72
The Collective Straight Up Yoghurt	8.9	5.7	3.5	0.27	109
Muller Light Greek Style Lemon Yogurt	9	0.2	0.1	0.2	69
Tesco Blueberry Yoghurt Drinks	9	1.1	0.7	0.1	68
Tesco Peach & Apricot Yoghurt Drinks	9	1.2	0.6	0.1	70
Morrisons Natural Yogurt	9	3.7	2.3	0.2	90
Yoplait Perle de Lait Coconut Yogurt	9.1	9.8	6.7	0.11	144
Tesco Strawberry Yoghurt Drinks	9.1	1.2	0.7	0.1	70
Tesco Yellow Fruit Split Pot Fruit Yoghurt	9.1	0.3	0.2	0.2	64
Yeo Valley Organic Little Yeos, Strawberry & Pear	9.2	2.6	1.4	0.12	91
Alpro Yogurt Alternative Vanilla	9.2	2.2	0.4	0.2	75
Muller Light Greek Style Raspberry Yogurt	9.2	0.2	0.1	0.2	69
Muller Light Greek Style Strawberry Yogurt	9.2	0.2	0.1	0.2	69
Activia 0% Fat Cherry Yogurt	9.2	0.1	0.1	0.1	59
Alpro Yogurt Alternative Blackberry, Elderflower & Pomegranate	9.2	1.9	0.3	0.28	74
Tesco Goodness Veggie Yoghurts	9.2	3.6	2.5	0.2	89
Morrisons Low Fat Natural Yogurt	9.3	1.3	0.8	0.3	75

Yoghurts

Product	Sugar	Fat	Sat	Salt	Cals
			per 100g		
Alpro Yogurt Alternative Strawberry & Rhubarb	9.4	1.9	0.3	0.25	74
Muller Fruitopolis Greek Style Peach & Passionfruit	9.4	0.1	0.1	0.2	65
Alpro Yogurt Alternative Blackberry, Raspberry & Cranberry	9.4	1.9	0.3	0.22	75
Alpro Yogurt Alternative Blueberry & Cherry	9.4	2	0.3	0.21	73
Yeo Valley Organic Little Yeos, Strawberry & Mango	9.5	2.6	1.4	0.12	92
Muller Fruitopolis Greek Style Strawberry Yogurt	9.5	0.1	0.1	0.2	65
Sainsbury's Fruit Fool Mango & Passionfruit	9.5	13.3	9.2	0.1	172
Morrisons NuMe Natural Yogurt	9.5	0.1	0.1	0.2	62
Alpro Yogurt Alternative Lemon & Lime	9.7	2	0.3	0.21	77
Muller Light Greek Style Honey Yogurt	9.7	0.2	0.1	0.2	71
Benecol Fat Free Garden Fruits Yogurt	9.7	0.5	0.1	0.1	62
Rachel's My First Yogurt	9.8	3.5	2.1	0.3	88
Muller Light Greek Style Cherry Yogurt	9.8	0.1	0.1	0.2	70
Asda Chosen by You Granola Split Pots	9.8	5.5	3.8	0.15	137
Rachel's Organic Greek Style Coconut Yogurt	10	10.1	6.9	0.1	145
Muller Rice Original	10	2.6	1.5	0.2	101
Morrisons Low Fat Smooth Strawberry Yogurt	10	0.9	0.6	0.1	72
Muller Fruitopolis Greek Style Cherry Yogurt	10.1	0.1	0.1	0.2	68
Muller Light Greek Style Mango Yogurt	10.1	0.2	0.1	0.2	72
Muller Light Chocolate & Toffee Corners	10.1	2.4	1.5	0.2	90
Sainsbury's Kids Yogurts	10.1	4.5	3.1	0.15	106
Morrisons Blueberry Yogurt Drinks	10.1	0.4	0.2	0	59
Sainsbury's Cholesterol Lowering Drink Originak	10.2	<.5	<.1	<.01	61
Yeo Valley Organic Little Yeos Tubes - Raspberry	10.2	2.6	1.6	0.19	95
Benecol Greek Style Yogurts - Strawberry	10.2	0.6	0.1	0.13	70
Alpro Yogurt Alternative Smooth	10.3	2	0.4	0.09	79
Sainsbury's Cholesterol Lowering Drink Strawberry	10.3	<.5	<.1	0.09	58
Tesco Goodness Pouches Strawberry & Raspberry	10.3	2.1	1.3	0.1	91
Tesco Goodness Pouches Strawberry & Apricot	10.3	2.1	1.3	0.1	91
Morrisons Savers Fromage Frais	10.3	2.9	1.9	0.1	98

Yoghurts

Product	Sugar	Fat	Sat per 100g	Salt	Cals
Actimel Yogurt Drink Original	10.5	1.6	1.1	0.1	71
Tesco Goodness Fromage Frais	10.6	3.1	2	0.1	105
Muller Light Strawberry & White Chocolate Corner	10.7	2.3	1.5	0.11	92
Tesco French Set Yoghurt	10.7	3	2.2	0.1	95
Yeo Valley Organic Little Yeos, Fruit Favourites	10.8	4.5	2.9	0.17	108
Morrisons Low Fat Strawberry Yogurt Drinks	10.8	1	0.7	0.1	63
Danio Strained Strawberry Yogurt	10.9	0.2	0.1	0.1	80
Tesco Finest Strawberry & Cream Yoghurt	10.9	6.2	4.3	0.1	116
Morrisons Signature Rhubarb Yogurt	10.9	6.4	4.4	0.1	130
Yoplait Perle de Lait Greek Style Strawberry	11	7	4.7	0.12	125
Sainsbury's Mixed Red Fruit Yogurt, Black Cherry	11	1.8	0.9	0.13	90
Sainsbury's Mixed Yellow Fruit Yogurt, Peach	11	1.7	0.9	0.13	89
Morrisons Signature Peach Yogurt	11.1	6.3	4.3	0.1	131
Asda Assorted French Set Yogurt	11.1	3.8	2.7	0.1	101
Asda Greek Style Split Pots	11.1	6.8	4.6	0.1	124
Actimel Yogurt Drink Kids Strawberry & Raspberry	11.2	1.3	0.9	0.1	74
Yoplait Perle de Lait Greek Style Mango	11.2	7	4.7	0.1	126
Sainsbury's Kids Fromage Frais Strawberry Pouches	11.2	2.6	1.8	0.08	93
Danio Strained Mango Yogurt	11.3	0.2	0.1	0.1	80
Tesco Red Fruit Split Pot Yoghurt	11.3	0.3	0.2	0.2	73
Morrisons Low Fat Blueberry Yogurt Drinks	11.3	0.8	0.5	0.1	65
Asda Chosen By Kids Raspberry Squidg'ems	11.3	2.3	1.5	0	92
Moma Bircher Muesli Wild Berry Yogurt	11.4	2.2	0.6	0.1	137
Liberte Greek Style 0% Fat Blueberry Yogurt	11.4	0.1	<.1	0.12	84
Liberte Greek Style 0% Fat Strawberry Yogurt	11.4	0.1	<.1	0.12	83
Yoplait Perle de Lait Lemon Yogurt	11.4	8.6	5.8	0.14	142
Asda Chosen By Kids Strawberry Squidg'ems	11.4	2.3	1.5	0	91
Asda Chosen by You Cholesterol Lowering Blueberry Yogurt Drinks	11.4	0.2	0.1	0.1	60
Danio Strained Cherry Yogurt	11.5	0.2	0.1	0.1	82
Danio Strained Peach Yogurt	11.5	2.3	1.6	0.1	99

Yoghurts

Product	Sugar	Fat	Sat	Salt	Cals
			per 100g		
Rachel's Organic Divine Rice Puddings	11.5	5.2	3.3	1	142
Morrisons Signature Vanilla Yogurt	11.5	6.3	4.1	0.1	130
Actimel Yogurt Drink Blueberry	11.6	1.5	1	0.1	74
Actimel Yogurt Drink Raspberry	11.6	1.5	1	0.1	74
Actimel Yogurt Drink Strawberry	11.6	1.5	1	0.1	74
Tesco Greek Style with Vanilla Yoghurt	11.6	7.7	5.2	0.1	130
Tesco Mango & Passionfruit Yoghurt	11.6	8	5.5	0.1	134
Activia Natural Yogurt with Fibre Topper	11.7	0.7	0.2	0.27	101
Danio Strained Blueberry	11.7	2.4	1.7	0.1	100
Danio Strained Passionfruit Yogurt	11.7	0.2	0.1	0.1	83
Sainsbury's West Country Glen Raspberry Yogurt, Taste The Difference	11.7	7	4.3	0.1	128
Morrisons Signature Raspberry Yogurt	11.7	6.5	4.4	0.1	137
Asda Inner Defence Blueberry Yogurt Drinks	11.7	0.7	0.5	0.1	65
Disney Frozen Fromage Frais	11.8	2.8	1.9	0.18	95
Sainsbury's French Set Yogurt	11.8	3	2	0.1	88
Morrisons Savers French Set Yogurts	11.8	3.1	2.1	0.1	98
Petits Filous Fromage Frais, Strawberry & Apricot	11.9	2.3	1.6	0.12	95
Ski Smooth Cherry & Blackcurrent Yogurts	11.9	2.6	1.7	0.1	87
Lactofree Yogurt Raspberry	11.9	2.7	1.7	0.08	104
Sainsburys Fruit Fool Strawberry & Cream	11.9	11.7	8.1	0.08	172
Tesco Free From Peach Yoghurt	11.9	2.1	0.3	0.1	83
Tesco Low Fat Strawberry Yoghurt	11.9	1.3	0.9	0.2	82
Peppa Pig Fromage Frais	12	2.3	1.6	0.13	95
Yoplait Thomas & Friends Fromage Frais	12	2.4	1.6	0.15	96
Yoplait Wildlife Fromage Frais	12	2.3	1.6	0.13	95
Onken Fat Free Vanilla Yogurt	12	0.1	0.1	0.2	75
Yeo Valley Organic Peaches & Cream Yogurt	12	4.1	2.6	0.16	105
Actimel Yogurt Drink Coconut	12	1.9	1.3	0.1	81
Sainsbury's Greek Style Yogurt, Orange & Mango	12	7.5	5.3	0.13	134
Sainsbury's Fromage Frais, Basics	12	1.5	1	0.09	87

Product	Sugar	Fat	Sat per 100g	Salt	Cals
Tesco Free From Raspberry Passion Fruit Yoghurt	12	2.1	0.3	0.1	85
Asda Low Fat Raspberry & Peach Soya Yogurt	12	2.3	0.4	0.03	89
Morrisons Signature Strawberry Yogurt	12.1	6.3	4.3	0.1	131
Asda Mango & Passion Fruit Soya Yogurt	12.1	2.3	0.3	0.1	89
Waitrose Strawberry Yogurt	12.1	6.8	4.8	0.08	125
Waitrose Champagne Rhubarb Yogurt	12.1	6.3	4.4	0.1	120
Actimel Yogurt Drink Multifruit	12.2	1.5	1	0.1	77
Yeo Valley Organic 0% Fat Greek Style Yogurt with Lemon	12.2	0	0	0.19	80
Tesco Finest Red Fruit Yoghurt	12.2	6.5	4	0.1	123
Morrisons Peach & Apricot Cholesterol Reducing Yogurt Drink	12.2	0.4	0.2	0	64
Fage Total 0% Fat Greek Yogurt With Raspberry	12.3	0	0	0.13	85
Activia Prune Fruit Layer Yogurt	12.3	3.4	2.3	0.1	100
Tesco Everyday Value Low Fat Strawberry Yogurt	12.3	1	0.7	0.1	80
Tesco Finest White Peach Yoghurt	12.3	6.4	4.3	0.1	121
Asda Low Fat Red Berry Yogurts	12.3	1.2	0.8	0.2	86
Waitrose Good To Go Berry Layered Greek Style Yogurt Granola	12.3	4	1.5	0.13	133
Munch Bunch Fruit Yogurt	12.4	3	1.9	0.2	95
Petits Filous Magic Squares Raspberry	12.4	2.8	1.9	0.12	101
The Collective Suckies Peach & Apricot	12.4	2.9	2	0.1	91
Activia Intensely Creamy Peach & Cream Yogurt	12.4	3	2.1	0.1	98
Activia Intensely Creamy Vanilla Yogurt	12.4	3	0.1	0.1	98
Sainsbury's Strawberry & Champagne Yogurt, Taste The Difference	12.4	7.2	5	0.08	127
Sainsbury's West Country Rhubarb Yogurt, Taste The Difference	12.4	6.6	4.1	0.1	121
Tesco Finest Champagne Rhubarb Yoghurt	12.4	5.9	4	0.1	117
Waitrose Deliciously Fruity Raspberry Low Fat Yogurt	12.4	1.4	0.9	0.15	84
Calin+ Strawberry Yogurt	12.5	2.5	1.7	0.12	90
Activia Intensely Creamy Apricot & Nectarine Yogurt	12.5	3	2.1	0.1	99
Activia Intensely Creamy Orange & Passionfruit Yogurt	12.5	3	2.1	0.1	99
Activia Intensely Creamy Raspberries & Cream Yogurt	12.5	3	2.1	0.1	99
Tesco Finest Raspberry Yoghurt	12.5	6.4	4.3	0.1	124

Yoghurts

Product	Sugar	Fat	Sat per 100g	Salt	Cals
Tesco Free From Mango Yoghurt	12.5	2.1	0.3	0.1	86
Morrisons Low Fat Mixed Fruit Yogurt Drinks	12.5	0.9	0.6	0.1	77
Morrisons Low Fat Red Yogurt	12.5	0.8	0.5	0.1	81
Activia Mixed Berry Red Fruits Yogurt	12.6	3.3	2.3	0.1	98
Tesco Low Fat Hazelnut Yoghurt	12.6	2.8	1	0.2	100
Asda Chosen by You Cholesterol Lowering Original Yogurt Drinks	12.6	0.2	0.1	0.1	66
Munch Bunch Fromage Frais	12.7	3	1.9	0.1	103
Munch Bunch Strawberry Drinky	12.7	1.3	0.9	0.1	76
Rachel's Organic Greek Style Honey Yogurt	12.7	7.5	4.6	0.1	131
Yeo Valley Organic 0% Greek Style Honey Yogurt	12.7	0	0	0.14	84
Calin+ Apricot Yogurt	12.7	2.5	1.7	0.11	93
Activia Intensely Creamy Pear Apple Yogurt	12.7	3	2.1	0.1	100
Activia Intensely Creamy Strawberry Yogurt	12.7	3	2.1	0.1	99
Tesco Greek Style Honey Yoghurt, 0% Fat	12.7	0.2	0.1	0.2	81
Asda Strawberry, Raspberry & Cherry Split Pots	12.7	3.5	2.2	0.1	104
Waitrose Duchy Organic Strawberry Yogurt	12.7	4	2.6	0.13	105
Petits Filous Frubes Strawberry	12.8	2.8	1.9	0.13	102
Yoplait Wildlife Choobs Strawberry	12.8	2.8	1.9	0.13	102
Onken Fat Free Strawberry Yogurt	12.8	0.1	0.1	0.18	79
Yeo Valley Organic Raspberry Yogurt	12.8	3.8	2.4	0.18	106
Activia Fusions Blueberry & Acai Yogurt	12.8	3.5	2.3	0.1	100
Activia Rhubarb Yogurt	12.8	3.3	2.3	0.2	97
Muller Rice Strawberry	12.8	2.2	1.3	0.2	106
Sainsbury's Active Health Strawberry Yogurt Drinks	12.8	1	0.4	0.12	77
Waitrose Scottish Raspberry Yogurt	12.8	7.1	4.9	0.08	131
Petits Filous Frubes	12.9	2.8	1.9	0.13	102
Yoplait Wildlife Choobs Dessert	12.9	2.8	1.9	0.13	102
Yeo Valley Organic Apricot Yogurt	12.9	3.8	2.4	0.18	107
Yeo Valley Organic Strawberry Yogurt	12.9	3.8	2.4	0.18	106
Actimel Yogurt Drink Vanilla	12.9	1.5	1.1	0.1	79

Product	Sugar	Fat	Sat	Salt	Cals
			per 100g		
Ski Tropical Yogurt	12.9	2.6	1.7	0.1	91
Yeo Valley Organic Yogurt Fruit Favourites	12.9	3.8	2.4	0.18	107
Tesco Low Fat Berry Medley Yoghurt	12.9	1.8	1.3	0.1	91
Asda Low Fat Mango & Passion Fruit Yogurts	12.9	1.2	0.8	0.2	84
Rachel's Organic Low Fat Cherry Yogurt	13	1.7	1	0.2	87
Activia Garden Fruits Yogurts	13	3.4	2.4	0.2	98
Onken Fat Free Apricot Yogurt	13	0.2	0.1	0.18	87
Sainsbury's Mixed Red Fruit Yogurt, Raspberry	13	1.7	0.9	0.1	92
Sainsbury's Mixed Yellow Fruit Yogurt, Apricot	13	1.6	1.2	0.13	89
Tesco Strawberry & Raspberry Yoghurt	13	5.9	4.1	0.3	122
Morrisons Strawberry Yogurt Drinks	13	0.4	0.2	0.1	68
Asda Extra Special Strawberry West Country Yogurt	13	6.7	4.4	trace	124
Rachel's Organic Low Fat Rhubarb Yogurt	13.1	1.6	1	0.2	84
Activia Fusions Mango & Passionfruit Yogurt	13.1	3.4	2.3	0.1	101
Activia Fusions Raspberry & Lychee Yogurt	13.1	3.4	2.3	0.1	102
Muller Light Lemon Meringue Corners	13.1	1.9	1.5	0.11	90
Munch Bunch Jelly Delight Strawberry	13.2	1.6	1.1	0.1	86
Munch Bunch Seasonal Squashums Yogurt	13.2	2.7	1.8	0.3	94
Liberte Greek Style 0% Fat Honey Yogurt	13.2	0.1	<.1	0.15	91
Activia Pineapple & Coconut Yogurt	13.2	3.6	2.6	0.1	101
Activia Intensely Creamy Blueberry Yogurt	13.2	3	2.1	0.1	102
Muller Fruit Corner Blueberry Yogurt	13.2	3.8	2.4	0.1	106
Ski Smooth Strawberry & Raspberry Yogurt	13.2	2.7	1.8	0.1	94
Sainsbury's West Country Strawberry Yogurt, Taste The Difference	13.2	6.9	4.3	0.1	129
Asda Inner Defence Coconut Yogurt Drinks	13.2	0.8	0.5	0.1	74
Waitrose Duchy Organic Rhubarb Yogurt	13.2	3.9	2.5	0.13	105
Activia Breakfast Pot Vanilla Yogurt	13.3	2.5	1.1	0.1	115
Oykos Greek Style Peach Yogurt	13.3	8	5.2	0.1	140
Activia Fig Yogurt	13.3	3.4	2.3	0.1	99
Activia Mango Yogurt	13.3	3.4	2.3	0.2	99

Yoghurts

Product	Sugar	Fat	Sat	Salt	Cals
			per 100g		
Activia Mixed Yellow Fruits Yogurt	13.3	3.4	2.3	0.2	99
Activia Strawberry Yogurt	13.3	3.3	2.3	0.1	99
Muller Rice Apple	13.3	2.2	1.3	0.2	107
Muller Rice Banana & Toffee	13.3	2.2	1.3	0.2	108
Morrisons Signature Lemon Yogurt	13.3	8.1	5.5	0.2	157
Activia With Cereal Yogurt	13.4	3.5	2.4	0.1	104
Muller Corner Red Fruits, Red Cherry Compote	13.4	3.8	2.4	0.2	107
Muller Fruit Corner Cherry Yogurt	13.4	3.8	2.4	0.2	107
Sainsbury's Fab Fruity Low Fat Strawberry Yogurt	13.4	1.2	0.8	0.15	87
Sainsbury's Fabulously Fruity Low Fat Mango & Passion Fruit Yogurt	13.4	1.2	0.8	0.18	88
Sainsbury's Fab Fruity Mango & Passionfruit Yogurt	13.4	1.2	0.8	0.18	88
Munch Bunch Double Up Fromage Frais Strawberry & Banana	13.5	2.7	1.8	0.1	104
Petits Filous Fromage Frais, Fruit Layers	13.5	2.9	1.9	0.09	110
Yeo Valley Organic Blueberry Yogurt	13.5	3.8	2.4	0.18	109
Shape Dessert Chocolate	13.5	2.3	1.8	0.1	100
Muller Fruit Corner Blackberry & Raspberry Yogurt	13.5	3.8	2.4	0.2	107
Shape Chocolate Dessert	13.5	2.3	1.6	0.1	100
Morrisons Low Fat Yellow Yogurt	13.5	0.8	0.5	0.1	85
Asda Extra Special Scottish Raspberry West Country Yogurt	13.5	6	3.9	0.1	127
Waitrose Gooseberry & Elderflower Yogurt	13.5	6.5	4.6	0.15	125
Onken Wholegrain Strawberry Yogurt	13.6	2.8	1.7	0.15	111
Rachel's Organic Low Fat Vanilla Yogurt	13.6	1.8	1.1	0.2	90
Activia Pear Yogurt	13.6	3.3	2.3	0.25	100
Muller Rice Vanilla	13.6	2.5	1.4	0.2	111
Waitrose Madagascan Vanilla Yogurt	13.6	8.2	5.7	0.1	141
Waitrose Deliciously Chunky Black Cherry Low Fat Yogurt	13.6	1.2	0.8	0.13	84
Onken Mango & Passionfruit Biopot Yogurt	13.7	2.7	1.7	0.18	102
Rachel's Organic Fat Free Strawberry & Rhubarb Yogurt	13.7	0.1	0.1	0.2	77
Rachel's Organic Low Fat Gooseberry Yogurt	13.7	1.7	1	0.1	89
Morrisons NuMe Fat Free Raspberry & Blueberry Yogurt	13.7	0.1	0	0.1	79

Product	Sugar	Fat	Sat	Salt	Cals
			per 100g		
Tesco Coconut Yoghurt	13.8	2.7	2.3	0.2	100
Morrisons Savers Low Fat Fruit Yogurt	13.8	1	0.7	0.1	85
Rachel's Organic Fat Free Blueberry Yogurt	13.9	0.1	0.1	0.2	78
Benecol Fruit Medley Yogurt	13.9	1.7	0.8	0.13	87
Muller Fruit Corner Peach & Apricot Yogurt	13.9	3.8	2.4	0.2	109
Rachel's Luscious Peach & Mango Yogurt	13.9	5.6	3.4	0.1	121
Sainsbury's Fab Fruity Low Fat Strawberry & Rhubard Yogurt	13.9	1.2	0.8	0.13	86
Tesco Low Fat Garden Fruits Yoghurt	13.9	1.9	1.3	0.1	93
Morrisons NuMe Fat Free Strawberry Yogurts	13.9	0.1	0	0.1	80
Asda Greek Style Yogurt with Honey	13.9	8	5.5	0.1	147
Asda Greek Style Honey Rich & Creamy Yogurt	13.9	8	5.5	0.1	147
Waitrose Deliciously Exotic Mango & Passionfruit Low Fat Yogurt	13.9	1.4	0.9	0.18	88
Frubes Strawberry & Raspberry Pouch	14	2.5	1.7	0.15	95
Munch Bunch Apple & Strawberry Yogurt Squashums	14	0.3	0	0	67
Activia Breakfast Pot Honey Yogurt	14	2.5	1.1	0.1	118
Oykos Greek Style Strawberry Yogurt	14	8.3	5.3	0.1	146
Ski Greek Style Strawberry Yogurt	14	3	1.8	0.2	105
Yakult Yogurt Drink	14	0	0	0.04	66
Rachel's Luscious Raspberry & Rhubarb Yogurt	14	5.5	3.4	0.1	123
Sainsbury's Fabulously Fruity Low Fat Rhubarb Yogurt	14	1.2	0.8	0.13	86
Sainsbury's Fruit Selection Low Fat Yogurt, Basics	14	1.3	0.8	0.18	86
Sainsbury's Strawberry Yogurt, Basics	14	1.3	0.8	0.18	86
Asda Low Fat Coconut Yogurt	14	2.6	2.1	0.15	102
Asda Chosen by You Coconut Low Fat Yogurts	14	2.6	2.1	0.15	102
Asda Extra Special Black Cherry West Country Yogurt	14	7.1	4.9	0.1	135
Benecol Yogurt Drink Original	14.1	1.9	0.1	0.1	83
Muller Bliss Raspberry Yogurt	14.1	5.9	3.3	0.1	129
Tesco Finest Swiss Black Cherry Yoghurt	14.1	6.4	4.4	0.1	127
Waitrose Black Cherry Yogurt	14.1	6.7	4.6	0.08	132
Waitrose Duchy Organic Blackcurrant Yoghurt	14.1	4.3	2.8	0.13	114

Yoghurts

Product	Sugar	Fat	Sat per 100g	Salt	Cals
Ski Greek Style Lemon Yogurts	14.2	3	1.8	0.2	106
Muller Bliss Strawberry Yogurt	14.2	5.9	3.3	0.2	129
Ski Mousse Strawberry	14.2	5.2	3.6	0.2	539
Sainsbury's Greek Style Honey Yogurt	14.2	8.4	5.9	0.13	149
Rachel's Organic Greek Style Ginger Yogurt	14.3	7.4	4.6	0.1	137
Rachel's Organic Greek Style Lemon Yogurt	14.3	7.5	4.7	0.1	139
Yeo Valley Organic Greek Style with Honey Yogurt	14.3	8.3	5.2	0.14	149
Morrisons Signature Black Cherry Yogurt	14.3	6.3	4.3	0.1	146
Asda Low Fat Smooth R'berry & Blackberry, Cherry & Strawberry Yogurt	14.3	1.6	1.1	0.2	91
Muller Greek Style Corner Apricot Yogurt	14.4	4.6	2.8	0.2	124
Sainsbury's West Country Mango, Papaya & Passion Fruit Yogurt	14.4	6.6	4.5	0.1	130
Asda Chosen by You Low Fat Fruit Yogurts	14.4	1.8	1.1	0.1	90
Munch Bunch Double Up Fromage Frais Strawberry & Chocolate	14.5	3	2	0.1	112
Rachel's Organic Fat Free Peach & Passionfruit Yogurt	14.5	0.1	0.1	0.2	82
Oykos Greek Style Pear Yogurt	14.6	8	5.2	0.1	143
Sainsbury's West Country Black Cherry Yogurt, Taste The Difference	14.6	7.1	4.8	0.1	136
Morrisons Low Fat Rhubarb Yogurt	14.6	1.4	0.8	0.2	90
Morrisons NuMe Pineapple, Lime & Peach, Mango Yogurts	14.6	0.1	0	0.2	82
Rachel's Organic Low Fat Mango Yogurt	14.7	1.7	1	0.1	93
Benecol Summer Fruits Yogurt	14.7	1.7	0.8	0.16	91
Muller Corner Greek Style Blueberry Yogurt	14.7	4.6	2.8	0.15	125
Tesco Finest Vanilla Yoghurt	14.7	6.9	4.7	0.1	133
Tesco Low Fat Sunshine Fruits Yoghurt	14.7	2	1.3	0.1	96
Muller Greek Style Corner Rhubarb Yogurt	14.8	4.6	2.8	0.1	125
Onken Cherry Yogurt	14.8	2.7	1.7	0.2	107
Rachel's Organic Low Fat Raspberry Yogurt	14.9	1.8	1.6	0.2	95
Sainsbury's West Country Vanilla Yogurt, Taste The Difference	14.9	8.4	5.3	0.13	150
Tesco Finest Mango & Passionfruit Yoghurt	14.9	6.6	4.7	0.1	132
Sainsbury's Fab Creamy Hazelnut Yogurt	15	5.6	2.4	0.1	130
Sainsbury's Fab Fruity Blackcurrent Yogurt	15	1.2	0.8	0.13	93

Product	Sugar	Fat	Sat	Salt	Cals
			per 100g		
Tesco Everyday Value Strawberry Splitpot Yogurt	15	1.2	0.8	0.1	87
Morrisons Raspberry, Cranberry & Blueberry Bio Yogurt	15	3.4	2.1	0.2	113
Asda Chosen by You Lemon Low Fat Yogurts	15	1.2	0.8	0.18	92
Asda Low Fat Lemon Yogurt	15	1.2	0.8	0.18	92
Waitrose Deliciously Nutty Hazelnut Low Fat Yogurt	15	2.7	1	0.15	107
Muller Greek Style Corner Cherry Yogurt	15.2	4.6	2.8	0.2	127
Muller Fruit Corner Strawberry Yogurt	15.2	3.8	2.4	0.2	114
Morrisons Signature Toffee Fudge Yogurt	15.2	7.7	5.1	0.2	159
Tesco Low Fat Lemon Yoghurt	15.3	1.3	0.8	0.2	93
Tesco Split Pots Chocolate Ball Raisin Yoghurt	15.3	3.8	2.3	0.2	126
Sainsbury's Fab Fruity Low Fat Cherry & Blackcurrant	15.4	1.2	0.8	0.13	93
Sainsbury's Mousse Lighter Chocolate	15.4	2.6	1.4	0.13	115
Sainsbury's Fruit Fool Careless Gooseberry	15.4	10.2	6.6	0.1	173
Tesco Low Fat Greek Style Red Fruit Yoghurt	15.4	2.2	1.6	0.4	100
Collective Dairy Mango Yogurt	15.5	5	3.1	0.23	128
Yeo Valley Organic 0% Fat Vanilla Yogurt	15.5	0	0	0.23	87
Sainsbury's West Country Honey & Ginger Yogurt, Taste The Difference	15.5	7.7	5.1	0.1	144
Asda Low Fat Hazelnut Yogurt	15.5	2.8	1.2	0.2	109
Asda Low Fat Smooth Confectionary Yogurt	15.5	1.6	1.1	0.2	94
Waitrose Duchy Organic Butterscotch Yogurt	15.6	5.4	3.6	0.18	132
Sainsbury's Hazelnut Yogurt, Taste The Difference	15.7	9.9	5.5	0.08	169
Tesco Low Fat Sweet Treat Yoghurt	15.7	2.1	1.5	0.2	111
Asda Strawberry, Toffee & Banana Split Pots	15.7	6.2	3.9	0.2	153
The Collective Raspberry Yoghurt	15.8	5	3.1	0.23	130
Collective Dairy Passionfruit Yogurt	16	5	3.1	0.23	130
Sainsbury's Fab Fruity Low Fat Raspberry & Elderflower Yogurt	16	1.3	0.9	0.15	96
Sainsbury's Fab Fruity Peach & Nectarine Yogurt	16	1	0.7	0.18	93
Sainsbury's Mousse Chocolate, Basics	16	4.6	3.7	0.25	136
The Collective Passionfruit Yoghurt	16	5	3.1	0.23	130
Muller Greek Style Corner Strawberry Yogurt	16.1	4.6	2.8	0.2	127

Yoghurts

Product	Sugar	Fat	Sat	Salt	Cals
			per 100g		
Onken Greek Style Apple & Cinnamon Yogurt	16.1	8	5	0.1	150
Sainsbury's West Country Mango & Yuzu Yogurt, Taste The Difference	16.1	7.1	4.9	0.08	144
Rachels Organic Divine Chocolate Yogurt Pots	16.3	10.2	6.2	0.2	181
Morrisons Apricot Fool	16.3	10.2	6.5	0.1	174
Waitrose Honey & Stem Ginger Yogurt	16.3	8	5.6	0.1	151
Morrisons Mango, Papaya & Passion Fruit Bio Yogurt	16.5	3	1.9	0.2	112
The Collective Russian Fudge Yoghurt	16.7	6	3.7	0.3	145
Muller Crunch Corner Banana Chocolate Flakes Yogurt	16.8	5.1	3.2	0.2	143
Yeo Valley Organic Lemon Curd Yogurt	16.9	4.4	2.8	0.18	127
Sainsbury's Fab Fruity Low Fat Cherry Yogurt	16.9	1.1	0.7	0.15	98
Sainsbury's Mousse Strawberry	16.9	7.7	6.4	0.22	161
Waitrose Deliciously Smooth Madagascan Vanilla Low Fat Yogurt	16.9	1.4	0	0.15	98
Sainsbury's Fabulously Fruity Creamy Lemon Yogurt	17	3.3	2.3	0.15	118
Sainsbury's Fab Fruity Black Cherry Yogurt	17	1.1	0.7	0.15	98
Tesco Low Fat Toffee Yoghurt	17	1.8	1.2	0.2	104
Asda Low Fat Toffee Yogurt	17	2.9	1.9	0.18	117
Asda Chosen by You Toffee Low Fat Yogurts	17	2.9	1.9	0.18	117
Asda Extra Special Cappuccino West Coutry Yogurt	17	10	6.6	0.1	173
Tesco Yellow Fruit Split Pot Yoghurt	17.1	3.2	2.1	0.2	113
Morrisons Gooseberry Fool	17.1	10.6	6.6	0.1	182
Ski Mousse Lemon Meringue	17.3	4.7	3.2	0.3	534
Asda Extra Special Roasted Hazelnut West Country Yogurt	17.3	8.5	4.6	0.1	159
Tesco Custard Style Yoghurt	17.3	3.1	2	0.2	112
Muller Crunch Corner Biscuit Yogurt	17.5	5.9	3.4	0.2	157
Muller Crunch Corner Strawberry Shortcake Yogurt	17.5	5.9	3.4	0.2	157
Tesco Finest Fudge Yoghurt	17.5	8.5	5.5	0.1	163
After Eight Mousse	17.6	16	11.4	0.1	970
Sainsbury's West Country Creamy Fudge Yogurt, Taste The Difference	17.6	7.8	5.1	0.15	154
Morrisons Low Fat Hazelnut Yogurt	17.6	2.7	1	0.2	115
Oykos Greek Style Caramel Yogurt	17.8	8.5	5.3	0.3	162

Product	Sugar	Fat	Sat	Salt	Cals
			per 100g		
Morrisons Fig, Date & Grain Bio Yogurt	17.8	3.2	2	0.2	121
Rachel's Organic Divine Vanilla Yogurt Pots	17.9	10	5.6	0.2	184
Sainsbury's Fab Creamy Vanilla Yogurt	17.9	3.9	2.7	0.13	124
Twix Yogurt	18	8.4	5.3	0.31	168
Morrisons Low Fat Black Cherry Yogurt	18	1.3	0.8	0.2	101
Morrisons Low Fat Strawbery Yogurt	18	1.3	0.6	0.2	101
Sainsbury's Fab Creamy Toffee Fodge Yogurt	18.1	4.1	2.7	0.13	128
Muller Crunch Corner Vanilla Chocolate Balls Yogurt	18.2	5.3	3.3	0.2	148
Aero Finesse Mousse Milk Chocolate	18.2	14	9.1	0.1	953
Tesco Split Pot Strawberry & Cherry	18.2	3.2	2.1	0.1	117
Morrisons Lemon Fool	18.3	10.4	6.5	0.2	187
Waitrose Lemon Curd Yogurt	18.4	8.5	5.8	0.15	164
Asda Extra Special Lemon Curd West Country Fudge	18.7	8.7	5.5	0.2	166
Fage Total 0% Fat Greek Yogurt Splitpot With Honey	18.8	0	0	0.08	108
Morrisons Low Fat Toffee Yogurt	18.8	1.8	1.1	0.2	111
Muller Crunch Corner Toffee Hoops Yogurt	18.9	5.5	3.5	0.2	153
Mars Yogurt	19.1	8	5.2	0.31	166
Sainsbury's West Country Lemon Curd Yogurt, Taste The Difference	19.1	9	5.7	0.1	175
Tesco Honey Split Pot Yoghurt	19.1	0.3	0.2	0.2	104
Aero Mousse Milk Chocolate	19.4	5.6	3.7	0.1	653
Nestle Milkybar Desserts	19.7	14.1	9.2	0.3	231
Sainsbury's Crème Caramel, Basics	20	0.9	0.6	0.1	103
Waitrose Deliciously Silky Toffee Low Fat Yogurt	20	2.2	1.5	0.13	123
Petits Filous Little Desert Chocolate & Vanilla	20.4	5.5	3.7	0.22	154
Smaties Split Pot Yogurt	20.4	5.4	3.3	0.2	152
Sainsbury's Mousse Lemon	20.5	8.4	7	0.22	184
Sainsbury's Crème Caramel	21	1.6	1	0.2	110
Sainsbury's Mousse Chocolate	21	7.5	5.8	0.19	185
Aero Mousse Mint Chocolate	21.1	9.4	7.3	0.1	781
Muller Bliss Lemon Yogurt	21.3	5.9	3.3	0.2	161

Yoghurts

Product	Sugar	Fat	Sat per 100g	Salt	Cals
Cadbury Bubbles of Joy Mousse Chocolate	21.4	8.1	5.7	0.1	200
M&M's Yogurt	21.4	8.7	5.5	0.12	182
Sainsbury's Chocolate Surprise	21.4	8	5.4	0.1	183
Sainsbury's Mousse Colombian Coffee, Taste The Difference	22.3	17.3	11.5	0.1	271
Rolo Toffee Split Pots	22.5	6.3	3.8	0.2	166
Asda Extra Special Clotted Cream Fudge West Country Yogurt	22.5	7.7	5.1	0.2	176
Cadbury Twin Pot Flakes	22.9	12.6	8	0.25	240
Sainsbury's Mousse West Country Fudge, Taste The Difference	23.2	19.8	13.3	0.15	290
Cadbury Dessert Milk Chocolate	24.6	11.7	7.2	0.1	225
Sainsbury's Caramel Surprise	25	6.8	4.7	0.1	181
Rolo Dessert	25.4	11.8	8	0.4	243
Quality St Dessert Toffee Penny	25.5	9.2	6.4	0.5	228
Cadbury Dessert Milk Chocolate & Caramel	26	10.5	7.6	0.2	215
Cadbury Twin Pot Dairy Milk Chunky	26.3	13.5	8.6	0.25	250
Cadbury Twin Pot Buttons	26.6	13	8.3	0.25	245
Sainsbury's Mousse Chocolate, Taste The Difference	27	18	12.4	0.08	313

SugarSnub™ Testimonials

This book has proven an invaluable tool to help me and my family reduce the amount of sugar in our diet. The food group charts make it really easy to choose wisely when you're shopping, and were a real eye opener. It was crazy to see how much sugar is in some of the foods we would normally have eaten.

Alex

I've been following a reduced sugar diet with the aid of SugarSnub for a while, and it has worked really well for me.

After the first week of headaches and feeling tired I doubted if this was for me but I stuck to it and the second week I started to feel more energetic and in control of what I was eating. The biggest difference has been that I have broken the cycle of treating myself with sugary treats everyday, which means I now eat a wider variety of healthier foods. I've lost 6kgs and feel and look great, especially around my mid section. The book and SugarSnub advice has helped me to make informed choices about what I put into my shopping basket and my body. These choices have now become part of my everyday life. Thank you SugarSnub for educating me, and for making me a healthier, slimmer and happier person.

Faye

Shopping List Notes

Shopping List Notes

Acknowledgements

This has been a pleasure to research and write.

I've learnt a lot in the process, but I couldn't have achieved it without help.

With thanks to:

Carol Granger, Registered Nutritional Therapist, for her professional advice.

Judy Stewart, Practice Nurse, for her support and insight into the challenges of helping people with diabetes.

Bambi Gardiner and Ali O'Boyle, for their enthusiasm and being my editors.

Jay Gregory, a good friend and even better designer (who is also now sugar free!)

My amazing boys: husband Chris, and son Joseph. You are my world!